Institute of Social and Religious Research

CATHOLICS, JEWS AND PROTESTANTS

Claris Edwin Silcox
Galen M. Fisher

The Institute of Social and Religious Research, which is responsible for this publication, was organized in January, 1921, as an independent agency to apply scientific method to the study of socio-religious phenomena.

Catholics, Jews and Protestants

A Study of Relationships in the
United States and Canada

By
CLARIS EDWIN SILCOX
and
GALEN M. FISHER

GREENWOOD PRESS, PUBLISHERS
WESTPORT, CONNECTICUT

Library of Congress Cataloging in Publication Data

Silcox, Claris Edwin, 1888-
   Catholics, Jews, and Protestants.

   Reprints of the ed. published for the Institute of
Social and Religious Research by Harper, New York.
   "The study ... was undertaken by the Institute of
Social and Religious Research at the request of the
National Conference of Jews and Christians."
   1. Catholics--United States. 2. Jews in the United
States. 3. Protestants--United States. 4. Catholics--
Canada. 5. Jews in Canada. 6. Protestants--Canada.
7. Religion and sociology. I. Fisher, Galen Merriam,
1873-1955, joint author. II. Institute of Social and
Religious Research. III. National Conference of
Christians and Jews. IV. Title.
BL2530.U6S56 1979   301.5'8   78-21101
ISBN 0-313-20882-4

Published in 1934 for The Institute of Social and Religious
Research by Harper and Brothers, New York

Reprinted in 1979 by Greenwood Press, Inc.
51 Riverside Avenue, Westport, CT 06880

Printed in the United States of America

10 9 8 7 6 5 4 3 2 1

PREFACE

The study of which this volume is a report was undertaken by the Institute of Social and Religious Research at the request of the National Conference of Jews and Christians. This latter organization had been engaged for some time in bringing together representatives of the Protestant, Catholic and Jewish faiths in round-table seminars for mutual discussion and understanding, but had found its educational efforts handicapped by lack of accurate information of the actual situations in local communities in contrast with the prevalence of rumor and impression. The National Conference of Jews and Christians, therefore, saw fit to ask the Institute of Social and Religious Research to make "a series of community case studies in localities of various sizes, pointed to problems of interfaith relationships. These studies would include a survey of the actual contacts and relationships between Catholics, Jews and Protestants in communities; a study of the forces making for isolation, indifference and difficulties; a study of the social forces making for understanding and greater coöperation."

The directors of the Institute of Social and Religious Research approved of such a study in January, 1933, and work was commenced in the following month.

Such a study was difficult enough under the most favorable circumstances, but it was undertaken when the existing financial stringency made it particularly necessary to economize in time spent and in the means used. Approximately six months were allowed for the case studies and a little more than a year for the completion of the report. In regard to cities to be studied, it was evident that a sufficiently wide spread of case studies was desirable. It was obviously necessary to select the communities with a view to geographical distribution; but geographical distribution in itself was not a sufficient guide, since it was equally necessary to consider other differences, for example, the ratio of native-born to foreign-born population, the size of the community, the respective levels in the economic, political and social prestige of the three religious groups under consideration, and the racial constitution of certain of the groups in the localities. Almost every city which was suggested seemed to deserve inclusion in the study because of certain oddities in the constitution of its population. Some advisers urged that the study be limited to perhaps four communities and made more exhaustive; others insisted that such a study, to fulfil its fundamental purpose, should be made in not less than twenty cities. In the end, it was decided to begin at Baltimore and spend approximately one month in that city, leaving further decisions as to places until experience had provided a clue to the best subsequent procedure.

Meanwhile, those entrusted with the study had come to a very definite conclusion that certain particular areas of conflict ought to be explored, since these conflicts had repeatedly been hinted at in the various seminars held throughout the country and concerning them more data were obviously needed. Among the more important of these problems were: the relations of the three groups to participation in community chests and various social-welfare agencies; conscious efforts at proselytization carried on by one or more of the groups; difficulties created by differer..es of faith in the general scheme of public education; alleged industrial discrimination against members of a given faith; adjustments or failure to secure adjustments for the religious development of students belonging to members of the various groups at secular institutions of higher learning, and in general, the prevailing attitudes of members of certain given faiths toward those of other groups. These, therefore, became in a peculiar way the *foci* of the community case studies, although by selecting such major areas of emphasis, it was not intended to rule out other significant types of situations that might emerge naturally in the process of the investigation.

The case study was then begun at Baltimore, and it was here discovered that the widest spread of community studies possible in the limited time was both desirable and imperative, and that certain problems might well be studied with particular attention in some cities and practically ignored in others. It was further found that it would be highly undesirable to prepare a report that should be little more than a running commentary on the particular situation in given cities, since the most valuable information vouchsafed to the investigators was almost invariably prefaced by an insistence that the information was confidential and could not be quoted. Personalities were involved; business interests and professional positions were at stake, and had the confidence not been accepted in the spirit and under the conditions in which it was given, the information would not have been forthcoming. It was necessary, therefore, to conceive of the final report as something to be treated topically with illustrations from the case studies rather than as *exposés* of the cities themselves. The only alternative to such a method would be for those engaged in the study, after they had completed their report, to have departed hastily for some secluded island in the South Seas.

In the end, valuable but cursory studies were made in the following cities in the United States: Baltimore, Washington, Pittsburgh, Buffalo, Cleveland, Cincinnati, Chicago, Louisville, Atlanta, San Francisco, Los Angeles, Oakland and Berkeley. In addition, some more incidental studies were attempted in New York City, Philadelphia and Newark. The spread was also extended to Canada and included Toronto, Montreal and Ottawa. The Canadian studies proved particularly valuable as a contrast to American trends, since the history of Canada and the United States provide not only many striking analogies but also many dissimilarities. Some of these will become immediately patent to the reader, notably in the chapter on Education. Canada began with a French-Canadian minority question on its hands —strictly speaking, it began with a French-Canadian majority dominated by an English-speaking Protestant minority—and it had, at the outset, to face the whole question of minority rights. It is today the only country in the Western Hemisphere in which two languages are openly recognized in law and where the Protestant minority (in Quebec) and the Catholic minority (in Ontario) have definite assurances and legal status. Again, the Canadian census takes cognizance of both racial origin and religious preference, and thus affords opportunities for many correlations indicating trends which develop when ancient European cultures are transplanted to the soil of the new world under the aegis of the laws and customs prevalent in English-speaking countries. In the same way, the religious implications of inter-marriage, crime and general vital statistics are much more clearly read in Canadian reports than in American reports which, unfortunately, are often practically useless to students of socio-religious relations. Moreover, the inclusion of data from Canada seemed to make it possible to avoid a difficulty inherent in many social studies that are made in the United States and are carried out on philosophical presumptions peculiarly American. The use of the comparative method and the gathering of data in a country where the identical presuppositions are not posited provide a subtle means of challenging the very presuppositions themselves.

The deeper the investigators penetrated into the study, the more imperative became the necessity of historical orientation. The history of the individual cities threw much light on the general attitudes existing in the city at the present time, and an afternoon spent in the archives at the local historical society was never wasted. But one of the greatest difficulties confronting the research workers in the actual writing of the report was that of determining how much space should be given to such historical material. The difficulties encountered by various groups in the New World reflected preceding difficulties in the Old World, and a knowledge of the latter was often necessary to the understanding of the former. But how far back should the investigators go in stating their findings? Some readers will find the historical sections too full; others will not find them full enough. Problems are sometimes dismissed in a sentence or two when their fuller elucidation would require tomes, to so great an extent does religious interest interpenetrate the whole of life. The line, however, had to be drawn somewhere, and those directing the study had to make up their minds, for better, for worse, where to draw it.

It is perhaps inevitable that in such a study as this, the initiative must come from the majority group. It is easier for a member of the majority to secure from the minority the story of the disabilities to which it feels itself subjected than it is for a member of the minority to secure from the majority the real or specious reasons which determine the attitude of the majority. At all events, the study was made under "majority" auspices, and it may therefore betray an inevitable slant in interpretation even though those responsible for the study may have tried to lean over backward to understand the minority position. It is extremely doubtful, however, if a man who has no positive religious philosophy of his own can be of any service whatever in trying to untangle the difficulties between religious groups. An objectivity built on complete indifference is here perfectly futile. Perhaps, a scientifically inclined Mohammedan might have been able to have grasped the situation more succinctly and more objectively than have those who were entrusted with the study, but that is doubtful too, for such a study inevitably involves a variety of subtleties which can often be felt only by those who are themselves within a given culture. Even if the report does incline at times unduly to the majority philosophy, it is not necessarily invalidated, since, when everything has been said for minority rights that may properly be said, there are still certain important and inalienable rights inherent in the majority, especially in a democracy.

There are obviously, however, more serious deficiencies in the study, due less to the philosophical slant of those engaged in it than to the limitations of time and means. The case studies in many of the communities were too cursory for thoroughness, and in certain of the communities, only major aspects of the problem received their due attention. Interviews were, to a great degree, only with leaders; hence, the attitudes of the rank and file were largely mediated through the leaders rather than sought out directly. Above all, "hard data" were too often entirely unavailable, especially in the United States, and it is impossible to discover things that don't exist. On the whole, the investigators received excellent coöperation from the Protestants, Catholics and Jews whom they consulted. They were seldom suspicious that information which was available was being deliberately withheld.

Efforts were made, however, to correct these deficiencies. (1) Studies of various kinds which had already been made were eagerly sought and their data evaluated and appropriated. Among these were studies of intermarriage, industrial discrimination, comparative achievements of parochial and public schools, social surveys made by non-sectarian organizations. The investigators were given access to certain special and confidential studies made under Jewish and Catholic auspices, while the Institute of Social and

Religious Research had already conducted a variety of studies in aspects of Protestant efforts and relationships. (2) In addition to this, a fairly extensive study of religious journals—Protestant, Catholic and Jewish (including the Yiddish press)—was made during the investigation and matter involving either tension or coöperation was especially noted. Naturally, the peculiar exigencies of the times, including the excitement over Hitler and Nazism, on the one hand, and the economic difficulties of the educational and philanthropic organizations, on the other hand, may have distorted what would otherwise have been a normal picture. At the same time, moments of crisis do reveal and bring to the surface certain situations that might escape notice under ordinary circumstances. (3) Once again, a more intensive effort at statistical analysis was attempted in those districts or areas where such data as were desired were more readily available. As already indicated, Canada provided more "hard data" than could be found anywhere in the United States. The investigators only hope that in some way a recognition of the paucity of fundamental material in the United States may create a demand for the inclusion in the next census of questions concerning religious preference. It would be interesting for the country to know where it stood in this respect. Finally, (4) while the report was still in draft, the manuscript was submitted to representatives of various groups concerned for criticism and suggestion. To all who have thus assisted, the authors are deeply grateful.

This study does not claim to be inclusive. Many important points of tension or coöperation are barely mentioned or not mentioned at all. But it is felt that most of the important facts are here set down, and the investigators sincerely hope that with these used as a basis of further study and discussion, greater mutual understanding and respect may develop. Certainly they have not wilfully concealed any attitude or situation of consequence bearing upon the problem on the grounds that the presentation of such an attitude or situation might induce an hysterical rebuttal on the part of members of other groups. They have considered attitudes as significant social data, even though a more thorough-going investigation might clearly prove that such attitudes had been acquired on a meagre basis of knowledge or experience. When people in large numbers maintain such attitudes, however inadequately grounded, they must be considered as worthy of presentation.

It may be, however, that in certain cases the reader will recognize the legitimacy of the data or facts brought forward by the investigators while he may challenge their interpretation of the facts. This, of course, is quite within his province, and yet without interpretation some facts may in themselves be fruitful sources of bitterness. To take a specific instance, something is said about the alleged sharp practices of the Jews in business. Anyone who desires to do so can accumulate a considerable amount of evidence that many Jews do adopt business methods highly distasteful to the majority of Gentiles. He can also accumulate a good deal of similar evidence that many Gentiles, to say the least, do not regard their business as a kind of public philanthropy. Crime statistics do not shed much light on the allegations, since, after all, crime statistics only indicate the number of persons who have been caught, convicted and sentenced, whereas many crooks are never caught, either because they are too sharp or because the law is too ponderous. Business and professional men will tell their tale and justify their aversion, at least to their own satisfaction, to any more dealings with Jews than are necessary, but there is no way in which we can measure the fairness of their reports. In the end, we must judge for ourselves. How, then, shall their allegations be reported? Obviously, we must admit what the prevailing opinion is and indicate the type of reasoning on which the opinion is founded; but that is only part of the story. Behind the data is a long historical phenomenon in which we see the Jew repeatedly prevented from living a normal life, e.g., excluded from the medieval guilds on religious grounds and forced time and again in history to adopt the rôle of the financial "bootlegger." We see him excluded here and excluded there and forced to use his wits to keep body and soul together; we see him used and abused by kings and princes, robbed of his just earnings and then given a chance to recoup his losses by the control of the taxes; we see him forcibly urbanized and consequently dealing almost continually with the manipulatable rather than with the processes of nature. Shall we go beyond the assertion of the common belief in sharp and unfair business practices and provide the apologia which the Jew, in the light of his history, might properly make against his accusers? If we do so, we are irrevocably committed to a lengthy analysis of an historical situation which has been in the making for centuries and which certainly seems to go beyond the scope of our immediate study. Our dilemma was constantly reappearing; we had to decide whether to give the facts without much interpretation, or else to essay the rôle of an interpreter, no matter to what length an adequate explanation would carry us. While we have ventured at times to assume the rôle of an interpreter (even though we may not duly qualify as specialists in the field of history), every reader must, in the last analysis, make his own interpretation in the light of his peculiar knowledge and experience.

This book will, it is hoped, be implemented by a discussion outline to be issued by the National Conference of Jews and Christians. We suggest that discussion groups which may be formed to consider the material herein furnished might well begin by considering the history of their own communities and seek to secure first-hand information concerning the beginnings of Protestantism, Catholicism and Judaism and the course of their relations in the very places where they reside. There is nothing like a knowledge of local history to reduce the existing local problems, if there are any, to their proper proportions. After they are seen in their historical perspective, the more specific issues may be considered more intensively, more sympathetically and with less emotional tension.

If the investigators had any outstanding presuppositions of their own, it is in the belief that whether we reside in the United States or in Canada, all those who truly love their country must try to live with their co-nationals in peace and understanding, and to coöperate in the great tasks which challenge members of all three groups as they face the high emergencies of a new era. In such a period as this, we pay too much when we indulge in blind prejudice and bigotry. We must learn to work together even if many of the differences which divide us are real differences and rooted in our respective readings of the things which are of eternal worth. Perhaps, too, the investigators are naïvely of the opinion that all great social problems are in the last analysis spiritual problems. Even in a day when all things are reduced to the terms of a materialistic philosophy and the economic interpretation of history, a faith in the ultimate nature of the universe and in the inalienable rights and responsibilities of men and women has still, as it has ever had, a fundamental and inescapable priority. Tragic indeed would it be, if the forces of religion which have ever sought to bind man with man and man with God, should at this critical moment fritter their strength in needless antagonisms and petty internecine bigotries!

Because of the limited time permitted the completion of the report, it was impossible for the director of the study to write the entire report himself. The chapters on Social Work and on Coöperation were prepared by his colleague in this study, Galen M. Fisher, executive secretary of the Institute of Social and Religious Research. Other valuable services were rendered in the course of the study by W. F. Stier, of the Institute staff, and by many advisers in all three groups—Catholic, Protestant and Jewish. Throughout this book, in the interests of brevity, the word "Catholic" is, for the most part, used in the popular sense as relating specifically to the Roman Catholic Church. There are, of course, other kinds of Catholics. The word "Americans" is also used in the same popular sense as relating specifically to the people of the United States of America, although some Canadians insist that they too are entitled to be called Americans!

CONTENTS

Contents

Contents

CHAPTER I

Introduction

Few problems in the field of socio-religious relations can be more fascinating, more intricate and more far-reaching than those surrounding the actual relations of Protestants, Catholics and Jews living in the various communities of the United States and Canada. Some sociologists avoid the consideration of such problems, possibly because they are too full of dynamite, perhaps more because the fundamental data requisite to objective treatment are too often lacking.

Social Significance of Religious Differences

Nevertheless, the religious differences which separate the various groups in a community tend to color their whole existence. They determine the attitude toward the newly-born child—shall it be baptized or circumcised? In a large measure they define the type of education which is provided for the pre-adolescent and the adolescent. They influence, if they do not definitely restrict, the sexual selection of mates, provide the ceremonies with which marriages are solemnized, and except in a mongrel and hybrid civilization afford the orientation of entire groups toward the home. They select the pictures on our walls and the books on our shelves. They create a variety of institutions which minister to the orphaned, the delinquent, the unmarried mothers, the impoverished, the aged; and when we are caught in the bitter throes of financial depression, they determine most frequently the agency from which we seek the saving dole. They inspire the building of almost countless academies, colleges, universities and hospitals. To a very large extent they choose the circles in which we find our intimate friends and sometimes determine the way in which we exercise our franchise. They may prevent one group from eating pork or rabbits or oysters, while another group "religiously" refrains from beefsteak on Fridays. The law of Israel forbade the wearing of garments of divers sorts, such as woolen and linen together. This law may, at an early date, have contributed to the Jewish control of the clothing industry, and if such was the case, the fact provides an interesting example of the interpenetration of economic life by religious motivations. Thus, religious affiliation may affect all of life, and it even seems to cast its shadow over us in death, for when we are buried, the grave is dug in a plot which may have been consecrated by our co-religionists.

I

Religious differences divide us in various ways from the cradle to the grave. Why not, therefore, frankly face the issues created by such distinctions, and ask ourselves that solemn sociological question: What about it?

To be sure, religious differences are not as unyielding as racial differences. The leopard cannot change his spots, nor the Ethiopian his skin, and our racial inheritance is something which we can neither control nor modify. We are what we are—white, brown, red, yellow or black, and what we are, we remain. The religious inheritance is, however, modifiable. Through the process of conversion we may pass over from one group to another, although this process is far less simple in practice than it is in theory, for ancient moorings have a strange tenacity—the divisions follow us even into the penitentiaries and reformatories. Most of us inherit our religion as we inherit our nationality or our mother tongue, and far from encouraging people to select their religion on the basis of personal conviction, religious groups seek to immunize youth against any possible defection in later years, and they erect every conceivable type of barrier which may keep the over-adventurous sheep within the fold.

If religion were purely a personal matter, as some maintain that it is, society would rejoice at every manifestation of spiritual emancipation. When the Jewish boy reached thirteen years of age, we should not observe Bar Mitzvah for him; we should ask him to make his own choice from the ménu-card of available religious delicacies. We should ask the Christian boy of the same age if he would not care to join the Brahma-Samaj, or a Roman Catholic Christian if he would not consider possible affiliation with the Quakers or the Mennonites. But of course we do nothing of the kind. The adolescent, as he faces the *Sturm und Drang* of life, has as much sail as his bark will probably stand; what he needs is a chart and an anchor. Custom, tradition and the need of discipline wisely bid him follow in the steps of his fathers. No, religion is not primarily an individual matter; it is rather a method of social control and social discipline, and since it is so, any defection is interpreted as a form of high treason except among those who have already become déraciné, lost their essential loyalty to the group and grown careless and indifferent in the observance of its discipline. Conversion from one group to another, therefore, is not only infrequent, but its prevalence is an almost sure index of trouble.

What is more, the religious group may be, and often is, highly supranational. Nations, in their ardent chauvinism, have ever sought to control and dominate their churches, even as certain German Christians are seeking today to create a Nazi church, which, as the German Christians themselves attest, shall be, not so much the *conscience* of the nation as the *soul* of the nation. Here is a dichotomy of more than passing interest; here emerges the clear significance for all narrowly nationalistic ideals of a supra-national body of believers, a universal "household of faith." What is significant for Germany is also significant for the United States or Canada. Browning said, "A man's reach must exceed his grasp"—even his political grasp, and Kipling sang, "What should they know of England who *only* England know?" We must therefore always bear in mind, in our consideration of the significance of religious differences, the fundamental distinction between such groups as seek quite definitely an international discipline and those that express primarily the will and aspirations of a particular people. We must also remember that over against both the international and the national groupings are the "sects," whose idiosyncrasies are neither national nor international, but more purely local and individualistic. As our problem impinges on the field of national and international politics, it certainly becomes no less intricate; it becomes more involved, more interminable, more fascinating and more terrifying.

The sociologist, attempting to delineate the various problems created in the field of interfaith relations in either the United States or Canada, may begin with some case studies of Middletown or Cobunk's Corners, but before he has penetrated very far, he will inevitably be searching for the roots of the phenomena in the pages of history, and if, by some strange deficiency in early training, he has been led to believe that history is bunk, he had better abandon his study before he becomes too deeply involved. Indeed, in no other phase of sociological inquiry, is some knowledge of history more imperative. However difficult it may be to discover in annals of the past "the truth, the whole truth and nothing but the truth," the effort must be made if our social judgment on the functioning of religious differences is to be at all adequate. If the psychologist does not exaggerate unduly when he affirms the significance of childhood memories for later experiences, so the sociologist cannot fail to underscore the significance of the whole story of the struggle for so-called religious freedom if he is to appraise aright the social distance between religious groupings in his own day and in his own nation.

HISTORICAL BACKGROUNDS

Such an historical investigation must, of necessity, lie largely outside the immediate scope of this study. Some, indeed, aver that if we seek peace and understanding, we should try to forget the past and let the dead bury their dead. The Jews, they say, should forget their persecutions; the Catholics, their martyrs; the Protestants, the Inquisition. A well-known Catholic layman prominent in every work for interfaith good will writes on this point:

"I never could see much advantage in going into the details of the unpleasant things of the past which includes the Civil War, but rather prefer to paint a picture of what our relations should be and the progress being made. I know that Jews, Catholics and Negroes like to have told the many injustices to which they have been subjected, but it is not helpful with the people whose cooperation for better relations is desired."

He might have included in his category the Protestants who also feel their backs stiffen at the tales of the Waldensians in Italy, the Huguenots in France, the Covenanters in Scotland and that struggle for freedom which led to the landing of the Pilgrims on Plymouth Rock.

The immemorial observance of Purim on the part of the Jews, with the annual re-reading of the story of Esther and the wicked Haman, may create in the Jewish people an expectancy of persecution and induce in them attitudes that make for persecution, while every man who believes that he is right, or that his church is right, finds a strong rhetorical appeal in the picture of the Christians being thrown to the lions—"the blood of the martyrs is the seed of the church."

The historically-minded, however, seek in history not fresh appeals to fanaticism, but explanations, and not until all three groups adopt a more objective attitude towards their respective pasts can present peace be assured. Objectivity need not involve indifference; it does demand the effort to understand.

Although this delineation of the past does not fall within the exact scope of this study, it may not be amiss, in this general introduction, to indicate certain aspects of history which the student of interfaith relations has a duty to examine, and which shed light on present attitudes.

ANTIQUITY OF ANTI-SEMITISM

In the first place, the phenomenon of anti-Semitism is certainly not new in civilization. Frequently it has been interpreted by Jewish writers largely in terms of the relations of Jews and Christians. But the book of Esther is sufficient evidence that it antedated the Christian era. Whatever the cause, the historic fact seems to be that, wherever the Jews have existed in considerable numbers, anti-Semitism has arisen, sooner or later. The "Jewish problem" existed for the Pharaohs in Egypt, for Ahasuerus in Persia, for Nebuchadnezzar in Babylon, for Antiochus Epiphanes and his Seleucid successors in Asia Minor, for successive Roman emperors before Christianity became the state religion of Rome, for Mohammed and his followers, as well as in Nazi Germany. Even in ancient Palestine, the Jews had no dealings with the Samaritans. Anti-Semitism can never be reduced to a mere struggle between the Star of David and the Cross. Religion, folkways, race, economics, politics—all are involved, and possibly at no time in history was one of these elements the only factor in the situation. The Jews frequently allege that the accusations directed against them by the Gentile world are either false, or else possibly true but, if so, the results of the persecutions they have suffered. The Gentiles, on their hand, insist that wherever the Jew has gone, he has carried with him a superiority complex, a deep sense that he belonged to "a chosen and peculiar people," and as a result, that his full participation in the life of the nation among which he dwelt was always self-restricted. His refusal when in Rome to do as the Romans, his insistence on living by himself, unless trade or political advantages modified his attitude, eventually brought down persecution on his head.

LACK OF OBJECTIVITY IN STUDYING CHURCH HISTORY

In the second place, there has been far too little objective study of the history of the Christian church except among the experts. History has been used to stimulate faith rather than to understand how we got this way. The problem of the relation of Church and State has often been confused with that of Roman Catholicism and Nationalism, while fundamental differences in the partial reading of history keep apart and probably will continue to keep apart the Protestants and the Catholics, however loyal either or both groups may be to certain fundamental emphases in Christianity. Even among the experts few Protestants or Catholics approach the study of history dispassionately or without preconceived ideas, while for the rank and file the infinite possibilities of the story of the church as a means of spiritual culture have been neglected by both groups alike. The less men know about the past, the more they argue, and even when they know enough to know better, they select such facts as will give support to their own point of view and try to forget those facts that will upset their theories. To limit the whole question to only one phase, when may we expect the history of Ireland to be subjected by all concerned to objective analysis? The Catholic Irish who came to the United States and the Protestant Irish who came to Canada were nursed on tales of cruelty and persecution—which were probably true in both cases—and such tales made these groups quick to look for trouble wherever they went and to find it.

PROTESTANT AND CATHOLIC IN THE NEW WORLD

There is, however, for the student of interfaith relations in the United States and Canada, one great aspect of the Protestant-Catholic impasse which deserves far more extended treatment than such a study as this can give to it. The whole discovery of the New World must be read against the picture of the clash of two cultures—one dominantly Latin and Catholic, the other dominantly Anglo-Saxon (whatever that means) and Protestant. The capture of Constantinople by the Turks, in 1453, brought to an end all hope of a European advance into Asia, and turned the hopes of Europe to a possible road to Asia via the Atlantic. It also rendered the Eastern Church more impotent in the larger affairs of Europe. Then came the discovery of

America, in 1492, a date which, for the student of interfaith relations, is also significant because of the expulsion in that year of the Jews from Spain. While the Renaissance of learning and the revival of nationalism were paving the way for the Reformation, this latter movement was to affect Northern Europe rather than Southern Europe. Spain was at the height of her power when the Reformation broke upon her, and in a glow of religious ecstasy she had expelled both Moor and Jew and effected her new unity. She, therefore, remained peculiarly impervious to the shock of the Reformation and, enjoying with Portugal the division of the New World decreed by the Pope in 1493 and modified in the treaty of Tordesillas (1494), was free to undertake the further discovery and subjugation of the western hemisphere. With her mixed zeal for gold and for souls, her gallant adventurers and missionaries penetrated the valleys of America, circumnavigated continents, shook the dust of mountains behind them.

France and England were too badly shaken by the religious disputes of the time to participate actively in the conquest of the New World for nearly a century. The English Kings might establish certain rights to Newfoundland, and four hundred years ago (1534) Jacques Cartier made his "discovery of Canada," but no considerable efforts at settlement were attempted by either country. Neither France nor England was strong enough on the sea to venture much against the naval strength of Spain, while within their boundaries there was a constant struggle between Puritan or Huguenot, on the one hand, and the Catholic, on the other. Some French Huguenots under Ribault did try to make a settlement at Fort Caroline in Florida in 1562, but this was wiped out by Pedro Mendez de Aviles three years later. Legend—probably apocryphal—has it that over the bodies of the killed the Spaniard erected the ominous sign—

"No por francesos sino por Luteranos."

The Wars of religion in France (1562-1598) made any attempts at settlement without that country hopeless until the Edict of Nantes, in 1598, established a temporary inward peace. Almost immediately certain French Huguenots received authority to establish posts in Canada, while in that very year a French settlement was effected at Sable Island. These first settlements seem to have been due largely to Huguenot initiative, although in these early enterprises and until the rise of Richelieu, both Catholics and Huguenots engaged. Then, in 1627, it was decreed that French Canada should be closed to all Huguenots and only Catholics were permitted to go to New France. This was enforced until the Treaty of Utrecht, in 1713, gave Acadia to England, but continued in Canada proper until the fall of Quebec in 1759. It may be that Richelieu's policy of excluding Protestants, while temporarily successful, in the end led to the troubles at home which culminated in St. Bartholomew's Massacre (1572) and definitely cost France her hegemony in the New World. Had French Huguenots participated in the building up of New France, they might have carried the arts of France with them and made of Canada a great power paralleling New England; their removal might have solved the internal conflict in France; while the struggle between New England and New France might have been a purely political struggle and not, as it became, a struggle between two religions as well as between two peoples. At all events, it is futile to attempt to understand the religious backgrounds of America without making proper allowance for the constant threat of New England to New France, and of New France to New England. Out of this struggle came more than the story of Evangeline.

While England had sent expeditions into the northern seas and, along with the French, the Spanish and the Portuguese, fostered fishing, she made little attempt at permanent settlement until her first colonists touched the Virginia capes in 1607. From that time on, the struggle for the continent was waged between Protestant England on the Atlantic seaboard, Catholic Spain to her south, and Catholic France to her north. As the Protestant English pushed southward they made, despite the tolerant arrangements in Maryland in 1633, a rule against Catholic settlements. Thus, the first charter of Georgia, in 1732, excluded from the new colony liquor, slaves and "papists." The exclusion of "papists" was probably due to the fear of the Spaniards around the Gulf of Mexico, and perhaps accentuated by the bitter experiences of the English governors in persuading the Acadians to take the oath of allegiance. Certainly the struggle for the New World involved religious factors and gave to later generations a tradition of antipathies which died hard, if, indeed, they ever died.

The reality of this conflict is seen most clearly after the conquest of Quebec in 1759. The task of the English governors was that of pacifying an almost exclusively Catholic population, and by the Quebec Act, in 1774, the French were given the right to their civil law and to the free practice of their own religion "subject to the King's supremacy," while a new oath of allegiance was framed which, it was felt, could be taken by the French-Canadian subjects of the Crown. This Act also annexed to the new province of Quebec "all the territories, Islands and Countries in North America belonging to the Crown of Great Britain" except those of the thirteen colonies. This was undoubtedly an important factor in precipitating the revolutionary war, and both economic and religious motives combined to arouse the opposition of the inhabitants of the thirteen colonies. When the American colonists learned that the Act was passed and "saw the gates of the coveted western lands closed against them . . . they cursed the King, the Pope and the French Canadians with as much violence as any temporal or spiritual rulers had ever cursed heretics and rebels."[1] The First Continental Congress, meeting in 1774, a few months after the passing of the Quebec Act listed among the acts of parliament which are "infringements and violations of the rights of the colonists" the "act passed in the same session for establishing the Roman Catholic religion, in the Province of Quebec, abolishing the equitable system of English laws, and erecting a tyranny there, to the great danger [from so total a dissimilarity of religion, law and government] of the neighboring British colonies, by the assistance of whose blood and treasure the said country was conquered from France."

Although within a year the Continental Congress sent a deputation to Canada to induce the French Canadians to join in the revolt, and though the deputation included the wealthy Catholic layman, Charles Carroll of Carrollton, with whom went his brother, later the first Roman Catholic Bishop of Baltimore, the die had been cast, and when the Revolutionary War ended Canada remained British. "It is one of the amusing paradoxes of history that because Canada had been French it was destined in the hour of danger to remain British when nearly all that was of British creation in America broke from the old allegiance."[2]

After 1783, the American colonies, now having achieved their independence, ventured on their new experiment. Their population was almost exclusively Protestant, and the inner problem of interfaith relations was at first largely intra-Protestant. As the Catholics came in by immigration— some from France escaping the ravages of the French Revolution, others from Ireland escaping the endless internecine conflicts of that island, and still others with the increments of territory purchased from France—new problems arose which not even the constitutional provision for freedom in religious worship could solve. Canada, on the other hand, began with an almost compact French-Canadian Catholic population under the rule of the British Crown, which was pledged to Protestantism. The Protestant population of Canada was recruited from the Loyalists in the revolutionary war and later, after the Napoleonic wars, by immigration from England, Scotland and Ireland. Canada had, however, from the very outset of British rule, to deal with a minority which was at first really a majority, and the entire course of her subsequent history, including her future relationship with the United States, must be read in the light of her attempted solution of that fundamental problem. In time the French Canadians poured into New England, until today in many sections of those states one wonders whether New England has not become New France. At all events, neither

---

[1] Quoted in William Wood: *The Father of British Canada* (Toronto: Glasgow, Brook and Company, 1916), page 56.
[2] Quoted from George M. Wrong: *The United States and Canada* (New York: The Abingdon Press, 1921), page 53.

Americans nor Canadians can understand aright the tensions between racial and religious groups in their respective countries unless they are sensitive to the problems created or solved—as one cares to phrase it—by the Quebec Act of 1774.

An evidence of the attitude of colonial New England Protestantism towards Roman Catholicism may perhaps be gathered from the terms of the Dudleian lecture which was annually delivered at the Chapel in Cambridge, Mass., on the first Wednesday in September on one of four topics to be considered in rotation. The third of these topics was:

"For the detecting, convicting and exposing the idolatry of the Romish Church, their tyranny, usurpations, damnable heresies, fatal errors, abominable superstitions, and other crying wickednesses in their high places; and finally, that the Church of Rome is that mystical Babylon, that man of sin, that apostate church, spoken of in the New Testament."

Catholicism grew, however, by immigration and by annexation, but the Catholics who migrated to the United States did not for the most part move forward into the West as the territory west of the Ohio River was opened up. Father Shaugnessy, in his volume, *Has the Immigrant Kept the Faith?* says of the early dioceses of the Catholic Church:

"The struggling condition of these pioneer dioceses, it may be noted here, was due in great measure to the fact that while immigration contained a goodly number of Catholics, it was not generally the latter who pressed forward to the west, but rather the natives, the newcomers generally preferring to congregate in the cities." [Page 104.]

Although the Irish immigrants had been for the most part peasants in Ireland, they settled mostly in the cities, and when some laymen urged Catholic bloc settlement on the land, their efforts were apparently opposed by the Archbishop Hughes of New York. They settled not only in the cities, but in northern cities, for it was hopeless for the Irish immigrant to compete with slave labor in the south. Thus, during the nineteenth century, American Catholicism was largely concentrated in the great northern and eastern cities.[3] This was a factor in the large degree of municipal power exercised by the Irish Catholics in many cities, and as in New York State, in the political opposition which arose between the city of New York and upstate. Such concentration of the Irish in the cities may have had a baneful influence on the Irish themselves, for it has been stated on high authority that in New York City the Irish "have the highest mortality and the lowest

---

[3] See C. Luther Fry: *The U. S. Looks at Its Churches* (New York: Institute of Social and Religious Research, 1930), page 23.

expectancy of life."[4] The high urbanization of the Catholic population—
79.6 per cent. according to the 1926 census—also makes the whole question
of birth control much more serious for Catholics than for Protestants, since
the birth rates of cities are notoriously lower than birth rates in rural areas.
At the same time it accentuated the clash with Protestants; in city after city
Protestant churches were left enisled by the wave of Catholic immigration
and their membership hopelessly disrupted. Large capital investments in
such churches were of necessity wasted. The contact of the cultures also led
to the political clash; while the Protestants continued to be an overwhelmingly dominant force in the country as a whole, in the strategic cities of the
North, political control was largely held by the Catholics, of which Tammany in New York is perhaps the most conspicuous instance. Finally, in
the competition for jobs, an economic struggle was precipitated in which,
for many years, employers were supposed to discriminate against both the
Irish and the Catholics.

The control of the wealth of the East was largely left in the hands of the
older Protestant families, and thus were accumulated the gigantic fortunes which have made "rich Americans" almost notorious. But the fact is
clear that a large number of Protestants who might have stayed in the East
and kept the eastern cities Protestant went West in search of new lands, leaving the vacuum created by their departure to be filled by Catholic immigrants from other countries.

Had the Catholic immigrants been scattered over the rural areas as thoroughly as were the Protestants, much of the tension which later developed
might have been avoided, and the common struggle with the soil might
have done much to blend the two groups. The Protestants in the cities,
however, felt a menace in the waves of Catholic migration, and this stirred
their old inherited animosities. Behind it all, too, was the inevitable clash
between city and country—a clash which is far from resolved as yet. As
Elmer Davis says in his essay "Beds of Ivory,"

"The one cardinal issue, the one irrepressible ideology, is the antagonism between city and country. It appears in different forms—wet against dry, Catholic
against Protestant, older immigration against newer immigration—on all of
which there is room for difference of opinion. . . . The farm and the small town
look on the city as a reservoir of wealth to be taxed for the benefit of the back
country, and as a sink of iniquity to be forcibly reformed."[5]

Mr. Davis might have added that in nearly all the schemes for social amelio-

---

[4] Louis I. Dublin, statistician of the Metropolitan Life Insurance Co., in a paper read at the
Second International Congress of Eugenics, 1921; quoted by Father Shaugnessy, *op. cit.,* page
129.
[5] Elmer Davis, *Show Window* (New York: John Day Company, 1927), pp. 117 ff.

ration, the cities by reason of their denser population can force action from governments when the farmer is the last man to get any attention whatever.

Another factor that played a great rôle in Protestant development was the Negro. It was only natural that the African slaves should be instructed in the religion of their owners, whether the latter were Protestants or, as in Maryland, often Catholics. It was also natural that the more "aristocratic" types of Protestantism, whether Anglican or Calvinist, should yield to the more "sectarian" types in missionary activity among the submerged Africans. Hence, nearly all Negroes became either Baptists or Methodists. Indeed, had the great migrations from Europe to the United States in the 'forties never taken place, the complexion of the country today would be much darker, for in 1840, out of a total population of 17,062,566, there were no fewer than 2,878,458 colored persons, of whom only 386,245 were free. At that time 15.5 per cent. of the entire population was colored.

The effect on Protestant mentality of the combined influence of early African slavery and later immigration from Europe needs to be studied. Protestant whites, except perhaps the German and Scandinavian, tended to withdraw from all forms of menial service and to be decidedly "bourgeois" in their occupations and habits. With their wealth and their more "refined" occupations, their viewpoint became increasingly aristocratic. As the immigrant classes rose in the social scale and challenged not alone the political power but the social prestige of the Protestant, resentment was practically inevitable, and with the resentment was the fear that the institutions which reposed in part on Protestantism might be overturned. Thus, the religious issue permeated economic, racial, political and social problems.

PROTESTANT SOLIDARITY SHAKEN BY SECTARIANISM

Throughout the formative period of American life, Protestantism was handicapped by its sectarianism. The constituent elements of the population, while dominantly of English extraction, were quite mixed, and even the Protestant immigrants brought the form of faith peculiar to the country of their origin with them. Indeed, it has been estimated that approximately one-third of the more than two hundred Protestant sects which exist in the United States today have a European origin. Certain of these sects, such as the Mennonites, exercised a rigid discipline over their membership, forbade intermarriage with non-Mennonites and practised the ban. The denominationalists were, and are, tenacious of their peculiar loyalties, and coöperative effort within Protestant circles, while making headway steadily, has been a slow and difficult process. In general, within American Protestantism, two diametrically opposite tendencies prevail—in "bloc" settlements there is often found a certain narrowness and intensity of religious outlook and discipline with internal difficulties frequently leading to further schism, notably in the case of the Mennonites and the Quakers; in other and more sophisticated areas are found a certain latitudinarianism and religious indifference. Both these tendencies may be observed in almost any part of the country today.

THE JEWS IN THE UNITED STATES AND CANADA

A word, too, needs to be said in regard to the general history of the Jew in the United States and Canada. The Jew was shut out of Canada as effectively as the Protestant by the government of France after 1627 and until 1759. During the last years of the French régime, however, practically the entire provisioning of Canada was entrusted by the French King to a Jewish family of Bordeaux, named Gradis. When Quebec fell in 1759, the commissar of Wolfe's army was a Jew, and a few Jewish families resided in Canada from the date of British occupation down to the present. The great bulk of the Jewish population of Canada arrived, however, only in the eighteen nineties and after the turn of the century when the persecutions in Russia drove them to seek sanctuary in the New World.

When the British first colonized America, Jews were not allowed to reside in England. They had been banished from the kingdom in 1290. Cromwell, however, watching Holland closely, perceived that part of the success which the Dutch were winning in the commercial world was due to its Jewish merchants, and he sought ways and means to induce some of these merchants to come to England. In December, 1654, he called a committee of lawyers, theologians and merchants and put to them two questions: "Whether it be lawful to receive the Jews. If it be lawful, then upon what terms is it meet to receive them?" The lawyers answered the first question in a manner favorable to the return of the Jews. On the question of expediency and conditions, however, there was hopeless difference of opinion. In disgust, Cromwell put an end to the discussion and decided to let in whomever he chose.[6] In this year, 1654, Portugal expelled the Jews from Brazil. Some of these came to New Amsterdam (later New York) where they were reinforced by other Jews from Holland. At first Peter Stuyvesant, the governor, hesitated to receive them, but finally yielded when he was assured that "the poor among them shall not become a burden to the community, but be supported by their own nation."[7] In 1658 fifteen Jewish families arrived in Newport, Rhode Island, bringing with them, according to tradition, the first three degrees of Masonry. Rhode Island was probably selected because Roger Williams had said of his colony that "all these consciences, yea, the very consciences of the Papists, the Jews, etc. . . . . ought

---

[6] See Carlyle, Thos., *Oliver Cromwell's Letters and Speeches*, Part VIII: Letters CCVII-CCXIV. Also: Albert M. Hyamson, *A History of the Jews in England* (London: Methuen & Co., Ltd. Second edition, 1928), chapter xix.
[7] Samuel Oppenheim, *The Early History of the Jews of New York*.

freely and impartially be permitted their several respective worships."[8] We find also some Jewish names among the earliest colonists in Maryland, one of them, Jacob Lumbrozo, "late of Lisbone, Portugal," is usually referred to as "the Jew doctor." He was in Maryland as early as 1656.

GROWTH OF JEWISH POPULATION

The Jewish population of the United States grew, however, very slowly. The first synagogue was built in New York in 1728. In 1733 came Jewish settlements in Savannah and Philadelphia. It is claimed that certain Jews, viz. David Franks, Joseph Simon, Levi A. Levy, Barnard Gratz and Michael Gratz, were engaged in the fur trade with the Indians as early as 1754 on the site of what is now the city of Pittsburgh.[9] Jewish firms received large concessions when the Indiana Company was formed, but later lost their claims. In Philadelphia, David Franks was a commissar to the British forces during the revolutionary war while Hayim Solomon, a Polish Jew in New York, was a commissar to the continental army and assisted in financing it. In 1780 a pamphlet, attributed at one time to Moses Mendelssohn and addressed to the Congress of the United States, stated certain disabilities which the Jews of Germany suffered and urged that they be welcomed to America and allowed to colonize freely and practise their own religion. There were, however, few Jews in the United States before 1800. In 1818, Major Noah, who later served the United States as consul to Tunis, 1813-1816, and whose spectacular effort to establish a Zionist state on Grand Island in the Niagara River is one of the delightful episodes in the history of Buffalo, estimated the Jewish population of the United States in 1818 at about 3,000. Of these it is safe to say that over 80 per cent. were Sephardic, i.e., Spanish or Portuguese Jews who had come to the United States either via Holland, England, Brazil or the West Indies. About 1840, however, following the revolutionary periods in Germany, many German Jews began to arrive, and in 1848 the Jewish population was estimated at about 50,000.[10] Considerable numbers went to Cincinnati, Pittsburgh and other rising industrial cities. A few, however, went into the frontier areas, not as farmers but as pedlars, with packs on their backs. In states like Kentucky, they intermarried and the first Jewish settlers were absorbed by the Gentile population. Not all the Jews of this period came from Germany, for when the government in Poland sought to force them to serve their terms in the army, an exodus of Polish Jews began.

[8] J. Pereira Medes, "The Sephardic Jews of Newport" in *Early Religious Leaders of Newport* (Newport Historical Society, 1918).
[9] See thesis for M.A. of Julia Miller, presented to the University of Pittsburgh, "Jews connected with the history of Pittsburgh, 1749-1865."
[10] This estimate is probably based on the number of males. See chapter viii. The correct number would probably be nearer 150,000.

By 1859 the Jewish population had only increased to about 200,000, and of these more than 50,000 were found in New York. For the next twenty years few Jews arrived, for the Jewish population in 1880 was estimated at only 230,257. Then, between 1881 and 1886, 114,000 Jews arrived, mostly from Russia. The persecutions within the Pale were forcing them out, and there began a steady migration that ceased only with the Great War. The Jewish population of the United States increased as follows:

1877	229,087
1897	937,800
1907	1,776,885
1917	3,288,951
1927	4,228,029

At the present time the main Jewish centers of population are:

New York	1,765,000
Chicago	305,000
Philadelphia	270,000
Boston	90,000
Cleveland	85,000
Los Angeles	75,000
Newark, N. J.	65,000
Baltimore	68,000
St. Louis, Mo.	50,000
Detroit	75,000
Total for ten cities	2,848,000

Sixty-nine per cent. of the entire Jewish population in the United States live in these ten cities.

There are, therefore, three major types of Jewish migration to the United States:

> 1655-1840, nearly entirely Sephardic Jews
> 1840-1880, largely German Jews
> 1880-1933, mostly Russian and Polish Jews

EARLY TOLERANCE AND INTOLERANCE

There is little evidence of severe anti-Semitism in colonial or post-colonial days. To be sure, even in the liberal states, the law protected from molestation only persons "professing belief in Jesus Christ" and an act was passed in Maryland in 1723 to the effect that "if any person shall hereafter within this province deny our Savior, Jesus Christ, to be the Son of God or shall deny the Holy Trinity, he should, for the first offence, be fined and have his tongue bored; for the second, be fined and have his head burned; for the third, be put to death." Under such circumstances, it might be needful to guard one's utterances, although even in England the Acts of Toleration supposedly extended only to those who believed in the Trinity, but there, as in the colonies, the Jews were unmolested.

Occasionally, to be sure, the word "Jew" was used with an opprobrious content. Thus, a certain John Israel came to Pittsburgh from Philadelphia about 1800 and established an anti-Federalist organ, *The Tree of Liberty*. The Federalist paper was the *Pittsburgh Gazette*, and after the first issue of *The Tree of Liberty* appeared, which had for its motto, "And the leaves of the trees were for the healing of the nations," the *Gazette* published the following verse:

> Have you heard of the New Press?
> *Echo:* Of the Jew Press?
> What, is it published by a Jew?
> *Echo:* And by a Hugh?
> Of the Aurora another edition,
> *Echo:* The mother of sedition.
> Jacobinism imaginary is or is real.
> *Echo:* Israel.

One correspondent wrote to the paper complaining of the motto, taken from the New Testament, "with which you have no right to meddle." The editor was also accused of abusing the Irish, though he married, outside of his faith, the daughter of an Irishman. Thus, in politics, any brick is good enough to cast at your opponent.

In the debates on the Jew Bills in Maryland, Judge Young did use the crucifixion story as a reason why they should not receive political equality, thus:

"For it cannot be denied that they persecuted the Savior, and put him, as they vainly imagined, to a cruel death, in consequence of which and of the continual contempt of his name, they have remained a distinct nation, and are literally vagabonds in the world. As human beings, let them live, and be protected in the peaceable enjoyment of their property which they too often acquire by knavery, and the most sordid avarice. . . . The Jews have rejected, and while they continue such, will reject and despise that light and life, and are not, therefore, as I humbly conceive, to become members of the lowest order of any body or community that is willing to be marked among Christian countries." (Dated: Greenburg, January 13, 1819.)

Governor Worthington, however, in his plea for Jewish emancipation on January 29, 1824, made a rather typical Christian rejoinder:

"I know the great cry in this country against the Jews, is that they crucified Christ. It was specially preordained by God, that act should be done, and they should do it. It was for your redemption. What right have you to take into your hands vengeance and punishment? God can and will vindicate his own acts.

Are you commanded to it? No; you are commanded the very reverse, by the very victim, the very author of the Religion you profess."[11]

Jewish emancipation was obtained in Maryland in 1826, but the above quotations indicate certain current trends of thought in these days. It may also be added that in certain Mennonite settlements in Pennsylvania, settlement by "papists and usurious Jews" was prohibited.

Generally speaking, however, in the early days, Jew and Gentile moved freely, and certain Jews, such as Judah Touro, first of Newport and later of New Orleans, were highly respected. Christians often collaborated in protests made by Jewish groups against alleged discriminations in other countries. Thus, a meeting was held in Pittsburgh, August 13, 1857, of Jews and Christians to protest against the treaty just effected with Switzerland, and it was resolved:

"That we hold that the stipulations of this treaty in so far as the Jewish citizens are excluded from their benefits and proscribed are in conflict with the spirit if not the letter of our constitution and directly antagonistic to all those suggestions of amity and courtesy which should animate national diplomatic intercourse in a Christian and enlightened age."

The Swiss Constitution of 1874 later established religious liberty.

There was, on the whole, friendliness, respect and collaboration between Jew and Gentile. What troubles the Jews experienced were largely due to the clash between Reformed and Orthodox Judaism, and thus were intra-Jewish rather than Jewish-Christian. Many of the early Jews married Gentiles, and their descendants today are in Christian churches. This was particularly true of the Middle West and the South.

EFFECT OF COMING OF EASTERN EUROPEAN JEWS

The consciousness of tension arose only when the Russian persecutions drove great numbers of Jews to asylum in America. Their coming at first disturbed the Jews already in the United States, but they organized to help them and thus to facilitate their absorption into American life. At this point, it is wise to indicate that the Jews of England did what they could at the time to divert the possibility of any extensive immigration of eastern European Jews into England. They saw the danger of a rise of English anti-Semitism, as the following quotation from G. F. Abbott's *Israel in Europe* indicates.

"The persecution of the Jews in Russia, Roumania, Hungary, and Germany threatened to flood England with a crowd of refugees more industrious than the

---

[11] Both these quotations may be found in Breckenridge, H. M., *Recollections of the West* (Baltimore: Lippincott and Co., 1818).

English workman, more frugal, and far more temperate. The consequence would have been a fall in wages. The danger was too practical to be ignored; fortunately, both for the English workman and for the Jew it was temporarily averted by the Jewish charitable associations, which directed emigration into safer channels. But, though the immediate cause for alarm disappeared, the anti-Jewish feeling remained; and was fed by the influx of new crowds from Eastern Europe at a later period. Again, the Board of Guardians, the Russo-Jewish Committee and other organizations exerted themselves strenuously to prevent the immigrants from becoming in any case a burden to the British rate-payer. With that object in view, measures were taken that those victims of oppression which remained in England should be enabled without delay to earn their own bread by that industry for which they might be best fitted; but, wherever it was possible, a home was found for them in countries less populous than England and more suitable for colonization. At the same time, by means of representations addressed to Jewish authorities, and published in Jewish papers abroad, regarding the congested state of the British labor market, efforts were made to stem the tide of further immigration."[12]

Thus, England avoided the presence of the Jewish problem, and passed it on to the United States and Canada.

There must have been evidences of anti-Semitism as early as 1890, for in that year the *American Hebrew* published a symposium by foremost Christians under the caption "Prejudice Against the Jew." This symposium was republished in 1928.[13] This early anti-Semitism was in part social and manifested itself in the occasional rejection of Jews as guests in certain hotels (e.g. in Saratoga about 1875) and in part was due to the results of a visit of Pastor Stoecker, of Germany, to America.

While the Jews in the United States addressed themselves heroically to the task of absorbing their persecuted brethren from Russia it must be admitted that there was not a little feeling against the eastern European Jew on the part of many of them. As a matter of fact, the epithet "kike" applied to the eastern European Jew, is of Jewish, not Gentile, coinage. Whatever its origin, it was used to express the attitude of German Jews to their brethren from Russia and Poland. The peculiar situation in the United States and Canada has been largely created by the character of Jewish immigration into these two countries since 1880.

This general outline of the prevailing course of interfaith relations in the United States and Canada is given with a full appreciation of its inadequacy, but because it contains certain fundamental facts which must be taken into consideration in any proper study of the problems to be later presented.

---

[12] London: Macmillan and Company, 1907, pp. 443-444.
[13] *Prejudice Against the Jew,* with a foreword by Philip Cowen (New York: Philip Cowen, 1928).

Philosophical Backgrounds

Another complication that injects itself into such a study emerges out of the fact that religious differences involve philosophical differences. It has frequently been said that all men are Platonists or Aristotelians, although most of them are quite innocent of any conscious philosophy. The social engineer, however, would rather avoid theological or philosophical differences. Largely because of the vast number of white corpuscles shed in the past in debates between the advocates of predestination and voluntarism, between the sacramentarian and the evangelical, the nominalist and the realist, philosophy is today in ill repute, and it suggests a realm which the sociologist would be very glad to ignore. In his Weltanschauung, humanism may, for the most part, have replaced theism, and his universe—if it be a universe—is anthropocentric rather than theocentric. He openly rejects the deductive method, and builds his science of living together on inductive processes. But what is to be done with men and women who insist on the validity of deduction? They may deduce something from a fundamental principle which disarranges his tidy schemata for all social organization. Take birth-control for instance. The sociologist may argue that the further limitation of the human species is necessary to the happiness of mankind; that if we could only sterilize the feeble-minded and the criminal classes and give every couple, not necessarily two acres of ground and a cow, but at least a two-roomed apartment and a small bath, our social problems would begin to adjust themselves. But along comes the adherent of some religion which postulates certain definite principles as constituting the chief duty of man, and his definition does not begin with any conception of temporal happiness, even of the right to life, liberty and the pursuit of happiness, as the fundamental objective of life. So we discover that the day of the arguments between the stoics and the epicureans is not over, and that between the two conceptions, there is a great gulf fixed.

Now, the sociologist must frankly face the fact that philosophies—or at least religions built on certain philosophies—do persist and exert a vast influence on large numbers of the human race. Some of them hold these philosophies lightly enough; others adhere to them with tremendous intensity, and at a certain point there is a foreclosure on all further discussion. For them, the matter is definitely and finally settled. For this reason, a liberal professor of theology advised the writer of this paper that any study of Protestant-Catholic-Jewish relations in the United States and Canada would never get far unless it actually came to grips with the fundamentally opposing philosophies which, consciously or unconsciously, the respective groups accepted. In dealing, therefore, with these relations, the sociologist must not blink nor minimize the importance of real differences in belief and philosophy, nor can he understand his problem until he has some appreciation of the significance of those differences.

SOCIOLOGICAL PROBLEMS

But apart from these historical and philosophical difficulties, the sociologist will encounter still others which are, possibly, more germane to his normal processes of thinking. After all, who and what are Protestants, Catholics and Jews? In any strict categorical classification, are these the names of *genera* or of *species*?

A RACE OR A RELIGION?

To begin with the Jew, does the Jew cease to be a Jew when he becomes a Christian Scientist or a Two-Seed-in-the-Spirit Baptist? In all his criticism of the discrimination to which he is often subjected, the Jew usually speaks of religious discrimination, but the Gentile almost universally repudiates the allegation and claims that religion has little, if anything, to do with it. An anonymous anti-Semite, who signs herself a "business woman," thus addressed the writer in tones reeking with sweetness and light:

"Personally, I do not care if they believed in totem poles, but to continually use their religion as a cloak for their repulsive personality and habits, has about used all the patience one has. I have seen beautiful neighborhoods overrun and destroyed by them. One could weep to walk down or up Broadway, 70th to 96th Street, and see the once beautiful neighborhood dirty and full of push-carts. Cheap, open-face butter and egg stores every block. What has religion to do with that?"

Scholars sometimes say that the roots of anti-Semitism are to be found in the religious struggles of the first eight centuries, but most anti-Semites of our own time assert with great emphasis that their controversy with the Jews is due not to their faith (of which they know little or nothing, and care less), but to their social manners and habits; that they have no objection at all to "nice" Jews whose way of living approximates their own, but that they have no use for "kikes." This stereotype is familiar to all students of the problem, and suggests that the major difficulty here may not be religious at all, but purely economic or social. Further, the bitterest comments against the Jews come, not from the people who are the most intimately associated with the churches, but from those on the periphery, if not entirely outside church life altogether. In their expressed antipathies, they distinguish between Jews and Jews, and their principle of differentiation is hardly ever religious. Indeed, while the difficulty of converting Jews to Christianity is well known, it is perhaps not as well known that an almost greater difficulty confronts the missionaries to the Jews when they seek to persuade Christian churches to receive their converts.

We face, then, the persistent question, *What are the Jews?* Do they constitute a racial group, a religious group, a national group, or just *a* group? There is little unanimity in the answers to this point to be found among Jewish writers themselves. Attention is frequently called to the fact that because of the Diaspora, Jewish blood has been greatly attenuated in the group which now calls itself Jewish. Some insist that the ancient Hebrews have practically disappeared from the face of the earth. Thus, in his recent book on *The Jews Across the Centuries* Dean Willett, of the University of Chicago, writes: "It would be as appropriate to speak of the English people of the times of Henry VIII as Americans, as to describe the Hebrews of Isaiah's day as Jews" (Page 134).

It is a wise race that knows its own ancestry, and the modern Jew is the child of many races. There is at least one notable case in history where an entire people, the Khazars, living between the Caucasus, the Don and the Volga, accepted Judaism about the year 740 A.D., and continued as a powerful Jewish state until about 1016 A.D., when it was extinguished by a joint expedition of Russians and Byzantines. What happened to these Jews? It may be that some of them migrated in a northwesterly direction and became the nucleus of the so-called Eastern Jews of today, while their children mingled their blood with that of the Jews of Western Europe who migrated eastward in the time of the Crusades and the Black Death and sought refuge in Poland. If this be true, then it may be claimed that the Eastern Jew has little connection with the ancient Hebrews, and is Jewish only in faith. At the beginning of the Christian era, these Khazars were already a mixed people—Scythians, Finns and Sclavonians—and they are hence no more the blood descendants of Abraham, Isaac and Jacob than are the Falasha Jews of Abyssinia. Nor must it be forgotten that the "lost ten tribes" have always haunted the imagination of such pietists as stress "the promises." The Spanish Jews of the Middle Ages, learning of the Jewish Khazars, thought that possibly they were the ten lost tribes, while the British-Israelites today believe that the British people are the descendants of the chosen race, the children of the Ten Tribes who escaped from Assyria to Britain via Ar-Sareth, a region in the south of Russia. Thus they permit themselves the option of two superiority-complexes.

At all events, there is possibly no such thing today as the purity of Jewish blood, and as a result so many Jews do not look Jewish—or perhaps, to be more accurate, Hittitish—while so often Gentiles do look Jewish! To revert to our former classification, it may be that the "nice" Jews are those who do not look Jewish, while the Jews that are not "nice" are those with pronounced Jewish features. Even so, in the early struggles between Judaism and Christianity in the first eight centuries, we learn that the Christians appropriated the Jewish scriptures and then went through the Old Testament, designating all the noble Jews of history as pre-Christian Christians, while all the "dirty" Jews in those sacred pages were definitely classified as Jews.

Are we then to accept the contention of many of the Jews that they must be considered primarily as a religious group? Rabbi Philipson, in his book on *Reformed Judaism* insists that "the national existence of the Jews ceased when the Romans set the Temple aflame and destroyed Jerusalem. . . . The Jews are a religious community, not a nation." The Canadian census secures from each resident both his religious affiliation and his racial origin (by father). In its classification of religious affiliations, it includes "Jews," while in its classification of racial origins, it indicates "Hebrews." Interestingly enough, while the Dominion census for 1931 gave a total of 155,614 Jews, it reported 156,726 Hebrews. Hence, it would seem apparent that the overwhelming majority of those who admit their Hebrew racial origin, wish to be included as Jews in religion. Nor does it diminish our difficulty when we frankly recognize a large number of "unsynagogued" Jews. We all know that there are many radical Jews who disown all religion and a small number who call themselves "Hebrew Christians"; there are, in addition, a considerable number who for economic or other reasons do not identify themselves with a synagogue, just as there are many Protestants whose loyalty to any particular church is, to say the least, most spasmodic, although, on occasion, they may easily develop a very boisterous type of Protestantism. On the great Jewish festivals, however, the synagogues will be crowded, even as on Easter lukewarm Christians throng the churches, and on Yom Kippur and Rosh Hashana these semi-Jews testify to their solidarity with the Jewish community. But if the community be essentially religious, then one may aver that it is far from a unity. Judaism reveals almost all the colors of the theological spectrum, from unadulterated humanism to unadulterated fundamentalism and orthodoxy. So-called Liberal Christians, for instance, reveal little difficulty in coöperating with Liberal Jewish leaders, but within Judaism there is hardly any whole-hearted coöperation between Reform Jews and Orthodox Jews, except perhaps in social work and education. Moreover, while Liberal Jews work heartily with Liberal Christians, Christian missionaries to the Jews seem more antagonistic to Liberal Jews than to Orthodox Jews, partly because they respect the greater definiteness of Orthodox Judaism in faith and practice, and partly because they seem to sense in Liberal Judaism the greatest barrier to their missionary activities. Where such diversities of religious outlook exist as within Judaism, it seems somewhat difficult to consider it as essentially a religious unit.

The answer of the Zionists is that the essential unity of Jewry is neither racial nor religious; it is national. The Jews are a people—to be sure, a people without a home, a wandering people but with the possibility of a

national home in Palestine before them. They are a nation, an international nation, an *imperium in imperio*, or better still, an *imperium in
imperiis*. To this, the Jewish group responds with its inner division between Zionists and non-Zionists, while the Gentile world reminds the Jewish
nation, if you insist on identifying religion and nationhood, why should you
blame us if we do likewise? Are you not wishing to claim for yourselves a
favored position? While you insist that other nations grant religious toleration to you, how can you insist that all those who constitute "your nation"
identify themselves with Judaism? You cannot have your cake and eat
it too.

Moreover, while the Gentile world might be very glad if the Jews had a
national home, it is subject to constant irritation by its uncertainty whether
to treat the Jews as a race, or religious group, or nation, and the net result
of it all is that in the Gentile mind, the Jew emerges essentially as an international irritant, resisting assimilation and finding ever-shifting grounds on
which to found his right to a separate existence. Meanwhile, his effort to
resettle in Palestine creates fresh international complications with the Arab-
Mohammedan world, while many Gentiles believe that the majority of the
Eastern Jews who are now knocking at the gates of Jerusalem and Tel-Aviv
are descended, for the most part, from tribes as far removed from Abraham,
Isaac and Jacob as were the pagan ancestors of the so-called Aryan. In
short, the whole situation is a frightful mess, and by his strange dexterity
in playing the triple rôle of a racial, religious and national group, the modern
Jew brings down upon his head a triple type of antipathy.

WHAT IS A PROTESTANT?

If we have found it difficult to answer the question, "What is a Jew?" we
find it also difficult to answer the question, "What is a Protestant?" The
Jew divides the human race into Jews and non-Jews; the Catholic into Catholics and non-Catholics. Where does the Protestant come in? In the
province of Quebec, the law of 1903 classifies Jews as, for purposes of education, Protestants, but when the Jews sought representation on the Protestant Board of Education in the city of Montreal, all the courts ruled that
this was not permissible under the special minority rights guaranteed to the
Protestants of that province by the British North America Act of 1867.

We all know the wide variety of Protestants, but only those who study
religious statistics realize the complications of classification. Shall we include Mormons and Christian Scientists, Theosophists and Spiritualists as
Protestants? Where in the doctrinal spectrum of Protestantism shall we
find a place, if any, for Unitarianism and Universalism? Or may there not
be more important lines of differentiation *within* any of the recognized
Protestant denominations than *between* them—between Harry Emerson

Fosdick and the late John Roach Stratton, for instance, or between Henry Sloane Coffin and John Gresham Machen? Then again, is the Protestant Episcopal Church Protestant or Catholic? No student of Protestant coöperation fails to appreciate the almost endless complications that inhibit Protestant action. Some Protestant ministers consistently refuse to attend the meetings of local ministers; some denominations will give only a restrained coöperation to certain movements, and some will give not even that; too frequently, the only successful bit of coöperation involves something that nobody cares about anyway. The differences here are largely temperamental, sometimes racial and historical, occasionally doctrinal, and not infrequently almost purely social—the social set go to the church where their social standing is reinforced, while the bourgeois middle class seek out their own little conventicles where they can indulge their sense of self-importance, and the proletariat can go to a mission, join the Pentecostals or the Salvation Army, or go nowhere. Then there is that large number of American or Canadian people who, when asked their religious affiliation, reply simply "Protestant," meaning for the most part that at all events they are not Roman Catholics. Sometimes, indeed, it seems that the most inclusive definition of a Protestant is one that stresses his repudiation of the authority of the See of Rome.

VARIETIES OF CATHOLICS

Then, we have the Roman Catholics, and in the interest of simplicity, we put aside for the time being the much-discussed problem involving the Catholicism of Anglo-Catholics and Old Catholics. We limit ourselves to Roman Catholics, although of course we recognize the importance of the Greek Catholics, and of the Uniat Church, which is of growing importance in the United States and Canada. We also pass over the Catholic group which calls itself the Polish National Church, although in some cities this is a very important communion. Limiting ourselves strictly to *bona fide* Roman Catholics, we discover here a much greater unity and less ragged edges than in either the Jewish or Protestant community. There is more centralization in administration and general policy; there is a more fundamental recognition of territorial responsibility through definite parishes with the enhanced emphasis on community life which such parochial responsibility inevitably means; there is far less overlapping and wasteful duplication of institutions and effort than in Protestantism.

NATIONAL DIFFERENTIATION

With all such apparent unity, however, there are still within Roman Catholicism manifold differences and perhaps the superlative genius of the organization is its extraordinary capacity to deal with human idiosyncrasies.

We must recognize, however, that racial lines are not obliterated entirely. Thus, we have national churches almost side by side with parish churches. The Irish Catholics, the French Catholics, the German Catholics, the Italian Catholics and the Polish Catholics—just to mention a few of them—seem to require special handling, while the Uniats have their own administration for the entire country. In early days, the struggle between the various racial groups within Catholicism was intense. If the German Catholics built an orphanage, as in Rochester, the Irish Catholics straightway built another. There was rivalry in establishing cemeteries, and one of the early cemeteries in Buffalo was to be used for the interment only of Catholics of the *Irish* race. Quite recently, in Rhode Island, some French-Canadian Catholics haled the Irish Catholic bishop to the courts in an effort to prevent him from using certain school funds in a way they considered unfair to the French-Canadians. In another New England town, the Poles desired a church of their own. The Irish priest announced in church one Sunday that there should be no division of his parish, but on the following Sunday he admitted that the Bishop did not agree with him. Montreal represents a most interesting superimposition of national churches on parish churches. The fundamental division within Roman Catholicism in Montreal is into French-Canadian parishes; but directly superimposed on these are the English-speaking parishes, consisting of persons of Irish, Scottish and English descent; superimposed again on these, in of course smaller number, are other national churches—Hungarian, German, Italian, etc. In Canada, too, one discovers complications not only between Protestants and Catholics but also between French-speaking Catholics and English-speaking Catholics. In Montreal, the Protestants say that they get on famously with the English-speaking Catholics but not so well with the French-speaking; in New Orleans, the Protestants say that the French Catholics are charming and delightful and even coöperative, but that the Irish Catholics are intransigent and aggressive. So it goes.

ORDERS AND COMMUNITIES

Catholicism not only provides inner variety by reason of its multiplicity of racial and national groupings, but also because of its various orders and communities. The Directory of Catholic Colleges and Schools for 1932-33 gives the names of no less than 139 different orders or communities in the United States engaged in teaching alone, and in addition to these there are communities devoted to hospital work, the redemption of fallen women, the care of the poor, etc., to say nothing of the better known communities such as the Jesuits, the Dominicans, the Vincentians, the Sulpicians, the Basilians, the Marists, the Paulists, etc., each with its own distinctive personality and its own distinctive privileges and responsibilities. In some instances, the charters of these organizations complicate the possibilities of coöperation, even within Catholicism. For instance, since 1920 efforts have been made to develop Federations of Catholic Charities in many American and Canadian cities, but the Little Sisters of the Poor are not permitted to have a stated income and must secure their funds from begging. Because of this, they find themselves unable to become members of a Community Chest or even to accept a budgeted allowance from the Catholic Federation. However, in one city a sum is earmarked for them and paid over by the Federation to an individual who gives it as a sort of personal alms to the Little Sisters and everybody's face is saved. Numerous complications have also arisen even within Catholic circles because of the feeling on the part of the members of the St. Vincent de Paul Society that charity work was highly confidential and that any clearance of cases with the Social Service Exchange would constitute a breach of confidence.

There is no doubt that these various communities within Catholicism do develop rare skills in their chosen field of service. Thus, an outstanding Protestant in Montreal commented on the high quality of management in the Catholic Women's Gaol and the poor management of the Protestant Women's Gaol: "The Sisters of the Good Shepherd," he said, "know how to handle such cases; we Protestants do not." Again, Protestants often comment most favorably on the atmosphere of the hospitals administered under Catholic auspices and they compare the peace of such institutions with the too commercial atmosphere of many non-sectarian institutions. On the other hand, however, it is easier to create such communities and to secure canonical standing for them than it is to eliminate them when once established and when, perhaps, a truly efficient solution of the problem would involve their elimination. Even in the field of education, it has not always been easy for dioceses to develop their own diocesan normal schools because so many of the sisterhoods that work in the diocese have their own mother-houses in some other diocese and their own normal training-schemes. There is also something of a Catholic analogue to feminism in the large influence which the various sisterhoods quietly exert in the various provinces and dioceses of the church. In the educational and social-work programs of the church, the bishops have to deal with them as well as with the parish priests.

Because of their greater centralization, however, many Protestants or non-Catholics come to believe that in their relations to the larger community, all Catholics tend to feel and act alike. It must, however, be urged that while unity is a note of Catholicism, diversity is also present, and coöperation between Catholics and non-Catholics is dependent in a large measure upon the personal attitudes of given parish priests, and especially of the various bishops. Some types of coöperation between Catholics and non-Catholics are quite definitely forbidden or inhibited by canon law, but much more might be done than is done were the bishops in some areas more coöperative. There are areas in the United States where the Catholic bishop is most popular in non-Catholic circles; and he is often the best apologetic for Catholicism in non-Catholic circles; there are other areas where the bishop is aggressively disliked and, by his ecclesiastical seclusion or his uncompromising manner, does more to intensify anti-Catholic feeling than any other factor in the situation. In not a few dioceses, the non-Catholic, whether Protestant or Jewish, looks upon the local Catholic bishop as perfectly hopeless, and in such instances a fighting, militant attitude on his part evokes a fighting, militant attitude on theirs. Many Protestants have expressed their astonishment that a church with such experience in diplomacy and administration as the Catholic Church should so frequently select bishops who seem to go out of their way to disregard non-Catholic susceptibilities and who undoubtedly make the position of all Catholics—including other Catholic bishops in the country—all the more difficult. Not only so, there is evidence that where the bishop is uncompromising and domineering, he irritates his own parish clergy just about as intensely as he irritates the non-Catholics—but with this difference, the clergy have to bear it, the non-Catholics do not. A lone Protestant happened recently to sit in with a number of Catholics who were discussing the recent elevation of a priest to the episcopal throne, and one enthusiastic layman remarked: "The Holy Ghost made no mistake that time." But there have been occasions in the naming of bishops when the choice was less happy. It is impossible to exaggerate the importance of the personal factor in considering the future coöperative adjustments between Catholics and the larger community.

SOCIAL SIGNIFICANCE OF MINORITY GROUPS

Each of these three major groups is thus still in process of inner integration—although this condition is more patent in certain groups than in others. In the matter of inner unity, a minority group has frequently an advantage over the majority groups provided the minority group believes not only in the possibility of its own survival, but perhaps in the possibility of its emergence as the majority group as well. Whenever any group becomes so powerful that it fears no competition, then it is in danger of disintegration, and the allegiance of its members often becomes nominal. Pride and self-confidence may precede a fall, and sometimes there are greater antipathies between members of the same group than between groups. Thus, in the South, not infrequently the Baptists and the Methodists, both Protestant, watch each other more carefully than either of them watches the Catholics who may be in an almost negligible minority. They do not *fear* the Catholics; they fear each other. In many parts of the South, any attempt at Protestant coöperation is almost a forlorn hope; but in Canada, where the Catholics constitute 40 per cent. of the population, a United Church of Canada has been formed.

The Jews, on the other hand, are well aware they cannot dominate by force of numbers. Conversions to Judaism are relatively rare and not encouraged, and if they were encouraged and actually took place with frequency, they would soon render the ethnic foundations of Judaism even more untenable than at present. It is, moreover, fairly clear that the Jewish birth rate is low, so low indeed that if it were not perpetually fed by immigration, the Jewish group would seem destined to disappear in both the United States and Canada in a relatively short time. This low birth rate is due in part to the urban characteristics of the Jew, and in part, probably, to economic ambition. Hence, the Jewish group can hardly hope for great accessions and it must content itself with a constant struggle against all forms of discrimination and an attempt to deserve well of the country through quality of achievement. The Jewish group counts less on numbers than on the individual success of its members, while the significance of the group as a group is largely due to its high concentration in a few of the major business and cultural centers of the country. The Jewish group may number less than 4 per cent. of the entire population in the United States, and only 1 per cent. of the entire population in Canada, but if it numbers over 30 per cent. of the population of New York City, and 10 per cent. of the city of Montreal, and if its leaders in business, in professions, in political life constitute a significant percentage of the total leadership of the country, then it certainly cannot be ignored. Thus, we find within Jewry, despite its inner disharmony, a tense struggle for success which non-Jews too carelessly attribute to materialism.

STATISTICAL PROBLEMS

Unfortunately, the sociologist, in his effort to analyze socio-religious groups in America, is further handicapped by lack of adequate statistics. In the first place, there has been no real religious census in the United States. The various religious censuses taken in 1890, 1906, 1916, and 1926, under Government auspices, are all incomplete and untrustworthy. Were religious preferences included among the questions which must be answered for each resident of the United States at the decennial census, we should have a much sounder guide to the religious complexion of the country and the basic material necessary to all correlations with other figures. It was, indeed, the absence of such fundamental data in the United States and their existence in Canada which constituted a major reason for the inclusion of Canada in this study of interfaith relations.

INACCURACY OF CHURCH STATISTICS

The figures gathered by the 1926 Census of Religious Bodies by the Federal Government of the United States are furnished directly by church bodies themselves—incomplete and inaccurate as nearly all church statistics are. Indeed, one might extend Bagehot's famous definition to read, "there are lies, damned lies, statistics, and *church statistics*." The Jewish estimate is furnished by enumerating heads of families and multiplying this by an arbitrary figure which may or may not indicate the average number in a Jewish family. Catholic statistics have been frequently challenged by Catholic sociologists themselves. Not infrequently the parish priest, in transmitting his reports, minimizes the number of Catholics in his territory for fear that the diocese will expect too large contributions from the local parishioners; the same motivation operates in Protestant parishes. Again, Catholics include all baptized children as members, but certain Protestant denominations do not believe in the baptism of pre-adolescent children and hence membership is construed in an entirely different sense. Still further, Protestants do not attach the same importance to actual membership in a communion as do Catholics. Where there has been good reason to study carefully the membership rolls of a given church, as in the case of the Presbyterian Church in Canada just before and during the nation-wide poll as to whether it should enter the United Church of Canada or not, upwards of 25 per cent. of all the names on the roll were found to be of persons who could not be located. On the other hand, the first Dominion census taken subsequent to the formation of the United Church of Canada indicated that the continuing Presbyterian Church, with barely 180,000 members, had more than 840,000 self-professed adherents in its ranks. To discover the potential constituency of any Protestant denomination, American church statisticians usually multiply the reported membership by 2.7, but a comparison of Canadian church statistics with the figures provided in the Dominion decennial census suggests that in the case of denominations with churches fairly ubiquitous in the area, it is necessary to multiply by 3.1 or more, while in the case of denominations with fewer and more scattered churches, it is sometimes necessary to multiply by 4.5, or even more. This diversity is due to the nomadic character of the age and a tendency of persons who have belonged to one communion and then moved into an area where there is no church of that denomination, not to affiliate themselves with any church, while their names are in time frequently dropped from the roll on which they had been originally entered.

INADEQUACY OF U. S. CENSUS

Many feel that the United States should include religious affiliation in the questions asked at its decennial census and take cognizance of religious preferences in other fact-findings. Without it, great social movements of the first consequence can not be adequately studied. Every now and again, for instance, some person writes an article on the religious affiliations of criminals or juvenile delinquents and he provides an interesting array of statistics, but if we do not know the actual number of people who wish to call themselves Protestants or Catholics or Jews in a given area in the country, how can we ever determine the respective criminal tendencies within these groups? The Catholic papers frequently call the public schools "godless," but who knows what would be the results of the study of the respective contribution of public and parochial schools to juvenile delinquency? We can guess and theorize and grow rhetorical, but we do not have the fundamental facts.

Again, intermarriage is a social phenomenon of first importance. Nothing, perhaps, is a clearer index of assimilation, on the one hand, or of the growth of a kind of tolerance, on the other; but where is the state which requires the individuals taking out a marriage license to state their religious affiliation or preference? We all suspect intermarriage of Protestants and Catholics to be a social fact of significance, but who knows what is its actual extent in the United States? In the Dominion of Canada we have definite information on this point, as outlined in Chapter VII, but in the United States we do not have the fundamental facts upon which to make any studies of intermarriage. We can only talk and theorize. Again, while a study of the records of the Courts of Domestic Relations may help us to know how many purely Catholic marriages or mixed Protestant-Catholic or Jewish-Christian marriages are broken by separation or divorce, there are no fundamental figures by which proper percentages can be properly estimated. While the Catholic Church declares an attitude on divorce which is well known, it is asserted in one major city that 35 per cent. of all the cases which passed through the Court of Domestic Relations in that city involved either purely Catholic or Catholic-non-Catholic marriages. Surely, it is as important to know these fundamental facts as it is to know how many homes are supplied with radio. It is unfortunate that the United States should build up a tremendous service of information on unimportant matters and neglect to ferret out information of first consequence. Bitterness exists in many communities, for instance, because it is said that while Catholics scorn the public-school system, far too many Catholic teachers are employed in these schools. Let some one ask for the facts, however, and the city authorities will piously announce that religious affiliations are none of their business, and thus under the benign protection of the powers of darkness suspicions thrive, hatreds are developed and periodically burst out during a political campaign. Then, to make matters worse, some hypersensitive groups have laws passed making it an offence to ask any applicant for a teaching position concerning his religious affiliation, thus compelling those who have good reason to secure teachers of a certain religious persuasion, to adopt subterranean methods of finding out the information they wish. Thus, the very social fact whose elimination is desired is actually underscored.

Again, in one city the Catholic bishop asked those entrusted with the study what, in their opinion, was the Catholic proportion of the population of that city. "The politicians tell me," he said, "that we number 60 per cent. of the population; I do not know how they found out, for I have been unable to discover myself what the Catholic population is." Now, one may believe that in that city the politicians may have been right; but if they were exaggerating, their exaggeration may have unduly influenced their own political action. In short, there is every reason for the American nation to know with the greatest accuracy possible the religious affiliation of its people. These groups are fundamental groups, and without sufficient data concerning them, we are victims of fears, suspicions and noise. One illustration: Even in Canada, where a certain approximation to accuracy is furnished by the census, gross exaggerations occur. The census of 1931 gave the number of Jews in the greater city of Montreal as slightly over 57,000. In 1933 one of the leading Jewish citizens intimated to the director of this study that there were 65,000 Jews in that city. Two hours later, one of the leading lawyers, commenting on the seriousness of the local situation, said: "You know we have 85,000 Jews in Montreal." The following day, a leading educationalist went one better and stated that there were more than 100,000 Jews in Montreal. If such is the situation where the facts are available, what is not possible where the facts are not available?

Finally, without a religious census which provides the churches with a fair estimate of the potential constituencies of any given denomination in a definite area, how can church boards make their plans for the planting of new churches? They are forced to take chances and doing so, they frequently establish competitive enterprises on insufficient data, and thus communities are shattered when some fundamental facts, properly studied, might have saved the situation. The prevailing American attitude on this matter of a religious census is doctrinaire.

While we have thus indicated chiefly the points of difficulty that confront the scientific student of interfaith relations, we have also sought to emphasize the fundamental importance of the more accurate and unimpassioned study of the differences and similarities between religious groups. Tensions develop which, not properly studied and relieved, create various types of social conflagrations. Intransigence breeds intransigence, and unless the roots of these difficulties are adequately traced and provided against, complications of the first magnitude develop for all social relations, as will be pointed out in succeeding chapters. The main point to remember is that while these various groups are all seeking passionately to develop their inner solidarity, they find it necessary at the same time to make terms with one another and with that larger group—the community or the nation—to which all belong. This larger integration between the household of faith and the household of economic and political interest is far from easy, and hence much of the criticism directed today against the international Jew and the international Catholic. But this integration must be made—not on any basis of complete indifference, not by hoping that in time all the structures of faith will crumble away into nothingness and their place be taken by the purely secular state, but by a greater insight into the social function of religion. The sociologist who leaves such problems severely alone, trusting entirely to the erosions of time to settle the conflicts of religious groups and standing cynically, like Werther, "above it all—alone with the stars," will need to guess again. Temples may mix with the dust of the desert, but new temples arise, and ancient gods have strangely resurrective powers.

CHAPTER II

Discrimination and Social Distance—Industry, Employment and Real Estate

Serious tension between religious groups naturally results from the discrimination directed against members of certain of the groups who seek to secure employment, rent or buy property, join social clubs or obtain political office. It is difficult, however, to distinguish between religious and racial factors in such alleged discrimination. The group most universally the victims of discrimination is one that is overwhelmingly Protestant—the Negro—but it is obvious that the discrimination in this case is not due to the fact that the Negro is a Protestant. Roman Catholics suffer discrimination at times but—except in the sphere of political life where religious difference does undoubtedly create complications—the discrimination to which they are subjected is perhaps usually racial in origin. In earlier times, advertisements for "help wanted" might indicate that "No Irish Need Apply," while today the majority group may take alarm at a threatened invasion of a given district by "foreigners." The difference in religion may accentuate the difference in race or social standing, but the dominant fact would seem to be racial. In the case of the Jews, the situation is complicated by the uncertainty whether the Jews are essentially a religious or a racial group. Jewish leaders tend to consider the group as a religious community, but the majority of Gentiles, as we have seen, think of the Jews primarily as a racial unit, the identity of which, nevertheless, is largely sustained by religious habits and practices. The majority of Gentiles in the United States and Canada would plead "Not Guilty" to charges of religious prejudice against the Jews; they would admit a racial aversion and antipathy.

Whether discrimination is grounded fundamentally on religious or racial prejudice, it practically presupposes either a preference for those of one's own kind or a dislike of those not of one's own kind. Dislikes and aversions are highly complex phenomena. Considered in the light of their origins rather than of their manifestations, they fall roughly into four categories: the instinctive, the traditional, the empirical and the philosophical.

Various Kinds of Antipathies

Psychologists may differ as to the relative significance of these origins of antipathies, and it is difficult, in any particular manifestation of aversion, to disentangle the various elements and distinguish accurately between the influences of instinct, tradition, experience or philosophy. There *may* be no instinctive antipathies at all, but on the other hand it is not impossible that Nature, in her effort to effect racial heterogeneity, implanted in man the idea of race or tribal consciousness, and made it a means by which races were, for the most part, kept unadulterated. Sir Arthur Keith, in his recent rectorial address at Aberdeen on "The Place of Prejudice in Civilization," attributed much of the ability of Nature to effect "ever better and higher races of mankind" to race prejudice, thus involving race prejudice in the whole scheme of natural selection. Sir Arthur said: "The heart of modern man is still alive with the instinctive longings, desires and prejudices of the tribal man," and he insisted that those who seek to build a new social order must frankly "give our prejudices a place in our civilization, but keep them under the control of reason." The physical aversion which some races entertain towards other races may perhaps have some basis in instinct; indeed this aversion may quite easily be reciprocal. If it be instinctive, it will prove difficult to keep such prejudice under the control of reason.

It is a commonplace of modern social psychology that many antipathies are sedulously handed down from generation to generation. In the various efforts to determine and explain social distance between cultural groups, it has frequently been pointed out that the attitudes of children are conditioned by those of their parents and other adults who influence their early years. But the adults, in their turn, inherited such attitudes from their parents, and thus a chain of antipathy is woven by the generations. Dislikes are thus often rooted in history, and must frequently be traced to their source in ancient racial conflicts before they can be duly subordinated to the reason. While a diligent study of history, however, may serve to remove the source of the difficulty, it may also accentuate it, especially if one is predisposed to find in history the corroboration of his prejudices rather than their explanation.

Other difficulties are the results of actual contacts with cultural groups other than one's own under unfavorable circumstances. If an individual has a series of unpleasant experiences with members of other groups, he may easily develop a mind-set against the whole group in question. He readily believes the worst about them and may even seek evidence of the worst. He labels all Negroes as lazy, all Jews as unscrupulous, or all Gentiles as "Hamans." The only satisfactory method of correcting such stereotypes is by encouraging fresh contacts with the group disliked or despised, but under the most favorable circumstances. If the victim of the unhappy contacts has opportunity to meet persons of the despised group whose tastes, habits, moral standards and ambitions more closely resemble his own, he may perhaps learn to discard his ill-founded aversion and find a new bond of union through the recognition of the common humanity which he shares with the other group. Here again, the social engineer encounters new obstacles, since it is difficult to persuade the victim of a prejudice born of experience to seek a new contact. "Once bitten, twice shy"; all he asks is to be left alone, and for the most part all preaching of human brotherhood only leaves him cold at the point of his carefully articulated antipathy.

Antipathy is also apt to develop between groups which adhere to seemingly contrary systems of thought and philosophy. Here, too, birds of a feather will flock together and consider the theories regarding either the universe or social organization put forward by an opposing group as dangerous. If philosophical difficulties are less to the front today, it is probably because most people are not philosophers and neither contrive nor adhere to philosophies with absolute values. Where, however, such concepts gain absolute as opposed to relative values, one may expect not only a measure of suspicion and antipathy, but even, at times, of positive warfare. Groups which accept such philosophies—even if they have not thought them through —find themselves part of a struggle which they but dimly understand, even as the men in the trenches are often unable to tell what they are fighting for. Such conflicts, on somewhat shifting fronts, continue through the centuries. While time and further thought may modify the allegiance one brings to certain philosophical principles, it is often dangerous to disturb an individual in his inmost conception of the meaning of life. To challenge his fundamental beliefs may disorganize his whole method of living, destroy his fundamental anchorages, sap his powers of moral resistance and hurry him to the shipwreck of faith itself.

Whether our antipathies and dislikes are rooted in instinct, tradition, experience or philosophy, there they are. While we may and presumably should modify or even transmute them, we do well to remember the caution of Sir Arthur Keith: Prejudices may have their place in our civilization, provided we "keep them under the control of reason."

Degree of Antipathy and Discrimination According to Locality

It is perhaps not surprising that the degree of antipathy discovered in this study and, to a certain extent, the reasons alleged for such antipathies as did exist, varied considerably in the different communities studied, and these variations are perhaps as significant as a certain similarity in the forms which antipathy takes. Local conditions and local leadership exert marked influences, thus:

(1) Where a given group is in a hopeless minority, the fear of it by the majority—and consequently strong antipathy—is removed, since fear is a prolific source of hate. Wherever Jews or Catholics, for instance, are a comparatively small group, there is, on the part of Protestants, a greater willingness to live and let live than where these two groups are so large as to swamp

the usually accepted majority. Thus, in spite of the fact that the Ku Klux Klan arose first in the South, there is good reason to believe that the South is less conscious of the pressure of either Jew or Catholic and to that degree is indulgent toward them as persons, although deeply opposed to the system and dogmas of Catholicism.

(2) Where, from the very earliest settlements, Protestant, Catholic and Jew have been intimately associated in the building of a community, there is far greater tolerance than where one particular group has given the city its cultural pattern, only to have the persistence of that pattern challenged by the advent of large numbers of persons with an entirely different cultural pattern. Boston, for instance, had a flavor entirely its own and a distinctive culture which was perhaps not surpassed or even equalled in the United States; but the inheritors of that culture and tradition have their backs to the wall and know it. On the other hand, in some of the cities of the Middle West, Jew and Catholic each made his contribution in the formative period of the city's life, and hence the character of the city has been composite from the very first.

(3) Much depends also upon the dominant racial group or social standing of an important minority people. In certain southern cities, for instance, the Catholic group may be small, but they probably belong to the same stock as the majority and move in the same social class. Many of the Catholics in Georgia came into the state from Maryland, and these southern cities have never experienced so great an influx of southern Europeans as inundated the northern cities. In the nineteenth century, most of the southern Europeans and most of the Irish had to engage at first in most menial occupations; but in the South the Negro had a monopoly of that type of labor, and hence it was useless for the new arrivals to migrate there and compete with slave and semi-slave labor.

Thus, the difference between Protestants and Catholics in many conspicuous southern cities is purely a religious distinction, and where this is the case antagonism is at a minimum. What might happen should the growing industrial life of the South lead to waves of alien immigration is another question. In a sense in which he may not appreciate it, the Negro has been a great bulwark to southern Protestantism. In the northern cities, on the other hand, perhaps the majority of Catholics are of non-Anglo-Saxon stock and represent a class still largely employed in factories and trades. As members of this group acquire wealth and prestige, the longer-established group may tend to view them for a time as parvenus, and some tension may be experienced as a result. Nevertheless, Catholics do not seem to be subjected to any particular social discrimination as is the undoubted case with the Jews.

Distinctly religious antipathy, therefore, does not seem as cogent as racial or social exclusiveness. Again, in such a city as Cincinnati, where an influential group of German Jews had already well established themselves before the great waves of eastern European Jews reached American shores, the attitude of Gentiles toward Jews is much more friendly than it is in cities like Montreal or Toronto, where, despite the British tradition of tolerance and recognition of the Jew, the Jewish population is not only comparatively recently arrived but is almost entirely a legacy from the persecutions of the Jews in Russia, 1880-1920. It is also significant that since the 'forties Cincinnati has had always a large population of German extraction, whether Jewish or Gentile. German Catholics, German Lutherans and German Jews at least had a common interest in things Germanic. The somewhat unique position of Cincinnati Jews is due also to the fact that Cincinnati became the headquarters of Reform Judaism in the United States and the location of the Hebrew Union College which brought early to that city Jewish men of learning. These have left their mark on the life of the entire city. Wherever Reform Judaism has been comparatively strong, as compared with Orthodox Judaism, the antipathy of Gentiles towards Jews appears to have been distinctly modified.

(4) Where a delicate equipoise between Catholics and Protestants had already been established and recognized, as in Montreal, the influx of Jews has, in disturbing that equipoise, accentuated hostility. Evidences of this will appear later in the consideration of certain difficulties in the field of education. When in the late 'eighties and 'nineties the Jews began to arrive in fairly large numbers, they not only changed the character of many residential areas, occupying a strip of land situated between the French and the English sections of the city, but they even sought various types of adjustment in the educational and political spheres to meet their particular needs. This seriously disturbed the equipoise already existing, and has been not a little responsible for a real antagonism to the Jews on the part of Protestants and Catholics.

(5) In the matter of Jewish-Gentile relations, some cities seem conservative socially and liberal religiously, while others are liberal socially and conservative religiously. Thus, it has been pointed out by rabbis who have lived in southern cities and then gone to Toronto, that in the southern cities they were quite fully recognized on all civic occasions and invited to address luncheon clubs and municipal gatherings, while seldom if ever invited to speak from a Protestant pulpit; on the other hand, in Toronto, many churches are open to them, but the line tends to be drawn in social matters.

(6) The personality of outstanding leaders in minority groups is a factor of the first consequence in many cities. The character and coöperativeness of the leaders does much to intensify or to modify whatever antipathy may

exist. A Jewish rabbi of outstanding parts is the best defense of the Jewish group against outstanding Gentile prejudice, while an uncoöperative, intransigent bishop is the greatest enemy that the Catholic Church must deal with. Protestants as a group tend to judge other groups on the merits of their outstanding representatives. If sometimes they inveigh against a whole group for the sins of a few, they will at the same time defend a whole group for the merits of a few. In reality, they care less about systems of thought than they do about people.

(7) One final generalization might perhaps be made. There are indications not only that minority groups frequently tend to work together sympathetically, but also that all groups which might under normal conditions engage in frequent conflicts forget their animosities in the presence of some other danger common to them all. Thus, the presence of the Negro in the South may tend to make people impatient of social complications between Protestants, Catholics and Jews, while the presence of the Oriental in California may similarly tend to create a greater solidarity among all those of European origin. It is not easy to appraise, however, the reality or extent of such solidifying tendencies. The Great War provided the superlative opportunity for demonstrating the possibilities of coöperation in face of a common danger.

Against these general and varying tendencies, we may now proceed to consider some of the more specific forms of social distance.

FORMS OF SOCIAL DISTANCE

The tests of social distance which were roughly applied in the various cities studied were:

(1) *Industrial, etc.* Do employers, in their selection of employees, discriminate against members of certain groups?

(2) *Real Estate.* Do owners of property refuse to rent or sell their property to members of certain groups, and deliberately seek to keep all persons belonging to these groups out of their neighborhood?

(3) *Social Clubs.* Do social clubs of various kinds refuse to consider application for membership from individuals belonging to specific religio-ethnic groups?

(4) *Political.* Do voters refuse to vote for candidates for public office on the ground that such candidates belong to specific religio-ethnic groups?

(5) *Intermarriage.* To what extent is the degree of intermarriage between members of various religio-ethnic groups an index of hostility or tolerance?

(6) *Immigration.* Does the governmental policy in respect to immigration reflect a definite desire and intention to restrict the incoming of any considerable number of certain groups on religious grounds?

These tests of social distance will be considered in this and the following chapters, with the exception of intermarriage, to which subject a separate chapter has been devoted.

DISCRIMINATION IN BUSINESS AND EMPLOYMENT

Those in charge of this inquiry sought to secure whatever studies had been made locally in the cities visited on the subject of discrimination in business. In addition they interviewed some of the more significant employment bureaus. They did not seek to discover new and unknown forms of discrimination in this area, but where definite instances were alleged, these became the basis of interviews with persons who might be supposed to throw light on the particular instances.

PROTESTANTS AND CATHOLICS

The various employment agencies admitted that discrimination did exist. Indeed, they often found it necessary to secure information concerning the religious affiliation of the applicant before sending him to interview a prospective employer. (In several instances, it was charged that the agency was often responsible for the discrimination.) Most frequently, Protestants were preferred. In one unusual instance, the manager of an important motor agency insisted not only on Protestants but on red-hot evangelicals. In many other cases, it would seem that it was largely a case of "birds of a feather flocking together." Employers felt disposed to emphasize the congeniality of their employees and did not care to introduce disturbing influences, and there were intimations that fraternal orders worked diligently to place their own "brothers" wherever it was possible. Many of these fraternal orders operate employment agencies, and it is natural to expect that their clientele—both employers and prospective employees—would largely belong to the order. It is difficult to overestimate the extent to which "pull" thus determines the securing of jobs on the lowest as well as on the highest levels. Nor does the activity of a fraternal order on behalf of its own imply any conscious discrimination against others. Social relationships are frequently a determining factor in economic opportunities. A man gets a job because he knows somebody who belongs to an organization in which another somebody is prominent. This has always been the story, and it is difficult to see how society can ever be reconstructed so that individuals will find their places purely on merit. Again, where a foreman is identified with a particular group and has the last word in filling vacancies and the first intimation that there is to be one, he may, consciously or unconsciously, show preference and favoritism to his own acquaintances or members of his own group. One surmises that this law operates with all three groups—

Protestants, Catholics and Jews. If it be discrimination, it is perhaps less discrimination *against* than discrimination *in favor of* a particular type. Then again, many employers ask for letters of testimony as to moral character, and the natural person from whom many applicants seek such testimonials is the clergyman. Such letters tend to label the religious complexion of the candidate and thus accentuate the possibility of discrimination.

Reputable persons in Washington alleged that in certain departments of the government Protestants predominated to the exclusion of Catholics, whereas in other departments Catholics predominated to the exclusion of Protestants. It was further stated that when a lone Protestant got into a bureau dominantly Catholic by mistake, or a lone Catholic got into a bureau dominantly Protestant, the "white crow" in question would seek to be transferred to a more congenial atmosphere. It was impossible to check on the accuracy of this information for reasons which are obvious, but if true, it would only corroborate the trends already indicated.

Again, like tends to attract like, and Gresham's law seems to operate in industry, for if a certain plant employs a large number of people of a given group, the tendency toward homogeneity encourages others to withdraw or seek employment elsewhere. Italians attract more Italian labor, and Poles attract Poles. Among the more skilled artisans, some races seem to show distinctive abilities. Thus, it is claimed that in some kinds of garment-making, Italian women are the more acceptable, since the prevailing shape of their thumbs gives them for certain specific tasks a superiority. If Jews predominate in a given industry, Gentiles tend to abandon it and let the Jews have it.

Generally speaking, however, any discrimination in employment against Protestants by Catholics or against Catholics by Protestants seems to be on the decline, and if an advertisement in a paper indicates a preference for Protestants, it may suggest a racial preference rather than a religious predilection. In certain more intimate types of domestic employment, involving the care of children, a religious stipulation may connote a desire to surround the child only with those whose religious ideals will harmonize with those of his own home, while occasionally a Catholic maid may complicate cooking arrangements on Fridays and fast days when the members of the family in question have a hankering for a thick juicy steak.

SELECTION OF SCHOOL TEACHERS

It is, however, very difficult for Catholics to secure employment as public-school teachers in small towns, or even in cities where their influence may not be strong politically. On the other hand, in cities where they are strong politically, as in Chicago, there is alleged to be a preponderance of Catholic

teachers. Part of the opposition is due to the fact that the non-Catholic majority do not see why Catholics should seek to teach in schools which some
of them reject as "godless" and to which many of them refuse to send
their own children. If the children are overwhelmingly Protestant, the non-
Catholics argue, why should the teachers not be overwhelmingly Protestant
too, and would not the ideals inculcated be more consonant with those of
the parents under such circumstances? An additional motive operates, however, in the small towns and rural areas. Here the teacher is much more
than an employee of the school board. The teacher is looked upon as a social
acquisition and a potential instructor in the Sunday school. A Catholic or a
Jew in such a community would be inhibited from performing the extra-
school functions which the teacher is expected to assume, and for this reason
is *non grata*.[1] Where such have been employed, the result has been unsatis-
factory both to the community and to the teacher. One Jew who managed
to camouflage her race or religion sufficiently to secure such an appointment
did her best to fit in; to use her own words, she went to prayer-meeting and
she attended all the strawberry festivals, but it was no good. They found
her out, and she had to leave.

Some cities where a large percentage of the population is Catholic require
an applicant for a teaching position in the city to show evidence that she has
already had one or two years' experience elsewhere. This means that a
graduate of the normal school or college of education in that city must find
some place out in the country before she will be considered by the board of
education in the city, and in perhaps most cases where this rule prevails,
Catholics and Jews are automatically eliminated. A few years ago, the foreign
accent of many Jewish teachers was adduced as one reason for not employing
them in the public schools; this argument has, however, more recently fallen
into desuetude, although occasionally around New York City Protestant
parents frequently object to Irish-isms which their children bring home from
school and state that they must work hard to break their children of certain
slight inaccuracies of speech. It is also not without significance that in many
of the best private schools, Gentile teachers are almost exclusively and intentionally employed, for reasons given in chapter vi. It is held that the
Jewish child in particular needs this cultural contact with the Gentile world
if he is to learn how best to comport himself in a nation where there are one
hundred and twenty five million Gentiles to five million Jews. On the basis
of the numerical ratio alone, it hardly seems of equal cogency that the Gen-

---

[1] In Ontario, Canada, hardly any Jews are teachers in the public schools. The Public Schools
Act, Section 100, includes among the duties of all teachers: "to inculcate by precept and
example respect for religion and the principles of Christian morality, and the highest regard
for truth, justice, loyalty, love of country, etc."

tiles should put themselves out to understand the Jewish mentality any more than they need to understand the mentality of a dozen other cultural groups. Against this allegation of discrimination against prospective Catholic and Jewish teachers, one must note the experience of cities like Chicago and New York in which there are large numbers of Catholic and Jewish teachers in the public schools. In New York City, there are separate federations of teachers for Protestant, Catholic and Jewish groups. In some of the cities the superintendents of schools are Catholics or Jews. A Jewish superintendent of schools in an eastern city was especially held in high regard and had done much to secure fair-play for the Negro school population in that city. It should also be noted that part, if not most, of the opposition to Catholic teachers emerges out of the unreadiness of Catholics in general to support the public-school system except in the payment of taxes as required by law.

Where Catholics are in an overwhelming majority, as in French Canada, the Protestants allege that they are apt to be discriminated against by the Catholics, even though much of the big business is in Protestant hands. In French Canada many of the labor unions are directly under the church and controlled by it. The priest, it is alleged, keeps the workers reasonably satisfied, and employers look to him to intervene in case any labor difficulties threaten. In return for such services, he is supposed to have access to the wage-lists of the workers, and the corporations frequently deduct a certain percentage of the wage for ecclesiastical uses. Partly because of this, manufacturers find that they can secure cheaper labor in Quebec than in English-speaking Ontario, and hence there is a tendency to remove from Ontario to Quebec. Of course, Quebec presents a unique situation, but the possibility of future collision because of such situations as this hardly requires further elucidation.

AGAINST JEWS IN BUSINESS

While there seems to be little discrimination against Catholics in employment, there are many handicaps confronting the average Jew or Jewess who seeks employment with Gentile firms, or for that matter, with Jewish firms. Excellent studies of this condition have already been made public.[2]

EXPERIENCE OF EMPLOYMENT AGENCIES

A good deal of data has already been gathered by the B'Nai B'Rith Society, and notably by the Committee on Unjust Discrimination in Chicago and the Committee on the Study of Racial and Religious Problems in New York City. In nearly every city visited, the Federation of Jewish Philanthropies operated or supported an Employment Bureau which sought to place unem-

---

[2] Heywood Broun and George Brill, *Christians Only*. Bruno Lasker, *Jewish Experiences in America*. Herman Feldman, *Racial Factors in American Industry*.

ployed Jews. Those directing these bureaus gave further information concerning their difficulties in finding suitable employment for Jews, particularly during the depression when every agency was seeking to place its unemployed, and, under such competition the tendency to favor members of one's own group is accentuated.

In several instances, we were informed that department stores had been advised that their continued refusal to employ Jewish sales girls would, if made an issue, alienate Jewish customers, and only such strong-arm methods had proved effective. In part, the difficulty was accentuated by the fact that Jews do not engage largely in certain forms of manual labor, although there are not a few Jewish carpenters, bricklayers, teamsters, etc. Another difficulty lay in the fact that Jewish girls seldom sought employment in domestic service or as waitresses in restaurants, etc. It was quite difficult to find adequate opportunities for Jewish stenographers. Public utility corporations, such as the telephone, gas and electric companies, were criticized for not employing Jews, although correspondence was examined in which some of these companies insisted that they did employ some Jews. Banks, too, were pointed out as striking examples of institutions which seldom used Jewish employees except in the limited areas where a knowledge of Yiddish was imperative. In addition to these handicaps, Jews felt particularly the difficulties confronting Jewish women who wished to go into teaching or nursing and Jewish men who wished to study for the medical or legal professions.

The general employment agencies, as already indicated, corroborated the existence of such discrimination. In many instances, they maintained, it was useless to send Jews to employers, for to do so would only annoy them. The agencies also divulged one reason which may be responsible, in part at least, for the allegation made in Jewish circles that the agencies themselves discriminated. Almost unanimously they insisted that they had exceptional difficulty in collecting their fees from Jewish applicants for work whom they had successfully placed.

It was frankly admitted, even by Jewish agencies, that many Jews who fail to secure jobs attribute their failure to discrimination when the real difficulty was really quite different—sometimes a personality problem, sometimes general unfitness. Even so, there was so much unwillingness among employers to engage Jews and so much unwillingness among Gentile employees to be associated with them in employment, that Jews are probably justified in expecting to be the victims of discrimination. Here is a typical instance of a young Jewess who wished to train for a nurse. She applied to a certain hospital and her recommendations and appearance were satisfactory. She was told to call at a stated time and begin her duties. Then the question of her religion came up, and she was informed that they were very sorry but it was their policy not to accept Jews. In this particular city there is no adequate Jewish hospital and her chances of studying for her desired profession are practically non-existent. A great many more Jewish women would study for teaching were there opportunities before them, but so many have already taken the professional training only to find the doors barred that others are discouraged. Indeed, there is a glut of teachers on the market both in the United States and in Canada. One came across so many Jewish men and Jewish women who had been trained to teach and were now engaged in social work, that it seemed as if the very exclusion of unusually well-educated Jews from the teaching profession had contributed in part to the extraordinary efficiency of Jewish social service. Perhaps, in the same way, not a few Jews who might have been absorbed in the teaching profession have gone in for journalism.

Jews claim that even Jewish employers, as already indicated, frequently discriminate against Jewish applicants for employment. The Jewish employers who plead guilty to this charge, in part at least, put up as a rule one or more of the following reasons:

(a) They do not wish to be known as too exclusively a Jewish firm.

(b) They occasionally distrust the loyalty of Jews to the firm, believing that the ambitious Jew will work hard to master the firm's trade secrets and then set up a rival business on his own.

(c) Gentiles are often more satisfied with a subordinate position than Jews who may want to run the business in their own way.

(d) The presence of a large percentage of Gentiles in the sales force attracts Gentile trade, and it is often impossible for Jews, by reason of the existing feeling against them, to establish the necessary business and social contacts.

It is well known that many Jewish firms operate under a non-Jewish name in order not to frighten away Gentile business. As a matter of fact, Gentiles frequently suspect any business which seems to conceal the names of the management and assumes a semi-patriotic appellation.

While the Gentiles admit a large measure of discrimination—which they could not well deny—they also point out that certain of the positions alleged to be closed to Jews are in some measure closed to them by prevailing tendencies among Jews themselves. Thus bankers indicate that the clerical work in the banks is tedious, the pay small and the chances of rapid advancement meagre. These conditions prove self-excluding to many Jews, since they prefer to enter a business where there are better chances of rapid advancement or where, failing this, they may in a short time be able to go into business for themselves. One cannot well do that in banking, especially when the whole tendency is towards fewer and bigger banks, nor in the public utilities. This point of view was stated quite definitely by a prominent Jewish financier, himself a director of a large bank. He affirmed that he had tried to secure a Jewish bookkeeper for his own office, but he had not been able to find one who was satisfactory or would stick. He had, however, in his office a young Jew, and he suggested that we call him in and ask him why Jews did not go into banking, adding that he had never discussed the question with him. The young man was duly called in, and the question put before him. His reply was: "I think that the average Jew would find the chances of promotion in a bank too slow. They want better pay and a chance to get ahead quicker, and preferably to be on their own." Other Jews who were consulted agreed with this statement, but added, by way of exception, that many Jewish stenographers would be quite willing to work in the bank's marble halls if they had the chance.

In certain types of work, Jews may, therefore, exclude themselves, while they show a particular desire to enter other kinds of work in which Gentiles are also keen to engage, especially when there are so many applications for every white-collar job, and when much modern education has caused young men and women to consider manual work beneath them. In short, the Jews are after the very jobs that the Gentiles want and they are not eager for the very jobs which the Gentiles would be glad to avoid and let them have.

Since discrimination does exist in spite of manifold efforts to prevent it, one is naturally led to consider some of the more basic causes of discrimination.

Why Gentiles Discriminate Against Jews

It is far from easy to find any general categories under which to classify the reasons put forward by Gentiles why they do not care to employ Jews or to be associated with them in business or employment any more than is necessary. Perhaps, the simplest classification would be three-fold:

(a) They prefer to surround themselves with persons more like themselves.

(b) They do not like Jews as a group.

(c) They fear Jews and their growing importance in professional life, in national and international finance.

The preference for one's own kind is so obvious that it may be overlooked, but it is of vital significance. Some reference along this line was made in connection with the activity of fraternal orders in finding places for their "brother-members." Such a preference may be, perhaps, a survival of that tribal consciousness which Sir Arthur Keith considers a device of Nature to secure better and higher races. It may be considered as a kind of social narcissism. At all events, Kipling has expressed it in his poem "The Stranger":

> "The Stranger within my gate,
>   He may be true or kind,
> But he does not talk my talk—
>   I cannot feel his mind.
> I see the face and the eyes and the mouth,
>   But not the soul behind.
>
> "The men of my own stock
>   They may do ill or well,
> But they tell the lies I am wonted to,
>   They are used to the lies I tell,
> We do not need interpreters
>   When we go to buy and sell."

One may deem this provincial, if he cares to do so. It is, however, probably true of all but closely-related groups.

The dislike of the Jews as a group is so common that discrimination is frequently defended on highly rationalized grounds when a far simpler explanation would be that the discriminators disliked the discriminatees. To be sure, certain Gentile groups indicate on the whole a high regard for Jews. Perhaps, their strongest advocates are the social workers with whom Jewish social workers cordially coöperate and with little competition. Next come teachers in the public schools who find Jewish pupils gratifyingly alert in intelligence and eager students. In artistic, musical and literary circles the dominant attitude is one of friendliness and appreciation. Liberal Protestant ministers are apt to be particularly friendly with Liberal Jews, since they admire the solid intellectual backgrounds of many Jewish rabbis, and approve the absence of a certain theological dogmatism which they may have discarded. When, however, one turns to the commercial and financial classes, to Gentiles "in high society," and to members of certain professions to which Jews are contributing "more than their quota," and where Jewish competition is most keen, he finds that the dislike of the Jew becomes exceedingly vocal and active. While there are notable exceptions to all these generalizations, it is from the latter groups that one may gather the most complete anthology of reasons why they sympathize with Hitler.

Those who confess to a dislike or distrust of most Jews will make exceptions. They will usually refer to some Jews who are "white," and for whom they have high regard, although it is quite evident that in their judgment the "white" Jews are exceptions. Others again distinguish between the Jews who have been for a long time in the two countries concerned in this study and those who have entered, mostly from Eastern Europe, within the last thirty years. Of the former they spoke with respect and no little admiration; for the latter they undoubtedly cherished a deep aversion. Perhaps, the spokesman of this distinction was a prominent lawyer who said: "The Jews will be perfectly all right after they have been in the country for two or three generations. By that time, certain traits that now offend Gentiles will be ironed out. Meanwhile, it is difficult to be cordial towards them."

This, of course, raises a fundamental question; is it possible, despite the eloquence of Edmund Burke, to indict a whole people? Most apostles of good-will answer in the negative and urge that men be considered in the light of their individual merits, and not as members of a group. The more one studies the situation, however, the more difficult does it become to avoid generalizations. Scientists certainly speak of national or racial trends even though they know full well that there are many exceptions to the rule, but mass judgments are made, not on the basis of exceptions, but on the proclivity of a given group toward a certain pattern of conduct or behavior. Are there distinctly Jewish characteristics, especially among those who have come to the country recently and have barely escaped from the intense Jewishness of the European ghetto? It would be strange if there were not characteristic virtues and characteristic weaknesses, and out of this admixture of virtues and weaknesses there emerges what seems to be a "Jewish type" to which the Gentile may react either favorably or unfavorably—usually unfavorably.

The Jewish group is frequently praised for perseverance, vitality, intellectuality, and the ability to survive the manifold persecutions to which it has been subjected. At the same time, it is frequently condemned for other characteristics, notably, for aggressiveness, "sharp business practices," clannishness and lack of sensitivity to the feelings of Gentile groups. It may be that neither the virtues nor the weaknesses are inherently Jewish; it may be that in both cases they are the accidents of history and environment, but that this archetype of the Jewish spirit does exist in the Gentile mind and is responsible for much of the antipathy displayed toward him is a fact which may be explained, but cannot be denied. Furthermore, many Jews themselves dwell on their distinctive characteristics. A prominent rabbi in the Middle-West expressed his surprise at Shakespeare's uncanny knowledge of the Jew as revealed in certain passages in "The Merchant of Venice," though it is hardly possible that he had ever known a real Jew. Yet, he makes Shylock plead his common humanity at one moment—"Hath not a Jew eyes . . . fed with the same food, hurt with the same weapons, etc." while at another moment he indignantly declines Bassanio's invitation to dinner— "Yes, to eat pork." Today the Jew will be pleading that he is just the same as the Gentile, the rabbi commented, and tomorrow, he will be insisting that he is quite different.

At all events, many Gentiles do feel a positive physical aversion when confronted with the dominant Jewish type. Whether this physical aversion is the result or the cause of their dislike is another matter. It may be both. The fact unfortunately exists and often makes Gentiles exceedingly uncomfortable when Jews with these marked characteristics are around. It may be that some Jews feel a similar aversion for Gentiles, but at this point we are considering the grounds upon which Gentiles discriminate against Jews. Moreover, Gentiles complain of Jewish manners which, they say, are usually either too aggressive or too insinuating, although they may fail to appreciate that both aggressive and insinuating manners frequently connote an inferiority complex, or to say the least, an uncertainty of status. They also particularly complain of the ethical standards, and especially of the business practices of Jews, and assert that Jews seem to have a different moral outlook from that of the average Christian. Prominent ecclesiastics who obviously desired to be fair quite sincerely expressed their belief that certain Jewish circles in America were a demoralizing influence, while men of business dwelt on the so-called "sharp practices."

Finally, discrimination is often due, in part, to fear. Dislike is at a minimum where competition is negligible and at a maximum where the Gentile is brought into open competition with the Jew. The Jew seems irrepressible; he succeeds in spite of handicaps; he thrives despite persecution. Many Gentiles refuse to credit this success to superior brains or superior ability, but suspect a "plot," and thus the soil is prepared to harbor any seeds which the anti-Semitic propagandist may sow. The fantastic idea of a world conspiracy of Jews to gain universal control of the economic forces dies hard. The Protocols of the Elders of the Wise Men of Zion continue to be circulated and to be believed, after they have been proved to be a forgery, because so many Gentiles are disposed to believe in the reality of such a conspiracy. Seeing Jews so prominent in the management of the theatre, the motion picture, the book publishing business, etc., the Gentile feels that the Jew is seeking to control him by controlling the organs of public opinion, and instead of admiring the enterprise he resents the influence of a minority. At times, the very efficiency of Jewish communal organization, whether local, national or international, seems to corroborate his fears, while the very recital of Jewish achievements, whether attempted by Jewish propagandists or Gentile apologists, only accentuates his suspicions. The motion picture, "The House of Rothschild," shows the founder of the house advising his sons to seek wealth so that they may force a situation where the Jew may "walk the earth with dignity," and even this seems to suspicious Gentiles to indicate an economic policy. Most notably, the advocacy by Jews of the boycott against Germany strikes many Gentiles as an example of a self-centered indifference to the serious effects of a boycott on trade and international relations. Such Gentile critics, it may be remarked, seem oblivious to the fact that the boycott to many of its supporters, whether Jews or Christians, is a righteous protest against intolerable wrongs.

The fear that breeds discrimination is aroused in Gentiles by Jewish capitalists, on the one hand, and by Jewish radical agitators, on the other hand. It is such fear that secures ready acceptance of Nazi propaganda. Over and over again, in casual conversation, business and professional men in the United States and Canada have disclosed their willingness to condone Hitler's destruction of constitutional liberties because his anti-Semitic policy chimed in with their own antipathies.

Behind the all too common discrimination by Gentiles against Jews, therefore, there lie easily aroused dislikes and rivalries and fears. How deep-seated and hard to eradicate they are will only appear as we look back through the centuries of Jewish-Gentile relations. We therefore offer a limited number of considerations, far too briefly sketched, which do seem of major significance.

The Anatomy of Anti-Semitism

There are five major factors in anti-Semitism—the racial, the religious, the social, the political, and the economic, although it is impossible to define sharply the boundaries that separate these various areas of friction. To begin at the beginning, the Jews emerge in history as a fairly clearly defined racial type, although far more mixed than is generally admitted. Very early they evolved from their nomadic status, passed through a brief period of more settled agricultural life and soon developed into a dominantly mercantile group. They were characterized by a certain intensity of life, a mental keenness and alertness, a highly developed tribal feeling, which was later accentuated by unique experiences in contacts with surrounding peoples and especially by the evolution of their religious outlook.

HISTORICAL ANTECEDENTS

The Jewish religion evolved in such a way that it became a force making for racial separation and cohesion. While monotheism may not have been the product of the Jewish mind alone, the concept of the peculiar relation of the God of gods to His chosen people, Israel, had certain distinctive features. The Jewish religion also came to be identified with a vast body of ritual law, against which some of the prophets sounded warnings. These laws, carefully prescribing for almost every conceivable action in life, including dress and food, made normal intercourse with other peoples next to impossible. In the absence of any metaphysical emphasis such as characterized the Hellenic peoples, ritual became increasingly central in the pattern of Jewish behavior and undoubtedly tended to the self-exclusion or seclusion of the Jews from the Gentiles. It is not without significance that the attitude to Jewish ritual law was the first grave question to engage the attention of a Council of the Christian Church. In lifting the ban on certain acts of ceremonial importance, the Council of Jerusalem made the schism of Christianity from Judaism inevitable. Henceforth, Christianity moved definitely in the direction of universalism, while Judaism continued to prescribe in the interests of racialism. Henceforth, wherever the Jews went, they remained, largely because of their religion, a people apart, firmly resisting assimilation. One of the leading Christian thinkers on this continent today stated that the main question he wished to put to modern Judaism was this: "Is Judaism today essentially *ethical* or *ethnical*?"

This deep race-consciousness, heightened by the prescriptions of a ritualistic religion and the lack of normal social intercourse with non-Jewish peoples, made the group so self-conscious that it sought and received certain political privileges. The Jews asked and received a large measure of self-determination in the countries in which they sojourned. They sought a certain extra-territoriality, as they established their own Beth-Din, or ecclesiastical courts of law which adjudicated in all matters relating to disputes between Jews. (There were of course more or less analogous courts in the Christian Church.) They frequently paid their taxes as a group, and used their own methods of collection from within the group. The fact that the Jews were often a favored and a protected people made them unpopular, and in Europe the story of the Jews vacillates between periods of special privilege and high favor, on the one hand, and periods of unspeakable oppression, on the other. The Gentile world seemed unable to live either with them or without them. The fact, too, that the Jews had no "national homeland" after the fall of Jerusalem made them politically *déracinés*, and their loyalty to the prince in whose realm they resided was always suspected. They were a wandering people, citizens of the world, or citizens of a hypothetical messianic kingdom which might come at any moment. They were not rooted in the soil nor did they gladly accept the lot of the majority of the people among whom they came.

Moreover, they were essentially a commercial people. Long before the city of Jerusalem fell, the Jews had been scattered throughout the Mediterranean world, and large colonies resided in the major commercial cities. There was a notable Jewish colony in Alexandria long before the Christian era, and even at that time the Jews, were stigmatized as "the mercenary race," never popular with their fellow-citizens, but, as the article in Hastings Dictionary of the Bible states, "protected by the rulers, Greeks or Roman, who recognized the value of their services to the commercial prosperity of the city. When Alexandria became part of the Roman Empire, B. C. 30, and a granary of Rome, the important corn trade fell into the hands of the Jewish merchants."

While Gentiles were more frequently rooted and attached to the soil, the Jews lived in certain specified towns and cities, often in definite areas in these towns and cities, and were engaged in banking, money-changing and various forms of trade. Until the advent of the Caorsini and the Lombards in the mediaeval world, the Jews had a practical monopoly on banking and money-lending, since the law of the Church forbade usury. Gentiles in financial need were forced to seek loans from Jewish money-lenders at high rates of interest. Often unable to pay when the loans fell due, they lost their all and bitterness developed against the "usurious Jews." When feeling ran too high, the Jews became the victims of pogroms or expulsions. Because they learned to fear pogroms or expulsions, they kept their wealth in bullion or precious stones which could be concealed or hastily removed. Such removals would undoubtedly complicate the ability of the country they had left to engage in foreign trade. At last Gentiles were permitted to engage in banking and money-lending, and the monopoly formerly enjoyed by the Jews was broken, but the legend of their control of international finance has persisted down to the present time, as is clearly indicated in the current phrase "the Jewish international bankers." The Jews thus continued to be essentially a trading and commercial people, and because of the location of some Jews in almost every commercial city of importance, much of the international trade was inevitably placed in their hands. Their talent and prominence in mercantile affairs gave point to the gibe of the ancient Alexandrians, that they were "the mercenary race."

All this while, they had no national home but continued to cherish the pious hope that once again, in the light of prophecy, they would return to their Holy City. A conventional greeting at the time of their great festivals was "Next Year in Jerusalem." *Déracinés,* they found it difficult to put forth new roots; they were inhibited from doing this by the repeated persecutions to which they were subjected, by their aversion for agricultural life and by that Messianism which promised them the land of Palestine as their own.[3] They became objects of political suspicion, men without a country, international Jews, here today and gone tomorrow, socially resisting assimilation.

The Catholic Encyclopaedia states the principal causes of the hatred of the Jews to be the following:

"(1) The deep and wide racial difference between Jews and Christians which was, moreover, emphasized by the ritual and dietary laws of Talmudic Judaism.

"(2) The mutual religious antipathy which prompted the Jewish masses to look upon the Christians as idolaters, and the Christians to regard the Jews as the murderers of the Divine Saviour of mankind, and to believe readily the accusa-

---

[3] Silver, A. H., "Messianic Speculation in Israel" (New York: The Macmillan Co., 1927).

tions of the use of Christian blood in the celebration of the Jewish Passover, the desecration of the Holy Eucharist, etc.

"(3) The trade rivalry which caused the Christians to accuse the Jews of sharp practice, and to resent their clipping of the coinage, their usury, etc.

"(4) The patriotic susceptibilities of the particular nations in the midst of which the Jews have usually formed a foreign element, and to the respective interests of which their devotion has not always been beyond suspicion."

The article concludes:

"In view of these and other more or less local, more or less justified, reasons, one can readily understand how the popular hatred of the Jews has too often defeated the beneficent efforts of the Church, and notably of its supreme pontiffs, in regard to them."[4]

The chronic maltreatment suffered at the hands of Gentiles, and the groundlessness of such allegations as that pertaining to the use of Christian blood, naturally rankled in the hearts of successive generations of Jews. Cruelty and antipathy were answered by distrust and antipathy.

It is futile to consider modern anti-Semitism except against the general background sketched above. It is because of this interweaving of racial, religious, social, political and economic factors that the problem today is so complex and so difficult to attack.

RELIGIOUS DIFFERENCES NOT NOW IMPORTANT

What, however, is the reason for the present feeling in the United States and Canada today? By and large the rank and file of Jews attribute modern anti-Semitism to religious prejudice, and tirelessly reiterate, even against the judgment of their Gentile friends, that they are hated because the Christians regard them as the Christ-killers. In the opinion of the writer, this insistence is ill-founded and only alienates the philo-Semites among Christians. It is true that the charge of Christ-killing does appear in various kinds of anti-Semitic literature from the epistles of Paul down to the present time, and in Europe the popular hatred of the Jews was fanned by such appeals to religious fanaticism. We find it even urged in various attacks on the bills brought forward in Maryland between 1818 and 1826 for the legal emancipation of the Jews in that state. The phrase may occasionally be used by thoughtless school-boys in their desire to hurt the Jews, but where it appears in either the United States or Canada today, it is a symptom and not a cause. This opinion is put forward on many grounds, among them the following:

(1) The charge of Christ-killing was practically never mentioned in any of the many discussions which the writer has held with Gentiles on the Jewish question, or if intentionally introduced, was vehemently denied.

---

[4] *Catholic Encyclopaedia;* article on "The Jews," by Francis E. Gigot, column viii; page 404.

(2) Practically no one even hinted at a religious reason why Jews should be discriminated against in employment or in the transfer of real estate. The only serious exception is a mild recognition of a certain interference with business caused by the absence of Jewish employees on Jewish holidays, especially those in the early fall when offices and stores may be particularly busy.

(3) Neither in the United States nor in Canada has religious homogeneity been a matter of governmental policy, although in Canada the special status of French Canada, and the early recognition of the Church of England as the established church have tended to stress the "Christian" character of the country. The national hymn in Canada includes the words "For Christ and the King" and links "altar" and "throne." But the entire background of the two nations' thoughts in regard to religious liberty is utterly at variance with that of Czarist Russia or Poland whence most of the Jews have come.

(4) Most of the Protestants interviewed stated that they had heard the phrase "Christ-killers" first from Jewish rabbis and had never heard it used in Christian circles. Some of them stated that they had been brought up in conservative circles, in communities without Jews, where the teaching in the churches stressed the unique character of the people of Israel and made them predisposed to view the Jews with peculiar favor.

Practically the only people who stress the religious motivations of anti-Semitism today are the Jews themselves and members of certain more or less negligible and esoteric Christian sects. The antipathy to the Jews in the United States and Canada is clearly not religious prejudice, although by constant iteration it might possibly become an issue.

The fundamental causes of anti-Semitism in the two countries under consideration are economic, social and, to some extent, political, but dominantly economic. The basis of the antipathy of many Gentiles to Jews as a whole is, in the opinion of the writer, largely due to one or more of these factors:

(1) The inherited conception of the Jews as international mercenaries.

(2) The excessive urbanization of the Jew, with the inevitable congestion of the Jewish population at strategic centers of commerce, finance and culture.

(3) Unfortunate personal experiences of Gentiles in their dealings with Jews which have tended to give some validity to their suspicions of "Jewish sharp practices."

(4) Gentiles, finding it profitable to discredit Jewish competitors, welcome evidence unfavorable to Jews as justification of their attitude.

So far as such attitudes are inherited stereotypes, they can probably only be changed by the development of a realistic and generous attitude toward the whole problem in the light both of history and of present conditions. In attaining this, both Jews and Gentiles must seek as far as possible to shed their preconceptions and make their inquiry *de novo*. So far as it is due to the abnormal distribution of the Jewish population and its excessive concentration at a few strategic centers, it is difficult to see what can be done, especially as the Jews may find it extremely hard to adjust themselves to certain changes in social organization which would inevitably follow. So far as it is due to "Jewish sharp practices" the Jews must take particular pains not to give the Gentiles just grounds for criticism, even though Gentiles may themselves indulge in similar sharp practices.

Excessive Urbanization of the Jews and Its Consequences

It is of importance that the vexed question of the distribution of the Jewish population be frankly faced. So far as the writer has been able to ascertain, the Jews since the beginnings of the Diaspora have ever sought the cities and centers of world trade. It has been said that the law of Israel regarded the soil as "unclean" and consequently diverted the Jews into commerce. This, however, is surely fallacious, since the entire law of Israel postulates, as several authorities point out, an agricultural people.[5] Whatever the reason, the Jews emerged at an early period as traders and financiers, although there is some evidence that the Jews of Babylonia did engage to a certain extent in agriculture in the seventh and eighth centuries, while in recent times absentee landlords in Hungary and Russia entrusted the administration of their estates to Jewish overseers. At times the Jews have been forced to reside in towns and were not permitted to own the land or to till the soil, but some scholars believe that such prohibitions were enacted to save a penurious and somewhat spendthrift peasantry from becoming the practical slaves of Jewish money-lenders. On this point, James Parkes says in *The Jew and His Neighbor*: "It is difficult for the Jew to degrade if there is no one willing to be degraded. . . . Where there is a provident and saving peasantry, as in France or Denmark, they are indebted to neither Jew nor Gentile." This is a partial but not quite complete exposition of the situation, and at all events the Jews have settled for the most part in countries where the Gentile peasantry has been either poor or improvident.

It may be that the Jews have, through long centuries of exclusion from agriculture, lost all love of the soil. At all events, few of the Jews who came to the United States or Canada in the great homesteading days took to farming or made good in it when they did so. A few agricultural colonies were started by Jews in the United States, but they came to little. There are today, it is estimated, about 80,000 Jewish people living on farms in the United States and engaged in agriculture. Numerous Jewish agencies are

---

[5] For an interesting view of manual labor held by the Jews, see Ecclesiasticus XXXVIII: 24-38.

abetting this effort "back to the land," believing that it is essentially a move in the right direction.

In Canada, the government approved the settlement of Jews in the Canadian West and the Hirsch Foundation poured considerable sums of money into such Jewish agricultural colonies, but the Jews did not stick.

Much has been said about Palestine, but the following statistics in regard to its Jewish population taken from Leonard Stein's excellent volume on *Zionism* (London: Kegan Paul, Trench and Trubner) are significant:

GROWTH OF THE JEWISH POPULATION, 1922–1931

Locality	1922 Census	1931 Census	Increase	Per Cent. Increase	Per Cent. Total Jewish Increase
Jerusalem, Tiberias, Safed, Hebron, and other towns not included in next list.	42,240	59,807	17,567	40	19.2
Tel Aviv, Jaffa, Haifa.	26,382	68,734	42,352	161	46.5
Rural Areas.	15,172	46,465	31,293	206	34.3
Totals.	83,794	175,006	91,212	108	100.0

It will thus be seen that while rural areas show relatively the larger increase since 1922, the cities and towns between them account for 65.7 per cent. of the total increase, while the rural areas account for only 34.3 per cent., and 25 per cent. of all the Jews in Palestine have taken to agriculture.

The *American Jewish Yearbook* for 1932-33 gives the Jewish population of the United States as 4,228,029, of whom 4,077,042 live in urban areas, i.e., in communities of over 2,500 population. This means that American Jewry is at least 96.4 per cent. urban. These figures are, to be sure, estimates, since we have no means of verifying them by an actual census taken in the United States under governmental auspices. In Canada, however, the facts are available. Of 156,726 persons of Hebrew descent counted in the Dominion census of 1931, 151,167 were located in urban areas and only 5,559 in rural districts.[6] The writer submitted the census figures to some further analysis and selected the ten Canadian cities in which there were at least 1,000 Jews. These ten cities (including Greater Montreal and Greater Toronto) had a total population of 2,699,084 which represented approximately 25 per cent. of the entire population of the Dominion; the ten cities had a Jewish poulation of 135,209, or 86.3 per cent. of the entire Jewish population of the Dominion.

It may be urged that Jewish migration to the United States was at its height when the free lands were exhausted, and when the country had definitely shifted from an agricultural predominance to an industrial pre-

---

[6] In Canada, "urban" areas include all cities, towns and incorporated villages.

dominance, and that naturally the Jewish immigrant fitted in with the existing trends. But while there is evidence that the Jew pioneered in the fur-trade and peddled his goods in the countryside in the early days of the last century, there is no evidence that he ever took up land to any considerable extent even when he had the chance. Further, Canada, in her effort to open up the West in the late 'nineties and the first decade of the present century, favored agricultural immigrants, but though the land was theirs for the asking, the Jews did not take it and settled down in the three major cities—Montreal, Toronto and Winnipeg. Even when certain agricultural colonies were milk-fed by the Hirsch Foundation, they withered, while the Ukrainian, the German and the Pole settled down and made good.

It is sometimes said that the Jewish immigrant, ignorant of the English language, required to settle among his own folk. The same thing, however, was equally true of the Ukrainians, the Poles and many other nationalities that poured into the Canadian West, and the government encouraged and facilitated bloc settlement. It is also urged that the Jews naturally tend to gravitate together since they must have a minyon of ten heads of households before they can initiate a synagogue, and Jewish orthodoxy forbids driving on the Sabbath or even walking more than half a mile. Hence, the practice of religion would be practically impossible on the great farms of the American and Canadian West, with the Jewish farmers isolated on their quarter-sections. This may have been a contributory reason to the urbanization of the Jews, since to this extent it would seem that the very law of Israel might make against large-scale agriculture and encourage village or town life. At all events, the Jew is not an agriculturist but an urbanite, and here is resident to a great extent the economic rub.

What does excessive urbanization do to the Jews? Lewis Browne, already quoted, points out in *How Odd of God* certain results best described in his own words:

"Our bondage to the asphalt." (Page 191)

"Makes us obtrusive in the world." (Page 192)

"We have roamed the jungle of urban life not as lone wolves, but in packs." (Page 195)

"With the marked waning of religious zeal . . . our virility seems to have followed suit." (Page 196, referring to the declining Jewish birth-rate, etc.)

"It estranged them from the physical." (Page 198)

"We have always had to make our way in the ruts; we have never been able to walk the paved Highway." (Page 201)

"We have but one weapon, our wits. . . . We learn to think quickly and talk glibly, to parry nimbly and thrust hard. We learn to be shrewd, artful and tirelessly aggressive." (Page 209)

"We are a city-folk, and cultural leadership is universally vested in such."
(Page 211)
"Our inclination for radicalism." (Page 215)

The three salient traits, he claims, which distinguish the Jew are "our alien-
ation from the physical, our proclivity for the intellectual, and our addiction
to the revolutionary." (Page 222.)

Urbanization, however, does other and perhaps more baneful things to
the soul. The city man is always dealing with forces and material that
can be manipulated; this makes him restive and eternally aggressive. The
countryman, on the other hand, who "slowly plods his weary way," has
to deal with Nature, which may be assisted but cannot well be hurried.
No amount of milking will draw out of the cow more milk than is
already there, and when milking is done, the cow must be allowed to
depart in peace until the next time. The countryman learns, therefore, to
do the best he can and to leave the rest to Nature. The city man is
always thinking up some new deal by which he can improve his general
position in society. While the countryman's mind may, as a result, be
somewhat sluggish, his close contact with the soil and with the world of
growing things may give him an emotional simplicity which the city man
lacks. The cities are always being recruited from the country. Few urban
Gentiles, moreover, are far removed in actual number of generations from
rural life and most of them have a romantic hankering, once they are
financially independent, for a country-seat where they once again dig their
hands into the soil. The difference between the urban and the rural point
of view is fairly fundamental. Even the average Jew, it is claimed, who
moves into a good residential area in the city does not take the same pride
in maintaining the grounds, the shrubbery and the garden of his home
as does the Gentile, unless he is financially able to employ a gardener, and
perhaps because of this the Gentiles expect that when the Jews move into
residential areas, the appearance of the district will usually deteriorate.

Today the cities dominate the country, and the Jews, by reason of their
high concentration in cities, at the very centers of finance, wealth, industry
and commerce, gain an economic prominence and influence out of all
proportion to their population. Whether they possess intellectual powers
superior to those of the Gentiles, or not, one fundamental cause of their
success is their concentration where the channels of commerce converge.[7]
Gentiles who assume that Jews by this concentration stand a chance of

[7] Nearly one-third of all the life insurance in force in America, both ordinary and industrial,
is held in New York. Approximately half the nation's imports, measured alike by tonnage and
value, enter the United States through the custom-house at the mouth of the Hudson, and more
than half of our total export tonnage clears through that port. One-seventh of all the net retail
sales in the United States were made in New York in 1929—seven billion out of forty-nine billion. Article in the *National Geographic Magazine* for November, 1933.

dominating business, inwardly resolve to do what they can to prevent it. Hence, discrimination.

Since cultural leadership in America, as Lewis Browne says, is vested in city-folk and since the Jews are concentrated in the cities, it is not to be wondered at that they are prominent in cultural as in commercial pursuits. In Chapter VI the statistics given show a high proportion of Jewish students in institutions of higher learning, due partly to Jewish preference and talent for intellectual pursuits, partly to concentration in cities where colleges are readily accessible. A recent survey has been made also of the Jews in musical fields. A newspaper report, dated January 31, 1934, quoted the maker of the survey, Dr. Keith Sward, of the Pennsylvania College for Women, as follows:

"Eminent American musicians number more Jews than you would expect from the Jewish ratios in the general population. Roughly, fifty per cent. of the violin-virtuosi, the maestros and the first violinists of American symphony orchestras are of Jewish origin. One quarter to one-half of the piano-virtuosi and of all symphonic and amusement instrumentalists are Jewish. Ten per cent. of American composers are of Jewish extraction."

Dr. Sward also pointed out that this stood in sharp contrast with European orchestras where there was an "extremely low ratio of Jewish players" despite the large size of the Jewish population. In twenty-three nationally known amusement orchestras in the United States, 73 per cent. of the violin players are Jewish, but in the same organizations, clarinet, trombone and horn are "strikingly non-Jewish."

It may be fair to suggest that the Jewish dominance in music in the United States is due to four major factors: (1) the excessive urbanization of the Jew and consequently his enhanced opportunity to secure a musical education; (2) the high concentration of Jews in New York City, the musical capital of the nation; (3) Jewish dominance in the theatrical and amusement business generally; and (4) the fact that Gentiles in the United States and Canada tend to look upon music less as a vocation than as an avocation and are not so ready as Jews to devote to musical study the prolonged hard work that proficiency entails.

The predominant control of the motion-picture by a limited number of Jews is resented by many Gentiles and made the occasion for casting aspersion on the character of all Jews. The cinema is an institution of unique power in the formation of character and interests, and many Gentiles feel that it has fallen into the hands of a group who are racially inhibited from properly appreciating the real tastes and ideals of the vast body of the population.

DOMINANT BUSINESS ACTIVITIES AND ALLEGED STANDARDS OF JEWS

Next to the high urbanization of the Jews, a fundamental cause of Gentile suspicion is the alleged character of Jewish business ethics. A realistic approach to this problem may best be made by first considering some of the types of business in which Jews particularly engage.

Most of the early Jews who penetrated the frontier in American life were pedlars, and several of the longest-established Jewish commercial families in the United States were founded by one-time pedlars. Putting packs on their backs, or driving a horse and wagon, they ventured into the hinterland selling such goods as the farmer might find more convenient to buy at the door than seek in the nearest town. Here we have their novitiate in the department-store and mail-order business, much of which they later controlled, although Gentiles shared with them in these ventures. In Canada, on the other hand, Scotchmen and Ulster Irishmen had established department stores and mail-order houses long before the Jews arrived in appreciable numbers, and as a result, while Canada has some of the largest department stores in the world, Jews control only two of the smaller stores—one in Ottawa and the other in Quebec. Here the Jews arrived too late to secure the chance they had in the United States and consequently were diverted into other forms of business.

It must also be remembered that Jews not only flock to the cities, but they are at first usually concentrated in definite areas in the city. This is inevitable in view of the natural tendency of all immigrant groups to flock together, and it is especially true of the Jews since orthodoxy prohibits walking beyond a certain distance on the Sabbath. The Jewish immigrants, almost always orthodox, bring with them certain vital needs which only Jews can meet. Kosher meat, for instance, requires that the preparation of all meat consumed by the orthodox—one of the most important of all commodities—be supervised by Jews and practically entirely marketed by Jews.[8] Wherever Jews settle, therefore, not only Gentile residents withdraw, but the Gentile butcher and grocer are also forced out and their places are taken by the small Jewish merchant, occasionally financed by a Hebrew Loan Association. When the Jewish shop-dealer is thus definitely established among his own people and has begun to master the techniques and business methods of the people among whom he has come, he moves to deal with the Gentile world as well. For such reasons as these, the advent

---

[8] The *American Jewish Yearbook* for 1931-32 estimated the value of kosher meat consumed in New York City alone during that year at $250,000,000. In the Old World and in some places in the New, a tax is placed by the Jewish community on all kosher meat sales at so many cents a pound, and the revenue from this tax is used to meet certain types of communal expense. During the depression, Jewish social workers frequently explained their larger per capita expense of relief on the grounds of the higher cost of kosher meat.

of Jews into any community destabilizes the business in the district and practically serves notice on the business men already located there.

Small shops to meet the needs of the people of their own race—clothing, jewelry and watches, pawn-broking—these generally are the characteristic first enterprises of Jewish merchants, and from these they gradually extend their operations into various other business fields. Strangely enough, with few outstanding exceptions, banking is a business which the American and Canadian Jew has not entered, despite the great "ado" about Jewish international bankers, and the effort of certain anti-Semitic propagandists to assure the people in the hinterland that J. Pierpont Morgan's name was originally "Morgenstern." True, a prominent city bank in the United States will usually have some "show-window" Jew on its Board of Directors whom they consult principally when Jewish firms ask for credit with their institution, knowing that Jews would have sources of information in such matters superior to their own. But such a director is usually a lone figure, while Jews complain, as already intimated and partly explained, that they cannot secure clerical positions in banks except perhaps where the bank in question is in a district overwhelmingly Jewish and where a knowledge of Jewish idiosyncrasies or of Yiddish would be a particular asset.

Immigrant Jews entered the factories, especially those connected with the needle-trades, but they did not to any large exent enter the manual trades. They showed what Lewis Browne has called "an estrangement from the physical." Unlike Scotch, German or Finnish women, few Jewish women sought employment in household service, while the Jews often employed Gentiles as servants, since the more rigid observers of Jewish law are prohibited from lighting fires on the Sabbath and the presence of Gentile servants provides a happy solution of the difficulties and discomforts which a climate more rigorous than that of Palestine presents. This higher degree of selectivity in occupation and deliberate preference for specific types of work brought the Jews into keener competition for jobs with the more skilled Gentile workers, many of whom had graduated from the farms into the cities and wished to get away from the drudgery of menial labor. Jews can hardly be blamed for seeking the more desirable kinds of occupation; nor can the Gentiles be blamed for seeking to retain such positions for themselves. Immigrants from other cultural groups threw themselves into almost any kind of work which presented itself. The Jew was inevitably and from the beginning more selective.

But all Jews could not be small merchants and most of them were at first handicapped from doing what they would have preferred to do by language and other similar difficulties. Many of them, under the coercion of this variety of handicaps, became ingenious in developing new lines of business. It is generally believed, for instance, that the Jew was the pioneer in the salvaging of waste materials. "Rags, bottles and old iron" made fortunes for many Jews, and even today in cities where the Jewish immigrants are still comparatively recently arrived, the ubiquity and insistence of the rags and bottle men have not made for good relationships between Jews and Gentiles. In many instances, he is the first and almost the only business contact which the rank and file of citizens have with the Jewish business man, for he penetrates into the Gentile quarters seeking "anything to sell." His forbidding appearance, his dilapidated wagon, his mangy and immobile horse, his bargaining proclivities, his tendency to pile his accumulated junk in the yard of his place of residence—all this has been so conspicuous that the Gentile world has frequently judged the whole Jewish group on the basis of the junk-dealer. The Jews were limited in their choice of occupations, but when they once went into something, they became most assiduous and persistent and in some instances they created great business enterprises almost from nothing. The control of the clothing industry by Jews in America has been attributed in part to the fact that prior to the invention of the sewing-machine, farmers and laborers used second-hand clothing for their work clothes, and Jews secured a practical monopoly in this line as the college song "Solomon Levy" attests. Then, when the sewing-machine was invented, they discovered the possibilities of preparing large quantities of ready-made garments, distributing them from central warehouses through retail stores which were already largely in Jewish hands. Thus, as early as 1850, local records show that the clothing business in Pittsburgh and Cincinnati was overwhelmingly Jewish.[9]

Again, in the old world, the severe Russian legislation forced many of them to be the vendors of alcoholic drinks, such as vodka, and when they came to America, they found it possible to enter a field which was increasingly looked down upon by the Protestant majority, with its growing sentiment for total abstinence, and which had been largely in the hands of the Irish and Germans. Once again, when the motion picture became practicable, there was already a high degree of concentration of Jews at the financial capital of the United States, viz., New York City, and in addition there had been a strong antagonism to the theatre in the more puritanical wing of Protestantism. Jews had already been securing the control of many theatres, and with this experience behind them, they were

---

[*] In 1929, New York made clothing which at factory prices was valued at approximately $2,700,000,000. It included three-fourths of the nation's production of ordinary apparel and nearly one-half of the country's clothing for women. See *National Geographic Magazine* for November, 1933.

quicker than Gentiles to see the possibilities in the baby motion-picture industry.

Although the Jewish control of business—whether wholesale or retail—has probably been exaggerated, it was sufficiently marked in some lines of business to create suspicion and fear, especially on the part of the "older American group" who found themselves compelled in the less skilled trades to compete with the whole immigrant population. In this respect there is a marked difference between the industrial development of a country like England, with no serious competition from immigrant populations, and newer countries like the United States and Canada. At all events, as the Jews became increasingly dominant in some lines of business, the Gentiles withdrew where their relations could be preferably with their own kind.

When, at last, the Jews more than all other immigrant groups began to penetrate into the sanctuaries where the Gentiles had felt most secure, even the professions such as law and medicine, the opposition to them was no longer confined to business men—it penetrated the professions. Descendants of the older Gentile stock resented being pushed out of the more significant posts. Some of them began to fear that if the Jews were not checked, they would soon be wresting leadership in the professions, as well as in business, out of the hands of the children of the men who had tamed the wilderness and established the characteristic institutions of the United States and Canada. Their reaction was thus not only Gentile but also "nativist." This proprietary attitude toward national history and culture on the part of Gentiles betrays some of them into anomalous positions, as for example, in the case of an educator born in Canada but reared in the United States, where he had spent his entire adult life as a university professor. Although he had consequently had no direct share in developing Canada, he delivered himself of these sentiments:

"When in the States, I felt very cordial to the Jews, especially to Jewish students. It was only when I returned to Canada that I became conscious of resentment. I myself was sufficiently near to the pioneer days to know what had gone into the making of the country, and when I found the Jews 'talking Canadian' and aggressively pushing themselves here and there as if they were the custodians of the Canadian spirit, I resented it."

In the same way, Americans often resent the way in which certain Jewish writers, some of whom can only know Gentile home-life from the outside, write long dissertations on the spiritual development of America, when, despite their acknowledged acumen and objectivity, they are often innocent of certain subtleties which can only be appreciated from the inside and by those who have inherited the tradition. Such "nativist" sentiment has its analogy in a resentment felt by some Christian scholars toward cer-

tain liberal rabbis who venture to propound the essence of pure and unde-
filed Christianity. It is in place to ask how many Gentiles stop to consider
the resentment aroused in Jewish hearts by the sometimes shallow and harsh
criticisms levelled at Judaism by Christians.

However unjust it may be, it is "nativist" feeling, too, which makes the
average American especially cordial toward those Jews whose families have
long resided in the country, but critical of the more recently-arrived Eastern
Europeans. He begins to feel toward the latter as the ancient Canaanites
may have felt when the children of Israel began to occupy the land. As
one of the business men interviewed in this study put it, in the words of
the book of Deuteronomy: They had come into a land and inherited great
and goodly cities which they had not built, and houses full of all good things
which they had not filled, and wells of water which they had not digged,
vineyards and olive trees which they had not planted, and why, asked
the man we were interviewing, should we, like the ancient Canaanites, let
them have it?

Not all Jews, however, became merchants. Many were employed in factories at low wages and they became not infrequently labor agitators. True,
Jews were conspicuously absent from some of the largest unions, such as
the railroad unions and the United Mine Workers of the World, but in
the garment industry they were particularly active. Others, still bleeding
in spirit from the persecution received in Russia, were socialistic or com-
munistic, and because of their location in such strategic centers as New
York, they seemed particularly vocal. The head of the American Federation of Labor for many years was a Jew, and while some Jewish labor leaders
were eminently conservative and constructive in their philosophy and action,
Jews became characterized in the popular mind as breeders of revolt, in-
citers to communism and difficult to manage. This fear of the Jewish
radical was accentuated by the prominence of Jews in the Bolshevist revolution in Russia and their leadership in the neighborhood of Madison Square
in New York. Recently, the Scottsboro case in Alabama drew certain
Jewish advocates of human rights to the scene, and this attempt on the
part of the North to "dictate" to the South, added to a growing consciousness of the number of New York Jews attending Alabama educational institutions, created a feeling against Jews which was practically non-existent
before.

OBJECTIONABLE BUSINESS PRACTICES

We have already indicated the common allegation that the Jewish business man stands for sharp practices. This reputation is of almost immemorial age. To the degree to which it is founded on fact, it may be in
part an oriental tendency, since the same kind of allegation has also been

made in regard to the Armenian. The experience of the Jew in mediaeval Europe would inevitably have enhanced such a reputation for trickiness. As has already been indicated in the preface, the Jews could not belong to the mediaeval guilds because the guilds were organized on religious principles, and hence what business the Jews could secure, had to be secured in face of the handicaps placed upon them. On this point, James Parkes says:

"The Christian merchants of the Middle Ages had evolved a system of mutual protection by a complete code forbidding a merchant to rob his neighbour of his business. But in return he had complete security in his own. His clients were hereditary, and since trade was very static in its conceptions the clients of a merchant provided children to be the clients of his own. But the Jew had no clients ready waiting for him. He had to go out and get them, and inevitably he had to find ways of getting them which were foreign to the old system."[10]

When the princes were in need of money, they forced the Jews to come across, and when Jews were robbed so brazenly, they are hardly to be blamed if they clipped coins, debased the currency and engaged in other practices which are not unlike some of those which have been deemed not below the dignity of sovereign states in our own day.

When these considerations are urged today in discussions with Gentile business men, they repudiate their significance for modern life and insist that at all events the same emergencies do not exist now, and that what happened in the Middle Ages is no excuse for sharp business practices at the present time. When one inquires further concerning specific types of business behavior to which Gentiles object, the following are among those most frequently adduced:

(1) There is the "haggling"habit which most of the western world has outgrown, although the "one-price" system is much more modern than many assume. The idea of Jewish haggling is so ingrained in the Gentile mind that he uses the word "to jew down" with little thought of its etymology. He frankly expects that the first price suggested by a Jewish merchant is not the final price and anticipates a period of bargaining before agreement is reached. In its elementary form, such haggling is evident in dealings with the "rags and bottles" man with whom the Gentile has often his first Jewish contact; it is perhaps apt to be characteristic of all dealers in secondhand goods, whether Jewish or Gentile; but Gentiles believe that it is largely characteristic of Jews. Some Gentile doctors and dentists assert that they never present their bills to Jewish patients without being asked for a reduction, and often they make it a rule to collect cash from such persons at the time services are rendered. It is of course unfair to attribute such bargaining habits only to Jews, but it is not easy to draw

---

[10] *The Jew and His Neighbour* (London: Student Christian Movement, 1930), pp. 112 ff.

any conclusions as to the relative frequency of the habit as between Jews and Gentiles. Perhaps, it is fair to say that the Gentile expects it in the case of all Jewish traders, and acts accordingly.

A Jewish dealer in second-hand books provided an interesting anecdote in this connection. Visiting a sale of certain old books imported from Europe, he saw an excellent copy of a very rare book of miniatures, the listed price of which he knew to be nineteen guineas, or over $95. Those in charge of the sale were apparently ignorant of its value and offered it to him for a couple of dollars. He took it. Immediately he carried his find to a certain Gentile client who collected such miniatures. After showing him the book and before he could suggest a price at which he was willing to part with it, the Jew was surprised to be told that the would-be purchaser was not interested: "I wouldn't give you a cent more than twenty dollars for it." The Jewish dealer had intended to offer it for ten dollars, but the bait was too alluring. "I only ask twenty five dollars," he said, "couldn't you stretch your offer that much?" The Gentile took it for twenty-five dollars, but if he had kept his mouth shut and not anticipated the necessity of bargaining, he might have had it for ten dollars.

(2) Not infrequently the Jewish predilection for second-hand goods tends to make him a receiver of stolen goods, even when he may be innocent of any connivance.

(3) To get business, it is claimed, Jews will not abide by prevailing codes but "chisel in" when and where they can. During this study, the writer was speaking to a small group of Gentiles and endeavoring to state the Jewish point of view on certain debated questions. A man in the cleaning and pressing business interrupted the address by saying: "The Jews engaged in my business will obey neither our business codes nor the civic by-laws. On my way down to this meeting this evening, I saw my Jewish competitor's shop open after 7:30 when the by-law says that such shops must close at seven." Jewish shops are often the first to open and the last to close, and there is frequently a tendency to cut prices to the lowest possible rate in order to "get business." Certain Gentiles indeed praise the energy of the Jewish shop-owner and his willingness to work long hours, but his competitor sees the whole matter in a different light. Some indeed have said that if business codes such as the N. R. A. has proposed could be adequately enforced, much of the opposition to Jewish business men would disappear.

(4) The fact that the Jewish working-men occasionally have their own unions and that Jewish business men have similar associations of their own in some places creates suspicion. (In some cities Jewish business men, as will be pointed out later, are excluded from Merchants' Clubs and Associations.) There are no other labor unions organized on the basis of re-

ligious groupings in the United States or Canada except among the French-Canadian Catholics in Quebec.

(5) The Gentiles complain that there is a tendency for Jews to under-cut prices in the hope of securing new business so that the possibilities of fair profits are generally reduced. An investigation into business practices conducted by the Canadian government in 1934 revealed that shocking wages were being paid by Jewish clothing makers. But it further made clear that much of this scandalous wage condition was due to the pressure exerted on the industry by Gentile-owned department stores and other mass-buying agencies, which were able to set their own price for certain lines of goods. In notable instances, the Gentile manufacturers gave up the effort to provide goods at such prices, but the Jewish manufacturers, however unwillingly, accepted the contract at the price set and passed their losses down to their employees, violating the minimum wage laws as they did so.

The sin of under-cutting is, however, not limited to Jews. It is openly practised by great department stores, both Jewish and Gentile, which offer guarantees that their prices are definitely below the price for which goods of equal quality can be had in quantities in other stores. The N. R. A. experiment now being attempted in the United States is seeking to check this cut-throat competition, but no one seems positive as to what methods, if any, will succeed in stopping it. The evil, so far as it exists, seems implicit in the uncontrolled capitalistic system, and is less in the offering of goods at lower prices than a competitor, than in being enabled to do this by utilizing the pressure of mass-buying to purchase goods at unfair prices and produced with ill-paid labor in the first instance. Both Jewish and Gentile business men must move to find some satisfactory method out of the difficulty.

(6) The criticism is also made that in order to offer bargains, the Jewish business man will resort to the use of shoddy or poor materials, but here again it is a matter of opinion which group is most guilty of such practices. The writer has found some of the most brazen breaches of ethics in this particular in the building business conducted by Gentiles, where the proportion of sand to cement in the foundation has been found, upon analysis, to be nothing short of robbery. On the other hand, it is stated by some that one reason why the Jews became connoisseurs of dry goods as early as the Middle Ages was that the Jewish law forbade the wearing of a garment "of divers sorts, as of woollen and linen together" (Deuteronomy 22:11). Gentiles who wished to be sure what they were buying therefore resorted to Jewish in preference to Gentile merchants.

(7) Jews are considered by certain leading insurance companies as a poor fire risk. There seems to be little hesitation in accepting risks on Jewish lives, since the Jewish death-rate is quite low, but insurance companies pro-

fess that the number of fires in Jewish shops, lofts and homes is suspiciously high. They also hesitate to accept certain Jewish risks for automobile casualty insurance.

When an investigator asks for hard data on this point, he is told that it is difficult in all suspected cases to prove arson or connivance at arson, although it would not seem necessary to indicate a suspicion of arson when furnishing the fundamental data regarding the number of fires involving Jewish establishments. In one of the cities studied, there was fairly clear evidence that an arson gang was operating in Jewish circles, and some of the men in the gang were eventually landed behind the gates of the penitentiary. It is not easy to believe that this unreadiness to accept Jewish fire and casualty business is due simply to prejudice. Insurance companies are out to make money and they have to gather carefully the fundamental data on which to determine the element of risks. It is hardly conceivable that they would refuse business unless they had good reason to believe that Jews were, considered as a group, "poor risks." They say, when accused of prejudice, if the Jews are such goods risks, why do not Jewish financiers form an insurance company and especially deal with such risks? There seems to be some evidence that in Europe, at least, Christians have been more likely than Jews to be convicted of arson, as appears in the comment by Mr. Israel Cohen quoted below.

It may be said that a sound actuarial study of this situation would of necessity take into consideration not only the racial or "religious" complexion of the group under suspicion, but also the district in the city where that particular group resided. Not infrequently the Jewish quarter is among the most congested regions and the buildings are the least modern and the most inflammable. Again, it would be necessary to take into consideration the fact that many Jews are engaged in the merchandizing of goods, such as clothing and silks, which are highly inflammable. Even so, there is here an ugly situation which requires sound actuarial study and proper publicity.

(8) Gentiles say they dislike business dealings with Jews because of their reputation for securing postponement of debt settlements. Generally speaking, the Jews have a high reputation for maintaining their credit at the banks by meeting all payments on borrowings, but at the same time the assertion is made that it is difficult to collect from individual Jews or from Jewish firms when they do not feel disposed to pay their debts. Gentiles believe that Jews will become argumentative or even litigious, and as a result they prefer to have as few dealings with them as is necessary. There seemed to be no way of checking on the accuracy of such allegations, and they are mentioned merely because they are commonly asserted.

CRIMINAL TENDENCIES AMONG JEWS AND GENTILES

It is unfortunate that there is no way known to the writer by which to make any sound estimate as to the respective breaches of business codes, such as they are, by Jews and Gentiles. Criminal statistics do not help greatly for reasons given in the note on that subject in the appendix. Dr. Arthur Ruppin, in his volume, *The Jews of Today*, published in 1913, gave some interesting figures on the respective criminal tendencies of Jews and Gentiles in Europe, and Mr. Israel Cohen made the following comment on Dr. Ruppin's tables:

"An examination of this table shows that the penal offences of which the Jews are convicted in a higher degree are those of usury, fraudulent bankruptcy, fraud, disseminating immoral publications, blackmail, evasion of conscription, frustrating legal executions, forgery, libel and duelling. On the other hand, the penal offences of which Christians are convicted in a higher degree are defiance of State authority, theft, robbery, burglary, injury to property, arson, injury to persons and murder. It will be seen that most of the categories in which the Jews are more liable to transgress are connected with commercial occupations in which they are proportionately more numerously engaged than their Christian fellow-citizens."[11]

In the light of such uncertainty, the writer gives it as his opinion that if the Jews are more addicted to certain commercial malpractices than Gentiles—and he is not at all sure that they are—this is due primarily to two facts:

(1) The Jews are so much more largely engaged in commercial activities, as Mr. Cohen suggests, than the Gentiles.

(2) Because of the discriminating feeling against Jews as such, they have had a greater temptation, not only in historical times but even today, to resort to certain questionable and possibly unfair practices.

No one can accuse Edgar Ansel Mowrer of anti-Semitism in his book *Germany Puts the Clock Back*. Dealing with the public scandals which followed the revolution of 1918 in Germany, Mr. Mowrer seeks to prove that the Jews were not the only scoundrels of the time, and he names among the outstanding financial scandals of those years those involving the Erzbergers, the Sklareks, the Barmats, the Sklarz Brothers, the Dumkes, Ludwig Katzenellenbogen and the Davaheim. He then points out that in only four of these seven cases were the scamps Jews, viz., the Sklareks, the Barmats, the Sklarz Brothers and Ludwig Katzenellenbogen. But when one

---

[11] Israel Cohen, *Jewish Life in Modern Times* (London: Methuen Company) Second edition, 1929. Chapter vi. See also Arthur Ruppin, *The Jews of Today* (New York: Henry Holt and Company, 1913), pp. 220-226. In Dr. Ruppin's latest book *The Jews in the Modern World* (New York: The Macmillan Company, 1934) he omits all references to Jewish crime statistics.

considers that the Jews number only one per cent. of the population of Germany, four out of seven major scandals is a fairly high percentage, even though Mr. Mowrer deduces that "corruption under the German Republic was, sad to say, not limited to Jews and Republicans." Again, the French scoundrel, Stavinsky, may or may not have been Jewish, but the Swedish match king, Kruger, though often called a Jew, was not one, and a majority of those bankers in New York, Detroit and Cleveland, who gained so unsavoury a reputation for themselves as custodians of the nation's pocketbook, seem quite innocent of any Hebraic heritage.

Little can come of any effort to defend rascals whether they are Jewish or Gentile, and it is illogical to attack the victims of a system instead of the system itself. The essential thing is to develop such a new code of business morality that both Jews and Gentiles can "discriminate" more effectively between those who deserve well of their country and those who ought to be in the penitentiary. Meanwhile, because of the indiscriminate prejudice against them, the Jews have an especially cogent reason for avoiding every appearance of business slipperiness.

POLITICAL ANTI-SEMITISM

Antagonism to Jews in the United States and Canada seems to be due, as already shown, almost entirely to economic factors. As will be pointed out in the section of the next chapter dealing with political discrimination, there is little suspicion of the patriotism of the Jews, and consequently anti-Semitism in the New World is economic rather than political. During the Great War there was a current rumor that the ranks of the war-profiteers in New York City contained a large number of Jews, and anti-Semitic pamphlets have alleged that 74 per cent. of the war-millionaires in New York were Jewish, but the number of Gentile war-profiteers was so numerous that such an allegation falls on deaf ears. It is generally recognized that Jews took their places with Gentiles in the military. In Canada, on the other hand, where conscription was not attempted until the close of the War, the Jews did not contribute many men to the armed forces. Neither for that matter did the French-Canadians. A total of 2,574 Jews are known to have enlisted out of a Jewish population of approximately 100,000 during the war years. At the University of Toronto, few male undergraduates but Jews were in attendance during the War, with a consequent growth of anti-Semitism. The Jewish group in Canada, being comparatively newly-arrived, could hardly be expected to show much imperial sentiment, especially as Britain was in alliance with Russia, memories of persecution in which country were still too fresh in their minds. A greater enthusiasm developed, however, when Britain sponsored the scheme for a Palestinian homeland for the Jews.

The Zionist movement does not seem to have accentuated whatever suspicion of the essential patriotism of the Jews may have existed. Indeed, were the Zionists to succeed in their enterprise and were a national homeland to be soundly established, it might provide a way out for such Jews as could never fully feel at home in any dominantly non-Jewish country, while those who did not go to Palestine might merge more completely in the country of their residence. This would tend to remove the legend of the "international Jew," but at present one can only speculate as to such a possibility. As yet, Zionism has created more opposition in Jewish than in Gentile circles. The average Gentile is not much interested one way or the other; if he is antipathetic and expresses an opinion, it may be the cynical hope that all the Jews may find their way to Palestine.

A more immediate danger to the patriotic status of the Jews in the United States and Canada was that created of late by the boycott of German goods and by the clamorous demand of some Jewish organizations that the American Government intervene in Germany on behalf of their fellow-believers. Even though the Nazi policy was an affront to humanity and justice and deserved the denunciation expressed by Christians no less than by Jews, the agitation for boycott and for intervention in face of an inflammable international situation led to much unfavorable comment in Gentile circles. It was felt that some of the Jewish leaders, however much they acclaimed peace, were promoting measures which might lead to strife. Gentiles generally did not realize that some of the ablest Jewish leaders in America took a dispassionate view of the situation and courageously opposed these measures as un-American. Rather than invoke the Government's intervention on behalf of foreign victims of persecution, whatever their religious affiliation, they held that the American way is to depend on such unofficial pronouncements as were made in 1930 by the American Committee (Protestant, Catholic and Jewish) on Religious Rights and Minorities in connection with the Soviet prohibition of religious activities.

REAL ESTATE DISCRIMINATION

While there may be Protestants or Catholics who will not rent or sell property to Catholics or Protestants respectively, those entrusted with this study were unable to discover any trends in this direction. As a matter of fact, real-estate agents welcome the coming of a Catholic church into a community, for it is regarded as an evidence of permanence, and almost invariably it tends to increase the value of the neighboring property. Catholics are generally loyal in church attendance; the church itself is as a rule an architectural asset; the coming of a church means the building of a parochial school sooner or later, and the presence of the parochial school is an attraction for other Catholic families. This is so generally recognized that comity commissions in Protestant federations of churches sometimes advise against the building of a new Protestant church in the neighborhood of an established Catholic church. A Protestant church is not a community asset in quite the same way; it makes an appeal mainly to the loyalty of such members of a particular denomination as may be resident in the area and not to Protestants as a whole unless, perhaps, the church definitely aims to be interdenominational and community-wide in character. A community house may constitute an appeal to a prospective Protestant settler, but there is nothing to attract him similar to the appeal of the parochial school of the Catholic.

Certain real-estate difficulties, however, do exist between Protestants and Catholics in Canada. In Quebec, the ancient right of the Catholic Church to tax land for ecclesiastical purposes was retained in the final settlement of the problems emerging from British occupation, and so to this day all Catholic landowners may be called upon to submit to a tax levied on property in the parish which they may own when the Church is contemplating a new building enterprise. This tax may be collected over a period of years, but if the Catholic landowner in the meanwhile sells his property to a Protestant, the Catholic Church may continue to levy the tax against the Protestant owner. In the smaller towns where a protestant may be in an infinitesimal minority, he may hesitate to raise any objection, although it is probable that if the matter were carried to the courts, they would rule that the validity of the tax ceased with the transfer of the ownership of the property. So far as the writer is aware, the dispute has not been submitted to the courts in any instance for decision.

Again, where there are two kinds of public school, as in most of the Canadian provinces—one for Catholics and one for non-Catholics—and the tax rates vary according to the type of school, complications may arise. These difficulties are indicated more fully in chapter v. The disposition of the tax is determined in some provinces by the religion of the owner; in others by the religion of the tenant. In Montreal the tax rate for Catholic schools is set at 7 mills on the dollar, while that for Protestant schools is 10 mills. In Ontario cities, on the other hand, in most towns and cities the rate for separate school supporters is higher than that for public school supporters, and this may create complications in renting. For instance, a Toronto paper[12] recently published the following statement respecting six apartments that presumably were of approximately equal value:

"On Winchester Street, Toronto, there is an apartment house occupied by both Protestants and Catholics. There are six five-room apartments in the building. Note the manner in which these have been dealt with by the Assessor:

---

[12] *Jack Canuck*, issue of November 30, 1933, page 3.

Apt. No. 1   Tenant Protestant $2,450
Apt. No. 2   Tenant Protestant $2,600
Apt. No. 3   Tenant Protestant $2,450
Apt. No. 4   Tenant Catholic $2,960
Apt. No. 5   Tenant Catholic $3,050
Apt. No. 6   Tenant Catholic $3,050

"To show what this means. The tax bills of the owner of the property showed that he was assessed on a Protestant tenant (as No. 1 above) General Tax, $56.59; Public School, $25.24; or a total of $81.83. The tax bill on the Catholic tenant (as in apartment No. 5 above) was: General $70.45; Separate School, $45.29; or a total of $115.74."

The Separate School Board in Toronto, in spite of the higher tax rate which it collects, has difficulty in raising enough money to meet its needs, since the taxes collected from corporations, with few exceptions, go entirely to the Public School Board. It is not, therefore, impossible that the city assessor may find it simpler to raise the assessment on property with Catholic tenants than to increase the Separate School tax rate, and if this is true, then Protestant landowners might have two reasons for not welcoming Catholic tenants—the increased tax rate and the increased assessment.

These and similar complications are non-existent in the United States, but problems of this character need to be kept in mind should the traditional policy of the United States in respect to the public support of only one type of school be changed. In making such a change, assessments, tax rates and tenancy problems would probably arise, and opportunities for discriminating against Catholics in real-estate matters which do not exist might develop.

With the Jews, however, there is discrimination in real-estate transactions. Where such anti-Semitism exists as is portrayed in the preceding section dealing with discrimination in business, it is perhaps too much to expect that Gentiles would welcome them into their community with open arms. The invasion of any particular area by Jews is often accompanied by the withdrawal or flight of the Gentiles, unless—and often, even when— the Jewish newcomers are persons of recognized social worth.

The Jews that first invade a city in the United States or Canada are, for the most part, poor and they come from countries in which the Jew has been confined to the congested quarters of the ghetto. They, too, take up their residence first in the more thickly crowded areas of the city into which they have come, and accelerate the process of deterioration which had already set in before their arrival. The Gentiles move out, as they left Brooklyn for the suburbs of Queens, only to be followed by the "invaders"; for as Jews acquire an economic competence they too seek to escape the self-created ghetto and move into the better Gentile areas. Here a modified form of the conflict is renewed.

There is little doubt that the presence of Jews in large numbers in a given area tends to break down the relative homogeneity of the Gentile community, weakens the potential constituencies for the Christian churches and may force some of them to close their doors. It places certain limits to social intercourse, limits set quite as much by Jews themselves, especially orthodox Jews, as by Gentiles, e.g., bitter opposition to intermarriage, loyalty to group institutions and the rigidities of the dietary laws. Quite recently, a Protestant minister received a letter from a member in his former parish, in which pessimism and resentment are revealed in equal proportions: "Our community has changed; no more room for you there now nor for any other minister; all they need is rabbis." One wonders indeed if much of the alleged and real discrimination would not decrease if Jewish real-estate companies deliberately sought to develop residential areas of a desirable character *for Jews only*, putting the shoe on the other foot by excluding Gentiles. But there is little evidence of any such policy. The bitter resentment of the old system which placed chains across the gates of a ghetto at nightfall may have created a hankering among Jews to live among Gentiles, even though they are refused full entrance into the social activities of the community.

Whatever discrimination did exist in the field of real estate before the depression was largely eliminated, however, as a result of the depression, at least, in most of the cities studied. Landowners could not afford expensive prejudices with empty houses on their hands. If a Jew had the money, he could go almost anywhere or buy almost anything—but in the general depression he, too, often failed to have the money. Of course, in a few cities, definite restrictions were written into the sales contract and if the property were to be transferred the consent of the original owners must be secured, and these terms were frequently directed against either Jews or Negroes. But as a rule the discrimination in real estate against Jews was of one of three types:

(a) Certain choice suburban developments are restricted. Socially, the intent is in the interests of homogeneity, and economically, those responsible for the development believe that land values cannot be maintained without such restrictions.

(b) Apartment-house owners would lease certain houses to Gentiles only and other houses to Jews only. They insisted that by and large it was impracticable to mix the two.

(c) Summer resorts are a particular source of trouble, for individuals select their summer homes not alone for scenery, quiet and climate, but also for congeniality. In the city men must put up with their neighbors and they can often ignore them completely, but at their summer homes they are more dependent upon them for comradeship and social life. If, then, some summer neighbors prove uncongenial for one reason or another, the summer may be spoiled. Real-estate men stated quite frankly that it was almost impossible to hold their Gentile clientele at a summer resort if any considerable number of Jews moved in.

In some beach resorts, those responsible for this study found signs reading "For Gentiles only"; one of them was even more specific: "For English-speaking Gentiles Only." In one case, a beach had been surveyed into lots which were put up for sale; pending the disposition of the lots, and for advertising purposes, the proprietors allowed the public to use the beach for bathing, but only on the presentation of special tickets which were given gratuitously on *personal* application. We were informed that Jews did not receive such tickets, and that device was the means used to keep them out. Those who accepted tickets were later canvassed and urged to buy lots.

At another place, a few Jews did obtain houses in a resort quite close to the business district of a large city. Unfortunately, these Jews did not comport themselves properly and as a result the leases in the following year included restrictions directed against Jewish tenancy. Here, the reputable and desirable Jewish tenants suffered for the sins of the few obstreperous ones.

In some other resorts, the property is held largely by semi-religious corporations which desire, so far as possible, to retain the original character of the resort. This would be impossible if Jews were largely admitted.

When real-estate dealers told their reasons for such discrimination, several arguments were forthcoming, some of which may or may not have been rationalizations. Behind all such rationalizations, however, is the obvious fact that Jews are, as a group, disliked, and it is feared that if some are admitted, the area will be "swamped." The more significant of these rationalizations can be summed up under a few heads:

(1) There is a feeling that Jews are "dirty" and "noisy." In the opinion of the writer, this conception of them is based largely on the rather unkempt appearance of the homes and tenements in which the Jewish immigrants first reside, and on certain conditions which colored life in the ghettoes in Europe. In the next place, whatever may be said about the lack of cleanliness around the homes of Jewish immigrants, it is doubtful if their non-Jewish neighbors in the same general area are any cleaner. To be sure, the junk-dealers, who bring back the results of their daily quests and pile them around the house, have in a peculiar way added to this undesirable reputation, and it may be that Jews are, generally speaking, so far away from the soil that they show less inclination than Gentiles

to keep up the appearance of lawns, yards, and shrubbery. At all events, the Gentile believes that Jews allow property to deteriorate and do not reveal much pride in making these homes attractive—on the outside at least.

(2) A good deal of objection has been taken to Jewish neighbors on the ground of certain offensive odors from their cooking. This is particularly stated in regard to apartment houses, and while there may be no material difference between the cooking prevailing in certain strata of Jews and that prevailing in the same strata of Gentiles, the cooking odors that emanate from houses in which a certain class of Jews live is extremely obnoxious to many Gentiles. Some who have peculiar reason for knowing this situation have stated to the writer that the odors penetrate into the walls of the houses and it is most difficult to eradicate them.

(3) Frequent complaints are made, especially in the more conservative and puritanical neighborhoods, that orthodox Jews are apt to use Sundays for their day of entertainment or else for fixing whatever needs to be fixed, and that the resulting noise and hilarity disturb Sunday quiet. In this connection the following quotation from the *Canadian Jewish Review* is quite in line with certain criticisms received from real-estate men:

"Take the example of the Jew who has fallen so far from the old Jewish ideals of neighborliness that he will violate the Christian Sabbath by hammering at his automobile by day and making the welkin ring with a noisy card-party in the evening, etc."

In the apartment houses it is claimed that it is not only the Sunday quiet which is disturbed, but the week-day quiet as well. In short, while it is admitted that Jews have no monopoly on lack of consideration for their neighbors, and that in conspicuous cases they are most considerate, it is also asserted that the rank and file do not make agreeable neighbors.

(4) Many Gentiles hesitate to rent or sell to Jews, not because they themselves object to them, but because they know that certain neighbors would so object, and they do not wish to displease their friends.

Fundamentally, the reason why Jews are not wanted in certain areas, residential and business, is anti-Semitism. They are not wanted because they are not wanted. Under such circumstances, any lapse in a Jewish neighbor is immediately attributed to his Jewishness, while a similar lapse on the part of a Gentile would be interpreted more simply and perhaps more correctly as an evidence only of that individual's lack of culture.

No real-estate man interviewed in the course of this study indicated that the desire to exclude Jews was in any way based on a policy of preserving the *religious* homogeneity of the community. Such a significant omission on their part is corroborative evidence that the antipathy to the Jew is not motivated by religious considerations. Possibly, if the real-estate promoters had ever had any hope of maintaining religious homogeneity, they had long since given it up under pressure from the competitive Protestant groups. Nor did any ministers of Christian churches located in an area becoming increasingly Jewish urge the exclusion of Jews in the interests of religious homogeneity, even though they frankly recognized that the ingress of the Jews into their community had made the eventual closing of their churches inevitable. It is perhaps fair to say that the situation created by the incoming of Jews is more serious for Protestants than for Catholics because, in the first place, owing to the parish-system characteristic of Catholicism, only a single church of that order may be affected, whereas the same invasion may spell the doom of eight or ten churches belonging to various Protestant denominations; and, in the second place, because the loyalties in Protestantism are, to a large extent and "for better for worse," built around the individual church—the fellowship of congenial souls—and not around the whole ecclesiastical system and discipline. When a Protestant church is disbanded, members hesitate to transfer their loyalty to another church and too often drop out of church life altogether. Whether this loyalty to the individual church be regarded as a virtue or a defect, it is largely shattered when, under the pressure of population shifts, the church is abandoned. Even the possible sale of the property at a fair price to a Jewish synagogue cannot repair the damage to the organization itself. Nevertheless, while the ministers interviewed were quite conscious of the imminent danger to their churches from a Jewish incursion, not one of them suggested that Jews should be kept out because local church life would profit thereby.

So far as the future is concerned, the shutting off of promiscuous immigration into the United States and Canada may help to stabilize community development. This immigration in the past has almost shattered Protestantism in many cities of the northern states. Before successive waves of Catholics from Ireland, French Canada and Continental Europe; of Jews from Poland and Russia; and of Negroes from the South, the city churches have been subjected to heavy burdens and pressures. There can be no sound community life when it is subjected to the sudden strains of population change which have been characteristic of the last forty years.

DISCRIMINATION—ACTION AND REACTION

Fed by anti-Semitism, discrimination thrives. Part of it is based on sheer prejudice, part of it on physical aversion, part of it on a dislike for Jewish manners, part of it on bitter experience with some undesirable Jews, part of it on economic competition. Much of it is due to a reading or misreading of history, and represents the hangover of ancient antipathies. To a large degree it is due, as already pointed out, to the high concentration of the Jews in cities and their preoccupation with commercial and trading pursuits.

The Jews, on their part, feel bitterly the discrimination to which they are subjected. Some try to forget that they are Jews and encourage Gentiles to forget it. They conceal their Jewishness when it is possible to do so, e.g., by changing their names, only to discover too often that they are no better off when the deception has been uncovered. Others take refuge within their own group and seek to promote Jewishness throughout the world. The majority, however, realize that only by proving 50 per cent smarter than their Gentile competitor will they be able to get as far as he, and some of them consequently seem to the Gentile intolerably aggressive. Others turn revolutionary and abet any movement that promises a real New Deal, however specious; thus, they win for the group the reputation of radicalism and this only makes it more suspect. Thus Gentile discrimination against the Jews not only opens new sores, but brings out in the Jews the very qualities the Gentiles profess to dislike in them, and only on rare occasions do Jew and Gentile meet without the unhappy sense of feeling different from each other. As the film, "The House of Rothschild" suggested, the Jew should be made free to "walk the earth with dignity," but he cannot achieve this goal without Gentile coöperation. Anti-Semitism only aggravates the problem, while ultra-Jewishness is no answer to anti-Semitism.

CHAPTER III

Discrimination and Social Distance (Cont.)—Social Clubs, Political Life and Immigration

Discrimination is not only practised in matters of employment and in real-estate transactions, but it is also credibly alleged to be prevalent in social clubs. There are, of course, certain social clubs which are purely Protestant, or purely Catholic, or purely Jewish, such as certain of the fraternal orders, and such difficulties as these clubs create for society are not rooted in discrimination but in their aggressive partisan attitudes.

SOCIAL CLUBS

The allegations of discrimination by social organizations, against Jews at least, are supported by ample evidence.

FRATERNAL BODIES

Among the fraternal bodies, however, the Masonic order is often criticized by Jews because it sometimes fosters the segregation of Jews and Gentiles, especially in the higher degrees, although there is some reason to believe that the third degree of Masonry was introduced into America by the Jews who settled in Newport, Rhode Island, in 1658. The whole theory of Masonry stresses the loyalty of its members to one another, and there is a suspiciously Jewish flavor in the general conception of the "building of the temple," but in certain parts of the country Jews are encouraged to form their own chapters. In other areas, Jews may be permitted to go through the lower degrees with their Gentile brethren, but they must frequently form their own chapters in the higher degrees, where a larger emphasis is laid on social activities. This type of segregation is not universal, but many Jewish Masons in the affected territory feel bitterly about it. The usual defence offered by the Masons themselves is that in these higher degrees, the wording of the prescribed ritual is such that most Jews will refuse to make the promises required, and consequently the exclusion is self-exclusion.

EXCLUSIVE SOCIAL CITY AND COUNTRY CLUBS

Fraternal bodies are, of course, in a class by themselves and discrimination is far more seriously resented in those city clubs to which men of business and affairs resort as "to their downtown home" for lunch or where they entertain out-of-town friends, or in the country club with its lordly acres whither they hasten to enjoy a round or two of golf. In nearly all the cities studied, these clubs made no apparent distinction between Protestant and Catholic in their membership,[1] but did draw the line quite rigorously at Jews. The Jews, consequently, have been forced to institute parallel clubs of their own, such city clubs being called in a number of cases the Standard Club. Indeed, the by-laws of one of the associations of golf clubs, viz., the Western Golf Association, specifically states that Jewish country clubs are admitted to *associate membership only* in the association.

In many of these clubs, one may discover an occasional "pet" Jew whose presence seems to irritate the excluded Jews as much as their own exclusion; sometimes there may be more than one, but generally speaking the club would view any extended admission of Jews with extreme disfavor.

UNIVERSITY CLUBS

Certain of the rabbis feel in a peculiar way this type of discrimination mostly as it is practised in university clubs. While these rabbis may have more than the academic qualifications for membership and are often invited to lecture before the university clubs, they know quite well that they are considered ineligible for membership. In one city studied, Cincinnati, they are admitted to membership. The original club in Cincinnati was broken up about 1896 when the lone Jewish member proposed that they admit another Jew. In 1907 the club was revived and it was definitely agreed not to exclude Jews as a group but to exercise careful discrimination in the selection of their Jewish members. There are at present about 295 members, of whom approximately thirty-five are Jews. This club holds few social affairs where women and relatives are invited.

BUSINESS CLUBS

Though the rabbis feel somewhat hurt concerning their exclusion from the university clubs in which, one might expect, intellectual distinction should be promptly recognized, they tend to minimize the importance of the exclusion from the other types of city and country clubs and say: "Why should we seek to force our way where we are not wanted?" Jewish business men, however, see it from another angle, for to them a club is not only a pleasant place to lunch, smoke or play a game of billiards, but it is also pre-eminently the resort of the financiers when they wish to talk over or put through a big deal, and then, as Kipling sings in "The Puzzler":

---

[1] The writer has lately been informed that in certain social clubs in Montreal, Catholics are excluded. He is unable either to deny or verify this at the time of going to press.

"Yes, sometimes in a smoking-room, through clouds of 'Ers' and 'Ums',
Obliquely and by inference illumination comes,
On some step that they have taken, or some action they approve—
Embellished with the argot of the Upper Fourth Remove."

For men of business, therefore, the club is more than a rococo lunch-room. There one may mingle with those who know what's what on the Rialto and why, and to be excluded from this sweet communion of kindred souls is to be definitely handicapped in the struggle for financial success and power. Moreover, to be required to entertain an important Gentile guest at a club patronized only by Jews is certainly underscoring the host's descent.

REASONS FOR DISCRIMINATION

Of course, whatever validity there may be in our pretensions to democracy, class-distinctions in America are by no means wiped out, and the Jews are not alone in being excluded from these "ritzy" clubs. Many Gentiles who would like to belong couldn't get in even if they were able to pay the high entrance and annual fees. Indeed, some of the *nouveaux riches* could crash the gates of Newport or crawl through the eye of a needle as easily as they could force their way into these sanctuaries.

Then again a club is primarily built on the principle of congeniality. One belongs where his "set" or "crowd" belongs, and it is this opportunity for intimacy which gives a club its peace and distinction. To imperil the continuance of that congeniality is to threaten the very existence of the organization, and the more exclusive a club is, the more is its membership prized.

The fact, too, that many such clubs sponsor social occasions attended by the women-folk of the members provides an additional reason for caution. An individual Jew might in himself be perfectly acceptable to this group of business nabobs, but the members of his family might not mix so readily with the members of the Gentile family. Where social groups live apart in normal life, it is difficult to bring them together without running a variety of risks which lack of congeniality and social snobbishness encourage.

Hence the prevailing discrimination. Religion has little to do with it, except, perhaps, as religious differences tend to accentuate or justify social difference. Those who defend the discrimination urge in brief:

(a) If the bars are let down and a few Jews are taken in, the new members will soon be presenting the names of many other Jews for membership, some of whom would not "fit in." Let a club lose its reputation for exclusiveness, and it soon ceases to attract those for whom it was originally intended and who are most desired.

(b) At many clubs, family evenings are planned, and while many individual Jews are acceptable in themselves, they are not so acceptable when they travel *en famille*. Complications of various kinds ensue.

(c) Both of the above reasons operate in a peculiar way at golf clubs. The Jew and the Gentile will not mix readily. If they do mix, complications may develop as disconcerting to the Jews as to the Gentiles.

Of course, a great deal of social intercourse is stopped between real orthodox Jews and Gentiles by kosher restrictions. One is well aware that many ocean liners and metropolitan hotels are required to operate "kosher kitchens," but it is doubtful if the possibility of this complication is any factor in the exclusion of Jews from clubs, for those who might be considered for such membership would, for the most part, have long since ceased to worry about kosher. Nevertheless, it is necessary to stress the fact that the peculiar laws of Israel in regard to food have undoubtedly operated to widen the social chasm between Jew and Gentile. Even in Jewish institutes, it complicates arrangements in the kitchens and the cafeterias. In one such, the director found that he could not be served meat and ice-cream in the same section of the room. A meal may become and often is a sacrament of friendship, and if a certain group builds up a set of regulations which make it necessary for them to eat apart, they must themselves accept a measure of responsibility for whatever social ostracism they bewail. Shakespeare was conscious of this self-exclusion when he made Shylock say to Bassanio:

"I will buy with you, sell with you, talk with you, walk with you, and so following, but I will not eat with you, drink with you, or pray with you." (Merchant of Venice, Act I, Scene 3.)

COLLEGE FRATERNITIES

In this same type of discrimination, it is necessary also to mention the exclusion of Jewish students from Greek letter fraternities. This will be treated more fully in Chapter VI.

Y. M. C. A. AND Y. W. C. A.

The Y. M. C. A. was one of the very first organizations to provide social and recreational facilities under "uplift" auspices for those young men in cities who could not afford the privileges of the expensive clubs. The Y. W. C. A. followed soon afterwards with somewhat parallel activities for young women. Both these organizations were in their inception definitely Christian and evangelical, but they both sought to be, within those limits, non-sectarian. At one time, indeed, they drew considerable criticism, both at home and abroad, for alleged subtle methods of proselytization, while within the conservative wing of Protestantism they have been attacked for allowing their social activities to obscure their evangelical mission. Many Jews and Catholics have, however, been enrolled in their membership, and their presence may have had not a little to do with the constant modifications of their religious policy.

In 1932 the Young Men's Christian Association reported that in 800 associations in the United States and Canada, their membership was constituted as follows:

	United States		Canada	
Church Preference	Y. M. C. A. Members	Other Participants	Y. M. C. A. Members	Other Participants
Total number..................	764,068	327,218	32,649	7,477
Per cent. Protestants............	80.5	69.7	86.1	72.8
" Catholics..............	13.4	17.6	8.6	15.4
" Jews.................	3.3	4.2	3.9	2.8
" Others...............	2.8	8.5	1.4	9.0

If these 800 associations are typical, then 19.5 per cent. of all local members in the United States and 13.4 per cent. of all members in Canada are not in any way Protestant; 30.1 per cent. of all other participants in the United States and 27.2 per cent. of all other participants in Canada are not in any sense Protestant. There is, of course, a difference between voting members and ordinary associate members. Voting members have until recently been limited to members of evangelical churches in accordance with the Portland test, and only 42 per cent. of all members in the United States and 33 per cent. in Canada had such voting privileges in 1932. But for years the association has taken counsel on means to remove the restrictions on voting members to those with full standing in evangelical churches, and changes in the by-laws have been made. At present, and since the decision of the National Council in Chicago, 1933, a member of the National Council itself (i.e., a representative of the local association on the Council) must be a member of a Christian (formerly Evangelical) Church, and

"Each local Association shall determine the qualifications of its voting members, and of the members of its Boards of Control, providing such members be in accord with the purposes, ideals, and spirit of the Young Men's Christian Association."

In 1933 the Cincinnati Y. M. C. A. elected Rabbi James G. Heller, of that city, to its Board of Directors, and Rabbi Heller accepted the office.

Both the Y. M. C. A. and the Y. W. C. A. have in their discussions sought, wisely or unwisely, so to modify their by-laws that they might:

(a) Express their coöperation with constituencies of other than Evangelical Protestant affiliation in carrying on character-education programs in local communities, and

(b) State some religious convictions in such explicit ways that the relation of Protestants to Catholics and to Jews will be obvious.

It should also be mentioned that the motto of the World's Y. M. C. A. has always been the words from the Gospel of St. John "That they all may be one," and this has been interpreted as its charter for inter-confessionalism.

On the other hand, certain local Young Men's Christian Associations have found it necessary at times to limit Jewish membership and participation, especially in those communities where there seemed to be a real danger that the Association might easily become a Y. M. H. A. and not a Y. M. C. A. In certain associations there is still a quota of 10 to 15 per cent. fixed for Jewish members. Certain difficulties have also arisen with Jewish members, notably, a tendency on the part of some of them to monopolize the handball courts, and in several instances the physical director has found it at once necessary but difficult to enforce regulations which would give the Gentiles opportunities to which they were entitled.

In some cities, the Association has urged Jewish applicants for membership to join the Y. M. H. A. and has even coöperated in the establishment of this kindred organization. Again, it has evolved methods of accepting Jewish applicants only after consultation with a local rabbi. It has thus sought to maintain good relationship with the Jewish community, while protecting itself against the flooding of its membership by Jews or the entrance of particularly objectionable Jewish types.

The Y. M. C. A. and the Y. W. C. A. have both leaned over backward to be inclusive. Of course, neither of these organizations can be strictly classified as social clubs, but it is perhaps not without significance that these two organizations which have had a distinctly Christian and Protestant orientation have made a place for both Jews and Catholics, while more purely secular "clubs" have excluded at least the Jews. This would seem to corroborate the theory urged elsewhere that antipathy to the Jews is not based on religion. In the light of the Paris basis,[2] which determines the membership of all national movements in the Y. M. C. A., some Protestants feel that the Christian Associations have gone further than the second mile.

LUNCHEON CLUBS

In 1905 the first Rotary Club was organized in Chicago, and soon the organization spread to other cities and to other countries as follows:

---

[2] "The Young Men's Christian Associations seek to unite those young men who, regarding Jesus Christ as their God and Saviour, according to the Holy Scriptures, desire to be His disciples in their doctrine [in the original French, 'foi'] and in their life, and to associate their efforts for the extension of His Kingdom amongst young men."

1910 Canada   1919 Asia
1911 United Kingdom   1920 Spain
1914 Latin America   1921 South Africa and Australia

Clubs organized on similar principles rapidly followed—the Kiwanis, Lions and Civitan. The aim of these organizations included the development of camaraderie in business, the formulation of codes of business ethics, the promotion of community-mindedness and community responsibility, and the spirit of service. It sought to fuse together the various groupings which broke our common life into fragments by means of the typically American enthusiasm for boosting.

The Rotarians and the Kiwanians, by reason of the fact that they were first in the field, became in a measure the aristocrats of the luncheon clubs, and first choice of the material available for membership. They received consequently a larger share of the men of outstanding substance, prestige and experience, than the Lions or Civitans. Perhaps, to this is due the fact that in many cities there are more Jews in the last-named organizations than in the first two. The relative fewness of the Jews in Rotary or Kiwanis is particularly evident in those cities where the Jewish community has not long been established, or where social lines generally are drawn more rigidly. In some of these clubs, however, in practically all the cities, the Jews have their representation.

The Catholics are also well represented, and indeed all the luncheon clubs stress their non-sectarian character, and seem willing to have anything discussed except "politics" and "religion." The clubs take pride in their efforts on behalf of the melting-pot. The number of Catholics enrolled seems to have alarmed certain branches of the church at one time, for in Spain a spirited attack was made against Rotary about 1928 by a Jesuit priest in which he likened it to Freemasonry and the Y. M. C. A. and complained that it was designed to diminish the faith of Catholics by bringing them into harmful contact with non-Catholics.[3] Some official pronouncements were later made by the church in Spain which had repercussions in America, but apparently explanations forthcoming from the Rotarians, together with protests of Catholic Rotarians, put a stop to the attack.

POLITICAL DISCRIMINATION

If Jews suffer most from the types of discrimination previously discussed in this chapter, the Catholics in the United States complain most of political discrimination, although Protestants aver that in those cities where Catho-

---

[3] Father Barcena was the outstanding opponent of Rotary. He was answered by Jose Ros y Guell, in *Rotary, Rotarismo y Rotarios* (Barcelona: Libreria Catalonia, 1929).

lics are dominant they often have difficulty in securing the election of Protestants.

Behind this discrimination, there is a long history of suspicion and struggle. Even after the Revolutionary War, the religious qualification for office persisted in many states. As Leon Whipple says in *The Story of Civil Liberty in the United States*:[4]

"Religious qualifications for the governorship persisted into the nineteenth century in New Jersey, New Hampshire, Connecticut and Vermont. In Maryland, no Jew could serve on a jury, sit as judge or magistrate, practise law or be a member of the Assembly until the passage of the 'Jew Bills' in 1828; and it was only in 1851 that a special clause of a new Maryland constitution forbade all such discriminations."

HISTORICAL BACKGROUND IN THE UNITED STATES

In providing a background for understanding this type of political discrimination, the following considerations should be borne in mind:

(1) In England at this time, Catholics and Jews were still disqualified from public office, Catholic emancipation only being obtained in 1829 and Jewish Emancipation in 1858. In England the toleration extended in the first year of William and Mary did not reach beyond those who believed in the Blessed Trinity. The law might not be applied in all its rigor, but the status of Catholics and Jews was somewhat uncertain.

(2) In New England, the intimate relation between church and state continued for some years after the revolution. While freedom of worship was guaranteed, the religious test for office was abolished in Massachusetts only in 1821. In New Hampshire there still remain some vestiges of the ancient relation between church and state in the present constitution, which permits communities to provide at their own expense for "Protestant teachers of religion, etc."

(3) The First Amendment to the Constitution of the Federal Government merely forbade Congress to pass laws which might establish a given religion or prohibit the free exercise of some particular religions; it did not disturb the inner economy of the individual states nor abrogate the relations already existing between these states and various churches.

(4) The Pennsylvania Charter of Privileges, 1701, stated:

"All persons who also profess to believe in Jesus Christ, the Saviour of the World, shall be capable (notwithstanding their other Perswasions and Practices in Point of Conscience and Religion) to serve this Government in any Capacity, both legislatively and executively, he or they solemnly promising, when lawfully required, Allegiance to the King as Sovereign, etc."

---

[4] New York: The Vanguard Press, 1927.

The Virginia Bill of Rights, 1776, went a step farther:

"That religion or the duty, which we owe to our Creator and the manner of discharging it can be directed only by reason and conviction, not by force or violence and therefore all men are equally entitled to the free exercise of religion, according to the dictates of conscience; and that it is the mutual duty of all to practice Christian forbearance, love and charity towards each other."

The spirit of the times was toward a larger tolerance, although there still remains the implication in these early documents that the country is a Christian country.

A somewhat similar assumption that the country is a Christian country might possibly be deduced from the reference in the Constitution of the United States, Article I, section 7, where the phrase "Sundays excepted" seems to imply the acceptance of the Christian Sunday as a legal holiday.

(5) The fathers of the Constitution, many of whom were Deists or Latitudinarians, undoubtedly weighted the constitution in favor of religious liberty, but they do not seem to have frankly faced all the implications in the possible relations between church and state. Even today, sessions of Congress are opened with prayer, while chaplains are appointed to serve the men of the army and navy. Courts of justice are frequently opened with prayer, and the President has always issued an annual Thanksgiving message calling upon the people to betake themselves to their houses of worship and render their appropriate thanksgiving.

(6) At the time of the establishment of the Constitution, the country was so overwhelmingly Protestant that the solution reached seems to have been motivated by the desire to place all Protestant sects and groups on the utmost possible parity rather than to state the "last word" in respect to the relation of church and state, religion and politics. In the Ordinance of 1787 for the government of the territory northwest of the Ohio River, it was specifically stated:

"Religion, morality, and knowledge being necessary to good government and the happiness of mankind, schools and the means of education shall forever be encouraged."

Religion was thus assumed to be a good thing, however unwilling the legislators were to describe more specifically the kind of religion they meant.

Indeed, as we have pointed out in the introduction, the first charter of Georgia specifically excluded Catholics as settlers, while after 1627 no Protestant was allowed to enter French Canada, even though the Huguenots were at this very time protected in France itself by the operation of the Edict of Nantes. In certain of the Mennonite settlements in Pennsylvania tolerance was extended to all prospective settlers except "Papists and usurious Jews."

Directly after the Revolutionary War, pacifist groups suffered for their religious conviction. In Pennsylvania many of the Mennonites had refused to take up arms on behalf of the rebellion, and for this they were subjected to much local persecution. Because of this, many of them migrated to Canada and settled in the Grand Valley area in Ontario, feeling that the British government would be more indulgent of their religious peculiarities than would the Americans. This was not the last time that the United States has been called upon to face the problem of how much freedom should be permitted men and women whose religious scruples forbade them to bear arms. During the Mormon colonization in the West, the question of polygamy arose, and another struggle between church and state ensued, with results which are well known. So, too, during the federal election campaigns of 1928 some asked whether a voter who believed in the necessity of preserving the army and navy on a war footing should not be justified in voting against Mr. Hoover on the ground that he was a Quaker. A somewhat similar justification might be brought forward for rejecting a candidate who happened to be a Christian Scientist on the theory that a Christian Scientist might not show the proper attention to measures necessary to the public health. In spite of our theories regarding religious liberty, situations arise.

THE SITUATION IN CANADA

Inasmuch as the Catholic issue came to the front first with the cession of Acadia in 1713 and of Canada in 1759, and involved the British government in problems which are not yet solved, it may be well to begin by outlining certain of the problems which arose in that Dominion.

New England was delighted when the Treaty of Utrecht added Acadia to the British possessions, but it was easier to take possession of the new territory than it was to discover an oath of allegiance which the Acadians would accept. The desire of the British government was to insist on allegiance to the King, not qualified by any higher allegiance to the Pope, but every effort to frame a suitable oath met with equivocations, delays, and objections. The struggle went on for years, until the British governors in disgust decided to expel the Acadians, and as a result we have the story of Evangeline. There is documentary evidence in the archives of Nova Scotia that French-Canadian ecclesiastics abetted the colonists in their resistance to the demands that they take the oath of allegiance.

By the cession of Canada in 1759, Britain obtained a land in which there were only Roman Catholics, about 65,000 in number; but as soon as the English-speaking Protestants came in by immigration from the colonies and the motherland the clash of two religions complicated a situation involving the clash of two cultures and two languages. Soon the English colonists began to demand a legislative assembly and a measure of self-government. At the same time they felt that the French-Canadian Roman Catholics should not be allowed to dictate the policies, and that the members of such an assembly should be chosen from their own ranks. In a petition sent to the King, they stated:

"There is now a sufficient number of Your Majesty's Protestant subjects residing in and possessed of real property in this Province, and who are otherwise qualified to be Members of a General Assembly."

The fear of Catholic defection should such an assembly be created caused the government to postpone any such action until some time after the Quebec Act (1774) had been passed, an Act, which, we have already intimated, vouchsafed "the free exercise of the Religion of the Church of Rome, subjected to the King's Supremacy," and which further substituted for the oath required of all subjects by the act passed in the first year of the reign of Queen Elizabeth the following:

"I, A. B., do sincerely promise and swear, That I will be faithful and bear true allegiance to His Majesty, King George, and him will defend to the utmost of my Power, against all traiterous conspiracies, and Attempts whatsoever, which shall be made against His Person, Crown and Dignity; and I will do my utmost Endeavour to disclose and make known to His Majesty, His Heirs and Successors, all Treasons, and traiterous Conspiracies, and Attempts, which I shall know to be against Him, or any of Them; and all this I do swear without any Equivocation, mental Evasion, or secret Reservation, and renouncing all Pardons and Dispensations from any Power or Person whomsoever to the contrary. So help me God!"

Shortly after, an Assembly was created, but the executive power was vested in a Legislative Council appointed by the Crown and not responsible to the Assembly. This condition existed from 1791 until the Rebellion of 1837 forced the issue of responsible government. The struggle between the two cultures had much to do in retarding the political institutions of Canada, and religion was an important part of the picture.

JEWISH EMANCIPATION

In 1807 a Jewish gentleman named Ezekiel Hart was elected to the Legislative Assembly of Lower Canada from the constituency of Three Rivers. The French members, knowing that Mr. Hart's sympathies were English, sought to disqualify him because, as a professing Jew, he had not taken the oath with the usual formula "on the truth faith of a Christian." The English minority fought the French majority for the seating of Hart and lost, the resolution reading "that Ezekiel Hart, Esquire, professing the Jewish religion, cannot take a seat, nor sit, nor vote, in this house." He was re-elected, but though he this time agreed to take the oath in the usual manner, he was again unseated and a bill was presented aiming "to disqualify Jews from being eligible to sit in the House of Assembly." Whereupon, on the very day the bill was scheduled for its third reading, the Governor dissolved the house. Gradually, little by little, rights were secured for the Jewish minority, and in 1831 a bill was introduced, passed and received the royal assent, giving full political equality to the Jews. Such rights were secured in Canada three years after the "Jew bills" in Maryland, and twenty-four years before similar rights were obtained in England.

CONTINUOUS CATHOLIC-PROTESTANT STRUGGLE

The struggle between Catholic Quebec and Protestant Ontario has characterized almost the entire political history of Canada. After the Rebellion of 1837, Lord Durham was sent to Canada to report on the situation, and he recommended that Upper and Lower Canada, which had separate governments after 1791, should be reunited. Up to this time, the system of government had been, as Lord Durham pointed out, based "on the policy of perpetuating that very separating of the races, and encouraging these very notions of conflicting nationalities which it ought to have been the first and chief care of Government to check and extinguish." By the Act of Union of 1840, the two provinces became one, and this gave the English-speaking residents a majority over the French-Canadians; but the dualism of culture had become too firmly rooted, and among the first questions that called for settlement after the union were those related to education—a fruitful subject of discord—and in the very decade in which the issue of public vs. parochial schools was to the front in the United States. Nor must it be forgotten that by this time the Oxford Movement had begun in England and was interpreted by many Evangelicals as a new effort on the part of the Pope to capture England. The Evangelical temper was aroused, the World's Evangelical Alliance was launched, and a bitter controversy was waged around "Romanism" in England, in the United States and Canada.

RISE OF ORANGE ORDER

Protestant Irishmen were pouring into Canada about this time, even as Catholic Irishmen were pouring into the United States, and they brought with them all the suspicion and hatred of Catholicism which the internecine conflicts of that unhappy island had evoked. By 1827 an Orange Order had been started in Canada and it has had an unbroken and continued existence to the present time, ever watching Roman Catholicism and sounding the drum and the fife when it scented danger. Unlike the various anti-Catholic societies in the United States, which suddenly rose and vanished but never failed to fling their hat into the political arena, the Orange Order was always present.

Both in Canada and the United States, the literature of the period of the eighteen forties and fifties is controversial and bitter, but in Quebec the conflict was accentuated because of the status given to French civil law which has persisted to this day side by side with English criminal law. The *issues almost always involved politics.* So in Canada the controversy waged, paralleling similar controversies in the United States but intensified in Quebec by the determination of the French cultural forces to survive and the equally resolute insistence of the English Protestants to keep the hierarchy in its place. Efforts to solve the school question along the lines adopted by New York State became clearly futile, and parallel Protestant and Catholic schools were set up in Lower Canada. By 1867 it was clear that the union of Lower and Upper Canada could not well continue, and hence a method was found of dividing again, but enlarging the general domain by taking into the proposed union or confederation the other colonies of New Brunswick and Nova Scotia, and creating one Dominion with four provinces. On July 1, 1867, the Confederation of the Dominion of Canada was effected, and special protection was vouchsafed to the Protestant minority in Quebec and the Catholic minority in Ontario.[5]

CONFEDERATION AND THE SEPARATE SCHOOL ISSUE

Still, even after 1867, constant clashes arose. Perhaps the most notable and bitter struggles were over the return of the Jesuit Estates by the province of Quebec to the Jesuit order in 1889, and the Manitoba School Question in the eighteen nineties. As soon as new provinces were carved out of the Northwest Territory, the school question came up just as in the United States the slavery problem had to be faced. Manitoba, such a new province, insisted that it was under no compulsion to provide for a separate school system. Catholic leaders urged the spirit of the British North American Act of 1867, if not its letter. The Conservative administration, led by Protestants and fearing to alienate the support of Quebec, sought to put pressure on Manitoba and force her to provide separate schools. The whole country was aroused and great bitterness threatened, when, to the surprise of all, a young French-Canadian member, rapidly emerging into public notice, stood out against the leaders of his own church and insisted that Manitoba had a right to determine for herself whether she should have a separate school system in addition to its public-school system,

---

[5] See Chapter **V.**

or not. Because a French-Canadian Roman Catholic political leader espoused the right of Manitoba to exclude separate schools, while his political adversaries, Protestant though they were, sought to force the separate school system on Manitoba, the people rallied to the support of Sir Wilfrid Laurier, who became Prime Minister and held that post for seventeen years.

While Sir Wilfrid's defiance of the church at first offended some of his co-religionists, they eventually forgave him, and racial pride in one of her own sons soon made Quebec almost entirely Liberal in politics. Thus it acquired a balance of power which was only lost in 1911 when the Reciprocity Issue gave the more imperialistic conservatives a chance to break its power. A good many Canadians believe that it is highly doubtful if there will ever again be a French-Canadian Roman Catholic premier, although Laurier was highly respected, admired and loved.

The political solidarity of Catholic Quebec, the bi-culturalism and bi-lingualism, the ecclesiastical control of all things temporal and spiritual in the province, colors the whole Canadian situation and complicates the whole of Canadian life. A few illustrations will suffice.

PROHIBITION MOVEMENT

In 1908 a plebiscite on Prohibition was taken throughout the Dominion. The English-speaking provinces voted overwhelmingly for Prohibition; French Canada voted overwhelmingly against it, and as a result no government could afford to touch it. While prohibition was in force throughout Canada during the war, immediately after the Dominion ban was removed, Quebec was the first province to resort to government control, and the curious division of governmental authority between Dominion and Provincial governments practically forced the other provinces to follow suit. This division of opinion gave color to the identification of "Rum" and "Rome" and led many prohibitionists to attack the Catholics as well, quite forgetting that there was a strong temperance sentiment among many of the French-Canadian clergy.

MARRIAGE ANNULMENTS

Then, again, owing to the fact that in Quebec French civil law prevails, and the right to practice the Roman Catholic religion is specifically stated in the Quebec Act, countless difficult situations have arisen. One of the most troublesome and most resented by Protestants is the repeated annulment by the civil courts of marriages contracted by one or more Catholics before Protestant ministers. A more detailed treatment of this situation must be reserved for the section dealing with intermarriages, but ever since the *Ne Temere* decree was issued at Rome, August 2, 1907, cases have been judged by Quebec civil courts according to ecclesiastical law. In 1911, the case of Herbert vs. Clouatre was determined in the Superior Court of the Province of Quebec. Both plaintiff and defendant were Catholics who had been married on July 14, 1908, before a Protestant minister. The marriage was annulled on these grounds:

"Que dans les circonstances, le demandeur and la défenderesse ne pouvaient se marier qu'a l'église catholique, et ce en presence de leur propre curé en suivant les formalités de la loi et les règlements de l'église catholique Romaine a laquelle les parties appartiennent," etc.

Of course, on a similar basis, a marriage between a Protestant and a Catholic could be annulled by a civil court on the ground that the Catholic party could not be properly married except before a Catholic priest as prescribed by the *Ne Temere* decree and the canon law. In January, 1934, Justice Coderre of Quebec annulled the marriage of Charles E. A. Holmes, who was born an Anglican, and his Catholic wife. This marriage had been contracted December 18, 1909, before a Presbyterian minister, and there was one child who, at the time of the annulment, was of age. In his annulment, Justice Coderre stated that the minister, being Protestant

"had no jurisdiction to unite the plaintiff and the defendant as husband and wife; that the marriage contracted between the parties is absolutely null, seeing that there cannot be, according to the doctrine of the Catholic Church, any valid marriage between persons of the Catholic religion or of mixed religions, unless it be solemnized and contracted before a priest of the Catholic religion and recognized by the said religion as fit to perform the said marriage, and without a special dispensation."

Marriages have also been annulled in civil courts, although contracted in good faith, because it was discovered that the contracting parties were cousins in the fourth degree, and consequently should not have been married according to Catholic practice except with a special dispensation from the bishop. One case in particular, commonly known as the Despatie-Tremblay case, was fought out in the courts of Quebec between 1910 and 1921, only ending in a decision by the Privy Council, which clearly stated the subordination of ecclesiastical to civil law in the matter. Such interferences with the civil law, especially in cases involving Protestants and Catholics, create no end of ill feeling. The situation in Canada is complicated by the facts, first, that in the Dominion there is no civil marriage, and secondly, that in Quebec civil status is determined somewhat by one's religion, and a Catholic can only cease to be a Catholic by making public abjuration of his faith before a Protestant minister, who thereupon sends the abjuration to the bishop of the diocese. This confusion of civil and ecclesiastical law has its repercussions on the Protestant population, strengthens the hands of the Orange Order, and promotes political discrimination on religious grounds. It encourages the belief that where the Catholics have the power, they will overrule civil by ecclesiastical considerations. Hence, it is argued, the safe thing to do is to keep them out of power.

BI-LINGUALISM

Another fruitful source of dissension relates to bi-lingualism in Ontario. As the French Catholics moved into Ontario, and established separate schools along the Ottawa Valley, they began an agitation for instruction in the French language, contending that Quebec permitted instruction in the English language. An effort to control this tendency led to a celebrated regulation called No. 17, issued by the Minister of Education, which aroused such opposition that it was withdrawn; but under a law giving the Minister wide general powers, the use of French as the language of instruction in certain schools is permitted, much against the wishes of the Orangemen and their friends. Many Protestants outside the Orange Order who would welcome every straightforward effort to effect better understanding between the French and the English in Canada feel that such concessions only tend to perpetuate the bi-culturalism which, reinforced by religious diversity, has prevented any real national unity. Thus the struggle between cultures is inseparably intertwined with the struggle between religious groupings, and strange to say, at this point, some of the most pronounced opposition to French in the separate schools has come from the English-speaking Catholics of Irish extraction in the affected areas.

Again, in Quebec, efforts to spread Protestant propaganda have not infrequently been halted by resort to intimidation, physical and legal. Colporteurs have been subjected to various indignities, and the latest of these is the attempt to silence the Rev. Victor André Havard, an ex-Trappist monk, who was converted to Anglicanism seven years ago and has been pastor of the Anglican "L'Eglise de Redempteur" in Montreal. Twice within the last year, he has brought large numbers of French-Canadians to the Anglican Bishop for confirmation—on one occasion nearly 500, and on a second occasion nearly 300. He was arrested in January, 1934, on charges of blasphemy, because he had, *inter alia,* put placards outside his church attacking the Catholic clergy and comparing their practices with "biblical" precepts. This makes it easy for Protestants to believe that while Catholics may plead for religious liberty where they are in a minority, the moment they become a majority, they crush out all dissent.

One might elaborate numerous other tensions which thus develop in Canada, and which give vitality to the Orange Order. The situation has its repercussions in the United States, especially in the New England area where French-Canadian immigration has been a factor of considerable importance. There also has seemed to be a nexus between the Orange Order of Canada and some of the various anti-Catholic organizations that have arisen in the United States, and the American developments can be best understood in relation to the Canadian dénouement, just as in 1774 the special privileges conferred on the French-Canadians by the British government aroused great hostility in the thirteen colonies.

Such circumstances inevitably bring political consequences. Quebec is overwhelmingly Catholic in religion and Liberal in politics; Ontario is dominantly Protestant in religion and Conservative in politics, and while a Protestant might have little chance of election in any but Protestant constituencies in Quebec, a Catholic faces similar obstacles in Ontario, except where the Catholic population may be of vital significance. So tense is the situation that the politicians dread nothing so much as the introduction of religious emotion into questions of state. So far as local boards of education are concerned, there are no Protestants, of course, on the separate school boards and no Catholics on the public-school boards. On other civic or municipal boards the Catholics seldom have representation except where there may be a considerable number of them in the community. The city of Toronto itself has been regarded as more Orange than Belfast, and many of the outstanding municipal leaders are Orangemen. Until recently, however, the Catholic minority has usually been represented by one Catholic on the Board of Control, but during 1933 an active agitation arose in Catholic circles for a larger share of the public funds for separate schools and a "more equitable" distribution of corporation taxes for educational purposes based on the number of children attending public and separate schools in any given municipal area, as in Quebec, and when the elections took place on January 1, 1934, the Catholic representative failed to secure re-election. This was generally interpreted as the answer of the Toronto ratepayers.[6] Even in the western provinces, the issue of public funds for separate schools, in a variety of its forms, once dragged out into the open, can always "upset a government."

In the Maritime provinces, the relations between Protestants and Catholics are much more cordial and less strained. By an unwritten law, municipal offices pass in turn, now to Protestants and now to Catholics. Part of this

---

* Prior to the Ontario elections in 1934, the Catholic Ratepayer's Association asked Premier Henry to make some provision and a division of the taxes received from corporations more favorable to the separate school system than that which already existed. The Premier offered to seek a ruling on the matter from the Privy Council. A letter was later published in the *Evening Telegram* (Toronto) purporting to come from the Catholic Ratepayer's Association and directed to all Catholic voters, asking them to vote against Premier Henry's government in the coming election. The election took place in June, 1934, and the Conservative government was badly beaten after having been in power for thirty years. Catholic action may have been a contributing factor to the defeat although there were so many other factors, notably the economic depression, that it is impossible to draw any definite conclusions.

good-will is due to the fact that Scottish Catholics exert an unusual influence, and the relation between the Scottish Catholics and Scottish Protestants is intimate.

In the Dominion Government, on the other hand, the solid bloc of Quebec together with the bi-lingualism of the country has at various times given to Catholic French Canada a balance of power which is frequently resented by the rest of the country. Even in the provision of government jobs, Quebec is always pressing for more jobs, appealing to the bi-culturalism and bi-lingualism of the country as requiring a large representation of French, and there is thus a general feeling that by such pressure French Canada probably has more than its due share of political influence. This, in turn, makes Canadian Protestantism more alert and self-conscious in all matters relating to politics.

JEWISH PARTICIPATION IN CANADIAN POLITICS

So far as the Jews in Canada are concerned, they have seldom been a factor of any great political consequence except in the few cities where they are numerous. One of the first members of Parliament sent to Ottawa from the new province of British Columbia in the 'seventies was a Jew; today there are three Jewish members of Parliament at Ottawa, one each from Toronto, Montreal and Winnipeg. There are no Jewish members of the Dominion cabinet, and no Jews on the bench of any of the higher courts, although some of them serve in municipal courts. This is substantially what might be expected when it is remembered that the Jewish population is only 1.6 per cent. of the entire Canadian population, and is almost exclusively confined to cities and towns. In Montreal and Toronto the Jewish population is largely to be found in certain specified electoral areas. It may be, however, that the Orange opposition to Catholicism might accentuate, if a specific problem arose, opposition to the Jews.

THE SITUATION IN THE UNITED STATES

The situation in the United States, while it was influenced from colonial times by the efforts of the British government to deal with the French-Canadian Catholics, is, of course, quite different. Here the original settlers were largely of English extraction and Protestant in religion, and they assumed the appropriateness of but one language. The incoming immigrants from Ireland and southern Europe challenged the continuity of this cultural tradition, and hence in the United States from the outset nativism and anti-Catholicism went hand in hand.

FIVE WAVES OF ANTI-CATHOLIC FEELING

In the report of the Commission of the Knights of Columbus on Religious Prejudice, issued in 1916, five waves of anti-Catholic feeling in the United

States up to that time were indicated. The first came soon after the close of the Revolutionary War and "culminated in laws discriminating against Catholics being passed in most of the original states. The main causes of this movement were traceable to the French Revolution, which resulted in so many Catholics seeking refuge in America, and alarm for the security of our institutions was manifested, and strangely, the cherished institution of religious liberty was all but abolished." The second wave followed the outbreak of anti-Masonic feeling in the prosecution of the alleged abductors of William Morgan, who had published what were supposed to have been the secrets of Freemasonry in 1826. The third wave was that commonly called the "Know-Nothing" movement, 1851-1858.[7] It "strove to preserve the political ascendency of Protestantism in the states both by Federal legislation affecting the naturalization of emigrants and by preventing legislation in their respective states for the relief of Catholics from their religious disabilities which was necessary to give effect to the liberal spirit and purpose of the constitution." While the Know-Nothing movement was formally launched only in 1852 under the title of the "National Council of the United States of America," the first "formal organization" of nativist sentiment was effected in New York in 1835. It is perhaps fair to say that the bitterness of the controversy which preceded, and culminated in, the Know-Nothing movement was not due to Irish immigration alone, but also to the intense excitement over the issue of public vs. parochial schools in the forties,[8] and was accentuated by the repercussions of the Oxford Movement which had spread to America and convinced American Protestants that Rome was once again aggressively seeking to subdue England.

At all events, the Know-Nothings—the members of which always met any queries concerning their organization with the phrase, "I don't know."—sent forty representatives to Congress in 1854, and held seventy-five seats in 1855. In 1856 they nominated Millard Fillmore as candidate for the Presidency, although he carried only one state, Maryland, and polled less than one-fourth of the total vote cast. Only the more crucial issue of abolition and the shadows of an immense civil war between North and South sapped the energy of this party. During the period of its greatest and most intense activity, nativist uprisings occurred in many cities, culminating in Bloody Monday, August 5, 1855, when nearly one hundred poor Irish were killed and some twenty houses destroyed by fire at Louisville, Kentucky.

The crest of the fourth wave came with the organization of the first coun-

---

[7] An excellent summary of this movement may be found in the *Catholic Encyclopaedia*, Volume VIII, pp. 677-680.

[8] Governor Seward at one time favored the use of public funds for Catholic schools. A year later, in 1841, he modified his views, but his espousal of the Catholic schools is supposed by many to have been the fundamental reason why the Republicans in 1860 had to pass him by and nominated instead a young Kentuckian named Abraham Lincoln for the presidency. See chapter on Education.

cil of the American Protective Association (A.P.A.) in Clinton, Iowa, 1887. "Members were bound by oath to endeavor to exclude Catholics entirely from public offices," and between 1891 and 1897, it created considerable commotion; but it was finally all but killed in its futile effort to prevent the nomination of William McKinley.

The fifth wave, according to the Knights of Columbus Commission on Religious Prejudice, began to develop in 1908 when the United States was advanced by the Pope from the status of a Mission country to that of a Province, and transferred from the "jurisdiction of the Propaganda to that of the Holy See." Following this important step, the first American Catholic Missionary Congress met at Chicago in November, 1908, and was followed by the Eucharistic Congress at Montreal in 1910. During the nineties, says Charles A. Beard, in *The Rise of American Civilization,* the Catholics possessed a majority, "or at least a plurality of the Christian communicants in thirteen states; twenty years later the number of such commonwealths had increased to eighteen, mainly the industrial sections with large factory and mining populations."[9] The excessive Catholic immigration was frightening many Protestants, and resolutions were frequently passed asserting that the Catholic Church was a menace. A widely circulated anti-Catholic paper which featured Catholic scandals helped by its very name, *The Menace,* to disseminate this fear. But it was not the mentally unclean alone who were troubled. President Theodore Roosevelt once addressed a Methodist audience thus:

"I would rather address a Methodist audience than any other audience in America. You know for one thing that every one there is an American. . . . Next to the Methodists I prefer to address Episcopalians. They are all American likewise, usually representing the higher or else the lower social class. The Methodists represent the great middle class and in consequence are the most representative church in America. I think the Methodists and the Episcopalians increase more rapidly than any other churches in the country. They appeal to the genius of our institutions, more than any other denominations. . . . The Catholic Church is no way suited to this country and can never have any great permanent growth except through immigration, for its thought is Latin and entirely at variance with the dominant thought of our country and institutions."[10]

During the World War, there was a moratorium on religious hatred and a specious national unity was effected, but following the War, the ancient bitterness broke out afresh. The anti-Catholic complex of the Ku Klux

---

[9] The director of this study has doubts concerning the validity of Professor Beard's deductions. The census might perhaps show a plurality of Catholic communicants, owing to Catholic inclusion of baptized children under thirteen years of age under that category. What, however, of Protestant affiliates?

[10] Beard, *The Rise of American Civilization,* Volume II, pp. 399-400.

Klan was due to many factors, among which four major situations should perhaps be noted:

FRIENDS OF IRISH FREEDOM

(1) The activities of the Friends of Irish Freedom, in the latter days of and immediately following the War, alienated a great many Protestants who felt, rightly or wrongly, that the Catholic Church was a party to the conflict which aimed to cripple the British Empire. At their Buffalo meeting in 1919, the Supreme Council of the Knights of Columbus passed resolutions of sympathy "with the aspirations of the Irish people for a government of its own" and urged "the recognition of the national independence of Ireland by the nations of the world" (August 7, 1919). While Irish independence had its sympathizers among the people of England and among some Protestant liberals in America, the vast majority of Protestants felt that this effort on the part of a group in the United States was at once an intrusion into the domestic affairs of a friendly and recently associated power, and a subtle effort on the part of the Catholic population to break the integrity of an empire dominantly Protestant.

THE PROHIBITION CONTROVERSY

(2) The Prohibition issue was at the front and the 18th Amendment had been passed. The Anti-Saloon League avowed itself—perhaps somewhat too hastily—as an agent of the Protestant churches. It had, in general, the support of the majority of the large Protestant denominations, although Protestants were by no means unanimous concerning the desirability of Prohibition. While there was an Association of Catholics Favoring Prohibition, and while certain Catholic ecclesiastics were known to support prohibition, Catholics in general seemed violently opposed, and many of the infringements of the law and subsequent bootlegging were believed to be the work of persons of foreign lineage and Catholic background. Some of the most vigorous campaigners for law enforcement openly attacked the Catholic Church in this connection, and the general result was that the struggle between wets and drys became in part a contest between Protestants and Catholics, with some notable defections from both groups.

Y.M.C.A. WAR WORK AND AFTER

(3) The Y.M.C.A. had undertaken a tremendous work in connection with the War, and on the whole had achieved considerable distinction in the accomplishment of the tasks assigned to it, although it was inevitable that in the very nature and magnitude of the work, some mistakes would

be made both in the selection of personnel and in the determination of policy. Criticism of this organization was commonly believed to have been stimulated by its rival organization, the Knights of Columbus, and undoubtedly the attitude of many Protestants toward Catholics hardened because of these attacks. Following the War, the Y.M.C.A. advanced aggressively in many new countries and met a bitter resistance from the Catholic Church. This also deepened a distrust of the ecclesiastical machine on the part of some American Protestants.

NATIVISM

(4) War almost inevitably stimulates a suspicion of all elements in the national life that show a negative tendency to assimilation. The passion—one might almost say, the mania—for Americanization work and the rigid restrictions against continued immigration were but symptoms of the feverish desire not to be caught again so weakened by internal divisions and subject to the partisan propaganda of scores of "national groupings" within the country. Because the foreign groupings were so largely Catholic, the nativism of post-war days became easily enough anti-Catholic.

The complication of religious antipathy with racial antipathy has thus influenced political development in the United States almost from the earliest days, even as the struggle between the French and the English in Canada has created a situation in which religion is hopelessly involved with racial and political factors. Thus, a Protestant literary man writes to the director of this study:

"The bulk of it [i.e. the antipathy] is felt not because the objects of this animosity are Catholic, but because they are Irish of a rather low order. That is, it is racial rather than religious, and racial only in the sense that in both Boston and New York—and in other cities as well—the Irish have come to be identified (because they have identified themselves) with the worst forms of graft, corruption and political crookedness generally. The Tammany politician (using Tammany as a generic term for a type that is prevalent in most of our larger cities) is by and large, with of course individual exceptions, the kind of a creature that one doesn't want to associate with. He happens also to be an Irish Catholic, usually of rather a blatant type, the variety of Irishman known as a 'mick'."

Had the early Catholic immigrants been Irish from the same general social level as the people to whom they came and at the same time Protestants, would the antagonism that actually developed in America and which only now shows signs of a permanent recession, have been so deep? In the answer which individual readers may give to that question may be found some clue as to their opinion whether the discrimination which finds its fullest expression in politics is founded on racial or religious attitudes.

In this connection it is well to indicate that in a recent analysis of the Canadian census returns for 1931, "Religious Denominations by Racial Origins," it has been made clear that over 69 per cent. of the persons of Irish extraction in Canada are non-Catholic. No Canadian who is at the same time familiar with the situation in the United States can fail to note the comparison between the esteem in which the Irish-Canadians are held in Canada and the usual contempt in which Irish-Americans were held in the States until the partial settlement of the perennial question of Ireland removed the fear of an "Irish vote" in the average American city.

No one who knows the tragic history of Ireland will fail to appreciate why the Irish who came to America after the Revolutionary War were bitterly hostile to England; nor is it remarkable that the Society of, or the Columbian Order of Tammany, founded in 1789 largely as a social and benevolent order, was for the most part an answer to the aristocratic Society of the Cincinnati and from the very first drew the incoming Irish to its fold. Their early espousal of the party of Jefferson was largely an expression of their antipathy to the Hamiltonians. As Claude Bowers says in his *Jefferson and Hamilton* (page 148),

"It was rabidly republican and wholly democratic . . . it sympathized with the revolutionists in France and resented the property disqualifications of our Revolutionary soldiers for the suffrage, while the wealthy, the notoriously friendly to England whom these soldiers fought were being accorded political recognition and place."

At all events, especially in New York, the immigrant group soon actively campaigned against the older and more established families, and a line was drawn which has continued, more or less, to our own day. As the immigrant group grew numerous, the feeling intensified; as they became preponderant, they rewarded all who had kept them out of office in their own coin, and for long years, as everybody knows, New York City was governed by Tammany Hall. Whether the reputation is deserved or not, that government has become notorious the world over for wholesale graft, political chicanery and lack of all sense of political honor. As most of these followers were Irish-Catholics, Catholicism in America has drawn to itself the nationwide antipathy to Tammany, and Tammany rule has been pointed out as a conspicuous example of "what happens when Catholics get in power."

THE POLITICAL CAMPAIGN OF 1928

Long before the elections of 1928 the Ku Klux Klan had been subsiding— Protestant leaders themselves being conspicuous in the efforts to provide the necessary antidotes—but the nomination of Alfred E. Smith for the Presidency fanned fires which might otherwise have died out. He combined against him a variety of antipathies:

(1) He was a Roman Catholic and never had a Roman Catholic been elected to the Presidency. Only once before, in fact, had a Catholic been nominated, viz., in 1872, when Charles O'Connor, running on the Labor Reform ticket, received 29,048 out of over 6,400,000 votes.

(2) Mr. Smith was avowedly wet, and this lined up. against him almost all the drys in the country who were still far from convinced that the prohibition law had been a failure.

(3) While he had fought Tammany from within, people generally considered him as belonging to the ring which had cursed New York for generations, and which was feared throughout the country as one of the most sinister influences in American life.

(4) He came from New York City and that is no asset in one who seeks the support of almost any other part of the United States.

(5) While many recognized his undoubted instinct for social justice, they felt that he lacked the background of personal culture desirable in the high office of President.

Other factors, too, entered into the picture, some of them perhaps cruder than those already mentioned, and the opposition finally deprived him of all the electoral votes except those furnished by Alabama, Arkansas, Georgia, Louisiana, Massachusetts, Mississippi, Rhode Island and South Carolina. Of these states, the vote in Massachusetts and Rhode Island would seem to represent an almost cleancut division between Protestant and Catholic. Louisiana not only was largely Catholic, but it also was normally Democratic; the other five states were dominantly Protestant and one of them, Georgia, has the smallest percentage of Catholics in its population of any state in the union. The vote was:

Hoover	21,392,190
Smith	15,016,443
Thomas	267,420
Foster	48,770

It is thus apparent that the vote was by no means conducted on religious lines, for less than 20 per cent. of the population in the United States is Catholic—and of these many are small children—while Mr. Smith obtained more than 41 per cent. of the total vote. Nevertheless, the religious issue was undoubtedly introduced, and the arguments put forward by Mr. Charles C. Marshall and others in the *Atlantic Monthly* clearly revealed that a certain section of Protestants did not trust the Catholic Church to the extent of permitting one of its communicants to occupy the Presidential chair.

RELIGIOUS AFFILIATIONS OF PUBLIC MEN

In this connection, it should be stated that in several of the cities studied, instances were uncovered where a defection from the Democratic party during the election of 1928 was remembered by the Catholic voters in subsequent efforts to secure office.

Of the thirty-one Presidents of the United States, the following denominations have been represented:

Episcopalian	9
Presbyterian	6
Unitarian	4
Methodist	3
Reformed Dutch	2
Baptist	1
Disciples	1
Congregational	1
Quaker	1
Without affiliation	3
	31

There has been neither a Catholic nor a Jew on the list, but studies of the religious affiliations of those who appear in *Who's Who in America* indicate that a very meagre percentage of the prominent people in the United States is Catholic or Jewish.[11] The available presidential material may be more limited in Catholic or Jewish circles. At least twelve of the Presidents have been connected with the Masonic order.

It is also pointed out that few Catholics have ever been awarded posts in the federal cabinet. Thus, when President Franklin D. Roosevelt named Senator David A. Walsh and James A. Farley as members of his cabinet, he broke a precedent which had continued for. twenty-nine years. Before these appointments, the only Catholic cabinet ministers had been: Roger Brooke Taney, Attorney-General, 1831-1833, Secretary of the Treasury, 1833-1834; James Campbell, Postmaster-General, 1853-1857; Joseph McKenna, Attorney-General, 1897-1898; Robert John Wynne, Postmaster-General, 1904-1905; Charles J. Bonaparte, Secretary of the Navy, 1905-1906, Attorney-General, 1906-1909. It is significant that since the Civil War until the accession of President Franklin D. Roosevelt, only Republican Presidents (McKinley and Theodore Roosevelt) had included Catholics in the cabinet.

In respect to Jewish and Catholic members of Congress and the Supreme

[11] See *The Scientific Monthly*, March, 1933; article by Dr. C. Luther Fry, on "The Religious Affiliations of American Leaders," and the same magazine for December, 1931, article by Dr. Harvey C. Lehman and Dr. Paul Witty on "Scientific Eminence and Church Membership."

Court, a list, admittedly incomplete, was prepared by the *Fellowship Forum,* which gave the religious affiliations as of April, 1933, as follows:

	Total	Protestants	Catholics	Jews	Unknown	Masons
Senate	96	71	5	0	20	54
Representatives	435	277	44	8*	106	160
Supreme Court	9	6	1	2	0	1

* A report in the *American Hebrew*, May 9, 1934, gives the number of Jews in the House as 10.

As a large number of those listed as Masons gave no religious affiliation, and were consequently included under the category "unknown," we may at least assume that they were not probably Catholics.

In the matter of Ambassadors, the *Jewish Yearbook* for 1932 lists sixteen Jews up to the date of publication who have ever been ambassadors, ministers, or consuls-general in various foreign countries. The only Jews representing the United States at the time of the publication of that statement (1932) were the Minister to Albania, the Minister to Siam and the Ambassador to Cuba.

Despite the fact that the United States must send many ambassadors and ministers to countries nominally Catholic, few Catholics have ever been entrusted with such positions. At the present time, the only American Catholics representing their country in foreign countries are the Ambassador to Poland, Mr. John Cudahy, and the Ambassador to Cuba, Mr. Jefferson Caffery. A Catholic authority writes:

"I think that most of the diplomatic corps representing foreign countries in America, are of the Catholic faith. I judge this from their attendance at the various exercises of the Catholic University of America and at the religious services at St. Matthew's Church, Washington, which is located in the diplomatic section of the city."

It is of interest to note that even Protestant England has been represented at Washington in recent years by a Catholic, Sir Esmé Howard.

Generally speaking, so far as these major offices are concerned, there is no great evidence that the Protestant majority should worry unduly about Catholics and Jews running the country.

In state politics, the Jews have at present a somewhat unusual representation in the gubernatorial chairs. Governors Seligman, of New Mexico; Meier, of Oregon; Lehman, of New York, and Horner, of Illinois, are Jews. Prior to 1930, however, only four Jews had ever been elected as governors of American states or territories. In the recent elections in Illinois, a distinguished native son who had just driven King George out of the country appealed to race prejudice in the state countryside to prevent the election of Mr. Horner, but his anti-Semitism did not keep a Jewish governor from presiding at Springfield.

At present Catholic governors are: Frank H. Cooney, of Montana; William Langer, of North Dakota. Governor Fred Murphy, of the Philippines, is also a Catholic.

RELIGION IN MUNICIPAL POLITICS

In municipal politics, Catholics and Jews figure more prominently, and since the Catholics and Jews are both so largely urbanite, Protestants complain that in many cities they have no rights except that of paying the largest share of the taxes. In the cities studied, Catholics have usually a fair representation of all municipal offices, even in the board of education, and the same is true of Jews. In the report of the Commission on Religious Prejudices of the Knights of Columbus (1916) we read:

"We have repeatedly stated that to vote for a member of any denomination solely on account of his religion or to vote against one solely on that account, are equally reprehensible. . . . Without doubt Catholics are often defeated for office on account of their religion, but we find that often there are other reasons for their defeat, and they are not always bad reasons." (Page 37.)

Instances are alleged where a party seeking to elect a Catholic has anonymously distributed literature against its own candidate and attacking his religious affiliation in the effort to secure a Catholic solidarity on his behalf. Often, too, because no one really knows the accurate number of Protestants or Catholics or Jews in any given community in the United States, there being no proper census, the fear of a Catholic or Jewish vote has been held over the heads of the politicians, when perhaps, if the facts were known, there was no need for any alarm. Again, as Protestant churches have often threatened ostracism to a candidate who voted wet, the Catholic leaders have held a club over the heads of politicians who flirted with the idea of a birth-control clinic.

Is there a Catholic, Protestant or Jewish vote? Whether under normal conditions such a vote exists or not—and, in the opinion of the writer, the existence of such a vote is extremely dubious—it may nevertheless be created with the raising of certain issues. Possibly the repercussions of the Nazi attacks on the Jews in Germany were responsible for the lamentable injection of the Jewish question into the recent mayoralty campaign in New York City. A suspected raid on the public treasury by the Catholic school system or the Catholic charities might easily arouse a fighting Protestantism. Efforts to establish birth-control clinics in public institutions or legislation to effect the compulsory sterilization of the feeble-minded might cause Catholic ecclesiastical authorities to marshal their hosts; suspicion that the Silver Shirts were becoming a political force might cause unity to prevail, perhaps for the first time, in Jewish circles. But if such issues as these are not raised, prejudices find little to feed upon, and the more one group establishes close personal contacts with the other, the quicker do the antagonisms vanish. Coöperation at every point, and especially acquaintance and friendship, do more than reams of arguments over theoretical situations and hypotheses.

Those consulted in the course of this study, especially those in the larger cities, stated their opinion that there was no longer a Catholic vote, and that the settlement of the status of Ireland had broken down the solidarity of the Irish Catholics in politics; they did assert, however, that there were in nearly all major cities "national groupings" which tended to vote more or less as a unit. There was a Polish vote, a Czech vote, an Italian vote, a Negro vote, and a much greater menace to American political life than any religious vote was the continued jockeying of politicians to capture these national or racial blocs.

By and large there does not seem to be much political opposition to the Jews. The Silver Shirts may decry the presence of many Jews in strategic administrative positions in the government and affirm their intention to keep the "Jewish mentality" out of America, but the greatest danger is that American Jews themselves will take these Silver Shirts too seriously. The anti-Nazi activities of a certain Jewish congressman will probably do more to make anti-Semites than all the Silver Shirts could accomplish by themselves in a millennium. It is the candid opinion of the writer—given on his own responsibility for what it is worth—that the somewhat unemotional approach of the American Jewish Committee to the present situation has saved America from an outbreak of anti-Semitism which the fulminations of the American Jewish Congress would have eventually produced. The boycott of German goods might have been far more effective if carried out quietly and without any publicity. But the endeavor on the part of a considerable number of Jews to bring Germany to time by cutting off their trade has had serious political and social consequences to the Jews themselves. Not only has it created counter-propaganda and suggestions that Jewish business might itself be boycotted, and aroused much feeling among German-Americans, but it has also alienated a great host of Americans and Canadians who have felt that the more insistent Jews were seeking to plunge both the United States and the British Empire into an economic impasse with Germany at a time when there was every reason for economic stability and when Europe itself was constantly hovering on the brink of war. It must, however, be stated that many Jews did not approve of the boycott, and that certain of the foremost Jewish periodicals, such as the *American Hebrew*, consistently declared against it.[12] Much must be ig-

---

[12] See especially the issues of March 17 and 31, 1933.

nored in the interests of mutual peace and understanding, and gentle irony is often a more emphatic and incisive weapon than prophetic fire. The latter often consumes the prophet more completely than it devours his enemy.

There are at the same time undoubted intimations that a member of a minority group who is elected to high governmental position is placed in an embarrassing position. Many of the members of the minority to which he belongs naturally look to him for leadership and favors which he can bestow only at the price of his personal prestige. In the case of a certain Jewish governor, it was thus found that since his election he seemed to have changed. The Jews found it increasingly difficult to understand him, for he seemed to be holding them off, while the Gentiles were equally sure that he was surrounding himself with too many Jewish councillors. A member of a majority group can bestow a favor or office with greater grace on a member of a minority than would be the case if the person conferring the honor were himself a member of the same minority.

Differing Views on Church and State

It would be unfair to conclude this section, however, without calling attention to three rather persistent factors that tend to develop political discrimination against Catholics:

(1) Catholics must continually face the implications of the struggle between papal internationalism and nationalism. If the issue were simply the issue of internationalism vs. nationalism, many Protestants would stand with them. But papal internationalism and internationalism are two different things. While the revolt of Luther was primarily religious, Protestantism soon found champions among those who wished to exalt national freedom above that type of internationalism represented by the papacy. The countries which adhered to Protestantism were those which did not care to have their inner policies reviewed by authorities at Rome and by ecclesiastics whose personal ambitions sometimes outran their idealism and whose prevailing mentality was too largely Latin.

(2) Protestants, especially those of the Calvinist tradition, strongly insist on democratic forms of government. This was never interpreted as signifying that a church could do without standards, nor that the voice of the people was always the voice of God. Any casual study of the Westminster Confession of Faith and the Form of Presbyterial Church Government, for instance, will reveal the fact that standards were definitely set and officers appointed to see that order and discipline were established. In the Congregational churches of New England, a high degree of autonomy was given to the local church, and this inevitably stressed the will of the people and made the town meeting and the parish meeting analogous. Protestantism

perhaps originated less in the democratic movement than it absorbed the democratic trends which followed in the wake of both Reformation and Renaissance. At all events, as Protestantism became more and more identified with democracy in government, its antipathy to Rome was not only nationalistic but democratic in emphasis; and it assumed, perhaps too readily, that a democratic state could not flourish side by side with an autocratic church, and that citizens could not be properly fitted for life in a democracy if they were nursed in a church which ever suspected laicism and stressed authority. Protestants thus tend to believe with Loofs:

"Rome remains the mother of obedient children, but to religious and moral independence she cannot educate them. Where moral independence exists, it has come to pass not through the Church's training, but in spite of it."[13]

(3) There still remains the perennial problem of the relative authority of church and state. Protestants would admit the supremacy of the loyalty to a spiritual ideal over any merely national allegiance, but they refuse to identify a spiritual ideal with an ecclesiastical system, and consider the ecclesiastical system as but another type of political system which by its very nature demands a first allegiance. This supra-national system which claims authority over all baptized Catholics seems quite Latin and analogous to the Italian concept of "once an Italian, always an Italian." The elucidation of this issue would take tomes, but without such an effort to understand the real significance of the difficulties involved, a certain amount of political discrimination, whether directed against Catholics or against Protestants, will probably continue. In situations of this character, Protestants and secularists tend to draw together.

INTERMARRIAGE

The problem of intermarriage is treated in detail in Chapter VII.

IMMIGRATION

It is alleged that the Protestant majority in the United States is seeking to reduce or cut off the extensive immigration of Catholics and Jews, and by the application of the system of "national quotas" to encourage only immigration from countries dominantly Protestant.

In Canada there has been a similar restriction of immigration, especially during the depression and without the use of a quota system. While the total immigration into the Dominion, 1925-32, amounted to 836,639, in 1932 the lowest mark of immigration was reached, only 25,752 being admitted, while more than 7,025 were deported. The recent figures are:

[13] In *Symbolik* (vol. i:387), quoted by John Oman in *The Church and the Divine Order* (London: Hodder and Stoughton, 1911), page 149.

Origin of Immigrants	1925–1932	1931–1932	Deportations 1931–1932
British	295,320	7,088	4,248
Continental Europe	376,645	4,367	260
United States	164,674	14,297	2,517
Total	836,639	25,752	7,025

While Canada's great need is for a larger population, the Dominion has become quite dubious of the value of too mixed an immigration, and in general shows a preference for those of Anglo-Saxon origin. Nevertheless, in the last eight years, the great bulk of the immigration has come from Continental Europe, while the majority of those deported since 1902, as in 1932, were of British extraction.

It must be remembered that Canada's career under British rule has ever been characterized by bi-culturalism, and her statesmen have confronted from the very beginning problems relating to minority groups to an extent unknown in the United States. Moreover, in the first decade of the twentieth century, the problem of assimilation which confronted the Canadian people was two and one-half times as great as that confronting the American people in the same period. The infiltration of non-Anglo-Saxons has been so large that in 1931, for the first time, the Dominion census revealed that one of the western provinces (Saskatchewan) had by that time become more non-Anglo-Saxon than Anglo-Saxon.

In the last few years, the races from Europe supplying the largest number of immigrants to Canada were:

	1925–1932	1931–1932
British	295,320	7,088
German	69,510	727
Ukrainian	58,159	502
Polish	35,203	554
Hungarian	29,021	397
Hebrew	22,309	202
Finnish	22,167	92

If we consider the denominational affiliations of these racial groupings, except the British, according to the analysis made of the Canadian population in the 1931 census (Bulletin XXXV), "Religious Denominations by Racial Origins," we discover that practically all of the Finnish and 80 per cent. of the Germans are Protestant; 70 per cent. of the Ukrainians, 90 per cent. of the Poles, 75 per cent. of the Hungarians are Greek Catholics (Uniats) or Roman Catholics; practically 100 per cent. of the Hebrews are of course Jewish. The British are overwhelmingly Protestant. Virtually 40 per cent. of the entire population of Canada is Roman Catholic, but over 66 per cent. of the Roman Catholic population is of French origin, and so far as immigration is concerned it stands to gain most from the incoming of the

Ukrainians who belong in part to the Orthodox Church but largely to the Uniat (Ruthenian Rite).

Next to British immigration, Canada shows a predilection for German immigration, since experience proves that the Germans readily settle in the rural areas and make excellent farmers. Thus, in 1831, of 473,242 persons of German descent residing in Canada, only 174,921 were in urban areas while 298,623 were in rural areas. The same rural tendency is particularly true of the Danish, the Dutch, the Icelandic, the Norwegian, the Russian, the Swedish and the Ukrainian. All of these, with the exception of the Ukrainian are dominantly non-Roman Catholic. The Poles and Roumanians are also largely rural, although these groups are more evenly distributed between urban and rural areas.

On the other hand, in addition to the British, who show a predilection for the towns and cities, those who incline to urban life are the Greeks, the Hebrews, the Italians, the Jugo-Slavs and the Czecho-Slovaks. These groups are dominantly non-Protestant and consist mostly of Jews, Eastern Orthodox and Roman Catholic.

CANADIAN POLICY BASED ON ECONOMIC GROUNDS

Canada, on the whole, does not seem to be concerning itself so much about racial (except in regard to Orientals) or religious inheritance in determining the qualifications of prospective immigrants, but rather concerning their adaptability to agricultural life. Because the Jews in Canada have proven themselves conspicuously unwilling to stick to farming, there is no inclination on the part of the government to let down the bars to Jews who wish to enter, beyond what is absolutely necessary. If there is discrimination here, it is due to the prevailing economic policy of the nation, and has little or nothing to do with religion. In French Canada, it must be admitted, a vigorous opposition has developed in the French press against any further immigration of Jews, partly based, one suspects, on the challenge of such immigration to the continuance of French Catholic cultural predominance on the St. Lawrence. In addition to this, when the Department of Immigration required each prospective immigrant to receive special permission to enter Canada, a racket, it is alleged, developed to facilitate Jewish immigration and in some cases even bribery on a large scale was attempted.[14]

COMPLEX BASIS OF AMERICAN POLICY

At the conclusion of the War, the United States decided to put the brakes on immigration. The serious situations created by the conflict of national

---

[14] The confidential character of the information received makes it impossible to disclose the sources of this statement concerning alleged bribery. The writer can only say that it came to him from significant quarters.

groupings within the country and their repercussions on international policies, combined with a conviction that the melting-pot was not melting, led to a new demand for national unity within the United States and a breathing-space in which to carry the work of "Americanization" to a more thorough conclusion. This determination was reinforced by a resentment of the presence in the country of many who avoided conscription because they were aliens and a fear that when Europeans were free to migrate after the shadows of the War had lifted, they would deluge the New World. There was also the new chauvinism created by the War itself, the anti-foreigner emphasis of the Ku Klux Klan, the sudden awakening to the fact that many factories under the pressure of war-contracts had geared themselves too high and that the increasing use of high-powered machinery was now making much man power unnecessary, and more important than all, a belief that many of the "alien" groups were coming from countries where they had never known the "disciplines of liberty" and hence soon converted the freedom of America into an excuse for license, threatening by their banditry and racketeering the very foundations of American institutions. Finally, the mental tests used in the army seemed to reveal that, despite the highly-developed educational system of the United States, an extraordinary percentage of the conscripted men were mentally under-age. There was, consequently, a vigorous insistence that the doors should be locked.

QUOTA SYSTEM FAVORS PROTESTANT COUNTRIES

The quota system was, therefore, developed to give preferential treatment to such peoples as were more inherently adapted to American modes of thought and government, and to exclude those whose previous training and temperament made them less readily assimilable. Indeed, many foreign critics felt that the stable door had been locked after the horse was gone. The quota system undoubtedly favored the Protestant countries of Northern Europe, over either Jewish or Catholic populations. The Jewish immigration fell as follows:

JEWISH IMMIGRATION INTO THE UNITED STATES

1921	119,036
1922	53,524
1923	49,719
1924	49,989
1925	10,292
1926	10,267
1927	11,483
1928	11,639
1929	12,479
1930	11,526
1931	5,692

In 1929, a new quota system was evolved, which increased the possible immigration from Czecho-Slovakia, Denmark, France, Germany (almost doubled) Irish Free State, Norway, Sweden (almost tripled) and Switzerland. On the other hand, reductions were given to the United Kingdom (almost halved), Italy, Netherlands, Poland and Russia.

Whatever one may think concerning the fairness of these restrictions, it seems reasonably clear that had they not been put into effect when they were, the depression of 1929 might have struck even greater depths.

While the preference for Northern Europe has aroused some Catholic criticism and while Jewish organizations have felt that special privileges should be provided for the persecuted Jews, it is difficult to believe that national policy either in the United States or Canada will revert, with the return of prosperity, to free and easy immigration. The free lands of the United States have long since been exhausted, and the essential problem now is to find ways and means of removing the population from lands that cannot be profitably worked and placing them where they can make a decent living. Large areas of arable land still remain in the northern parts of the western provinces in Canada, but where shall the settlers find adequate markets for what they can produce? The industrial life of both countries is in sore need, not of new workers, but of new markets, and the life of the world demands a new tempo. The methods which gave the United States and Canada great prosperity in the past will not do for the immediate future and, if continued, may even spell the ruin of these two great and resourceful countries. For some time to come both nations must concentrate on the reorganization of their inner economics, during which time it appears imperative that they keep all immigration at a minimum.

ADVANTAGES OF RESTRICTION TO CATHOLIC AND JEWISH AGENCIES

What is more, Roman Catholicism and Judaism in America have really profited by the cessation of immigration. The burdens of adequately caring for the new arrivals were almost intolerable. To furnish new schools, new churches, new synagogues and to adjust the difficulties which "national groupings" within both Catholicism and Judaism created, taxed the resources of both of them to the limit. The cessation of mass immigration has provided the breathing-space whereby the two religious groups have been enabled to catch up with themselves, and an outsider can not but believe that the two groups are infinitely better prepared to deal with new situations because of opportunities for inner consolidation which the cessation of immigration has made possible.

So, too, with the return of some measure of normalcy, the relief work of Jewish philanthropic agencies will be curtailed and some greater synthesis of the whole problem of associated philanthropic action may, perhaps, be effected. It is difficult for the writer to believe that we must continuously act on the assumption that, in the care of the unfortunate, Jew should look after Jew, Catholic after Catholic and Protestant after Protestant. If ours is a commonwealth, then the more fortunate must meet the needs of the unfortunate, irrespective of their racial, creedal or national complexions.

NATURAL INCREASE OF IMMIGRANT POPULATIONS

There seems to be little likelihood of any reversion in the near future to unrestricted admission of immigrants to the western hemisphere, and the United States, at least, has probably permanently relinquished her rôle as an "asylum" for the persecuted. Practically all South American countries, with the possible exception of Brazil, are following suit, and hence immigration, in our modern world, is perhaps, free only to Africa. But the person who migrates to Africa, if he is an unskilled laborer, must compete with the native African. That prospect is hardly alluring. In short, it seems that from now on, the channels of immigration will be largely blocked for many years.

This means that for all the countries of the New World, the "alien" races must depend for their growth upon natural increase rather than immigration, and in this connection, several considerations bearing on birth-rates are to be borne in mind:

(1) Nearly all immigrant groups are drawn, for the most part, from those in their prime. The aged seldom face the trials of such adventure as immigrants must face unless they are escaping persecution. Hence, for the period immediately following the arrival of any new ethnic group in a country, their birth-rate may be inordinately high. The larger percentage of the women are of child-bearing age.

(2) Much of the high natural increase of certain groups of the immigrant population is due less to racial origin or to religious conviction than to the hangover of peasant behavior. The fertility of the French-Canadian has long been well known, but the birth-rate in Quebec shows a marked decline with continued urbanization.

(3) The birth-rate throughout the United States, especially in its cities, has shown a marked decline during the years of the depression, and this decline has been registered in cities with a large foreign population, where higher birth-rates might have been expected.

(4) So far as the Jews are concerned, what facts are available indicate that, of all races, their birth-rate is the lowest. In Canada, where the number of Jews of the first generation must be fairly high, the birth-rate per 1,000 Jewish women and girls of all ages was but 27, when compared with some other birth-rates, as follows:

CANADA: BIRTHS BY RACIAL ORIGINS OF MOTHERS—1931

Racial Origin	Total No. Females	Total Live Births	Rate per 1,000 Females
Hungarians	15,516	1,305	84
Ukrainians	102,341	6,849	66
French	1,454,615	93,904	64
Polish	63,415	3,842	60
German	225,700	12,112	54
Italian	43,032	2,288	52
Norwegian	39,706	1,979	49
Russian	40,018	1,723	43
Swedish	33,257	1,436	43
British	2,627,406	107,185	41
Hebrew	7,639	2,135	27

Infant mortality rates, on the other hand, indicate clearly that the Jews have an unusually low death-rate while the French have a high rate, exceeded only by that of the native Indians. In 1931 the percentages of children of mothers of various racial origins, who died under one year of age, were as follows:

CANADA: INFANT MORTALITY, 1931

(Exclusive of Stillbirths)

Racial Origin	No. of Live Births	Deaths Under One Year	Percentage of Deaths Under One Year
Indians	3,316	532	16.0
French	93,904	10,512	11.2
Hungarian	1,305	126	9.8
Polish	3,842	338	8.7
Ukrainian	6,849	582	8.4
Russian	1,723	138	8.0
Italian	2,288	184	8.0
German	12,112	727	8.0
British	107,185	5,984	5.6
Swedish	1,436	81	5.6
Norwegian	1,979	93	4.7
Jewish (Hebrew)	2,135	103	4.7
All races	240,473	20,360	8.4

Situations of this character raise, of course, the whole issue of birth-control—a subject of such vital importance to the general relations of Protestants, Catholics and Jews that an extended treatment is included in the Appendix.

CHAPTER IV

Relations in Social Work

HISTORICAL BACKGROUNDS

A comparison of the social ideals proclaimed by bodies representing Protestants, Catholics and Jews discloses a high degree of agreement among them. To this fact, presumably, is due the considerable degree of friendly coöperation among the social-work agencies of the three faiths. Yet there are not lacking instances of friction. Our later review of the data gathered will show that in the cities studied not a little of the friction is due to rather deep-seated differences in religious and social tradition and structure. It is also due in part to the unconscious assumption by the Protestant majority of Anglo-Saxon extraction that their standards and ways of doing things should be followed by all other groups in the population. As one Catholic social leader has observed:

"The majority hold that America has one basic culture: woe betide him who does not conform to it. He shall be judged by the culture of the majority and not in terms of his own. The liberal non-Catholic group have caused trouble by trying to impose on us a stereotyped Calvinistic individualism. We think the Catholic point of view also should be tolerated and allowed for."

Few Protestants probably are at all aware of this assumption, and possibly even the writer of this chapter has unconsciously allowed it to influence his presentation of the data. If so, the reader is well warned. At any rate, it undoubtedly accounts for some of the tensions in the field of social work. In order, therefore, to understand the present relations in social work among the three faiths and to be better able to remove causes of irritation, it is important to have some appreciation of the underlying historic process. Accordingly, the first part of this chapter will be given to tracing successively the development of social ideals and activities, first among the Jews, then among early and later Catholics, and lastly among Christians other than Catholics, together with the rise and spread of the secular system of social work.

In Europe many forces have impeded the free development of the three systems, but in America, with its guarantee of religious liberty and its early elimination of established churches, each faith has been left comparatively

113

free to give play in social work, as in worship and teaching, to its distinctive genius. It is not to be wondered at that in this process there have arisen various kinds of misunderstanding and conflict, and also various forms of coöperation and mutual appreciation. To their consideration the bulk of this chapter will be devoted.

The whole world has been enriched by the stream of charitable ideals and ordinances which has flowed from the Old Testament. The Mosaic law made charity an obligation: hence charity and justice early became synonymous, as in Second Isaiah. The mainspring of Jewish philanthropy was based on the religious beliefs that the poor were the wards of God, and that He is a God of both justice and compassion. As Professor Mordecai M. Kaplan observes: "The prophetic championship of the cause of the poor left its indelible impress upon Jewish character. . . . The Jewish civilization certainly stands alone during the pre-Christian Era in upholding the cause of the poor and in regarding their condition as brought on not by themselves but by the evils of the social order."[1]

One distinctive feature of Jewish, as contrasted with Buddhist and Christian, history is the absence in it of any attempt to construe poverty as a blessing in disguise. With the possible exception of the Essenes, no Jewish class or order adopted destitution or mendicancy as a way of life. But, "this very sanity of Judaism prevented Jewish charity from . . . that complete self-effacement, that eager and mystic self-abandon which expressed itself among Christians in loving ministrations to the outcasts of society."[2]

It is interesting to discover that the Jewish communities initiated the lay administration of philanthropy in the second or third century before Christ. The most trustworthy men in the synagogue and the community were made overseers of the poor fund. For several centuries, "the Overseers, like the Presidents of congregations, were chosen by election or by general consensus of opinion . . . men who usually combined wealth with learning and achievement, and a strict sense of justice."[3] The fund was maintained by a system of taxation.

During the Middle Ages Jewish charity was directed especially to caring for orphans and travelers and to ransoming captives. After the twelfth century all over Europe there were Jewish charitable societies devoted to educating poor children, rearing orphans, caring for the sick and aged, ransoming prisoners and providing dowries for needy maidens and free burial

[1] Faris, Laune, Todd, *Intelligent Philanthropy* (University of Chicago Press, 1930), p. 64.
[2] Frisch, Ephraim, *Historical Survey of Jewish Philanthropy* (New York: The Macmillan Company, 1924), p. 180.
[3] *Ibid.*, p. 109-10.

for the destitute. Thus it appears that from ancient times the Jewish communities have been marked by a sense of communal responsibility. A strong unifying influence in Europe was the right given by various rulers to the Jewish communities to lay their own taxes, of which part was remitted to the government, and part applied to their communal and social-welfare needs. In some parts of Europe this custom still holds and in America the influence of the tradition is felt.

Until recent years Jewish charities appear to have had no further original development, but to have utilized the improved methods evolved by the Gentile world around them. In the United States, however, the serious relief problems precipitated by the large Jewish immigration after 1880 have taxed the benevolent resources and organizing ability of the Jewish communities and have made their social work second to none in the federating of agencies, in the standard of services given, and in the quality of professional personnel. The Communal Federation of Jewish Charities and its united financial campaign long antedated the Community Chest movement and helped prepare the way for it.

The Jews in America have always striven beyond most other religious and racial groups to care for their own people in need. They are credited with having given, between 1914 and 1930, eighty-one million dollars for the relief of persecuted fellow-Jews in Europe. The older Jewish residents have also had to shoulder a heavy burden of social service for the hosts of Jewish immigrants who have poured into the United States since 1880. Although the demands for primary relief grew lighter after the War, the financial pressure was not relaxed, because the Jewish social agencies improved the quality and expanded the range of their other activities, especially in the care of families and in the development of recreation and education at Jewish community centers. Of the modern educational activities a Jewish authority writes:

"In some instances the intense activity of the Jewish educators resulted in antagonism to their programs on the part of those who are inclined toward assimilation. On the other hand, the modern spirit and activities in these schools occasion opposition from the orthodox and fundamentalist groups in the Jewish Community. These antagonisms, however, have not been sufficiently strong seriously to threaten the development of this movement."[4]

In every sizable Jewish community there are likely to be two or more sets of certain social agencies, as of synagogues, a reflection of the social and economic contrast between the well-established older settlers from Western Europe, and the newer immigrants from Eastern Europe. Religiously, the

[4] Karpf, Maurice J., "A Decade of Jewish Philanthropy," *B'nai B'rith* magazine, February, 1932.

former tend to be attached to the Reform or Conservative synagogues and the latter to the Orthodox synagogues.

CHRISTIAN CHARITIES TO THE MODERN ERA

The early Christians were nearly all Jews and they accordingly carried over into the infant church the keen social conscience characteristic of Judaism. There was, however, a radical difference between the two. Judaism was originally centered in the family and the tribe, and care for needy individuals was primarily a family responsibility. But by the time Christianity arose, family ties had become weakened, and among Christians they were not strong enough to ensure adequate care of unfortunate members. Furthermore, the tendency of the early church to draw its converts from the cities rather than the country, doubtless made it difficult then as now for families to be self-protecting. The resulting need of some Christian believers for aid from their fellows was met by the overflowing spirit of brotherhood which marked the young church. At first, "they sold their lands and other property, and distributed the proceeds among all, according to everyone's necessities." A little later the administration of relief was systematized by being placed in the hands of seven laymen.

The new principle in social service was the higher value that Jesus Christ placed on the individual:

"Out of the faith in the fatherhood of God flowed this other new faith in the brotherhood of man, and it made one of the great transitions in the evolution of the human race. The poor and rejected, the submerged of mankind, were regarded in a wholly new light when they were thus accepted as essential parts of the body of Christ. . . . The 'Caritas' of the Christians gave a quality and color to human relations which classic civilization never knew."[5]

But the expansion of social sympathy due to this new valuation of the individual "brought its own new danger. . . . The new philanthropy brought a new mendicancy. Poverty grew by what it fed on."[6] "As the church became an institution administering progressively larger revenues its service of the poor degenerated, partly from worldliness, and partly from 'other worldliness.' "[7] The teaching of St. Paul that "it is more blessed to give than to receive" was distorted to mean that there is merit in the very act of giving and that the future welfare of the giver is in a measure dependent on his generosity.[8] These conceptions found expression in the

---

[5] Peabody, Francis G., *Charities Review*, III, p. 4, 1893.

[6] *Ibid.*

[7] Warner, *American Charities* (New York: Thomas Y. Crowell Company, 1918), 3rd ed., p. 6.

[8] *New International Encyclopedia*, 2nd ed., volume 5, p. 53.

medieval monasteries, which formed the earliest considerable institutions in Europe for the dispensing of charity.

Throughout the centuries, down to the modern era the vast bulk of philanthropy was marked by three defects: it was for the most part indiscriminate and palliative; the laity ceased to function actively in its administration, the work being absorbed by the clergy and the monastic orders; and the people were taught that the giving of alms was one of the chief forms of good works essential to salvation.[9] So far did the pendulum swing away from the lay "overseers" of the Jews and the lay "deacons" of the early church that during the early Middle Ages the right to distribute alms was declared to be "the exclusive right of the bishop" or his immediate representatives.[10]

It remained for a Roman Catholic priest, Vincent de Paul of France, shortly before the Pilgrims landed on Plymouth Rock, to become the pioneer in rebuking indiscriminate giving and in providing work as well as alms, and also in enlisting lay women as visitors and distributors of aid among the poor. The beneficent society now known in many countries as the Sisters of Charity grew immediately out of the Ladies of Charity whom Vincent de Paul enrolled in Paris. Thus, in a rudimentary way, he was the forerunner of the modern era of organized charity, and his example led Ozanam and Père Bailly, two centuries later, to name after him one of the foremost lay agencies for social work, the Society of St. Vincent de Paul, which will appear in our later discussion.

THE INAUGURATION OF SECULAR CHARITY IN EUROPE

The church had laid such stress on almsgiving that support was provided for a great volume of relief work, but the church was not primarily equipped to administer charitable funds, nor to devise measures to eliminate dependency. At length it became clear, in northern Europe, at least, that the ecclesiastical machinery could no longer carry the load. It was inevitable that the state itself should undertake relief work; but, as has been well observed, "that relief work, and the great access of sympathy for our fellowmen which impelled it, would never have existed except for the influence of the church."[11]

---

[9] In a recent survey made by the Mexican Government entitled "Mendicidad en Mexico" the section on "Relacion de la Iglesia Catolica con la Institucion de la Mendicidad," pp. 46-51, contains this statement: "The attitude created in the mind of the masses by the doctrines and preaching of the Catholic Church regarding charity has contributed in an appreciable degree to facilitate the existence in the normal life of Mexico of mendicity as a permanent social institution." It is also stated that by the establishment of the mendicant orders, the Catholic Church seemed to have put its blessing on mendicancy.

[10] Hannan, Jerome D., "The Bishop and Social Work," *Ecclesiastical Review* (Philadelphia, December, 1932), Vol. 87, No. 6.

[11] Warner, *op. cit.*, p. 9.

Simultaneously with the tendency in northern Europe to rely increasingly on the state dawned the recognition that scientific methods should be applied to social problems. Both of these tendencies doubtless received a remote impulse from the Renaissance, but probably the more immediate impulse toward the secularization of relief came from the sectarian religious fragmentation accompanying the Reformation, and from the spirit of self-reliance and experiment developed in the aggressive commercial centers of the North. As to the former, the church was split into numerous denominations, which no longer had the old church endowments. Since it was manifestly impossible for each of the new churches to maintain an adequate system of social agencies, they naturally looked to the state to carry the load. As to the latter, the cities of the Hanseatic League, such as Hamburg, had developed a measure of independence of both Church and Empire and had come to rely on their own enterprise and wealth. Among them, Hamburg was one of the most progressive, and it was there that efficient and comprehensive social work under municipal auspices was first firmly established early in the eighteenth century. Two centuries earlier abortive attempts in that direction had been made by various German cities. With Luther's blessing they had developed a system of poor relief administered by city "deacons" who served one or two years. But many difficulties were encountered. "The short term of the deacons made systematic effort impossible; the existence of old orders and institutions caused cross currents, and the plans gradually failed."[12]

Professor Queen has made the interesting observation that, from the time of the Council of Trent, thirty years after the beginning of the Reformation, "charity was urged as a means of defending the [Catholic] Church and strengthening its position. It was insisted that charity is a function of the Church exclusively. Hence it was that the modern development of relief by civic agencies came first in northern Europe and has not even yet really established itself in the Catholic countries."[13] In view of the standing of present-day social agencies in Belgium and France, this statement may call for some qualification, but there is little room to doubt that Protestant Germany, Great Britain and the United States have played a leading rôle in the secular and scientific development of social work ever since the eighteenth century. Parenthetically, it may be noted that the extraordinary burst of progressive social reform in Catholic Munich late in the eighteenth century was due to the genius of a New England Protestant, Benjamin Thompson, later Count Rumford. A résumé of some of the stages in the process started

    [12] *New International Encyclopedia*, Vol. 18, p. 191.
    [13] Queen, *Social Work in the Light of History* (Philadelphia: J. B. Lippincott Company, 1922), pp. 245-6.

by the North German cities will throw light on the present-day situation in American cities.

Hamburg's preëminence as a pioneer in social work under municipal auspices did not come about by accident. The huge increase of vagrancy and beggary, caused by a severe plague, convinced her officials that the prevalent methods of poor relief, whether by the unsystematic doles of the rich or by the indiscriminate ministration of the church, were at once inadequate and demoralizing. Accordingly, by degrees, between 1711 and 1788 the citizens evolved a secular municipal system in which the distinctive features were a central supervising bureau, the subdivision of the city into sixty small districts, each under the supervision of a competent volunteer, the provision of work for the unemployed, the emphasis on keeping families together, the opening of crêches for the children of parents going out to work, the maintenance of free schools for children up to sixteen, and the support of the whole system by a combination of public taxes and private contributions. The marked success of the Hamburg experiment exerted a powerful influence abroad on thinkers like Malthus of England and on social pioneers like Chalmers, the Scotch divine, and Count Rumford in Bavaria.

Thomas Chalmers, in Glasgow about 1820, adopted a number of the progressive ideas already demonstrated in Hamburg, but his original contribution was to show that a single neighborhood—a parish of 10,000 souls—could be so organized and its altruism so aroused as to care for all its own relief needs by voluntary contributions and a system of volunteer visitors.

The system of relief developed early in the nineteenth century at Elberfeld, Germany, carried to a higher pitch some of the ideas originated earlier at Hamburg. But Elberfeld's distinctive contribution was in the organic unification brought about between voluntary and public relief activities.

In England, the organization at London, in 1869, of the first Charity Organization Society was the culmination of a movement covering two-thirds of a century. The Society from the beginning laid stress on fostering self-help rather than giving doles, and on coördinating the vast amount of benevolent activity throughout the city. The London Society set the pattern for the hundreds of similar agencies that gradually dotted the United States.

Right across the bows of the spread of secular charity in modern Europe arose a lay organization with a religious basis, the Society of St. Vincent de Paul. While this Society derived inspiration from the noble life and progressive leadership of St. Vincent de Paul two hundred years earlier, it owed its formation, in 1833, to a layman, a young Catholic student of law at the Sorbonne in Paris. Stung by the charges of the followers of Saint Simon "that the Catholic Church really did nothing for the poor, Ozanam persuaded seven of his companions to organize for the more effectual aid of the needy. . . . While the suggestion which led to the organization of the first conference came from Ozanam, it is likely that the method and spirit of the society came from Père Bailly, a journalist who befriended them and was first president of the Council-General."[14] Their distinctive principles were that there should be no religious test in the distribution of alms, that all cases should be personally investigated, that the members should do friendly visiting in the homes of the poor or distressed, and should "unite in a communion of prayers." In each parish a "conference" or group was to be organized and its counsels were an important factor in deciding what aid should be given. This practice has been widely adopted in modern social agencies.

CATHOLIC CHARITIES IN THE UNITED STATES

The effects of the Reformation on Roman Catholic charities in northern Europe were drastic, notably in England, where the monasteries and church hospitals, alms-houses and schools were confiscated. In most of the American colonies, also, Roman Catholicism was proscribed until the Revolution, so that the early Catholic charities were able to develop normally only in Pennsylvania, and for a time, in Maryland. Their steady development in the United States since 1800 has been due to a combination of clerical and lay efforts. At first the leadership was taken almost entirely by religious orders introduced from Europe. But the establishment at St. Louis, in 1845, of the first American conference of the Society of St. Vincent de Paul marked an increase in voluntary lay activity and also in service to the family.

Religious disabilities, such as the Catholics and Jews had suffered from in some of the colonies, were removed by the federal constitution of 1789, but Catholic authorities allege that the strongly Protestant character of the majority of the population in most sections of the country resulted, until late in the nineteenth century, in frequent discrimination against Catholics by social agencies of a public or supposedly non-sectarian character. Protestant child-caring agencies exerted themselves to place Catholic foundlings or orphan children in Protestant families in order "to preserve them from the errors of Romanism." Father O'Grady goes so far as to say that "the history of Catholic Charities in the United States is almost a history of the struggle of the immigrant for the preservation of the faith of his children."[15] In order to meet this situation the Catholics worked for legislation requiring that children be placed in homes of the same religious faith as the parents. This agitation reached a successful climax with the enactment of such a law in Connecticut, in 1893. Catholics kept establishing child-caring homes as

---

[14] Watson, *op. cit.,* pp. 38-9.
[15] O'Grady, John, *Catholic Charities in the United States: History and Problems* (National Conference of Catholic Charities, 1930), p. 147.

fast as their resources made possible and between 1885 and 1928 they opened no less than 125 new homes.

During recent decades Catholic authorities say that they seldom have had occasion to complain of discrimination at the hands of public agencies. But when the relations among the charities of the three religious bodies are presented later, it will be well to bear in mind the background factors of majority-minority relations which have been described.

The organization, in 1909, of the National Conference of Catholic Charities gave an impetus to the adoption of scientific methods and the employment of trained workers. During the last two decades the numbers and influence of professional Catholic social workers have steadily increased, and they are now in charge of most of the diocesan central offices for Catholic charities.

PROTESTANT SOCIAL WORK AND THE SECULAR TREND IN THE UNITED STATES

That Protestant Christians in the United States have played a dominating rôle in charities and social service is only what would be expected in view of their preponderance in population and in wealth. But both the Catholic and the Jewish groups have during recent decades come to play a larger part, although their relative increase seems even larger than it really is because Protestants, in accordance with their historic principles, have tended, during the same period, to function as individuals more than as churches, and to place social work on a non-sectarian or secular basis.[16]

The application in America of the Protestant philosophy of social work is thus expounded by Dean Shailer Mathews:[17]

"Many of the motives to which it [Protestantism] appeals are identical with many of those which Roman Catholic and Jewish leaders can utilize, but they do not include some of the most influential to whom the others can and do appeal. . . . It does not expect meritorious reward from almsgiving as a compensation for other forms of penance, nor can it appeal to ethnic pride and loyalty. Protestants have been forced to develop their conception of charity as *something to be outgrown in the same proportion as society is more intelligently organized*. This may be said to be the point at which Protestantism joins hands with a frankly scientific social service. Just as Protestants have brought about the separation of church and state are they bringing about the separation of church and the administration of charity. Removal of charities from ecclesiastical control has given opportunity for the appearance of scientifically trained workers, as profes-

---

[16] It is important to point out that Jewish social work is not synagogue-centered, but community-centered. In this respect, therefore, it resembles the non-sectarian agencies more closely than it does the Catholic agencies. On the other hand, it differs from the non-sectarian agencies because in control and, with the exception of such institutions as hospitals and certain social settlements, in constituency served, it is Jewish in the communal sense.

[17] *Intelligent Philanthropy*, pp. 120 *seq.*

sional social service agents . . . a new vocation. Such administrators of the social service are the counterpart of the brotherhoods and sisterhoods of the Roman Catholic organization."

The substantial truth of these statements is evidenced by the fact that general agencies in America, like the Charity Organization Society and the Family Welfare Organization were founded largely, although not exclusively, by Protestants. There are still thousands of charitable institutions under Protestant denominational auspices, but Protestants have been foremost in converting the general agencies created by them from a religious to a non-religious and non-sectarian basis.

It is this fact that largely accounts for the lack of powerful federations of Protestant charities, corresponding to the Catholic and Jewish federations. The Protestant Welfare Federation in New York City, for example, was created a decade ago primarily to represent child-caring agencies in their dealings with municipal departments, and has no authority over either the standards or the budgets of its members; although proposals have repeatedly been made for conducting a united campaign on behalf of the eighty-two Protestant agencies and of certain of the non-sectarian agencies, they have come to naught. The lack of specifically Protestant federations is thought by not a few Protestant leaders in various cities to have resulted in the neglect of needy Protestant clients, although Protestants give a large proportion of the funds raised by general appeals. The reason is that the Catholic and Jewish federations receive separate quotas from such funds and use them almost exclusively for Catholic and Jewish clients, whereas Protestant clients have to take their chances of receiving aid from the non-sectarian agencies which serve not only Protestants but persons of other categories.

Some time ago neither the religious agencies nor the non-sectarian agencies wished to form entangling alliances. Thus the Family Welfare Association of America, founded in 1911, until two years ago was exclusively non-sectarian in character, but since 1932 Catholic and Jewish agencies have become constituent members. The earlier policy was partly no doubt a reflection of the spirit of the times, but several national Jewish leaders have said that it was due in large degree to the fear of the Jewish and Catholic agencies lest their jurisdiction over Jewish and Catholic cases might be weakened if they joined non-sectarian agencies originally sponsored by Protestants. The gradual rise to control of well-trained workers in the religious agencies and the pressure of the recent hard times toward the pooling of resources have doubtless been contributory influences in breaking down the old barriers.

In contrast with the case just cited, the Child Welfare League of America, which was organized in 1921, from the beginning included religious as well as non-sectarian social agencies, a reflection possibly of the broader spirit prevalent at the time of its origin.

A few of the landmarks in the development of secular charities in North America should be mentioned. The Association for Improving the Condition of the Poor was founded in New York as early as 1843, and similar associations were rapidly formed in other cities. They generally had a non-sectarian character, but confined their services almost exclusively to giving material aid, and thus "sank into a sea of almsgiving." It was not until 1877 that a secular charitable agency was created in the United States which was intended to serve as a clearing-house for all the social agencies in a city and to sponsor a program of general social service. That agency was the Charity Organization Society established in Buffalo, after the pattern of the parent society in London. By 1900 the "C.O.S." or its equivalent could be found in a majority of important American cities.

In 1875 began the annual gatherings which later adopted the title, the National Conference of Social Work. For many years it has formed an arena where secular and religious social agencies have exchanged experience and developed standards. It has been a powerful factor in drawing together the social workers of the three faiths. The National Conference of Jewish Charities, now called the National Conference of Jewish Social Service, was organized in 1899, and the National Conference of Catholic Charities a decade later. The latter is quite independent, but the former is affiliated with the National Conference of Social Work and generally convenes at the same time and place.

The Pittsburgh Survey of 1908 gave a strong impetus to the more systematic and scientific approach to local social problems, and to the demand for trained workers. Various universities, such as Chicago, Columbia and Loyola, introduced courses preparatory to professional social work, but the need of more specialized curricula led to the creation of several separate training schools. The earliest was the New York School of Social Work, in 1898. The National Catholic School of Social Service (for women) was opened at Washington in 1921. In 1925 the Training School for Jewish Social Work was founded.

Calamities and emergencies have powerfully influenced the development and coördination of social agencies both secular and religious. The suffering caused by the hard times of 1907, and the consequent strain on relief agencies, were among the factors that brought about the Pittsburgh Survey. The Dayton flood of 1912 and the drain caused by it on the philanthropic resources of Cincinnati gave the impetus needed not only to federate nearly two score of the social agencies in the city, but also to inaugurate the joint financing which a few years later became known as the Community Chest.

During the World War the tides of patriotic devotion tended to submerge local and sectarian divisions so that the proposal to combine the war service financial appeals of Protestant, Catholic and Jewish agencies in the United War Work Drive met with tremendous response. In this campaign many of the early community chests were born, although the united community campaign had been originated in Cleveland in 1913. It now prevails in nearly 400 cities of the United States and Canada.

COÖPERATION AND NON-COÖPERATION AMONG AGENCIES

At this point the reader should be reminded of the self-imposed limits of the data on which this chapter is based. They were not gathered from all parts of the United States and Canada, but only from twenty larger cities, distributed, to be sure, somewhat widely. Even in the cities visited the data were symptomatic, not demonstrably representative of all agencies or of all shades of opinion and experience. An effort was made to tap different viewpoints, but more time was spent with employed executives than with laymen. Furthermore, while historical perspective was not forgotten, chief attention was focussed on the present and the recent past. Finally, the study was made during the depression, when relations among public and private social agencies were inevitably abnormal. Having stressed all these limiting and qualifying factors, it should be said that the data in this chapter are presented as being suggestive and stimulating, and as revealing real attitudes, dangers and potentialities in the relations of Catholics, Jews and Protestants in the social field.

The relations among the three faiths in this field were found in this inquiry to range all the way from the most friendly coöperation, on the one hand, to distrust and friction, on the other; but coöperation is decidedly predominant. Since one of the purposes of this inquiry—its only bias, it is hoped—is to help remove barriers to fuller coöperation, disproportionate attention is given in this chapter to instances and causes of non-coöperation.

JOINT FINANCING

In view of the central place occupied in these relations by the Community Chest, or Community Fund, and the Council of Social Agencies, it is but natural that much of the data to be presented should center around them.

The united financing of the social work of the three faiths obtains in all but three of the American cities that were studied. Generally this takes the form of the Community Chest. By common consent the plan of city-wide united fund-raising has done more to foster good relations among leaders of the three faiths than any other single influence. It has tended to dispel suspicion and animosity based on ignorance and traditional antipathies. At the same time, however, the operation of the Chest itself and the revelations in Chest committees of the differing social ideals and practices of the three religious groups have often caused offense and friction. Before dealing with specific cases of misunderstanding and friction it will be well to show the degree to which the three religious groups are participating in the Community Chest.

Both the Catholic and the Jewish charities have united with the various local Chests far more generally than Protestant observers sometimes think. A few figures will prove the point. Out of thirty-six of the larger Community Chests, the Catholic charities are coöperating in twenty-seven and the Jewish charities in thirty; albeit their coöperation, in several instances, dates only from 1930 or later, when failing income due to the depression made them readier to forego independence. There is no full-fledged Protestant federation of charities, but the degree of Protestant participation in these larger Chests is much heartier than would be inferred from the fact that only twenty-five out of the thirty-six Young Men's Christian Associations are coöperating. A more accurate index is probably the participation of thirty-four out of the thirty-six Young Women's Christian Associations. The lower ratio of participation by the Young Men's Christian Associations is partly due to the assumption by the Association in some cities that it would lose decidedly in income by participating, although this assumption is challenged by some men familiar with the Chest throughout the country. That some Associations have overcome their reluctance is due in no small measure, so they assert, to a desire to foster interfaith fellowship and community-wide coöperation in an inclusive altruistic endeavor.

It should further be noted that the individual Protestant social institutions almost invariably participate in the Chest. Furthermore, the non-sectarian agencies which were originally Protestant, as has already been pointed out, often take a leading part in Chest activities.

The participating Catholic federated charities in a few cities, like the Young Men's Christian Association, contended that they were sacrificing their own monetary advantage for the sake of the general good. A national Jewish authority maintains that no such contention on the part of the Jewish federations would be valid because sponsors of the Community Chest, in their eagerness to win the Jewish federations, "were willing to make terms agreeable to the federations, guaranteeing them autonomy in policy-making and safeguarding the differentials in agency expenditures."

In fifteen of the cities that have community chests of medium size, participation by Catholic charities is unanimous, whereas the proportion of participation by the Jewish charities and by the Christian Associations is about the same as their participation in the larger cities. But in the next group of forty-eight cities having smaller chests, the ratio of participation by the Catholic and Jewish charities drops to about 70 per cent., the obvious reason being that in many of these cities the Catholic and Jewish population is relatively small and therefore there is no Catholic or Jewish charity federation.

Attention will now be given to instances and sources of coöperation and non-coöperation or friction among the three groups, particularly in connection with the Community Chest and the emergency relief funds.

REPORTING CASES AND ACCOUNTING FOR FUNDS

The degree to which social agencies comply with modern standards of efficient social work is on the whole directly proportionate to the trained competence of their leadership. Violation of such standards is peculiar to the agencies of no single faith. In both the Protestant and the Jewish groups there are small societies working on a non-professional basis which are notably lax in keeping case records and in financial accounting. In this particular inquiry, however, the sharpest and most frequent criticisms of such laxity were directed toward certain Catholic agencies, and most of this section will refer to them. Since the picture is, therefore, knowingly out of proportion, the reader is reminded of the high reputation enjoyed by the professionally trained staffs of many of the diocesan Catholic charity federations. On this point a national authority on social work, himself a Protestant, expressed himself to this effect:

"The professionally trained directors of Catholic charities are almost all glad to coöperate with non-Catholic agencies and to practise good case work and accounting. Where they offend in these matters, it is generally because they are over-ruled by an unenlightened bishop, or blocked by stubborn parish priests. The officers of the National Conference of Catholic Charities at Washington are doing all in their power to advance progressive policies."

Having this general caveat in mind, the reader will be better prepared to interpret the specific cases that follow.

One of the sharpest criticisms aimed at the St. Vincent de Paul and certain other Catholic agencies in a few cities is that they refuse to "play the game"; specifically, that their workers in charge of field "cases" fail to clear through the Social Service Exchange, which is the common repository of information about persons aided by all the agencies; and also that they are lax in accounting for monies received from the Chest and from public relief funds. A fairly careful consideration of the facts, however, will show that occasions for such criticisms are rare and also that Catholics are not the only offenders. In the first place, it is important for non-Catholics to understand that, although the diocesan federations of Catholic charities, with their trained personnel, are steadily gaining in influence, the parish still remains the basic unit in the conduct of family social work. Protestants customarily assume that everything connected with the Roman

Catholic Church is highly centralized. This is true as regards ultimate authority, but not as regards either spiritual or social ministry to families or individuals. The Society of St. Vincent de Paul, as already explained, operates entirely through "conferences," each attached to one parish. Furthermore, the pairs of volunteer visitors sent out by these conferences to minister in the homes are supposed to give religious counsel and to strengthen people's attachment to Mother Church as well as to meet physical needs. Ordinarily, conferences follow the counsel of their parish priest and they are federated in a city-wide or diocesan Particular Council, but they are jealous of their lay character and their independence. They have been particularly hesitant to adopt the reporting methods of the trained social worker, lest they thereby violate the confidential relation between them and their clients.

In passing, mention may be made of the interesting inconsistency between the depreciation of laicism in general by some Catholic authorities and the glorification of laicism in particular by certain parish priests and Catholic social workers in their references to the Society of St. Vincent de Paul and the Ladies of Charity. On one phase of laicism, however, professional social workers of all the faiths are agreed, namely, in their opposition to the dictation of social-work policy in certain cities by narrow-minded business men whose yardstick is dollars and cents, not human need.

Against this background we are now in position to understand better the situations disclosed in the following series of quotations:

An official of a state relief commission:

"Until recently we couldn't recognize the Catholic work as up to par. They never would give us data. Even yet the St. Vincent de Paul records and reports are far from adequate."

The "even yet" refers to the fact that the diocesan authorities eight months earlier had formally agreed to clear and register all families receiving aid from the State funds. The partial failure to fulfill this agreement was attributed by Catholic authorities to their inability to enforce its observance by certain of the conferences. As a partial compensation for the technical shortcomings of the conferences, mention is made by Catholic leaders of the money saved by their unpaid service. Thus an executive of the Catholic Charities in a large city said:

"Our cost of distribution per capita was 5 or 6 per cent. before the emergency and is only 2.4 per cent. this year, far the lowest of any agency, because we offer 6,000 volunteer workers. We make a selling point of it to our people that we can administer so cheaply. We don't want to stress this point with the non-Catholic public, lest it make bad feeling and decrease their giving."

The difficulty experienced by diocesan Catholic authorities in inducing the parochial social workers, both volunteers and clergy, to make systematic reports to the Social Service Exchange is vividly illustrated by the following incident, as told by several leading social workers in a certain city. The parochial workers received allotments from the Chest and the public relief funds, but they gave little accounting of their disbursements "to anybody but God." This was a sensitive spot in their relations with the other social agencies. The director of Catholic Charities himself could not extract reports or accounts. Finally the parochial groups were brought to time by an ingenious device. The manager of a dairy, while on a committee that supervised the distribution of free flour by the Red Cross, had been disgusted with the way some of the volunteer Catholic workers had "thrown it around." So he decided that he would try a form of indirect pressure to prevent the recurrence of such laxity. He did it by offering to supply milk for relief cases at a big discount, but only to such agencies as would turn in records and financial accounts for all cases. Overnight the parochial workers yielded and began to flood the central bureau with case records.

A person connected with the public relief fund remarked:

"One of the Catholic officials laughingly told a social agency executive and me that the milk deal had accomplished at a stroke what he had tried in vain to bring about, because the priests had always insisted that only they understood their family cases and should therefore be allowed to disburse the funds as they thought best."

How irritating this was to the persons in charge of the funds and also to some non-Catholic workers is evident from these remarks by one of the former:

"Our relations with all the agencies have been free of irritation except with the Catholics. They don't play the game at all according to the ordinary rules. They say they can't be expected to because their set-up is entirely parochial and the priests must be trusted to handle all funds honestly according to their custom. But granted that they are all honest, it is our bounden duty to see whether they have made errors through ignorance as well as through possible design. So many persons of all sorts are distributing city funds in the parish conferences that the risk of mistakes and fraud is great. We have checked them up a little and found a few errors, but nothing important. Still the principle holds and we have only refrained from insisting on applying it rigorously in order not to kick up a public rumpus."

The whole situation was fairly summed up by a person in the Social Service Exchange:

"The Protestant, Jewish and secular charities give 100 per cent. coöperation, phoning in to us to see if a case has been taken by any other agency before they give the first interview. But the Catholic priests who handle all the Catholic cases have seldom done this and have not sent in case records until this month. This has naturally caused a lot of trouble and dissatisfaction, but Father X, of the central office, has always maintained that it was inevitable with their system. While the parish priests are in charge, they have in many parishes a Conference of laymen and sometimes Ladies of Charity, who being volunteers don't realize the importance of either reporting cases or checking up on new applicants through the Exchange. We have, in fact, about the same kind of trouble with the Protestant church workers. They don't do so much relief work, but leave it to secular agencies which were originally Protestant.

"But from this month a revolution has taken place among the Catholic parishes. It was precipitated by the milk deal. Now they are sending in their cards by the hundred—750 already, and they have a lot more ready, but are withholding them so as not to swamp the clerks who have to enter and check them. They are filled out even more fully than the other cards we receive.

"Until now we have tried in vain to ascertain how many cases the Catholic Charities had in each parish, but while Father X and his assistants have promised, and no doubt tried, to get the facts, they have never come across. Now we are likely to learn these and other data for the first time."

A Catholic Charities executive in another eastern city, who had labored successfully to bring about the reporting of cases by the Catholic agencies, told how the change of heart had been wrought:

"Because the St. Vincent de Paul cases had to be cleared through the central bureau for work relief it was discovered that 80 per cent. of the cases treated were already 'active cases' with some relief organization, although this fact was unknown to the St. Vincent workers. This naturally opened the eyes of some of the members of the Society to the dangers of 'clandestine' unchecked relief."

In still another city a notorious situation has developed, owing in part to the conflicting viewpoints of Protestant and Catholic leaders. It was thus summarized by an impartial outside authority:

"For years the Community Fund was successfully conducted without Catholic participation. Finally, in order to persuade the Catholics to join, the character-building agencies (Y.M.C.A., Y.W.C.A., and Boy Scouts) were excluded and assurance was given that the Catholic budget askings and accounts would not need to be submitted for review to the central budget committee. This is the only important city where such an exception has been made. The Y.M.C.A. was not in the good graces of every one, even in non-Catholic circles, but without its powerful support the campaign was a flop. It shows that such compromises are dangerous, even if a bishop's feelings may be ruffled by having his estimates scrutinized and pruned by a mixed committee. I presume this humiliating requirement may account for the unwillingness of the bishops in certain cities to join in the united campaign."

The sharp cleavage between Catholics and Protestants in Quebec has led to situations which are significant, even though not typical of relations between the two faiths in the United States. In Montreal, for example, the daily press during the winter of 1933-34 gave prominence to allegations of grave scandals in the distribution of public relief funds by the St. Vincent de Paul societies of the French-speaking parishes. In the end, the city officials, themselves dominantly French Catholics, refused to distribute public funds any longer through those societies. But an American Jewish social work authority, acquainted with the affair, stated that "the situation is attributable to racial and other social factors in Montreal rather than merely to the St. Vincent de Paul method of handling their funds." Confirmation of this statement is found in the fact that no such charges of scandal were made against the Montreal Catholic Federation of Charities, which represents the English-speaking Catholics.[18]

The coöperative attitude of most of the trained workers in the federations of Catholic charities in the United States is reflected in these remarks by one of them:

"I am delighted to be able to say that practically all our Catholic agencies now clear through the Social Service Exchange. The Society of Catholic women, for example, registered all their cases in connection with the Red Cross garment and flour distribution last year. The St. Vincent de Paul Society did the same. That was the first time, however, that these two Catholic societies had registered all their cases, but now that they have started and found the value of doing so they are likely to continue. We shall encourage them in it. I may say that the Catholic women made 40,000 garments practically all of Red Cross material.

"The importance of registering is illustrated by one case that I myself found where a woman who was being served by our volunteers got twenty-eight pairs of new shoes and several other articles of clothing besides money for rent and water, although at the same time she was receiving $50. a month from her brother-in-law."

Confirmation of the willingness of the professional Catholic social workers to play the game with the other groups is indicated by these comments of an eastern Chest executive:

"We have no trouble in the administration of funds by either Jewish or Catholic charities. They all report faithfully to the Social Service Exchange and do their best to avoid overlapping. Occasionally there is a knotty problem but everyone makes an effort to solve it fairly. Sometimes Father A virtually asks me to use the pressure that can be exerted by the budget committee of the Chest to jack up some laggard Catholic society. He says some of the Sisters used to

---

[18] A Canadian commentator thought that these malpractices might have caused the inordinate number of abjurations of the Catholic faith which have occurred during this period.

ignore his requests, looking on him as a mere priest, but they don't dare disregard the instructions or requests of the budget committee. Mighty is the power of the purse!"

That the peculiarities of the Catholic system are understood and charitably allowed for by some non-Catholics is indicated by the genial remark of a leading Jewish businessman:

"We have contributed as a rule to the Catholic charities and have never received a financial statement, such as I always insist on from our agencies, but I have thought nothing of it, knowing that it was simply a part of their way of doing things. Other non-Catholics probably feel the way I do about it."

HIGHER JEWISH STANDARD OF RELIEF

The higher standard of aid granted by the Jewish agencies is so frequently a cause of misunderstanding and irritation among Gentiles and is so revealing of Jewish ideals that it deserves exceptionally full consideration. Is the standard really higher, and if so, why? Does it cause much irritation? What are the pros and cons? These are some of the questions on which light will be thrown.

The fact that a higher standard of family relief is generally maintained by Jewish agencies is certified by the representative data gathered by the Russell Sage Foundation and by all the social workers interviewed in this study. The situation and the justification for it are well set forth in the following statements.

The executive of a Jewish Federation of Charities in a Southern city:

"Our standards of relief are frankly higher. This is in part due to the fact that so much of both Protestant and Catholic relief is given to colored people whose standard of living is lower than that of the Jews. Even the white people on relief are usually of the laboring class whose standard of living is lower. We would pay rent, for instance, when the other organizations might not. Our standard of relief runs about $37 to $40 a month a family. This higher standard is evident in practically all the cities, as may be gathered from reports gathered by the Russell Sage Foundation and also in the records of the Federal Children's Bureau. Such a disparity between Jewish and non-Jewish standards would not matter where the Jews raised their own funds entirely, but where they get their funds from the Chest, it may raise questions."

A national Jewish authority on social work supports this contention:

"It is inevitable that there will be conflicts on the standard of Jewish social services while the money for the support of Jewish clients comes either from the public treasury or from a community-wide Chest. Responsibility for balancing the issue by maintaining a high giving standard rests upon the Jews."

The secretary of a state emergency relief commission:

"In the early part of the depression, it was unfortunate that private charity agencies had to carry the entire load, and hence the lowered standard. The Jews especially insist on high standards, even through the depression, and the other agencies all want to reduce their load and maintain higher standards, except the Catholic Charities, who want to run up to an absurd number of cases. They can take proper care of four or five thousand cases but are ambitious to carry forty or fifty thousand. They never registered their cases until Emergency Relief. We had a struggle with them for years, but now they are reporting pretty well."

The higher Jewish standard is sometimes resented by Gentile laymen as connoting snobbishness or favoritism; but professional social workers heartily approve it and wish that all agencies could be raised to the Jewish level, except that they commonly object to any differential rate being allowed to Jewish agencies in the grants made by state or city emergency relief funds to private agencies. It is worthy of note that the tenacity of the Jewish agencies in insisting on a higher standard has tended to raise the level of other agencies. The following extracts will illuminate these various points:

The Protestant secretary of a Council of Social Agencies:

"The Jews have organized the best of all, and have maintained the highest standards of relief. On entering the Chest, they had a definite understanding that they would be allowed to continue their higher standard, but nevertheless, non-Jews have objected now and then in committee meetings and some feeling has been caused. The Jewish agencies maintain that their supporters insist on more liberal treatment; they are often approached by contributors with some such demand as this: 'what are you for if you are not our agents to give away the money we give you, and don't be niggardly about it.' If the Chest were to cut the Jewish standards down to the level of other agencies, I fear that the Jews would either raise funds separately to supplement the Chest appropriations or would withdraw entirely."

In the same city the secretary of the Jewish Federation said that "the differential in relief standards between us and other agencies is that we allow rent and they don't. We believe it is demoralizing not to do so."

A Protestant business man, long-time chairman of the Council of Social Agencies in a large city:

"The higher standard of the Jews has not aroused special feeling among Protestants but the Catholics have resented it a little; still it has resulted in the Catholic standards being somewhat raised."

A representative of a Jewish Federation:

"The compactness and strong organization of the Jewish Federation enables it to exert a stronger influence in Community Fund, and fighting our own battle for higher standards we believe we have been fighting for higher standards for all agencies."

An officer of the Catholic Charities explains the various ramifications of the problem and supports the Jewish contention:

"The Jews have sometimes proposed to merge their work in the general Welfare Federation but they are tending away from that idea of late. This recoil has been due to the fact that the Chest has objected to the higher standard of relief insisted upon by the Jewish Charities. I think there is considerable justice in the Jewish contention. It costs them more per capita to administer the work for 1,000 families than it does the Associated Charities for 12,500. Then, the cost of food for Jews is estimated to be 10 per cent. higher, and finally the Jewish Federation is accustomed to pay enough toward rent to prevent the frequent evictions which are inevitable when only dribbling amounts are paid toward rent by the Associated Charities. The Jewish Federation follows the estimated food budget compiled by the Department of Agriculture, but the Associated Charities allow about two-thirds as much. In Philadelphia and Chicago the amounts allowed are a little higher. The Jews feel that the Chest Committee forced them down to an unreasonably low level of aid per family."

A pointed comment on the Jewish demand is thus phrased by a Protestant student of social conditions:

"It is strange that a group which is but recently arrived in the country and which supposedly came in great poverty should insist that they cannot accept the standard of minimum living set by the longer-established groups."

A Protestant lawyer, prominently identified with the budget committee of a Chest takes a mediating position:

"Jews are more aggressive in social work as in all other realms. I sympathize with their higher standard of relief, but as practical humanitarians we have to strike a medium between the ideal and the possible or let some needy die of starvation."

The hard-headed attitude of a practical layman is expressed by the executive of an Emergency Relief Bureau:

"The difficulty in the case of the Jewish Charities has been that they as a group contributed very liberally, and so when their representatives on the Committee have argued that kosher food and the need of more cash for their predominantly white-collar needy required a higher rate, it would have been impolitic for the rest of us to protest and risk offending them and alienating the Jewish givers."

A prominent rabbi cites an actual case to show what dilemmas arise from a three-fold differentiated rate of aid:

"Jewish Charities have always spent more than United Charities and Catholics. The average family rates are $40, $32, and $21. In one recent case, in an apartment, there were Catholics on the first, Jews on the second and Protestants on the third floor, and the Catholic Charities chairman and I advocated the same rate for all. This was agreed on and all has been happy since then."

The social philosophy underlying the Jewish insistence on allowances for rent is well put by the secretary of the Jewish Charities in a city of medium size:

"Contrary to our wishes, . . . it is financially beyond the means of the community fund to pay rents and, as a consequence, much of the sense of security and stability, the very foundation stone of organized family life, is being taken away from numbers of families, and this in spite of the fact that our Jewish organization has probably done more in this respect than other organizations, barring only one."

This extended review of the evidence can hardly fail to convince an impartial mind that the Jewish maintenance of high standards in face of hostile pressure is deserving on the whole of praise rather than of blame.

DISCRIMINATION AGAINST MINORITY FAITHS

Occasionally Catholics and Jews charge that they suffer discrimination at the hands of the Chest and non-sectarian agencies because the boards of managers and the budget committees are always composed predominantly of Protestants. While there may be a modicum of truth in this charge, for the most part it seems to rest on fear rather than on fact. This attitude was publicly expressed by a southern priest at the 1933 National Conference of Catholic Charities in these words:

"While I think we should coöperate with non-sectarian agencies and get all we can out of them, we should not patronize them any more than we must, because they are never Catholic but always Protestant in their attitudes."

In every city the officials of the Chest or Community Fund were found to be on guard against partiality. The number of Jews and Catholics on boards of management or budget committees was never strictly proportionate to the ratios of the religious groups in the population: often the Jews were more numerous and the Catholics less numerous than their population ratios. But the Catholic leaders themselves acknowledged that this was seldom due to sectarian bias, but generally to the lack of an adequate number of first-rate Catholics who were willing to serve; whereas in most large cities there is a surplus of able, public-spirited Jews available. In one city the head of the Catholic Charities remarked that they fared better at the hands of the Protestant Executive Director of the Chest than they would if the executive were a Catholic.

A Chest executive bears this testimony:

"The set-up of the Catholic churches in relation to the Fund is very satisfactory. They have almost no direct administrative responsibilities for their member institutions, but coördinate them with reference to the Fund. We have no more differences of opinion with the Catholic than with the Jewish and Protestant agencies. One reason is that the Catholics have been in the Fund from the beginning and feel like equal partners, even though they have few representatives on the committee. We are especially fortunate in having such a Catholic executive as Father X."

In another city an officer of the Council of Social Agencies:

"There is no log-rolling in the Board of Directors of the Chest. All parties get a fair deal. The relations and spirit are perhaps the best of any city in the country. This is partly due to X's extraordinary patience with delinquent or inefficient agencies. He realizes that the best method of reform is by indirection, such as persuasion and example."

From a Jewish welfare federation executive comes this emphatic tribute:

"The value of the Chest to me is largely its effecting of close contact and coöperation. If it only effected economies and administrative efficiency, I wouldn't consider it very valuable. We Jews are just as efficient when independent. The Chest helped immensely to draw leaders of Catholic, Jew and Protestant groups to understand and stand by one another. This is especially important here where demagogues and extremists are apt to inflame racial and religious prejudices. We need to have a group of strong sane leaders of all sects and faiths who know and trust one another no matter what happens."

In a medium-sized city an incident recounted by a Jewish social work executive betokens a Chest "without a religious rift."

"The Committee on Church Coöperation is worthy of particular note. At one meeting I noticed a Communist and asked him what in the world he was doing in such a group. He replied that he came to see how they ran things and that he was greatly surprised to see a Negro in attendance and being treated like any white man. This is typical. 'Gosh! I wouldn't believe it unless I had seen it with my own eyes,' he said. The annual rally of church people under this Committee has steadily increased from 100 to 600 attending."

Reference has already been made to the natural and, for the most part, unconscious tendency of supposedly non-sectarian agencies of Protestant origin to discriminate against persons of other faiths. But in the cities investigated this was found to be a negligible and diminishing abuse. In fact, the contrary tendency was sometimes complained of, that Chests and other agencies whose boards and officers were nearly all Protestants were discriminating a little against Protestant agencies. Complaints of favoritism are by no means heard only from persons of any one faith, but such occasional partiality as there may be, is so mild as to cause little irritation; and moreover, it is apt to be felt most by officials of inefficient sectarian institutions—of all three faiths. The trained professionals, of all the faiths, recognize that the weaker institutions in their own group deserve the drubbings they sometimes get from Chest budget committees, and are grateful to have discipline administered by a neutral body.

Occasionally spokesmen of the minority faiths complain that Jews and Catholics are debarred from becoming executives of a Community Chest or Council of Social Agencies. As far as the Jews are concerned, a group of Jewish authorities said the facts gave no warrant for such a complaint, and they named numerous Jews, both professionals and laymen, who have headed Chests, Councils of Social Agencies and emergency relief bureaus. As for Catholics, their representation in such posts may be somewhat smaller in proportion to their ratio in the total population, but in cities where the Catholics and Jews are strong evident pains are taken to see that the three faiths are represented on staffs and committees of general social organizations. In one recent instance an important committee, attended by ten Protestants, two Jews and two Catholics, elected as a new member a Catholic in preference to a Protestant on the ground of superior qualifications and without regard to faith. Occasionally, in places where there is tension between the Catholic and Protestant social workers, a Jew may be elected as a neutral mediating person.

STAYING OUT OF THE CHEST

A third source of friction or ill-will among the religious groups is the refusal of one or more of them to join in the general Community Fund or Chest. There is a tendency by the "ins" to stigmatize the "outs" as selfish dissenters. Even though all three of the groups are actually in a large majority of the Chests, inquiry reveals that sometimes a group is technically but only half-heartedly in, or, on the other hand, that the motives of a group for staying out are partly altruistic. These aspects of the question will be illustrated by excerpts from the data.

In one city where the Chest includes neither the Catholics nor the Jews nor the Y.M.C.A., business men of all faiths have threatened to force them all to join. One of the Jewish laymen, in commenting on the issue said:

"Catholic officials and priests opposed the united campaign because they claim their system is parish-centered and is based on a spiritual appeal which others lack. The latter we denied. There was no doubt some feeling aroused among Catholics, but I held that they would gain by uniting and that the Jewish charities would be taking a loss."

The Catholic view was pithily expressed by a priest:

"We feel that it would be very difficult and undesirable to try to unite. People give more to the three than they would to one. Naturally we also stress the religious appeal and church loyalty."

The most influential Protestant clergyman in the city fully agreed that the plan of three separate federations is better in this particular city, so long as they are coördinated by a joint Council of Social Agencies. The newspapers here and elsewhere are inclined to favor an all-inclusive campaign, because they could then cover it at one time instead of having to give space to three separate campaigns. An outside observer, of national reputation, well acquainted with the situation in this city said:

"The Catholic bishop is the chief obstructionist. In their last campaign the Catholic solicitors approached people in factories and firms regardless of faith, on the ground that the Catholic Charities were serving the whole community!"

Non-Catholics would lose some of their distrust of the Catholic Church if they realized that the Church follows no uniform policy on such matters as its relations to the Chest. The truth of this statement is pointedly illustrated by the fact that in two neighboring cities embraced in one diocese, the Catholic Charities in the one are in the Chest whereas in the other they are out. The reason for this lies in local conditions and personalities, just as might be the case with Jewish or Protestant agencies. A Catholic authority in City B summed it up by saying: "They are probably out in A because of old traditions and vested interests." A Protestant leader told how the tendency of the Catholics in B to follow the precedent of A and stay out of the Chest had been overcome:

"The head of the Catholic Charities had violently opposed forming a Chest but prominent Catholic laymen said, 'Why not?' They felt the importance of the three faiths standing together to neutralize the divisive influence of organizations such as the Klan. The question was finally referred to the bishop and he said: 'If you local men want to there is no reason why you should not join the Chest.' That settled it, and the head of the Catholic Charities was man enough to say, 'From now on I'll play heartily with you.' And he has. His associate once said that the Chest had treated them better than if the secretary of it were a Catholic."

This instance of the decisive part played by Catholic laymen is not as singular as non-Catholics are apt to assume. In another city a Chest official told this story:

"The Catholic Charities were being severely criticized, not only outside but inside their group. They were getting the big load of unemployment and they were utterly falling down in meeting it. One of the Catholic laymen said he was sick of the situation, and tired of hearing the criticism leveled at Catholic Charities. We advised him to get an outside Catholic expert to make a report on the situation. This was done and the report convinced them of the desirability of joining the Welfare Federation."

The upshot of it all was that they reorganized and put in a trained executive and fulfilled all the other requirements for joining.

Non-Catholics occasionally misconstrue the refusal of the Little Sisters of the Poor to join the community fund, not knowing that to do so would violate their constitution, as a Catholic professor explained:

"It is against their principles to have any fixed income. They depend on begging for alms and receive whatever comes in cash or kind. The day of miracles has not passed for them, as I can testify from an incident that I myself saw. On a hot summer day the Sisters had just poured out the very last ginger ale for the poor old men and women in their care, when unexpectedly a coca-cola truck drove up and the driver offered them a whole load of bottles that had been improperly labeled."

In only two of the cities studied were the Jewish charities outside the community fund, and in those cases the Catholics and the Y.M.C.A. were also out, so that no one of them was the target of special criticism. To be sure, the remark was occasionally heard that it took the depression and a sharply falling income to make the Jewish or the Catholic federation or the Y.M.C.A. yield and join the Fund; but in the case of the Jewish federations a more potent reason is said by a Jewish authority to be the reluctance of Jewish laymen to lose the close control and participation they enjoy when their agencies are independent and which they surrender to mixed committees when their agencies are affiliated with the Fund.

Most of the Jewish federation leaders who expressed any judgment on the matter held that affiliation is rarely an advantage to the Jewish agencies, but that social pressure by the other groups or an honest desire to help the entire community impels them to stand by the Fund. Four opinions may be quoted:

The Jewish executive in one large city put it thus:

"I felt the Chest could help a lot in lifting the level of a lot of inferior non-Jewish agencies. I saw we could either say to the rest: 'God bless you but we'll not go in; or, we'll go in on a trial basis; or, we'll go in for good and help the whole community, even though the Jewish agencies might lose thereby.' I persuaded the Jewish group in two cities to adopt the last. In one it has not been beneficial financially to the Jewish charities, but in the other it has been: and in both cities it has been a moral and civic benefit."

An emphatic claim of altruistic motive is made by a Jewish federation official in another city:

"Our federation joined the Chest with reluctance and we did so largely in order to help the community as a whole. We had had no trouble in raising all the funds needed by Jewish charities and believed that we would gain no financial advantage by joining, but rather, that our institutions might be forced to lower their standards of relief and that Jewish givers might give smaller amounts because they would tend to follow the average givings of non-Jewish givers."

Non-Jews might well note this judgment by a national authority on Jewish social work:

"The affiliation of our Jewish federation with the Chest has tended to weaken the Jewish community, because it has distracted the energies of Jewish leaders from the Jewish to the general community, and has lowered the standard of giving of Jews. Before our federation entered the Chest they had got the Jewish giving up to a high average, but when our givers saw what non-Jews gave to the Chest they tended to slump to that level."

Another national Jewish authority:

"The transfer of financial responsibility of Jewish agencies from Jewish federations to community chests resulted in a loss not only in the number of Jewish contributors to the Chest, but also in the degree of active interest in Jewish social work by the Jewish group."

The participation of the Y.M.C.A. and the Y.W.C.A. in the Chest is resented by Catholics in a few cities on the ground that their character as educational and character-building agencies cannot be dissociated from their distinctly Protestant bias. A Jewish leader attributes the opposition to other than religious factors:

"I do not feel that the Church opposition to the Y.M.C.A. was ever a serious factor. Those elements in the Chest who felt that relief needs should have first claim on its funds have objected to giving to the character-building agencies, and others have objected equally to the tendency of Chests to raise all funds on the relief appeal, and then to allocate a large part to other purposes."

As a rule non-Protestants recognize the non-sectarian spirit of the Associations and appreciate the financial sacrifice they sometimes make by entering the Fund. A Catholic charities officer states the case in an Eastern city:

"The presence of Y.M. and Y.W.C.A. and Scouts and other character-building agencies in the Chest was resented a while ago by Catholics but now they understand the situation and make no complaint, realizing that without the backing of these agencies the chest could not be carried on here."

On the other hand, a Catholic bishop in another eastern city opposed the inclusion in the community Fund of character-building agencies like the Christian Associations, maintaining that during the depression the Fund should be confined to relief purposes.

The way it looks to the president and secretary of one Y.M.C.A. is shown by these observations:

"There has been some talk of an inclusive Financial Federation and the Y.M.C.A. would join it gladly. The chief reason why we didn't join the Fund when it was started was that our Directors believed it would stamp the Fund as Protestant, since neither the Catholics nor Jews were going in, and that would be unfortunate for the community as a whole. So far as I know the Fund has been fairly administered.

"The Y.M.C.A. is not in it because we feel the Fund ought to be either inclusive or purely secular. We thought it was better for both the Fund and the Y.M.C.A., and the Y.W.C.A., for that matter, to stay out unless both Jews and Catholics came in."

In another city both Protestants and Jews long blocked the formation of a Chest. The Protestants gave as reasons that it would give big business still further control of social activity and that it would be just another device to get Protestant money to carry the Catholic load. The Jews maintained that they needed to achieve the unification of their own communal life before they could safely branch out in a community enterprise. The deadlock was broken when the Y.M.C.A. took a more coöperative attitude and a group of influential business men—nearly all Protestants—decided to go ahead regardless of clerical opposition.

CARRYING A FAIR SHARE OF THE LOAD

One of the commonest innuendoes is that this or that religious group is shirking its load in the community. Proof is never offered nor can it be, for the officers of the community chests invariably declare that neither they nor anyone else can unscramble the Fund and classify gifts by religious groups. One of the few definite statements on this point is made by Rabbi Barnett R. Brickner in his unpublished *History of the Jews in Cincinnati*. He writes:

"In the Community Chest campaign of 1929-30 Jews contributed 20 per cent. of the gifts of $100 and over. Five hundred and eighty-five Jews gave 14 per cent. of the total."

Since the Jewish population of this city is only about 5 per cent. of the total, these contributions are obviously large, but the exceptional wealth of the Jewish group in Cincinnati makes it fallacious to assume that these figures are typical of most other communities. With Rabbi Brickner's figures should be bracketed this statement by one of the best informed social workers in Cincinnati:

"The Jewish and Protestant groups measure up well in their gifts in relation to their wealth. In 1927 the Catholics were taking out about what they were putting in. When, however, such neutral agencies as the Scouts are taken into account, the load of the non-Catholics is increased, but Catholics often mention with justice the large sums of which they relieve the public treasury by maintaining their parochial schools. The Lutherans are not as large givers as several other denominations; this being partly due to the carry-over of wartime feeling."

There is, however, good ground for believing that in some cities, if population is taken as the basis, the Catholics give less than their proportion and that in certain cities where the Negro population is considerable, the Protestants fall just as far short. Even the Jews, during the depression, are thought in a few cities to have broken their almost invariable record of more than pulling their weight.

The situation is everywhere complicated by the uneven distribution of wealth among members of the three faiths. Broadly speaking, the Protestants are held to be more well-to-do than the Catholics. Wherever the Catholic population includes a large proportion of recent immigrants, it is unable for decades to meet all the relief needs of Catholics, and the burden inevitably has had to be carried in part by the "non-sectarian" agencies. But since these agencies were originally Protestant and are still supported almost exclusively by Protestant contributions, it means that Protestants are often carrying some of the Catholic load. This situation is well described by a Protestant minister who is acquainted with all parts of the country, but especially with New England.

"In my Connecticut parish practically all the poverty is Catholic and all the benevolent giving is Protestant. In much the same way, in most places that I know, there is but one non-sectarian hospital, largely carried by Protestant money; but once the Catholic population increases to the point where they can swing their own load, they build their own hospital, drain off Catholic contributions, and leave the Protestant community to shoulder the entire support of the non-sectarian, quasi-municipal hospital. Because the Catholics were recently arrived, they constituted the poorer group, and to a large extent their benevolences went into the building of Catholic churches and institutions, while the Protestant group, being the longer established and the wealthier, carried the burden of general charities."

A Canadian historian, commenting on this point of "bearing the charitable load," observes:

"In the United States the Jews have looked after their own more adequately than any other group, but in Canada, where the Jewish population is small and the number of wealthy Jews very limited, much of the Jewish relief is provided by non-sectarian or public agencies."

Apologists for one or another religious group frequently attempt to prove its superior generosity by reference to the special loads that it carries.

No conclusive data have ever been compiled on the issue, but certain considerations will throw some light upon it. The Catholics have to maintain not only their own churches and charitable institutions but also a vast system of parochial schools, which entails the payment every year of possibly 150 to 200 million dollars by American Catholics. The large sums contributed by the Jews in America for relief of fellow-believers abroad and for supplementary religious education at home have been mentioned in an earlier section. As for the Protestants, they are often the mainstays of non-sectarian relief agencies, settlement houses and the endowment of educational institutions, but three other heavy demands on their generosity are generally overlooked: the first is the high per capita cost and the multiplicity of small overlapping Protestant churches, staffed by a married clergy; as contrasted with the low per capita cost and the limited number of Catholic churches, staffed by a celibate clergy, and serving parishes that do not overlap, except in the rare cases of racially differentiated churches. The second demand is the support of "home-mission" extension work among the rural population. As the Religious Census demonstrates, both Catholics and Jews are concentrated mainly in the cities, whereas a considerable proportion of the Protestant population is scattered over the rural areas. The third demand is educational and charitable work among poor whites and Negroes. The only non-Protestant agency of note in this field is the Rosenwald Fund. The fraternal orders with their heavy financial demands are common to all three faiths. These considerations will suffice to show that the honors in monetary generosity are more nearly equal than might on first thought be supposed.

From a broadly humanitarian viewpoint, however, it is beside the point to assess praise or blame on a population basis. Once grant that the only sound basis is to gather from each according to his means, and distribute to each according to his need, and it becomes obviously unfair to expect recent immigrants, such as still compose many Catholic and Jewish communities, to give as much per capita as the old Protestant stock gives. This point was well put by a priest in a wealthy industrial city:

"Perhaps the Catholics here are not bearing their full share of the load; but there are extenuating circumstances: they represent to a large degree the working classes, who have small incomes. They have done much of the work in the industries which made possible the big fortunes held by Protestants."

In Chicago a leading Protestant social worker spoke in somewhat similar vein:

"Catholic laymen have given as well as others in proportion to wealth, but there are very few wealthy Catholics. Roman Catholics worked hard in the campaign. They know they get more out of the Fund than if they were not in it.

"The Jews give far more than they get out of the Community Fund. They would prefer to be on their own, if community sentiment would tolerate it."

A sharp stricture on Catholics was uttered by a Jewish philanthropist in a city where the Catholics are unusually strong:

"The Roman Catholics put strong pressure on Jewish and Protestant merchants to contribute to their charities. They use rather strong language sometimes. This is felt to be unfair by a number of the victims, especially as the Roman Catholics have refused to join in the Chest and thus dodged their full share of the community load."

Even the Jewish community sometimes lays itself open to criticism on the score of giving less to the Chest than it has previously given to its own agencies. One instance of this kind drew the following comments from a Chest executive:

"The Protestants seemed antagonistic. In part their argument seemed to be that this was just another means of getting Protestant money to carry the Catholic load.

"The Jews, however, have fallen off, to judge from the comparison of the contributions made to the Jewish philanthropies before they joined the Chest with those made by Jewish contributors now. In short, the Chest has not gained any financial support from the Jewish group commensurate with the added obligations which the joining of the Jewish group has caused. The Jewish philanthropies last year received from the fund $396,000 and this year their allotment is $368,000."

He added this revealing information on the Y.M.C.A.:

"There has been a drop in the contributions from those men who specially favored the Y.M.C.A. This is typical of the persistent problem which arises when men are urged to shift their loyalties from some particular cause to a more inclusive but less clearly defined one."

Mutual recriminations by social workers in the three groups were most frequently heard in a city where the Community Fund did not include the Catholic and Jewish federations, and where the patronizing air of certain Catholic authorities ruffled the sensibilities of the other people. In another city the domineering attitude of certain Protestant leaders in the Chest was resented by non-Protestants. In almost every city the inquirers found similar evidence of the power of a few dominating personalities to create an atmosphere of pervasive good will or of irritation, regardless of the formal relationships among the agencies.

NATIONAL AGENCIES AND COMMUNITY CHESTS

The relation of the Chest to appeals for national and foreign undertakings has caused some controversy. Local agencies participating in the

Chest have often argued that if they could not include in their askings amounts in support of national enterprises, such as the Jewish national tuberculosis sanitarium and the work in foreign countries conducted by the Young Men's and Young Women's Christian Associations, then they should be allowed to canvass separately for them, as they had done before the Chest was formed. As a rule the Chest has granted the request, but according to the estimate of an authority on the Chest movement, in perhaps 50 out of the 400 chests, it has been deemed wiser to include amounts for such objects in the Chest rather than permit constituent agencies to violate the slogan, "only one appeal for everything," by making a separate canvass. In one city, for instance, where the Young Men's Christian Association leaders have been the backbone of the Chest campaign the Association has been allowed to include $2,000 or more a year for the work in foreign countries. To reverse this policy might alienate the Association constituency to such a degree as to imperil the entire Chest. The refusal of the Chest in other cities either to include such an amount or to allow a separate canvass has been one of the obstacles to the Association's affiliation with the Chest.

In another city the Jewish Federation was assured, upon its entry into the Chest, that certain national agencies could be included in its askings, but the protests of a few Gentile leaders have been so persistent that the Federation has refrained from claiming the privilege.

PROSELYTIZING AND DISCRIMINATION

The amount of friction arising from alleged proselytizing and religious discrimination is surprisingly small. Catholic social workers rarely alluded in interviews to discrimination by Protestant or non-sectarian agencies. The former unfair allocation of Catholic children to Protestant agencies, to which allusion was made in an earlier section, seems today to be almost unknown, at least in the cities studied. On the contrary, occasional complaints were made by non-Catholics against the excessive religious zeal and occasional discrimination practised by Catholics. The various facets of the situation can best be illuminated by a series of extracts from the testimony.

In the placement of dependent children the courts have ruled that the religion of the parents should be followed or in case of a mixed marriage between a Catholic and a Protestant, that the baptismal relation of the child should be determining.[19] This principle has so long been followed by social agencies that disputes seldom arise. In Cleveland, for example,

---

[19] In New York State the following decisions are cited by Rev. W. H. Meegan, Director, Child Placing Department of the Catholic Charities of Buffalo, in letter of February 22, 1930 to the Secretary of the Children's Aid Society: 139 N.Y.S. 685; 52 Misc. Rep. 66, 102 N.Y. Supp. 440; 112 N.Y.S. 591; 82 N.Y.S. 986; 13 Wall, 679, 728, 20 L. Ed. 666.

the director of the Catholic Charities, Father Le Blond (lately elevated to a bishopric) described substantially as follows the practice and some of the perplexing situations that arise in applying it.

"In children's work we have arrived at a pretty satisfactory basis with the Cleveland Children's Bureau. We rely on them absolutely to handle Catholic cases in the first stage. We made the agreement with them years ago, that the baptismal religion of a child, or if none, the religion of the parents, should be accepted. In case of mixed marriage, the baptismal religion of the child is the determining factor in its assignment. We never change this classification after its first determination, even though this gives rise to some puzzling situations. For example, there was a child of an Italian Roman Catholic father and a Protestant mother. The court decided that the child should be given to the mother's care and therefore placed in a Protestant home; but although after six years the mother became a Catholic, we refused to change the classification as long as the child was under institutional care. If we did not hold to this agreement we should be plunged into hopeless confusion and competition.

"Our Catholic Homes take Protestant boys if the Protestant homes are full and they do the same with our children but transfer them as soon as practicable. Very seldom does a worker show bias and if discovered she is fired."

A tragi-comic illustration of the kinds of complications that sometimes arise to tax the patience and sense of humor of the religious authorities occurred in Washington:

"Strange situations arise where borderline cases create complications. Thus a child with a father who has no religious interest and an Episcopalian mother gets sick. A kind neighbor thinking it ought to be baptized Catholic-style calls a priest and the child becomes a Catholic. The child is now a Catholic, and the Associated Charities cannot take up the case because it is a Catholic case, although the parents have no Catholic affinities at all."

In several cities the secretaries of the Council of Social Agencies and similar bodies bore witness to the fidelity of nearly all agencies of all the faiths in living up to the principle. The prevalent consideration of Catholic sensibilities is indicated by this statement of a Welfare Federation executive:

"There is no discrimination against Catholics in the various non-Catholic charitable institutions except that certain of the children's agencies decline to handle Catholic children because the Catholics themselves object and wish all cases turned over to them."

In parts of the country where religious rivalry is still intense, there may still be a good many acts that squint towards proselytizing, such as this instance given at the 1933 National Conference of Catholic Charities by the director of Catholic Charities in a southern city:

"I found one Protestant children's agency that was caring for seventy Catholic children, who had been turned away from Catholic homes by red tape or by our strict requirements; whereas the Protestant agency was strict only with Protestant applicants and readily let down the bars for Catholic applicants."

Upon hearing this another priest made these comments:

"We can't possibly care for all our Catholic cases and can't blame them for going to Protestant and non-sectarian agencies. The people in charge aren't evil or wilfully undermining the morals of our people. To them birth control and sterilization are not evil at all, but desirable—strange as it may seem to us. Our remedy is to become voting members of the various community boards and committees that pass on funds and charity policies and see that funds aren't used for such deplorable ends."

In the allocation of adult cases, except in Quebec,[20] no such clear and uniform principles have been worked out as obtain in children's cases, the reason being that adults are free agents and themselves may prefer to receive aid from an agency of a faith different from their own. Naturally, ambiguous and controversial situations arise and cause unpleasantness. In one city, for instance, the Catholic authorities resented the refusal of the Charity Organization Society to give a list of Catholic families cared for by it, although the Society explained that this was partly due to the fact that records of church connection were often lacking. In another city, "there has always been bitter rivalry between the United Charities and the Catholic Charities because the United Charities care for many Catholic cases whom the Catholic Charities would like to get hold of."

No specific instances of alleged proselytizing or discrimination in connection with the placement or handling of Jewish cases were brought to the investigators' attention. The following description of the friendly relations in a southern city would come near to fitting most of the cities studied:

"The Family Organization is housed in the same building as the Jewish agencies, and all Jewish cases are dealt with by the Jewish agency directly. In certain cases of Jewish-Gentile mixed marriage, the decision as to who shall handle the case is usually left to the Jewish agency, and if they do not care to handle it, the Family Organization does. In general, it would seem that the principle of decision revolves on the whole tendency of the particular family to incline to the Jewish or to the Gentile world. If, in a particular case, the family of the party applying for aid is Jewish and may perhaps help, then the Jews take it; if the family of the party most likely to help is Gentile, then the Family Organization looks after it. But there is no friction and complete coöperation."

In mixed marriages involving Jews the amicable arrangement worked out in San Francisco may be considered typical:

[20] In Montreal, for example, Catholics must apply to Catholic, Protestants to Protestant and Jews to Jewish agencies.

"The Associated Charities and our Federation have always shared the expense in case either husband or wife were Jewish. But during the depression, if the mother was a Jew, we would take care of the family. If the mother was a non-Jew we referred the case to the Associated Charities."

Complaints were made by Jews, however, in several cities that certain of the less scrupulous Christian Missions to Jews, in their zeal to attract converts, were inclined to extend aid to Jewish applicants who could not qualify for help from the Jewish agencies.

The Catholic philosophy of social work insists that religious and physical ministration should always be combined; that if a choice must be made, the religious should take precedence; furthermore, that the divinely appointed channel of spiritual grace and eternal salvation is the Catholic Church; and therefore, that fidelity to its sacraments and observances is a paramount duty. It is the failure of non-Catholics to realize how rigorously this philosophy dominates Catholic social work, both lay and professional, that causes much of the irritation. Repeatedly the investigators heard complaints from secular and Protestant agency workers that the Catholics were apt to refuse aid to Catholic applicants who would not fulfill their church obligations.

A secular agency executive of Protestant affiliations terms the Catholic practice an "exaggerated emphasis," a judgment, of course, which depends on one's basic assumptions. That it is the unwavering Catholic position was pungently stated by a prominent Catholic layman in a city where Catholicism is deeply intrenched:

"Our Catholic principles of doing relief differ fundamentally from those of the 'A', originally a Protestant society, now the chief secular agency, because we insist on linking the religious and moral rehabilitation with the rest. We don't want the 'A' to mess in our field on that account. We agreed to let them continue caring for Catholics whom they already had on their lists, but Catholic Charities take on all the new cases."

From the viewpoint of interfaith harmony it is in place to note the effect of the Catholic attitude as it appears to an official of a public relief fund in a large city:

"If applicants to the public welfare fund request to be transferred to the Catholic Charities or Jewish Charities it is done. Many prefer not to transfer, because Catholic Charities are not so prompt. But others prefer to apply to Catholic or Jewish Charities because they are reluctant to be on the public list. On the other hand, Catholics have to renew contact with the Church every week, through the St. Vincent de Paul committee of two or by seeing the priest. When cases refuse to have a marriage validated or what not, the Catholic Charities may return them to the public welfare fund. Their practice of refusing to take cases that do not comply with church requirements is a constant source of friction."

In similar vein speaks the Community Fund executive in another city:

"The Catholic practice of using relief aid to bring pressure on recipients to stay by the Church and perform religious duties is resented, especially in the case of families where one spouse is a Protestant."

In several cities, non-sectarian workers said that the Catholic Charities seemed

"quite willing that we should handle straight Catholic cases where there is no danger of defection from their faith, but quite unwilling that we should deal with cases of mixed marriages or cases where Protestant relatives might be called in to assist in the family rehabilitation."

Discrimination in hospitals against applicants for service on the basis of their faith happily appears to be rare. Not only did persons of all faiths who were interviewed mention no case of this kind, but they refrained even from innuendoes and hearsay charges. Catholic hospitals often include non-Catholic physicians on their staffs and Protestant patients testify to the open door and kindly ministration of various Catholic hospitals. The tolerant spirit of nearly all the hospitals may be epitomized by the emphatic declaration of a Catholic bishop, who said: "We make no discrimination whatever as to faith of patients in Catholic hospitals." That this tolerance may be sometimes inadvertently strained is indicated by the words "should be" in a report of the Los Angeles Society of St. Vincent de Paul for 1932:

"A hospital is a great field for the saving of souls. One of the great objects of Vincentian work in a hospital, besides cheering and comforting the patients, is to discover those inmates who are, or should be, Catholics, and who need priestly service."

The only explicit complaints against Catholic hospitals came from two widely separated communities. A minister in the far South stated that the Protestant ministers of the city had more than once conferred regarding certain impediments encountered in visiting Protestant patients in Catholic hospitals. A minister in a small city adjoining New York City said that many of his Protestant fellow-clergymen had complained of similar treatment and that some years ago a number of them had met to see if they could develop some code of procedure to handle such cases.

Attempts at proselytizing by social-work visitors to clients in their homes is occasionally alleged. A Polish National Catholic ecclesiastic, in a city where the St. Vincent de Paul visitors are notably active complained:

"Very few of our people serve as friendly visitors, but there are many Roman Catholic visitors and their proselytizing of people in other communions whom they visit is a source of provocation to us and to persons of other faiths."

The granting of public funds derived from taxes to private welfare agencies has long been practised in connection with dependent and delinquent children, and little interfaith tension seems to have been caused by it. But the case has been otherwise in reference to the award of public relief funds during the present depression to private agencies. Although Catholics have not been alone in agitating for this practice, they have been the most active and influential in several localities, and consequently unpleasant feeling between Catholics and non-Catholics has been aroused. The reaction of Protestant leaders in a midwestern city is reflected by the statement of a sociologist that "the Roman Catholics have used the money they have received from public relief funds for ecclesiastical advantage. This is so marked that Protestants may feel forced to federate in self-defense."

The Federal Relief Administration in 1933 issued a ruling against making grants to private agencies, but in some localities, such as Chicago and St. Louis, the ruling was formally observed but practically evaded by an agency's posting a sign claiming to be a branch of the State Public Relief Administration. The hollowness of the claim was revealed in Chicago, so informed persons allege, when the Diocesan Catholic Charities, which displayed such a sign, refused to allow a representative of the county Relief Administration to exercise any authority over its disbursement of public funds.

In another Illinois city a study of the relief situation made by a non-sectarian national agency had recommended that no private agency should be granted public relief funds. The local Catholic Charities referred the matter to the officers of the National Conference of Catholic Charities, who objected to the recommendation. Meanwhile the local Community Chest leaders, including some Catholic laymen, supported the recommendation. At this writing the president of the Chest is a Catholic layman and he has shown no signs of yielding.

In a large city in another state a study of the relief and welfare agency situation has been directed by a staff of three specialists, Catholic, Jewish and Protestant, the Catholic being the secretary of the National Conference of Catholic Charities. When it came to the recommendation as to disbursing public relief funds through private agencies the staff were deadlocked, one in favor, two opposed.

Again, in Chicago an effort was made, in 1934, to organize a permanent Chest, one of whose proposed rules would exclude private agencies which receive public funds, on the practical ground that to do so would handicap the appeal for gifts: the prospective giver would inquire why he was being asked to support private agencies already in receipt of grants from public funds derived from taxes paid by himself and others. This rule would apply to all private agencies, but it was interpreted as discriminating mainly against the Catholic Charities, since they have been the chief private recipients of public relief funds.

The issue, however, has not been drawn sharply according to religious groupings. The Catholic laity, in the case cited and elsewhere, sometimes refuse to follow their ecclesiastical authorities, and among the Protestants, bodies like the Lutherans, that operate many hospitals, object to losing aid from public funds. When the whole issue was discussed at a national conference summoned by the Federal Council of the Churches of Christ in America in March, 1934, the recommendation regarding public funds was qualified in deference to such Protestant objectors, as follows:

"Public funds, raised by taxation, should be administered by public agencies and should not be allocated to private agencies except when the proper care of the people makes it imperative."

Furthermore, in New York and other places it has long been customary for the Department of Public Welfare to make grants to child-caring agencies, of all three faiths, for the maintenance of children of the respective faiths who have been allocated to the agencies by the courts. In still another field, the Citizens Conservation Camps, the question of the propriety of the Government's granting expenses to either Protestant or Catholic volunteer camp chaplains is a moot question.

It is thus abundantly clear that no thoroughly consistent policy has been everywhere accepted or applied. Nevertheless, the issue in its most aggravated form, the granting of public relief funds to private agencies, has lately been a disturber of the peace primarily between Catholics and Protestants.

In view of all the facts recited, it is important for the leaders of all the faiths to grasp the fact that the issue roots in deep and sincere differences of conviction. On the one hand, are those who believe that the private agency is more efficient than the public and that spiritual and physical ministration should not be separated. On the other hand, stand those who dread any reversion to the entanglement of church and state and hold that American traditions demand the public disbursal of public monies. In view of the general expectation that relief must continue for many years to depend predominantly on public funds, the issue is likely to remain a live one, and to call for thorough discussion without aspersions against the motives of any religious group.[21]

During the depression, the relief of single men in some cities was left largely to the Salvation Army or to the Gospel Missions. A common source of antagonism to these missions, especially on the part of Catholics and Jews, is that they force the unfortunate to listen to gospel harangues—

[21] The kindred issue of granting public funds to private educational institutions is by no means dead, as will be shown in Chapter V.

a rather glaring instance of luring men to undergo spiritual treatment as a condition of receiving material benefits. A student of relief agencies in one eastern state criticized the gospel missions "for confusing the claims of Jesus with a cup of coffee." With the assumption of material relief by public agencies this malpractice has doubtless diminished.

Catholic leaders frequently voiced to the investigators a protest against those non-Catholic social workers who were advising Catholic clients to practice birth control and submit to sterilization. Medical men attached to public clinics and hospitals and social workers to whom Catholics apply for aid often conclude that the best and perhaps the only fundamental solution would be one of these practices. In several instances the investigators were told that such Catholic patients were reminded of their church's prohibition of these practices and were warned of the risk of excommunication. The Catholic authorities felt that even after receiving the patient's free assent, the practitioner was not absolved of complicity in a crime. In one city, where non-sectarian social workers had referred Catholic cases for such treatment to a municipal hospital, the Catholic authorities protested so vigorously that thereafter similar cases were referred to a Protestant hospital. Early in this chapter reference was made to the offense given to adherents of minority faiths by the unconscious assumption of the Protestant majority that their standards and customs should be followed by the minority. A large number of liberal Protestants as well as Jews are equally offended by the Catholic insistence on imposing their moral code as to birth control on others, and preventing the adoption of laws which would allow physicians to give information regarding contraception to such as desire it, among whom are many non-Catholics.

OVERCOMING IMPEDIMENTS TO COÖPERATION

The principle of Salmon P. Chase's adage about specie payments—"the way to resumption is to resume"—is pat with reference to interfaith coöperation: the way to develop a coöperative spirit is to work together. As a Lutheran professor in Chicago phrased it:

"The best way to get interfaith understanding and harmony is to put men to work together on something non-ecclesiastical that they all care about, like civic welfare."

Such a rapprochement is begotten not by formal agreements but by growing acquaintance and avoidance of controversy over the deep and apparently permanent religious differences. In Louisville, for example, it was stated:

"There seems to be a very fine piece of collaboration between the Family Service Organization and the Society of St. Vincent de Paul without written agreements or formal colloquies, but simply through the coöpting of the President of the St. Vincent de Paul Society on the board of the Family Service Organization and his making himself thoroughly sensitive to its aims and objectives and procedures. He in turn has transformed the temper of his Society in his own way and in harmony with its own genius.

"Frequently, non-Catholics find themselves in need and go to the parish office and ask if Mr. Vincent de Paul is in. The local parish may provide immediate relief, but non-Catholics it is only too glad to turn over to the Family Service Organization."

The immense contribution made by the joint-financing organizations like the Community Chest toward bringing leading men and women of all faiths into face-to-face, shoulder-to-shoulder relationships and thereby exorcising fears and stereotyped religious antipathies is one of the clearest findings of this study. The nub of the matter was well stated by a Catholic financier in a mid-western city:

"I have long been a member of the Community Fund and in close touch with the Catholic Charities. I believe that the Fund has been a leveler of castes and cliques in the city at large. It has had a wholesome effect also on relations among the churches, because leaders in the various churches were enabled by the discussions in committees to get an idea of what the other churches were trying to do and they found they were not so different from themselves after all."

A Chest executive in the same city spoke in similar vein:

"The spirit of coöperation and understanding among men of all faiths developed by the Fund has spread to other areas and is probably the chief factor underlying the strong spirit of community coöperation in the city."

Although "accommodation" rather than "coöperation" may perhaps more accurately characterize the relations between Catholics and non-Catholics in the last community-wide drive for charitable funds in Ottawa, Canada, the experiment is worthy of citation because "the good feeling generated by it was a happy contrast with the suspicion that had accompanied some previous drives." The plan was briefly as follows: the two city-wide charitable organizations, one Protestant (including the Jews, after the Quebec educational law precedent), and the other Catholic, joined hands for the drive. All committees consisted of an equal number of Protestants and Catholics. The Catholic solicitors followed parochial divisions, while the Protestant solicitors followed general community lines. But a distinctive device was the use of three pledge cards, one for Protestant, one for Catholic and one for non-sectarian charities, so that the tabulations showed clearly whether each group of believers was giving its reasonable share to the non-sectarian agencies as well as to its own.

With the Chest should be bracketed the Council of Social Agencies, which brings into intimate contact the leading minds in the social agencies and thus promotes appreciation of one another's good faith and ability as well as problems. In fact, the Council has one marked advantage over the Chest as a promoter of disinterested coöperation: it is less engrossed with money. In the Chest the emphasis is on the raising and dividing of funds, and the temptation to bargain and compete for sectarian advantage is strong. In the Council of Social Agencies the emphasis is on professional standards and social problems. On the other hand, the Chest appeals to the masses and arouses camaraderie and generous emulation among a large number of campaign workers of all the faiths, whereas the Council comprises a few persons who work soberly and seek little publicity. To the exceptional value of the Council the social executives of all three faiths give emphatic testimony. Thus a director of Catholic Charities said:

"All the social and relief agencies are drawn into effective relations by this Council. Through it we keep matters adjusted with the Family Organization, Jewish Charities and Salvation Army."

Among the religious groups in another eastern city the friendliest relations obtain, a happy condition chiefly due, in the common judgment of a leading attorney, a Protestant bishop and a local journalist, to the fact that the federations of the Catholic, the Jewish and the non-sectarian social agencies are "each independent but are smoothly coördinated through the Council of Social Agencies, a set-up which unites the advantages of self-determination with coöperation in matters of general concern."

In view of various instances of friction among the social agencies of the three faiths that have already been disclosed, it is almost superfluous to call further attention to the rifts in the lute of coöperation. Yet the record shows that some blocking of coöperative relations can be charged against all three groups, although very seldom against the liberal Jews. Some Protestant leaders are always in the forefront of coöperative efforts, but there are not a few Protestant laggards, especially among the socially untrained laity and clergy. Their ignorance of scientific social work combines with traditional offishness and suspicion of the Catholics to make them refuse the right hand of fellowship. In one city, for instance, where interfaith relations are exceptionally good, a Protestant leader, describing the Chest Committee on Church Coöperation, said:

"Each church is asked to name a key man, through whom the committee may communicate with the church. When he hears some 'libel' about the Chest, he may communicate with them and enable them to run it down. He also may secure speakers for men's clubs, etc.

"Six out of thirteen synagogues have named such men. About 50 per cent. of the Catholic churches have named them—not a few being priests instead of laymen, but Protestant coöperation is lower than either Catholic or Jewish. The

Southern Baptists provide such representatives in only one or two cases; the Southern Methodists in three or four; the Lutherans relatively few."

The data already presented show a rather high degree of participation by Catholic charities federations in the Chest; indeed, it is surprisingly high in view of the jealousy of many parish priests and St. Vincent de Paul conferences of any infringement on their prerogatives. The trained Catholic social workers, increasingly in charge of the diocesan charity headquarters, are nearly always inclined to be coöperative. Non-Catholics, who think only of the rock-like refusal of Catholics to unite with Protestants or Jews in religious rites or any other activity that implies ecclesiastical equality, are prone to overlook the good Catholic record in relations like social work, where no ecclesiastical or doctrinal questions are, involved. At the same time, in several cities leaders in community welfare activities complained of the difficulty of finding Catholic laymen and women to serve on boards and committees. This is to be explained partly by absorption in Catholic activities and partly by the long-standing diffidence of a minority toward a dominant and not always cordial Protestant majority.

The extent and heartiness of interfaith coöperation was everywhere found to hinge most of all on a few outstanding personalities. Success or failure may depend on whether some eminent ecclesiastic smiles or frowns. This is preëminently true in the case of Catholics, for the obvious reason that an archbishop or a bishop is literally an authority, and laymen, however coöperative and determined, can seldom successfully defy his will. Evidence for these observations was found in every city. Not only the living but the dead ecclesiastic may wield tremendous influence: witness the potent and reconciling spirit of Archbishop Ireland still pervading the city of St. Paul and the irenic influence of Cardinal Gibbons in Baltimore.

The blocking by the Catholic bishop of coöperation in Chest campaigns is notorious in certain cities. In one of them a secular agency executive said:

"He held 'thumbs down' on Catholic participation in the Federation, except that on account of the abnormal burden of relief during the depression he allowed his name to be used and sent instructions to all his clergy that the people were to coöperate to a certain degree, because the entire community must get under the emergency load."

In striking contrast is the cordial support given to the Community Fund by other Catholic bishops, like one in California, whose praise was on all lips:

"In the Chest all groups work cordially together. The Archbishop is always the chairman and the leaders of other faiths are very active. Before the first drive for the Fund the Archbishop invited the leaders of all faiths and groups to luncheon at a delightful convent and there were many speeches and every one was delighted. Next year the Jews gave a similar affair and later, the Episcopalians and others."

Naturally, the example of the bishop or archbishop is contagious among the lower clergy. In one western city a parish priest has been one of the most active leaders in the Chest as well as in the Rotary Club, and the secretary of the local Y.M.C.A. related with warmth how this priest had publicly supported the Y.M.C.A. interest at Chest committee meetings when no representative of the "Y" was present and had repeatedly refuted charges against the wartime work of the "Y".

The influence of the clergy, whether Catholic, Jewish or Protestant, over the community as a whole seldom appears to be as strong as that exerted by outstanding laymen, about whose ecclesiastical affiliation no one stops to think, and whom all men delight to honor. Such first citizens were spoken of in nearly every city. They represented all the religious groups and various professions, such as law, industry, education and banking. In one city the chairman of the Chest Committee on Church Coöperation was an educator, and he remarked: "They said they wanted me because I was not a churchman; they really pull together with surprising enthusiasm."

GENERAL OBSERVATIONS

A variety of criticisms of one religious group or another and many instances of friction among the three groups have been reported in this chapter, but a fair appraisal of the entire situation would declare that as a rule a friendly and coöperative spirit is predominant among them. The purpose in giving disproportionate space to the shadows in the picture has been to help each group to see how it looks to the others and to show how petty are some of the common causes of friction and how readily curable are others. It should have become clear that a sovereign remedy for such ailments is to bring about closer contacts and more accurate information among the three groups.

The discussion, however, has also referred to the sharply contrasted emphases characteristic of the three groups. The majority, by the very genius of Protestantism, stresses the liberty to differ on matters of religion but prizes all the more the compensating principle of unity in common devotion to community and to country. The Protestant majority also tends to be intolerant of variants from its own standards of culture and of conduct. This means that Protestants, on the one hand, take the lead in coöperative social endeavor and, on the other, that many of them consider to be socially divisive the church-centered emphasis of the Catholics, and the communal-centered emphasis of the Jews. Granting, however, that these differing emphases should be respected, it is generally agreed that in social work, at least, special effort should be made by the three groups to magnify their points of agreement and to multiply the occasions for working together.

The experience of social workers during the present hard times has led many of them to conclude that hereafter the State should bear the full burden of meeting primary relief needs. If this policy were adopted, it would automatically prevent repetition of the dispute over the allocation of public funds to sectarian agencies, which has been a source of irritation, not only among the three faiths, but also between civil and religious officials. But, in addition, the adoption of this policy would relieve the religious and other private agencies of the burden of handling physical relief and would leave them free to concentrate their energies on the more difficult and intimate services of personal and family rehabilitation and counselling, and the equalization of cultural opportunities for all. The historical student of social work can discern that a slow evolution has been taking place, from the elementary and indiscriminate physical ministration to the individual by medieval charity to the more comprehensive and discriminating ministration to the whole person and to the family by modern social work. If the depression has hastened that evolution, who will deny that it has thereby compensated somewhat for the grievous damage it has otherwise inflicted?

Attention has been so frequently drawn to the friction or misunderstanding among the various groups that the reader might naturally ask whether it would not be a good idea to eliminate all separate religious social agencies and pool everything under non-sectarian and public auspices. Plausible as this may sound, it overlooks certain vital considerations. As private social service becomes less physical and more psychical, increasing importance must attach to the ability of the social worker to understand and stimulate the subtle energies that form and re-form personality. Prominent among these energies are those that spring from religion and from other embodiments of the racial and cultural heritage. Who can minister to a loyal Jew or a faithful Catholic or a convinced Protestant quite so well as one whose heart vibrates to the same chords? The time seems far in the future when any social minister, however generously disposed, can be all things to all men in these deeper reaches of life. This apologia for separate Jewish and Catholic and Protestant social ministries argues also for separate social agencies to provide them; but does not the chapter as a whole argue with equal force for an increasing degree of collaboration among all the agencies?

If, however, the case for separate agencies for Jews and Catholics is sound, is it not also sound for Protestants? The logic so far as it goes, seems inescapable, but it does not go far enough. It does not take account of the strong sweep of Protestant evolution toward secularizing all social service, as sketched in an earlier section. Nevertheless, why should Protestants assume that the secularization of social work which they have fostered for a century past must be accepted as the final term in the series? History cannot be revised, but it can be made. So the question may properly be raised whether, with the trend of private social service increasingly toward the psychical realm, the Protestant churches should not focus their social energies in a system of clinics and counselling bureaus and orders of family visitors, in which religious motivation would be freely employed. Supposing that the Catholic and Jewish social agencies adopted a similar emphasis, the question then would arise: Would it not be a further step toward efficiency to establish central clinics, where clients of all the faiths and of no faith could be diagnosed by the most advanced scientific methods and then referred for specific treatment to whatever religious or secular agency or agencies could best meet their needs?

The anomalous situation growing out of the secularizing policy of Protestants deserves mention. Protestants for the most part have converted the relief societies that they started, and still in large measure sustain, into broad non-sectarian social agencies. In so doing have they become victims of their own humanitarianism? Charitably construed, their liberalism and community-mindedness impelled them to dispense with distinctively Protestant agencies. Realistically construed, their sectarian fragmentation would have compelled them ultimately, in any event, to forego the too expensive luxury of a host of parallel denominational agencies. Both forces, no doubt, have been at work. The upshot of it all may be, as one Protestant observed, that "Protestants get it coming and going. We give more than our quota of money and time to agencies that serve all faiths, and then if we try to ensure a square deal for unfortunate Protestants we are called grasping and sectarian." Wherever the minority faiths are well organized and group-conscious, while the Protestant majority is unorganized, and in danger of being penalized on that account, the situation is fraught with strain. Actual ruptures can best be averted by a determination on all sides to play fair and subordinate sectarian advantage to the general good.

Finally, in the judgment of most of the experts consulted, the best relations among the social agencies are found where the employed leaders are professionally trained. General efficiency as well as willingness to coöperate are both highly correlated with trained leadership, whereas much of the friction and lack of coöperation among the agencies is due to narrow-minded, untrained leaders. The conclusion, of course, is not that lay volunteers should be dispensed with, but that they should be yoked with professionals. The happiest interfaith relations also seem to require that the professional worker who is likewise an ecclesiastic should not allow his ecclesiastical connection to outweigh his function as a social worker. It is at this point that lay boards of control and of counsel exert a decisive influence in the direction of a coöperative and broadly human approach.

CHAPTER V

Elementary Education

In the preceding chapter it has been shown how social work became steadily secularized, and how, with the secularization, religious organizations engaged in social work were required to explore new areas of coöperation and relationship both with the state and with one another. In much the same way, education was originally a function of the church which has been constantly brought more and more under the aegis of the state or of non-sectarian organizations. It was inevitable, therefore, that religious bodies would be compelled to define their own position in regard to the control of education, and in this process some conflicts have arisen not only between religious bodies, but between specific religious bodies and the body politic itself. In approaching this subject, it is very necessary to remember that the present trend toward the secularization of education is quite modern.

HISTORICAL RELATION OF RELIGION TO EDUCATION

In the history of Europe, the training of the child was regarded as primarily the responsibility of the parents and as or when provided, was designed to "fit him for his station in life." In England, education was made compulsory only in 1876, and during the ministry of Lord Beaconsfield, although a preliminary step in that direction had been previously taken in 1870. In the United States, the laws providing for compulsory attendance were passed by the various states at different times, that of Massachusetts in 1852 and that of Mississippi only in 1918.[1] In the Canadian provinces, education is still not compulsory in Quebec, although other laws stipulating the minimum age at which a child in Quebec can be engaged in industry operate to secure much the same ends, except perhaps in agricultural districts.

PROTESTANT EMPHASIS ON EDUCATION

It is sometimes asserted that the great emphasis on popular education is essentially due to Protestantism which, in shifting the center of authority from an institution to a book, supplied an added impetus to the desire to read. Those who argue thus point out that Protestant countries usually led

---

[1] For Summary of Laws Relating to Compulsory Education in the United States, see *Bulletin*, 1928, No. 28, published by the Department of the Interior, Bureau of Education, and prepared by Ward W. Keesecker.

the way in common education, even as in New England a major reason for the Massachusetts Law of 1647, which Horace Mann regarded as epochal for universal education, was couched thus:

"It being the chief project of that old deluder, Satan, to keep men from the knowledge of the Scriptures, as in former times, keeping them in an unknown tongue, so in these later times, by persuading them from the use of tongues, etc."

They also maintain that the urge to literacy was as real with Protestants as it was with the Jewish people, "the people of the book," whose educational system was based on a knowledge of the Torah, and aimed to create a nation who would "fear God and keep His commandments."

It is necessary, however, to qualify this theory by pointing out that:

(1) Devotion to an authoritative book may be accompanied by fairly wide-spread illiteracy. The Koran is deeply venerated by all Mohammedans, but in recent years Mustapha Kemal has made extraordinary efforts to wipe out the appalling illiteracy of Turkey.

(2) While such countries as Sweden, Scotland, Germany and Switzerland were quick to establish schools to serve the general population, England— another Protestant country—continued for years to stress aristocratic ideals in education and made little provision for the education of the common people. This backwardness was probably due, at least in part, to the struggle between the Established Church and the Nonconformists. According to Professor Wilhelm Dibelius churchmen in England felt that "too much knowledge might lead to Deism or to a sectarianism perilous to Church and State. A perfectly blank face was presented to every effort at improving popular education; the Church's interest was confined to preventing the foundation of Dissenting schools which might prove hostile to it."[2] Even as late as 1902, the attempt to give larger financial assistance to church schools in England led to the Passive Resistance movement on the part of the dissenters although the church seems to have won out, for in 1926-27, the number of schools under the church outnumbered the "provided" schools, 11,533 to 9,170.

So far as the universities were concerned, it is well known that religious tests were abolished at Oxford and Cambridge only in 1871, although before this time the organization of the University of London and certain other universities had made provision for dissenters. When this was the condition of popular education in England, it is fair to assume that a veridical picture of educational conditions in the thirteen colonies would be far from rosy.

(3) To a certain extent, the emphasis on public education in Protestant countries was probably due, not only to the desire for a Bible-reading public,

[2] Dibelius, W., *England* (New York: Harper and Brothers, 1930), p. 443.

but also to the concomitant growth of democracy and the recognition that a democratic government, to prove at all permanent, must rest upon an educated citizenry; and further, to the nationalistic ambition to provide a citizenry, trained and well able to compete with the best among other nationals.

(4) In part, the emphasis on popular education in Protestant countries was due to the rise of manifold sects, once the unity of the church was shattered, which made the control of education by the church or churches no longer practicable and consequently diverted this control to the state. Thus, not Protestantism in itself, but the sectarianism which emerged from Protestantism, paved the way for the state control of education, and once this control was vested in the state, and political institutions became increasingly democratic, universal and compulsory education naturally followed. So, too, when the state had achieved in certain Protestant countries the control of education, the state in other non-Protestant countries began to claim a similar control, even though there the challenge of sectarianism might not have existed to the same degree.[3]

(5) Popular education could hardly have existed prior to the invention of printing. Gutenberg may be considered not only one of the fathers of the Reformation but also of popular education.

It is true, however, that certain Catholic countries did not give the same emphasis to popular education as Protestant countries, as the literacy statistics of Spanish and Portuguese cities to this very day testify. While the church may have sought within certain limits to provide an education which "fitted a man for his station in life," it moved very slowly in the direction of popular education, especially in Latin America, where its task was greatly complicated by a diversity of racial factors.

THE PROCESS OF SECULARIZATION

Education, both in the Motherland and in the colonies, began at the top and worked down. In England, first came the great universities of Oxford and Cambridge, and then the "endowed schools" such as Eton and Harrow. Schools for the common people slowly followed, first the Sunday schools, founded by Robert Raikes in 1780, then the free schools established either by Joseph Lancaster, a Quaker (1801), or by Andrew Bell (Anglican) in connection with his National Society for the Education of the Poor (1811). So, too, in the colonies the colleges came first and were designed for the training of ministers. Of ten colleges founded between 1637 and 1776, only one was non-sectarian, i.e., the University of Pennsylvania (1749). Harvard, Yale and Dartmouth were Congregational; Princeton and Hampden-Sidney were Presbyterian; Columbia and William and Mary were Episcopal; Brown was

---

[3] Argentina copied the educational structure of the United States.

Baptist; Rutgers (Queen's) was Reformed; Dickinson was Methodist. Between 1782 and 1796, fourteen more colleges were established, but of these ten were non-sectarian. A new trend is clearly evident.

Below the colleges and sometimes integrated with them were the academies. These were modelled after similar schools in England which had been founded by the dissenters after the Act of Toleration made such institutions possible. Most of the academies in the thirteen colonies go back to the middle of the eighteenth century, although, as Boone says in his *History of Education in the United States*, the universities of Harvard, Yale, and William and Mary "were for many years not superior to the best classical schools of the English Dissenters."[4] In Fleet's *Pocket Almanac* for 1790, published in Boston, appears a list of the incorporated academies of learning in the state. Those mentioned are Dummer Academy at Newbury (1763); Phillips Academy at Andover (1778); Leicester Academy (1784); Derby School at Hingham (1784); another at Williamston in Berkshire County— apparently the present Williamstown—"which is yet in its infancy" (1785); a Grammar School at Ipswich (1765) and a similar school at Roxbury, incorporated 1789. The *Almanac* adds:

"These academies have very handsome funds and are flourishing. The designs of the trustees are to disseminate virtue and true piety, to promote the education of youth in the English, Latin, Greek and French languages, to encourage their instruction in writing, arithmetic, oratory, geography, practical geometry, logic, philosophy and such other of the arts and sciences as may be thought expedient. At these academies, as also at the Grammar Schools (which by law almost every town is obliged to provide) young Gentlemen are fitted for admission to the University."

The Massachusetts law of 1647, already referred to, provided that every town of fifty householders should appoint one within the town to teach

"all the children as shall resort to them to write and read; whose wages shall be paid, either by the parents or masters of such children, or by the inhabitants in general, by way of supply, as the major part of those who order the prudentials of the town shall appoint; provided that those who send their children be not oppressed by paying much more than they can have them taught for in the adjoining towns."

In addition, every town of one hundred householders was required to set up a grammar school, failing which they must pay the sum of five pounds per annum "to the next such town." This law remained in force until 1780. A somewhat similar law was passed in Connecticut in 1650 and continued in force, practically unchanged, until 1795.

---

[4] Boone, R. G., *Education in the United States* (New York: D. Appleton and Company, 1893), p. 71.

These laws in Massachusetts and Connecticut were unique, however, and not at all typical of the existing regulations relative to education throughout the colonies. Pioneer conditions, the pushing back of the frontier, the exigencies of existence, the presence of a large slave population—all were factors in the somewhat limited provision for education while, even in Rhode Island, where perhaps the theory of the complete separation of church and state was first articulated, education was not considered the responsibility of the state, but of the family.

Even after the Revolutionary War, the Constitution made no mention of education, although in the Ordinance of 1787, providing for the government of the territory of the United States northwest of the river Ohio, Article III declared that "religion, morality and knowledge being necessary to good government and the happiness of mankind, schools and the means of education shall forever be encouraged."[5] There was everywhere, however, a feeling that self-government and republican institutions could only succeed in proportion as the citizens were educated and intelligent. Thomas Jefferson had said: "The diffusion of light and education are the resources most to be relied on for ameliorating the condition, promoting the virtue, and advancing the happiness of man."

Secularization of education, therefore, went forward rapidly, as the colonies, now self-governing states, sought to build up inclusive state systems of education. Not only did the favored denominations relax their control of elementary schools in such states as Massachusetts and Connecticut, but as has already been pointed out, ten of the fourteen colleges established between 1782 and 1796 were non-sectarian. School funds were created by the setting aside of state lands, lotteries were utilized to secure money for schools and colleges, school districts were developed, and Free School societies, similar to one founded in New York City in 1805, sprang up in many places. Rates, fees and donations all provided the necessary funds, but church schools continued to receive state assistance. In 1825 a contest arose between the Bethel Baptist Church in New York City and the New York Free School Society, as a result of which the government withdrew financial aid from clerically conducted education, and in 1831, the law committee of the New York Board of Aldermen reported that the public school "ought . . . only to prepare a child for the ordinary business of life . . . [and] religious studies are not necessary to prepare the child for the mechanical or any other business." The issue thus became clearly defined between public and sectarian schools. Educational interest developed rapidly, and by 1840 the census returns indicated that there were 173 universities or colleges, with 16,233 students; 3,242 academies and private schools, with 164,159 students; 47,209 primary and

---

[5] When the State of Ohio prepared its constitution, this reference to religion and education received considerable modification.

common schools, with 1,845,244 students. Of the children in the common schools, it was reported that 468,264 were being taught at the "public charge" —a statement which clearly indicates the extent to which fees were collected even in 1840. It is also significant that the same census reported that of 6,439,699 *white* persons over 20 years of age, 549,693 could neither read nor write. Part of this may have been due to immigration, since in the decade 1831-1840, the number of immigrants admitted had been 599,125.

SOME CAUSES OF SECULARIZATION

The so-called American ideal of the public school is, therefore, only faintly foreshadowed in colonial days, and the transition from a religious to a secular emphasis was somewhat gradual. The main causes for such secularization would seem to be as follows:

(1) As new territory was opened up, settlers with various religious backgrounds poured into these areas. It seemed hopeless to provide schools along specifically denominational lines for these pioneers, when the denominations found it difficult enough to plant even churches for them. Moreover, Archbishop Hughes opposed the establishment of rural colonies of Catholics and apparently sought to keep the Catholic population close together where church institutions could be provided more efficiently and economically. It was an almost analogous situation in Canada, 1900-1910, that precipitated the union of three Protestant denominations in Canada,[6] while even today in Saskatchewan, where separate schools receive government support and the Roman Catholics constitute 25 per cent. of the population, only thirty-one separate or minority school districts out of a total of 4,878 are reported. Within Protestantism, the men on the frontier had to learn tolerance, and they could choose between non-sectarian schools or nothing.

(2) Even in 1775 the number of religious sects existing in the United States was quite large although many of the sects were small. At that time there were Congregationalists, Church of England, Baptists, Presbyterians, Lutherans, German Reformed, Dutch Reformed, Associate Reformed, Moravians, Methodists (quite small), Roman Catholics, Mennonites and Quakers.

The Protestant immigrants, coming from different parts of Europe, brought their distinctive labels with them and soon the Methodist circuit-riders and other missionaries reached many lonely souls unknown to the more established churches. Perhaps the most thoroughly organized ecclesiastical system in the United States in the eighteenth century—the Congregationalists—was torn asunder by theological difficulties which culminated in the Unitarian schism of 1815. The Church of England in the United States was left, after the Revolutionary War, in an anomalous condition,

---

[6] Silcox, C. E., *Church Union in Canada* (New York: Institute of Social and Religious Research, 1933).

for there were no bishops and hitherto supervision had been vested in the Bishop of London. That church had to develop an indigenous organization, secure the episcopate and become the Protestant Episcopal Church. Hence it was too much preoccupied with its own struggle for existence to stand on ٧ny prerogatives which it might otherwise have claimed. Consequently, the sects grew and had to be reckoned with; the secularization of common education was therefore inevitable.

(3) The temper of the people was increasingly against the recognition of a peculiar status for any particular church or churches. The Virginia Bill of Rights, 1776, had affirmed that "all men are equally entitled to the free exercise of religion, according to the dictates of conscience," while the first Amendment to the Constitution, passed December 15, 1791, stated that "Congress shall make no law respecting the establishment of religion, or prohibiting the free exercise thereof." The spirit of these pronouncements and mandates not alone reflected a certain latitudinarianism but also created it.

(4) In the early years of the expressed opposition of the Roman Catholic Church to the "public-school system," the leaders of that opposition repeatedly objected to the inclusion of any religious matter at all in the curriculum, any bible reading or prayers or hymns, even any references in the histories which might be interpreted as a reflection on their church. With the devastating logic characteristic of Latin thinkers, and always irritating to the pragmatic Anglo-Saxons, they insisted that if the schools were not to be under the direction of the churches but at the same time tax-supported, all material, conceivably religious, should be eliminated from the curriculum. However the Protestant population might differ among themselves in theological theory and in their deductions from the Scriptures, they were agreed that the Bible in itself ought to be familiar to every citizen as it was "the charter of their liberties." Even the Deists of the period felt that observances which made a child conscious of his responsibility to his Maker were a necessary part of education. Catholic opposition to anything that smacked of religious instruction, direct or indirect, while it did not wholly succeed in determining the quality of public-school instruction, did, however, inevitably point to secularizaton.

(5) Later, when the Jews arrived in large numbers, fresh problems arose in the schools as efforts were made to eliminate any "Christian" emphasis— even Christmas celebrations. The Jews withdrew their children from the schools at the time of Jewish festivals and often resented Christmas and Easter programs in the schools. In one town in the environment of New York, a rabbi visited the school for several days before Christmas in an effort to make sure that no references to Christmas or to its religious signifi-

cance were made. Such an attitude also tended to eliminate any possibilities of even indirect religious teaching.

(6) In more recent years, as at White Plains, N. Y., the effort to provide for the possible inclusion in the curriculum of optional courses in religious education aroused the Freethinkers' Organization to prevent what the law specifically permitted and what, presumably, the majority desired.

In these various ways, minorities tended to restrain the majority from developing the type of correlation between religion and education which it desired.

Rise of Catholic Parochial Schools

In the whole development of popular education in the United States, the major tension has been created by the Roman Catholic insistence on the right to administer their schools, coupled with an effort to secure public funds for them. In the early days of the controversy, the Jews sought in many cities to develop their own schools similar to the Catholic parochial schools, but such a policy was soon abandoned. In 1927, according to a study made by Dr. Harry S. Linfield, Jewish parochial schools were maintained in only three of the communities in the United States and there were but twelve of them altogether. Practically all the Jewish children were, therefore, sent to the public schools.

In general, the majority were inclined to let the Catholics have their own schools, but only on condition that they pay for them entirely themselves. The principle was steadily asserted that no public funds should be used for any "sectarian" instruction or for schools under sectarian control. The Catholics were unable, however, to provide schools for all their children, and some Catholic families were unwilling to send their children to such parochial schools as were available. Hence, the Catholics felt justified in leaving no stone unturned to prevent indirect religious influence being exerted on such of their numbers as were instructed in the public schools. Thus, while they were building up their own schools, they continued to watch the public schools for any breaches of the principle which would eliminate all religion from them.

In certain states, notably Oregon, a definite effort was made to do away with all private schools and to force all children into the public schools, and a law to that end was passed November 7, 1922; but the judges of the Federal Court for the district of Oregon, in a decision handed down March 31, 1924, declared that the state legislature had "exceeded the limitations of its power" and the law was thus found to be *ultra vires*. In the majority of states, however, the diversion of public funds to private schools, whether Catholic or non-Catholic, is specifically forbidden by the state constitutions. As a result, the Catholics must pay the entire cost of the education of such children as attend the parochial schools, while they also pay their share of the taxes to support the public schools which their children, for the most part, do not attend. There are a few Lutheran parochial schools, but their number is negligible. A detailed history of Catholic opposition to the general principle of "neutral" schools is therefore in order.

In the early days the number of Catholics in the United States was extremely limited, except around Baltimore, Detroit and New Orleans. The first Catholic church in Boston was founded in 1789, and the first such church in Connecticut was established at Hartford in 1829. Between 1790 and 1830, according to Father Shaughnessy's computation,[7] the Catholic population increased from 35,000 to approximately 318,000. Part of this increase may be attributed to the number of Catholics already living in the territories added to the republic at the time of the Louisiana purchase. Catholic immigration must, however, have accounted for at least 77,000 between 1790 and 1820, and for 54,000 between 1820 and 1830—a total of 131,000. Unfortunately, there are no definite immigration statistics prior to 1820, but between 1820 and 1830, 143,439 immigrants arrived, of whom Father Shaughnessy estimates that 54,000 were Catholics and of these 35,356 were Irish.[8] The Catholic Church was diligently seeking to secure the necessary organization to meet the needs of the new immigration, and in 1829—the very year of Catholic Emancipation in England—the first Provincial Council of Baltimore was held, which laid down the general lines of procedure and discipline. Among the decisions of that council were:

"Whereas very many youth of Catholic parents, especially among the poor, have been and still are, in many parts of this Province, exposed to great danger of losing their faith, and having their morals corrupted, from the want of proper teachers, to whom so important a trust can be safely confided; we judge it indispensably necessary to establish schools, in which youth may be nurtured in the principles of faith and morals, while they are instructed in literature. (XXXIV)

"Since not infrequently many things are found in the books which are generally used in the Schools, in which the principles of our faith are impugned, our dogmas falsely expounded, and history itself perverted, on account of which the minds of the young are imbued with errors, to the terrible loss of their souls; zeal for religion, as well as the proper education of youth and the honor itself of the American Union, demand that some remedy be provided for so great an evil. Therefore, we determine, that there shall be published for the use of Schools, as soon as possible, books entirely expurgated from errors and approved by the

---

[7] Shaughnessy, Gerald, *Has the Immigrant Kept the Faith?* (New York: Harper and Brothers, 1925).

[8] Father Shaughnessy estimates 82 per cent. of the total Irish population at the time as Catholic. There is reason to believe that the percentage of Irish who were Catholic and migrated to the United States may have been higher than 82 per cent. since the Irish Protestants in the period were more prone to migrate to Canada.

authority of the Bishops, and in which nothing may be contained which might produce enmity or hatred of the Catholic religion." (XXXV)

The Catholics thus sought to establish their own schools and to provide innocuous text-books, but apparently they continued to hope that, in this plastic period when the educational policy was not yet crystallized, some arrangement might be effected whereby the state would give their schools some share of financial assistance.

Meanwhile, in the 'thirties, more than two hundred thousand Irish had arrived in the United States, and nativist sentiment blended with anti-Catholicism was rising, stimulated in turn by the repercussions of the Oxford Movement in England. Within the Catholic Church, difficulties respecting the legal incorporation of Catholic churches were being fought out, while warm disputes arose between Irish, French and German Catholics. By 1840 the question of the relation of parochial schools to public funds was raging.

It was under such conditions that the fourth Provincial Council of Baltimore met in 1840. In dealing once again with the problem of education the Council declared:

"As it appears that the system of public instruction, in most of the Province, is so devised and administered as to encourage heresies and gradually and imperceptibly to fill the minds of Catholic youth with errors, we admonish pastors that, with the utmost zeal, they watch over the Christian and Catholic education of Catholic youth, and to take especial pains lest such youth use the Protestant version of the Scriptures, or recite the hymns and prayers of sectaries. It must therefore be carefully provided, that no books or exercises of this kind be introduced in the Public Schools, to the danger of faith and piety." (VI)

The Catholics were meanwhile organizing their own schools, sometimes receiving assistance from public funds despite the nativist sentiment (Know-Nothing movement) which raged until the Civil War gave the entire population something else to think about. After the Civil War, the issue came up again. Some school districts had evolved a plan of assistance to Catholic schools on the ground that they "relieved the public schools from a burden which otherwise such schools would have to bear." So much opposition to this procedure arose that in 1875 President Grant asked for an amendment to the federal constitution forbidding the practice. On this point Carl Zollman writes:

"The constitutional provision was defeated in the senate while the campaign of 1876 was in progress, but the principle advocated was gradually incorporated into the great majority of the State constitutions. Under it today such parochial schools as remain must rely wholly on the support of their own followers."[9]

---

[9] Zollman, Carl: "The Distinguishing Marks of the Modern State," in *Religious Education*, March, 1927.

PROVISIONS OF STATE CONSTITUTIONS

At the present time, there are constitutional provisions forbidding the use of any public funds for institutions which are neither free nor non-sectarian in all but eight states. These eight states are Arkansas, Iowa, Maine, Maryland, North Carolina, Rhode Island, Vermont and West Virginia.[10] Even in such states, however, public policy usually takes the place of a constitutional amendment, while New Hampshire has steadily refused to repeal the constitutional provision in its Bill of Rights, which, as amended in 1902, still empowers

"the several towns, parishes, bodies corporate or religious societies within this state to make adequate provision, at their own expense, for the support and maintenance of public Protestant teachers of piety, religion and morality."

This odd provision in the New Hampshire Bill of Rights may perhaps only be adequately understood by one thoroughly familiar with the legal position of Congregational ministers in New England. The net result of this controversy was, as we all know, to establish a definite breach between the public-school system and the parochial school system, and to provide a situation which is still a source of discontent and a bone of contention.

COMPULSORY PUBLIC EDUCATION AND CHURCH REQUIREMENTS

Education in the United States is compulsory. Every state has laws to this effect, although the constitution of Kentucky, Section 5, declares that "no man shall be compelled to send his child to any school to which he may be conscientiously opposed." This provision does not seem to relieve him of the necessity of finding some school to which he is not conscientiously opposed and to which he may, therefore, send his children. Of course, most of the states admit certain exemptions to the general requirements of school attendance.[11] A Catholic is, therefore, under obligation to send his child to school, but he immediately runs into the legislation of his faith which he cannot ignore without incurring spiritual penalties.

CATHOLIC CHURCH EDUCATIONAL POLICY AND LAW

Roman Catholic legislation and the interpretation thereof may be found in a number of official documents listed or quoted below.

(1) *The Code of Canon Law:* The following citations are taken from the

[10] Excellent summaries of the present state laws governing private schools, and of recent legal decisions in regard to education, may be found in two Education Bulletins, issued by the National Catholic Welfare Conference, Bureau of Education, 1312 Massachusetts Avenue, N. W., Washington, D. C., *Bulletin* No. 2 (1926) and No. 4 (1928).

[11] See *Bulletin*, 1928, No. 28, quoted above, for full information regarding "Laws Relating to Compulsory Education in the United States."

digest of the new canon law prepared by Father Woywood (New York: Joseph F. Wanger, Ltd. 1929), Seventh Edition.

Canon 1113: "The parents are bound by a most serious obligation to provide to the best of their ability for the religious and moral, as well as the physical and civil education of their children, and to care for their temporal well-being."

Canon 1372: "Catholic children are to be educated in schools where not only nothing contrary to Catholic faith and morals is taught, but rather in schools where religious and moral training occupy the first place. Not only the parents, as mentioned in Canon 1113, but also all those who take their place, have the right, and the most serious obligation of caring for the Christian education of the children."

Canon 1373: "In every elementary school, the children, must, according to their age, be instructed in Christian doctrine. The young people who attend the higher schools are to receive a deeper religious knowledge, and the bishops shall appoint priests qualified for such work by their learning and piety."

Canon 1374: "Catholic children shall not attend non-Catholic, indifferent schools that are mixed, that is to say, schools open to Catholics and non-Catholics alike. The bishop of the diocese only has the right, in harmony with the instructions of the Holy See, to decide under what circumstances, and with what safeguards, to prevent loss of faith, it may be tolerated that Catholic children go to such schools."

Canon 1375: "The Church has the right to establish elementary schools as well as any kind of schools."

Canon 1379: "If there are no Catholic elementary, or mediate schools, spoken of in Canon 1373, the Ordinary should take care to have them established. Likewise if the public Universities are not imbued with the Catholic doctrine or spirit, it is to be desired that in the nation or province a Catholic University be erected. The Catholics should not refuse to contribute according to their means towards the building and maintenance of Catholic schools."

Canon 1381: "The religious teaching of youth in any schools is subject to the authority and inspection of the Church. The local ordinaries have the right and duty to watch that nothing is taught contrary to faith and good morals in any of the schools of the territory. They, moreover, have the right to approve the books of Christian doctrine and the teachers of religion, and to demand, for the safeguarding of religion and morals, the removal of teachers and books."

Canon 1382: "Ordinaries have the right, either in person or through others, to visit in reference to religious and moral instruction, any schools, oratories, summer schools, etc., and from this visitation the schools conducted by a religious community are not excepted unless it is a school exclusively for the professed members of an exempt order."

(2) *Decisions of the Plenary Councils of Baltimore:* Plenary (not provincial only) councils of Baltimore were held in 1852, 1866 and 1884. A

résumé of the decisions of these councils may be found in the *Catholic Encyclopaedia.* The first Plenary Council ordered that pastors themselves should teach Christian doctrine to the young and ignorant, while bishops were exhorted to have a Catholic school in every parish and to pay the teachers from parochial funds. The second council ordered that teachers belonging to religious congregations should be employed whenever possible in Catholic schools, which should be erected in every parish. Catechism classes were to be instituted in all churches for such children as were taught in the public schools. Industrial schools or reformatories, especially in large cities, were advised, and the desire was expressed that there should be a Catholic University in the United States. The third council reiterated the necessity of establishing schools and charged parents to send their children to such schools, unless the bishop should judge the reasons for sending them elsewhere to be sufficient. The wish was also expressed that the parochial schools should be free, and supplemented by suitable schools of higher education for Catholic youth.[12]

(3) *Instructions of the Holy Office to the Bishops of the American Church, November 24, 1875:* In reply to certain questions propounded by the American bishops, the Holy Office made an elaborate reply which probably determined certain new emphases in the findings of the third plenary council. Perhaps, the most striking part of this reply is the conclusion:

"Likewise, if any parents neglect to provide this necessary Christian training and education for their children, or permit them to attend schools in which the ruin of their souls cannot be avoided; or if, when a suitable Catholic school is located in the place, well-built and equipped, or an opportunity is provided for them to educate their children along Catholic lines in some other district, they send their children, despite all this, to the public schools without adequate reason and without those necessary precautions which might remove the danger of the perversion of their faith, then, if they continue to do so defiantly, *they can not, in accordance with the clear teaching of Catholicism, receive absolution in the sacrament of Holy Penance."* (Editor's italics.)

This ruling, therefore, gave large spiritual powers to the bishop of a diocese, and while it was enforced with more or less severity in the various dioceses, it did place the Catholic who wished to send his child to the public school in a difficult situation.

(4) *The Encyclical Letter, "Immortale Dei," November 1, 1865, issued by Pope Leo XIII, and dealing with the Christian Constitution of States:* A translation of this encyclical constitutes the preface to the volume on

---

[12] For Canada, somewhat similar decisions, *mutatis mutandis,* were handed down by the Plenary Council of Quebec, 1909. See *Acta et Decreta Concilii Plenarii Quebecensis Primi* (Quebec. L'Action Sociale, Ltd., 1912), pp. 252-275.

The State and the Church, prepared by Fathers Ryan and Millar.[13] While it does not deal so specifically with the question of education, it is fundamental to an appreciation of the Catholic attitude in regard to the inherent limitations in the authority of the State.

(5) *The Encyclical Letter, "On the Christian Education of Youth," December 31, 1929, issued by Pope Pius XI:* The complete text of this important letter, translated, may be obtained from the National Catholic Welfare Conference. Important sections dealing with the relative position of the church and state in matters of education follow:

"In the first place, it pertains to the State, in view of the common good, to promote in various ways the education and instruction of youth. It should begin by encouraging and assisting, of its own accord, the initiative and activity of the Church and the family, whose successes in this field have been clearly demonstrated by history and experience. It should, moreover, supplement their work whenever this falls short of what is necessary, even by means of its own schools and institutions. For the State more than any other Society is provided with the means put at its disposal for the needs of all, and it is only right that it use these means to the advantage of those who have contributed them.

"Over and above this, the State can exact, and take measures to secure that all its citizens have the necessary knowledge of their civic and political duties, and a certain degree of physical, intellectual and moral culture, which, considering the conditions of our times, is really necessary for the common good.

"However, it is clear that in all these ways of promoting education and instruction, both public and private, the State should respect the inherent rights of the Church and of the family concerning Christian education, and moreover have regard for distributive justice. Accordingly, unjust and unlawful is any monopoly, educational or scholastic, which, physically or morally, forces families to make use of government schools, contrary to the dictates of their Christian conscience, or contrary even to their legitimate preferences. . . .

". . . It follows that the so-called 'neutral' or 'lay' school, from which religion is excluded, is contrary to the fundamental principles of education. Such a school cannot exist in practice; it is bound to become irreligious. There is no need to repeat what Our Predecessors have declared on this point, especially Pius IX and Leo XIII, at times when laicism was beginning in a special manner to infest the public school. We renew and confirm their declarations as well as the Sacred Canons in which the frequenting of non-Catholic schools, whether neutral or mixed, those namely which are open to Catholics and non-Catholics alike, is forbidden for Catholic children, and can be at the most tolerated, on the approval of the Ordinary alone, under determined circumstances of place and time, and with special precautions. Neither can Catholics admit that other type of mixed school (least of all the so-called 'école unique', obligatory on all) in which the students are provided with separate religious instruction, but receive other lessons in common with non-Catholic pupils from non-Catholic teachers."

---

[13] The Macmillan Company, 1924.

The concluding sentence in the last paragraph just quoted must be kept in mind when the problem of weekday religious instruction on "released time" is considered.

ATTEMPTS OF CHURCH IN CATHOLIC COUNTRIES TO MONOPOLIZE EDUCATION

In the light of such official pronouncements, legislation and instructions, what could Catholics do but build up their own school system unless they were prepared to renounce their faith? This, they have done at great sacrifice, even though the disability to which they have been subjected is due, essentially, not to the action of the state but to the inner limitations of their faith. The public schools were open to them, but they were not "open" to the public schools. The distinction must be kept in mind. Further, while in some instances, as in Oregon, efforts were made to force them into the public-school system, these efforts have been frustrated, and their conscientious scruples have been respected, even though it has been insisted that those minorities who have conscientious scruples be willing to pay for them.

Catholics have been permitted to build up their own schools in Protestant America, while in certain Catholic countries a similar liberty has been bitterly fought by the Catholics. Thus, in 1929 (June 22), President Leguia, of Peru, issued a decree which stated that "although the constitution guarantees liberty of worship, this should not be carried on in such a way that the schools are converted into centers of sectarian propaganda, opposed to the religion which the nation professes," and ordered that in all educational establishments, "public as well as private," no doctrines may be taught which in any sense are opposed to "the religion of the State" and that in all such schools "moral and religious instruction should be given." Any private school which violated this rule would be closed. Such a law would, had it been put into operation, have closed all the Protestant mission schools in the country unless they had been willing to admit Catholic authorities to provide the moral and spiritual instruction. Only strong representations to the government nullified the result of such a decree. While North American Catholics can hardly be held responsible for the intransigence of their co-religionists in Latin America, there are many aspects to the whole question of religious liberty.

THE CATHOLIC SCHOOL SYSTEM IN AMERICA

Nevertheless, the effort of Catholics to build up their own school system in the United States, supported only by the free-will offerings of poor people who were for the most part but recently arrived in the country, deserves admiration. The Directory of Catholic Colleges and Schools for 1932-33 indicated that there were 2,123 secondary Catholic schools in the country, with a total enrolment of 241,869, and 7,923 elementary schools with an enrolment of 2,222,598.

TYPES OF LIMITED ASSISTANCE GIVEN FROM PUBLIC FUNDS

For the most part, this imposing educational structure has been raised with no help from public funds at all, either those which might have been contributed by State Departments of Education or those made available from local taxation. The few exceptions to this general rule are inconsiderable and would. seem to be as follows:

(a) In some rural areas, e.g., Iowa, Kentucky, etc., where the whole community is practically Catholic, the church has built a school, rented it to the district trustees, and then it has been operated practically as a Catholic parochial school, the district trustees maintaining it out of local taxes.

(b) In certain institutions such as homes and orphanages, the local Board of Education has felt itself justified in contributing to the maintenance of schools for the children in such orphanages, especially as frequently the counties were paying a *per capita* grant for the care of such children.

(c) In certain municipalities, where the parochial schools were unable to furnish manual training, arrangements have been made whereby the students in the parochial schools are permitted to attend the public schools where manual training was given to them twice a week, while they continued to receive the rest of their training in their own schools.

(d) Parochial schools have, of course, been able to avail themselves of the services of local Departments of Health, operating under mandates which govern health as well as education.

(e) Some municipalities and states, as indicated later, have made provision for the transportation of parochial school children in public-school busses, or for supplying free text-books to students in the parochial schools.

COST OF MAINTAINING CATHOLIC SCHOOLS

Outside of these exceptions, the Catholics have borne the entire financial burden of their system themselves. They have only been able to do this because of the sacrificial devotion of the teaching sisterhoods who accept a mere pittance—often no more than $25 a month *per sister*. They have dedicated their lives wholly to the instruction of Catholic youth. Because there is no common accounting within the parochial school system and no reports are required concerning the financing of such schools as distinguished from other forms of parochial expenditure, it is impossible to indicate with any degree of assurance what the Catholic Church actually expends each year in elementary education. The per capita expense in the institutions which have been studied carefully has varied quite widely—occasionally being as low as $25, but sometimes running into quite high figures. As there are nearly two and a half million pupils in Catholic elementary and secondary schools, it might be fair to estimate the annual aggregate cost of these schools at over $100,000,000. As we shall point out in another part of this report, it is necessary to remember this large expenditure on the part of Catholics, voluntarily contracted, when Catholic givings to the Community Chest are spoken of in a disparaging way, or praise is given to the generosity of the Jews, or to the contributions of the Protestants to philanthropy, foreign missions and higher education. The statistics of the United States Bureau of Education indicate that the per capita expense of public-school education in the United States is approximately $100. Hence, whatever the parochial schools actually cost Catholics, they do probably save the taxpayers of the nation no less than $200,000,000 a year, for should their schools be given up and their children suddenly thrown back into the public school system, new schools would have to be built, new teachers employed and new equipment purchased to take care of this unusual demand. Of course, in many instances the public school system as at present equipped would probably be quite able to accommodate the parochial school pupils, should parochial schools be for any reason discontinued. Nevertheless, it is doubtful if in the larger cities the public schools could add to their present load without making provision for new schools and new teachers.

EXEMPTION FROM TAXATION

Not only do they receive no help, but at least in one state, California, only colleges, and not parochial schools, are exempt from taxation. The Constitution of California provides:

"Any educational institution of collegiate grade, within the State of California, not conducted for profit, shall hold exempt from taxation its buildings and equipment, its ground within which its buildings are located, not exceeding one hundred acres in area, its securities, and income used exclusively for the purposes of education."

The fiftieth regular session of the Legislature of the State of California (1932) sought to amend this section by adding:

"Any private educational institution of less than collegiate grade, within the State of California, not conducted for profit, shall hold exempt from taxation its buildings and equipment, its grounds within which its buildings are located, not exceeding ten acres in area, its securities and income used exclusively for the purposes of education."

This amendment to the constitution passed the senate by a vote of 34 to 2, and then went before the people at the state election on June 27, 1933. The vote was taken on what was called "Proposition Four," but the proposition was defeated 518,374 to 772,043. Los Angeles was somewhat more favorable to the proposition than San Francisco, and among the possible reasons for this were: (1) In Los Angeles, the Catholics did not campaign so much for the proposition, in that way arousing Protestant suspicions. (2) There were more Protestant private schools in Southern California than in the San Francisco region. (3) The Protestants were preponderant in Los Angeles and hence inclined to be more generous—at least such was the case with the moderates.

The economic factor, the central principle of the separation of Church and State and the need of safeguarding the neutrality of the public school were the dominant arguments used by the Protestant opposition. In the case of some Masons in San Francisco the long-time policy of opposition to Catholic "attacks on the public-school system" seems to have been operative, whereas in Los Angeles this element seems to have played a negligible part. At all events, the proposition was defeated and bitterness left behind. Perhaps, the attitude of many moderate Protestants who opposed the Proposition might be summarized in the following statement from a prominent Protestant ecclesiastic:

"I am, in the first place, somewhat doubtful about the whole system of exemptions. I am not sure that if I had been actively concerned at the time that the exemption of church property came up I would have been prepared to support the project. Churches are of course somewhat different from educational institutions for the state cannot provide us with them and it can provide us with schools. Nevertheless, I am inclined to believe that the church is in a better position if it takes no favors whatever from the state.

"But while I still have perhaps some doubts as to my position in regard to churches, I do feel quite definitely certain in regard to educational institutions. . . . I am not saying that such exemptions are un-American or thinking in terms of any silly slogans of that kind. My position is quite simple. It is that the state provides public education from the earliest grades through the university and that if any people for school or religious or any other reasons do not wish to use the state schools, it is their responsibility, and the state or other citizens of the state ought not to be asked to contribute. I feel quite as strongly as you do the importance of religion as a necessary element in education. Our public-school system is definitely handicapped because through our manifold divisions we cannot have religious teaching included in its work. But the way out appears to me to be clearly the way which we have attempted several times to get through the legislature, namely, the released time system. My understanding of that project is that it does not necessarily include the giving of credits except in relation to time. But along some such line it seems to me we must work it out, for any system whereby appropriations were given to religious bodies for schools would lead to a situation quite perilous to the unity of our national life. Tax exemption is not appropriation, but the principle to which I have referred is involved in both plans."

The Catholics consider that they consequently have a grievance, and that the state should come to the assistance of their parochial school system, especially as they claim to be saving the American taxpayers no less than $250,000,000 a year. There does not seem to be, however, any disposition on the part of the majority to remove the grievance. The existing constitutional provisions stand in the way of such assistance in the great majority of states, and on this matter of public policy the majority has a very definite mind-set. Then, too, there is a fear that, if any exception to the rule of "no public funds for sectarian institutions" is made, it will prove the thin edge of the wedge and the Catholics will thereupon press for something else. It is useless to deny a fundamental distrust, on the part of the Protestants, of any compromise scheme that would satisfy Catholic aspirations. An expression was frequently used to those engaged in this study—"the Catholics are so grabby." On the other hand, detailed situations such as the following require further consideration:

(1) In one state, the state government made, in 1933, a per capita grant of $6 to each county, based on the number of children of school-going age in the county. Every year an officer of the county makes his census and includes Catholic children in the census; he then goes to the capital of the state and gets his grant for the county, but none of the money goes to the education of the Catholic children; it all goes to the aid of the public-school system.

(2) In several states the parochial school authorities have applied to the municipal board of education with the request that their children might be conveyed to school in the same busses used to transport public-school children. The State of Illinois passed a law, June 30, 1933, which became law after the legislature had adjourned without the signature thereto of the Governor. This law provided:

"In case children who attend any school other than a public school reside on or along the highway constituting the regular route of any public school bus or conveyance provided by any school district for transporting pupils to and from the public schools, the board of directors or board of education of such district shall afford transportation, without extra charge, for such children from their homes, or from some points on the regular route nearest or most easily accessible to their homes to such school, other than a public school, or to the point on such a regular route which is nearest or most easily accessible to such school."

A similar effort was made in Maryland where, however, the State Board of Education ruled that this was not a proper use of State funds. It should be pointed out in this connection that there is no provision in the constitution of the State of Maryland against the grant of public funds to sectarian institutions, and as a matter of fact, such grants are being made, although a movement under the League of Women Voters is seeking to effect the gradual elimination of all such aid to sectarian institutions.

(3) Again, in some states an effort has been made to secure for parochial school students the privileges of free text-books which are given to public-school students. The legislature of Louisiana passed a law to this effect, and an appeal was taken against the law on the ground that it contravened Article XII, section 13, of the state constitution: "No public funds shall be used for the support of any private or sectarian school." The Supreme Court of Louisiana, and later the Supreme Court of the United States decided, however, that such legislation was not unconstitutional, since it was not necessary to assume that aid to a pupil to enable him to prosecute his studies was, *ipso facto,* aid to the institution which he attended.

There would, therefore, seem to be no reason why other states which wished to provide free text-books to students in parochial schools as well as to public-school students might not provide the empowering legislation, unless the phrasing of their constitutions forbade such grants in terms more definite than those in the Louisiana constitution.

Slight measures such as these, taken in recent years by states with con-stitutional provisions against the use of public funds for sectarian institu-tions, may indicate, perhaps, a greater readiness to distinguish between the responsibility of the state to see that children are educated and an insistence that the state should further only such schools as it directly creates. Perhaps in no area of human activity is standardization less desirable than in edu-cation, but every measure to deflect state funds for education from the "public-school system" brings not alone great opposition, but also a feeling on the part of many that the ultimate goal of such measures is the destruc-tion of the public school. On the other hand, the Catholics feel that their schools should receive aid, especially if (a) the state was satisfied with the educational standards of the parochial schools. (*Per contra,* if the state is not satisfied, why should it permit the teachers to teach or the students to attend?); (b) the parochial schools were free (i.e., no fees were charged) and not run for profit or for "social exclusiveness." (If they can provide a training which fully measures up to the standards insisted upon by state authorities, and at a much lower *per capita* cost, why should they not receive state assistance in doing so?)

On the other hand, the opponents of state aid to parochial schools are quite sure that any concession that may be granted will be but the signal for new demands, until the public-school system will be hopelessly divided into two or more parts, and communities now struggling to maintain high standards in one school will be confronted with the necessity of dividing

their slender resources between two schools, neither of which will probably measure up to the possibilities of a single and unified school. The
whole situation abounds in difficulties, especially in the smaller places.

ARGUMENTS AGAINST PAROCHIAL SCHOOLS

Some of the more common arguments directed against parochial schools
may be briefly stated:

(1) *They are poorly equipped in comparison with the public schools:* So
far as the elementary schools are concerned, there may be some truth in
this charge, for the parochial schools have not had the money to spend that
the public schools have had. There are also marked differences between
parochial schools in poor parishes where the need is often greatest, and in
the richer parishes where there are frequently not so many children. It
must, however, be pointed out that in a great many of the Catholic schools,
excellent equipment with the most modern devices has been provided, and
at great sacrifice on the part of the parish.

(2) *The quality of their teaching is challenged:* This is gratuitous. As
there is frequently no check-up in states on the qualifications of teachers
in private schools, a statement of this character is based largely on opinion,
rather than on fact. It may well have been that at an earlier time, the
teachers were not always well-trained, but perhaps much the same might be
said for the public schools. Moreover, in certain states, e.g., Alabama,
Michigan, Nebraska and South Dakota, teachers in private schools must
be certificated the same as in public schools.

The most careful study of this aspect of the problem has been made by
the Rev. Sylvanus Schmitz, O.S.B., in 1926, and is available in print.[14]
Father Schmitz analyzed the training of the teachers in fifty religious communities, or to be accurate, of 10,666 teachers in the parochial schools. On
this data, he concluded:

"One fourth of all Religious teachers have had four years of advanced training.
This is more than 10 per cent. higher than the corresponding figures for the
public-school teachers in thirty-six states. . . . 57.2 per cent. of all Religious
teachers have had at least two years of higher training as compared with 50.6
per cent. of the public-school teachers. Of the thirty-six communities listed,
19, or slightly more than half, show a standard of teacher preparation whereby
50 per cent. of their teachers or better have had at least two years of training
beyond high school. As regards the public-school teachers, only 17 of the thirty-
six states have attained such a standard. . . . 17.4 per cent. of the Religious
teachers have had no training beyond the high school and more than one fifth
(20.1 per cent.) have had only partial high-school training. The corresponding

---

[14] *The Adjustment of Teacher Training to Modern Educational Needs* (Atchison, Kan.:
The Abbey Student Press, 1927).

figures for the public-school teachers in thirty-six states are 20.1 and 9.6 per cent. respectively. In the case of the Religious teachers, the proportion of teachers with only partial high-school training is appalling. One out of every five teachers employed in the Catholic schools has not had the equivalent of a complete secondary education. . . . Nine communities are chiefly responsible for this state of affairs. These nine communities include 1,424 or 66.3 per cent. of all Religious teachers so poorly prepared."

While this survey by Father Schmitz did not include more than a cross-section of parochial school religious teachers, it would seem to be a real cross-section, and the conclusions indicate that the better trained religious teachers are slightly more numerous, comparatively speaking, than the better trained teachers in the public schools; that the public-school teachers with only high-school training are slightly more numerous than the religious teachers with only high-school training; but that the religious teachers with only partial high-school training are more numerous than public-school teachers with only partial high-school training.

In recent years, the religious teachers have been most assiduous in their efforts to secure better and more thorough preparations. They haunt the summer schools both of religious normal schools and of secular universities. With a devotion that sometimes threatens to imperil their health they are seeking to take advantage of any possible opportunity to make themselves worthy of their vocation. Specialists in pedagogy who have opportunity of comparing the work of the sisters with that of lay teachers, speak highly of their efforts and especially of their quiet manners and courtesy which make them very effective in the class-room. If such assiduity and such single-mindedness of purpose are continued, it would seem almost inevitable that within a few years the training of teachers in the religious schools, considered purely from the point of view of professional attainment, will not be surpassed in the country.

(3) *The product of the parochial school is inferior:* This, again, is gratuitous. If there is one outstanding need in a research of this character, it is in a comparison of the achievements of public and parochial school pupils. Some efforts along these lines have been made in Pittsburgh and in Minnesota, and also in Chicago (referred to later), but the data to date are hardly sufficient to use as a basis for a sound judgment.[15] Superintendents of public schools interviewed in the course of this study have been reticent to express an opinion on this aspect of the subject. They admit quite generally that children trained in parochial elementary schools and later enrolled in public high schools are quite able to hold their own. In some respects, they seem

---

[15] See O'Connell, E. L., "1932 Diocesan Survey in Arithmetic: Grades Four, Five and Six," published by the Diocese of Pittsburgh (Multigraphed), and Koos, Leonard V., *Private and Public Secondary Education* (University of Chicago Press, 1931).

to show a high degree of efficiency.[16] In the various spelling-bees conducted under federal auspices, Catholic pupils have almost invariably walked off with the prizes. In all these studies, however, there is one fact which needs to be kept in mind; it is not sufficient to judge a school merely on attainment, it must also be judged on achievement. It is one thing to take a group of children who have had the advantages of the culture gained from the long residence of their parents in this country and lift that group to a still higher level of intellectual power; it is quite another to lift a group of children of recent immigrés to the same level of intellectual achievement, and the latter has been the challenging task of the parochial schools, to a rather remarkable degree.

Or, if we consider the comparison in terms of moral achievement, there is once again no adequate basis on which to make claims one way or the other. In a good many cities studied, the Catholics do seem to furnish more than their share of juvenile delinquents, but it is not always clear whether such delinquents were trained in the public schools or in the parochial schools. Even if it could be proved that parochial schools supplied more than their quota of delinquency, it is generally recognized that juvenile delinquency is in large measure due to the social and economic conditions of the children and families affected, and to the clash between the cultural level of the parents and the confusing cultural emphases of the new world into which the family of the immigré has come.

Perhaps, it is fair to assert at this point that some public-school administrators believe that the most unruly cases are often dropped by the parochial schools in midterm and have to be absorbed by the public schools where a more rigorous discipline may be enforced. In one city, especially, the public-school administration complained somewhat vehemently on this score.

(4) *There is too much time given to religion in the parochial schools:* If we take the Catholic parochial schools of Chicago as a basis, we find in their printed reports that in a total week of 1,500 minutes instruction, 150 minutes are devoted to Religion, Christian Doctrine, the Bible or Church History. This means an average of thirty minutes a day. Whether that is too much or too little depends entirely upon the point of view. If deemed important, the amount of time does not seem too demanding, provided that real teaching is done during the time.

On the other hand, it must be stated that in certain of the parochial schools, the students themselves do not always see the importance or value of much of the religious instruction. Thus, in one diocese, a questionnaire survey of 5,552 students brought out the following facts:

[16] One superintendent commented on racial characteristics in learning. He had found the Greeks most astute in arithmetic; some of them, he claimed, were almost uncanny in their powers of computation.

75, or 1.6% indicated the study of religion as something that would help in future work.

99, or 1.8% indicated that religion was the study they liked best.

6, or 0.1% indicated that religion was the study they liked least.

142, or 2.6% indicated that religion was the study they considered most beneficial.

20, or 0.4% indicated that religion was the study they considered least beneficial.

From which, one may draw a variety of conclusions.

(5) *Education, under authoritarian influences, is not the best for life in a democracy:* Such criticism opens the way, of course, to a philosophical discussion of primary significance such as the eminent German pedagogue, Friedrich W. Foerster, has treated in his volume "Autorité et Liberté."[17] Such a discussion, in so far as it deals with Catholic theory and practice, might well take into consideration the words of Pope Pius XI in his encyclical on "Christian Education of Youth" and an excerpt from the annual school report of the Diocese of Cleveland, 1931-32. In his encyclical letter (1929) the Pope said:

"Every form of pedagogic naturalism which in any way excludes or weakens supernatural Christian formation in the teaching of youth, is false. Every method of education founded, wholly or in part, on the denial or forgetfulness of original sin and of grace, and relying on the sole powers of human nature, is unsound. Such, generally speaking, are those modern systems bearing various names which appeal to a pretended self-government and unrestrained freedom on the part of the child, and which diminish or even suppress the teacher's authority and action, attributing to the child an exclusive primacy of initiative, and an activity independent of any higher law, natural or divine, in the work of his education.

"If any of these forms are used, less properly, to denote the necessity of a gradually more active coöperation on the part of the pupil in his own education; if the intention is to banish from education despotism and violence, which, by the way, just punishment is not, this would be correct, but in no way new. It would mean only what has been taught and reduced to practice by the Church in traditional Christian education, in imitation of the method employed by God Himself towards His creatures, of whom He demands active coöperation to the nature of each; for His Wisdom 'reacheth from end to end mightily and ordereth all things sweetly'."

In the annual school report of the Diocese of Cleveland (1931-32) we read:

"The principle of free-activity received a powerful impetus this year. Two factors especially had operated heretofore to prevent this principle being carried

---

[17] The French translation of this book is published by Edwin Frankfurter, Grand Chene, 12, Lausanne, Switzerland.

into practice. The first was the feeling that the function of the school is primarily to give pupils the traditional intellectual heritage rather than to guide their natural development. The second has been the fear on the part of teachers, that children, when not kept under close discipline, tend to indulge in wild disorder. "Both these objections lost considerable force during the past year. Teachers found it imperative to watch closely over the health of their charges and to take time out of the school day for this work. The teachers thus became more interested in watching the children develop than in ascertaining that they had covered any assignment of subject matter strictly according to the letter of the law.

"Then, too, after a teacher has opened her day by serving breakfast to a number of children in her class; after she has made arrangements for the noonday meal; after she has spent hours in the evening gathering and repairing clothing for the poor—she is no longer able to maintain towards her class the attitude of a disciplinarian. She has assumed the rôle of a parent.

"All this has reacted likewise upon the children. They have become freer in their class-room manner. They work at problems which have more vital connection with the life around them. Lacking text-books at times, they have learned to turn more to the actual world. They feel that they are not performing tasks set by an impersonal agency, but that they are learning things closely connected with problems of their own life. Engaged in work which has for them a real life interest, there is not much temptation to indulge in sheer disorder and noise, always the characteristic of an unintelligently and unsympathetically conducted classroom.

"In the schools as they are now developing, discipline is simply a non-existent matter."

(6) *The parochial school is divisive:* The criticism is repeatedly advanced that the larger interests of national unity require that all the children be trained in one system, while segregation fosters undesirable attitudes on the part of the segregated and non-segregated alike. Playing and studying together, it is urged, will break through the superiority complexes, prejudices and bigotries which, if allowed to develop, lay their devastating hand upon adult attitudes in later life. Donald Young, in his *American Minority Peoples* (1932) says:

"Voluntary educational segregation may become a serious threat only when it takes the place of the public-school system instead of supplementing it, and then inculcates ideals and standards at variance with those of the community. To the extent to which the Roman Catholic parochial school system supplants the public-school system and teaches cultural elements foreign and antagonistic to those of the United States as a whole, it delays the assimilation of Irish, Italian and other immigrants of that faith, and increases group conflict. In numerous children the parochial school tends to preserve old-world attitudes not altogether in harmony with American cultural patterns. In theory, at least, teaching is controlled from the Vatican and by church officials, the overwhelming majority of whom were reared in Latin cultures. This is of course offset by a teaching personnel of

American background, but it is difficult to see how a conflict of cultures and strained race relations can be avoided under such conditions."

Such a suspicion was probably justified prior to the war, when many of the parochial schools for the foreign-born, especially the Poles, were taught by foreign-born teachers, not a few of whom were even deficient in the English language. Today, however, the bishops are generally most insistent on the predominant use of English, while twenty-nine states specifically state in their school legislation that English shall be the language of instruction. Further, to quote one of the Catholic bishops, they are themselves "ironing out" the whole question of the national churches and national parishes. At the same time, many argue that a sort of purgatorial school standing betwixt the culture from which the immigrant has come and that to which he has gone, may make a special contribution to the sound development of his personality. Thus, in the same Annual School Report for the Diocese of Cleveland (1931-32), already quoted, we read that certain foreign languages are to be taught in the seventh and eighth grades.[18] The report reads:

"The foreign language program of the elementary schools will include not only Latin, French and German, but also any other modern inflected languages which are the vernacular of the ancestors of sufficiently large groups of our children. While these languages have not so universal an appeal as have the languages commonly selected for high-school study, yet they have more significance for certain groups of our children, since there is already existing a fair foundation on which to build.

"But the great purpose to be served is the ennobling of these languages, and the cultures and the peoples for which they stand in the minds of the children whose immediate ancestors used these tongues as vernacular. Due to a variety of circumstances, children of origin other than English, have been given a type of education which is not closely enough suited to their psychological needs. The contributions of the later immigrants and colonists have not been recognized. . . . All this has resulted in building up in many of our children a national or racial inferiority complex which is responsible for so many failures in later life, which produces a feeling of aversion or contempt for their ancestry, which drives them either to fling off whatever may remind them of their origin, or to accept defeat and fall back on a truculent 'nationalism.' . . . After all, the function of education is to minister to the needs of the children. Where these needs are different, different subjects must be offered. Every child not only has the right to, but the need of, a full and sympathetic knowledge of his origin, if only that his place in the universe and his reason for existence can be offered without variation to children of varying origins. Along with the core of established subjects applicable to all our children, in so far as they are Catholic and American, there

---

[18] The laws of Ohio forbid the instruction in any language but English in the first seven grades.

should be varying offerings of subjects and materials (mainly in the social sciences) which shall make a child feel proud of what his ancestral race has contributed to civilization."

If the parochial schools attempt such a program on a large scale, they stand a good chance of leading the way in a type of education, somewhat variant from the public-school training, which has long been needed. Incidentally, the pedagogical principles set forth in this report indicate that in some ways the parochial school may have a rôle in actual Americanization even greater than that which the public school itself can perform.

So far as the principle of segregation itself is involved, it need hardly be pointed out that in the section of the country which is overwhelmingly Protestant, the principle of the segregation of races is carried out—perhaps ruthlessly—within the public-school system, colored children not being allowed to attend white schools.

Whether segregation means the perpetuation of group conflict depends, perhaps, less upon the fact of segregation than upon the conditions of fairness or unfairness which gather around it; and upon the spirit in which the segregators and the segregated look upon their respective tasks and responsibilities. It may be an additional force making for intolerance, mutual ignorance and suspicion; on the other hand, people sometimes get on better, the more they are kept apart. Generally speaking, in any plan of segregation, the minority group may in the end suffer more than the majority, for social prejudices and social groupings enter far more than is commonly thought into all forms of social and industrial life in the after years. For instance, as will be pointed out later, the graduate of a Catholic college has probably less chance of acquiring the position he seeks than the graduate of a larger non-sectarian university.

INNER PROBLEMS OF PAROCHIAL SCHOOLS

While it is hardly within the province of this report to consider in detail certain problems of administration that arise in the parochial school system, it is perhaps not unfitting to indicate some of the problems inasmuch as they may have an indirect bearing on the relationship of that system to the public schools. It is hardly necessary to add, however, that the public-school system has perhaps quite as many problems of its own.

(a) The immediate relation of the parochial school to the parish creates special problems in a nomadic age. Sometimes the burden of support is unequally divided, the poor parish having the largest number of children while the rich, suburban parish may have a relatively small number. On the other hand, the poor parish frequently inherits a building already completed and paid for, while the suburban parish has a new building enterprise on its hands as well as the maintenance of the institution.

(b) The fact that the nominal control of the parochial system is in the hands of the parish priest, who is not always an "educator," may also create difficult situations. The parish priest is apt to be jealous of matters within the parochial precincts, and sometimes this may not tend to the maintenance of high educational standards.

(c) The multiplicity of communities at work in a single city or diocese may render the task of coördinating the teaching work in the area unduly complicated. In the United States there are no fewer than 139 such communities in charge of the secondary schools. These sisters are under the discipline of their respective superiors, and are frequently trained under the separate auspices of the community. To the outsider it would seem that such a distribution of the training facilities would almost inevitably create problems. Only a few dioceses, such as Cleveland, Cincinnati, Toledo, etc., have established diocesan training schools and are seeking thus to provide a more thoroughly coördinated and somewhat standardized preparatory course for teachers.

(d) Supervision also creates problems. While in each diocese some particular priest is assigned to the position of Diocesan Superintendent of Schools, in many dioceses he is a parish priest who has his own work to superintend in addition to these extra duties. Occasionally, he is at once an administrator and a teacher of teachers. The customary policy is to put inspection in charge of a group of special sisters selected from the major communities of women represented in the diocese, and these work together under the diocesan superintendent.

(e) Some of the states have legislation in regard to the fundamental courses of instruction; others have no such legislation. But, in the last analysis, the curriculum is determined by factors other than legislation. Owing to the increasing number of children going on to high school, the parochial schools must prepare their children to enter a high school, either public or Catholic, and this in itself assures that the subjects taught in the parochial school will be at least equivalent to those taught in the public school.

(f) The methods of financing the schools are diverse. Some schools charge fees from those able to pay, but forget to collect them in case of poverty. On the other hand, fees are often quite inadequate to meet the expense and general parochial funds must be made available. This problem is intensified in the financing of Catholic high schools to which reference must be made later.

(g) The difficulties of financing the parochial schools are not diminished by the increased outlay of public funds on the system of public schools. Just as the large endowments of Harvard, Yale and Duke create fresh problems for small colleges without much endowment, so every improvement or new course put into the public schools seems to create an additional challenge to the parochial schools to provide just as many of the attractive features of the public school as they can afford—perhaps, sometimes, more than they can afford. The only alternative is to be satisfied with less equipment and to emphasize rather the quality of the teaching.

(h) The only way in which such schools could be financed is by the use of the communities of sisters. Indirectly, however, this works a hardship on many Catholic laymen and laywomen who desire to teach but do not wish to join a community. The number of such lay teachers is comparatively small, thus:

	Religious	Lay	Total
Elementary schools...................	53,384	4,861	58,245
Secondary schools....................	12,217	2,090	14,307

Facts such as these account, at least in part, for the number of Catholic teachers in the public-school systems of many cities.

(i) Certain national groupings of Catholics do not take to the parochial school idea, partly because of the tuition fees and partly because they have been accustomed to think of education as essentially a matter for the state government. Thus, in one city studied, where the population was approximately 600,000, the Catholics themselves estimated that there were 30,450 Catholics in the public schools, of whom 11,873 were Italians and 7,915 were Poles.

These are only a few of the problems that confront the Catholic Church in the working out, on a basis of private support, of their vast system of parochial schools. The burden of expense is exceedingly great and shows no signs of diminution. On the contrary, it will probably continue to increase in proportion as the expense for public education increases unless the church definitely delimits its fields and says: this we will try to do; that we frankly cannot encompass.

RELATIONS OF PAROCHIAL AND PUBLIC-SCHOOL SYSTEMS

There is amazingly little relationship of any kind between the parochial and public-school administrations. Perhaps the situation in the United States is nowhere so drastic as in Montreal, where are two distinct systems—one Catholic and the other Protestant—both receiving public funds and neither of them coöperating in any form, shape or manner with the other. In the cities of the United States, parochial schools must report attendance to the Truancy departments and occasionally the complaint is made that such reports are not always made with care or sent in promptly. The parochial schools must frequently apply to the officials of the public-school boards for employment certificates. They also use the services of the Public Health department. Occasionally, the public officials are called upon to examine and judge the work done in the eighth grade of the parochial schools when the parochial school authorities ask them to do so, which, of course, tends to ensure the adequate preparation of their pupils for the public high schools. In one city studied, the Superintendent of Public Education arranged some special training, with the coöperation of his own teachers, for a number of teachers in the Polish parochial schools. One is struck, however, by the rather uniform absence of knowledge of the parochial schools on the part of the public authorities. There is a large area here of potential coöperation which deserves more extended exploration. It might be stated parenthetically that in one city, Cleveland, the local course of social studies authorized for the seventh grade includes sections not only on the various races that make up the population of Cleveland but also on religious toleration.[19] This is a very significant departure.

While there may be, on the part of public-school authorities, a general irritation with the complications that result from the existence of the parochial schools and the subsequent accentuations of the difficulties in planning effectively for the educational life of the whole city, the specific tensions mentioned are of no great significance. In one small town, it was reported that papers written by parochial school students and later sent to state officials for rating purposes, had been corrected in places by the teaching sisters before being despatched to headquarters. In another city, as already noted, the authorities complained that frequently the more unruly pupils in the parochial schools were discharged in midterm, whereupon it became necessary to take them into the public schools under most unfavorable conditions. Some of the public-school teachers complained that they were "spied upon" by the parish priests and were frequently called to account for teaching history in a way that might be interpreted as unfavorable to Catholic claims. It would seem that in some of the cases the priest had heard reports from the pupils, who may have garbled what the teacher actually said. In one instance where the documents were presented, the priest, instead of calling on the teacher to inquire, wrote a very high-and-mighty note warning her and definitely intimated that now that she had been warned, any further breach would be reported to the Superintendent. Instances of this character make the teachers feel that some priests are more than anxious to find some cause for discharging them, and replacing them, perhaps, with Catholics. In the main, however, the relations between the two systems offer few examples of administrative tension—for the most part, there are no relations.

THE MAIN GRIEVANCE AND POSSIBLE REACTIONS OF CATHOLICS

The main grievance put forward by the Catholics is, of course, financial. They feel that since they are paralleling the work of the public schools, they

---

[19] *The Social Studies,* Cleveland Junior High School, Grade VII; pp. 239-255.

should receive financial aid, and this issue has come to the front with particular urgency during the depression. The church labors under a sense of injustice, and the reference of His Holiness to the state's responsibility for "distributive justice" in the encyclical letter "On the Christian Education of Youth," quoted above, meets with a warm response in their hearts. The fact that the disability that they endure is brought about by their own inability to gear into the public-school system and is also shared by all others who develop private schools does not remove the feeling of "hurt." Their attitude to the public schools, therefore, is frequently tinged with some bitterness, and their references to the "godless" schools to the very "godlessness" of which—so far as it exists—they have helped to contribute, however undiplomatic they may be, must perhaps be read in the light of that bitterness. It would also not be surprising that, as voters, they may at times show little enthusiasm for the greater support of the public schools and great tenacity in promoting the cause of Catholic teachers in the public-school system. There are, indeed, several courses open to them, especially when, as in many American cities, they are actually in the majority:

(1) They can bring pressure to elect Catholics to the Board of Public Education, and frequently Catholics do hold prominent places on such boards.

(2) They can use political influence to elect Catholic superintendents of public schools. Whether they have done so or not is another matter, but there are several Catholic superintendents of schools.

(3) They can encourage their young women to prepare to be teachers in the public schools. It may seem anomalous for a church whose local representatives refer to the public schools as godless to encourage their young women to train for service in them, but on this point there is definite evidence, especially in Chicago. Thus, in an editorial in the *Christian Century*, August 16, 1933, the following is stated:

"A study of the records of the Chicago normal college shows that, in proportion to enrolment, the Catholic high schools furnish about ten times as many graduates of that college as do the public high schools. This can scarcely be the result of accident. Neither is it the result of general academic superiority of Catholic schools. Figures from the University of Illinois show that students from all private schools (including Catholic) have an average rating slightly below that of students who come from public high schools. A scholastic aptitude test of all secondary school seniors in Chicago, given by the Registrar of the University of Chicago in coöperation with the schools, showed that the seniors in Catholic high schools rated somewhat below, and seniors in other private schools considerably above, those in public high schools. Yet the Catholic schools continue to furnish more normal school graduates than the public schools by a ratio of ten to one, in proportion to the total enrolment in each class."

The facts would seem to be as stated, but Catholic leaders point out that many Catholic girls go in for teaching, for some of them, especially among the Irish, seem to have a flair for celibacy. At all events, if the girls want to go in for teaching, and the Catholic schools take greater care to assist them in "making the grade," it is difficult to see where they are blameworthy. The number of Catholic teachers is also marked in New York, where there are three different organizations of public-school teachers—one Protestant, one Catholic and one Jewish. But that is a story in itself.

(4) Finally, when there is an opportunity to vote a new bond issue for public-school purposes, the Catholics can vote "no" and in many cases—provided there is a "Catholic vote"—they are strong enough to squelch such an issue.

In short, it is high time for the American people to realize that in many of the large northern cities, they are confronted, as Grover Cleveland would say, not with a theory but with a situation, and they should begin to view the situation in other than doctrinaire terms. If the Catholics have not taken advantage of their potential political power along the lines of possible action mentioned above, all the more credit to them. If, on the other hand, they are taking advantage of such channels of power, the situation deserves to be considered on its own merits.

At this point, however, it seems desirable to shift our attention from the problems of the public schools in the United States to the field of elementary education in certain Canadian provinces where public funds are applied to Catholic schools, in order that an analysis of the problems that arise under those systems may furnish us with some guide as to what might be done or must not be done along such lines in the United States.

The Canadian Solution in Different Provinces

Various solutions of the problem presented by the apposition of public and Catholic schools have been attempted in the Canadian provinces. Manitoba recognizes but a single system of public schools, as in the American states, and the Catholic Church must provide entirely out of its own resources for such parochial schools as it establishes. The same situation exists in British Columbia, an immense but sparsely-populated province where the maintenance of one school system is financially exacting, and the maintenance of two might be ruinous. In most of the provinces, however, separate schools, or minority schools as distinguished from parochial schools, on the one hand, and from public schools on the other, are recognized by law and supported by public funds. In Ontario, separate schools may be established by Catholic, Protestant or Negro groups, but as a matter of fact there are but five Protestant separate schools and no Negro schools.[20] In the prairie provinces of Alberta and Saskatchewan the schools are more accurately described as

---

[20] The entire Negro population of Ontario is less than 7,000.

majority and minority schools. In Quebec, however, there are two—and only two—completely separated school systems, one Catholic and the other Protestant. For purposes of education the Jews are definitely classified by law as Protestants, and the resultant situation is perhaps unique in the world. For the purposes of this study, an analysis of the contrasting methods in Ontario and Quebec will suffice. Certain general facts need, however, to be kept in mind throughout.

(1) If the United States began under dominant Protestant influences, and the Catholics came in by immigration, Canada began as a dominantly Catholic country, and the Protestants came in by immigration, under—it must be stated—favorable and favoring circumstances, viz., the support of the Crown. In short, the first Protestants were a minority, aggressive and somewhat grasping since they were quite conscious of the fact that they "had captured the country." In time the Protestants became the majority. At present, 40 per cent. of the population in Canada is Catholic.

(2) At the time of British occupation, the Catholics had already developed a number of schools in what is now the Province of Quebec. It may perhaps be possible to romanticize unduly about these schools, or to exaggerate either their extent or their standards, but some such schools there undoubtedly were.

(3) After the cession of Canada, British policy, as stated in the instructions to the Governor, included the establishment of the Church of England as the established church in Canada, the division of the land into new parishes and the introduction of schoolmasters who should teach under a license issued by the Bishop of London. These plans tended to disorganize the existing situation without putting anything satisfactory in its place.

(4) At first, all Canada was governed as a unit. In 1791 it was divided for reasons more or less obvious into Upper and Lower Canada, or to use the more modern terms, into Ontario and Quebec, and so continued until 1840. During this period it was practically impossible to agree upon a system of education which satisfied the French in Quebec or the English in Ontario with the minorities in both provinces. When, after Lord Durham's report, Ontario and Quebec were reunited and received a central government, education proved as difficult as ever—perhaps more so. An attempt was made to copy the law passed in New York State in 1841, with necessary modifications and with special provisions for the right of a minority to establish its own school, but this system did not work at all, and eventually different methods were evolved even within the same central government for dealing with the situation. When at last, in 1867, the Confederation of Canada was formed, and once again Ontario and Quebec became separate political entities, one of the terms of the confederation laid down by the British North America Act, creating the confederation, section 93, was:

"In and for each Province the Legislature may exclusively make laws in relation to education, subject and according to the following provisions:

"(1) Nothing in any such law shall prejudicially affect any right or privilege
with respect to denominational schools which any class of persons have by law
in the Province at the Union.

"(2) All the powers, privileges, and duties at the Union by law conferred and
imposed in Upper Canada on the separate schools and school trustees of the
Queen's Roman Catholic subjects shall be and are hereby extended to the dissentient schools of the Queen's Protestant and Roman Catholic subjects in Quebec.

"(3) Where in any Province a system of separate or dissentient schools exists
by law at the Union or is thereafter established by the Legislature of the Province,
an appeal shall lie to the Governor General in Council from any Act or decision
of any Provincial authority affecting any right or privilege of the Protestant or
Roman Catholic minority of the Queen's subjects in relation to Education, etc."

It will thus be seen that by the terms of Confederation, Quebec promised
to respect the educational rights of the Protestant minority in exchange for an
assurance that Ontario would respect the educational rights of the Catholic
minority. As Sir John A. Macdonald stated in his notable speech dealing
with the proposed Confederation: "We will enjoy here that which is the
great test of constitutional freedom—we will have the rights of the minority
respected." The rights, therefore, of these two minorities are thus specifically guarded in the very constitutional fabric of the country, but while
similar rights might be extended to new and other minorities, such an extension would be done out of courtesy only, and no other minority could claim
any constitutional right to such privileges, as the Jews later discovered. Moreover, since at the time of the British North America Act, there were in
Ontario no Catholic secondary schools supported by the government, the
privileges of receiving government support for separate schools is even now
limited in Ontario only to elementary schools, and not extended to secondary
schools. Since, however, many of the elementary schools are at present permitted to teach fifth classes (or the first year of high school), while each year
sees some new step toward the creation of junior high schools, a no-man's
land between elementary and secondary education is created, which at any
time may raise new questions as to the propriety of government support for
separate schools beyond the elementary grade. We now turn to consider
more specifically the Quebec and Ontario systems.

THE QUEBEC SYSTEM

Owing to the overwhelming Catholic majority in Quebec and the duality
of culture and language, the attempt to organize a public-school system on
the lines suggested by the legislation of the state of New York in 1841 was
a complete failure. Between 1841 and 1879 there were many revisions of

the laws regarding education until in 1869 there was a complete cleavage within the system, with a Roman Catholic Committee and a Protestant Committee paralleling each other within the Council of Education, sitting separately and seldom together and making the regulations for their respective schools quite independently of one another.[21] In the municipalities there might be majority or minority schools; the majority schools were supervised by a Board of School Commissioners, while the minority schools were supervised by a Board of School Trustees, except in the larger cities where both boards are called commissioners. These two boards seem to have no more to do with one another than would be the case if one were in New Zealand and the other in Timbuctoo. The language of instruction in most of the Catholic schools is French, although in the elementary grades of such schools English is also taught; the language of instruction in nearly all the Protestant schools is English, although in the elementary grades of these schools French is also taught. In Montreal, where there is a large English-speaking Catholic population, the Catholics provide two types of schools—those in which French is the language of instruction and those in which English is the language of instruction.

These two school systems are supported to a small extent by the province but mostly by municipal taxes and rates. So far as the rural areas are concerned, such a duality of schools practically leads to the extrusion of the minority group. If, for instance, the number of Protestants in a given rural area is negligible, they find it practically impossible to support a school. Protestant parents in such cases therefore confront the necessity of (a) sending their children to the majority (Catholic) school, or (b) sending their children to certain boarding-schools which Protestants have erected specially for French Protestants, or (c) moving out of the community altogether and living in a community in which it is possible to develop a Protestant school. The net result has been the steady extrusion of the Protestant minority from many townships in Quebec.

The situation in the cities may be ascertained from an examination of the educational facilities in Montreal. In the first place, civil status is here determined to a certain extent by religious affiliation. If one is a baptized Catholic, he may only cease to be a Catholic by signing an open abjuration of the Catholic faith before a Protestant minister who, in turn, transmits such abjuration to the Catholic bishop of the diocese, whereupon the abjuror is no longer to be considered a Catholic and is free from any legal obligations to the church. So long, however, as his status is that of a Catholic and he owns property, his taxes on that property, in so far as they involve school rates, go to the Catholic School Board, even if the tenants in his houses are

---

[21] For an excellent description of this system, see Sutherland, J. C., *The Province of Quebec* (Toronto: Thomas Nelson & Sons, 1931), pp. 88-108.

Protestants or Jews, and by a provincial law the maximum Catholic school rate in Montreal is seven mills on the dollar. The taxes of a Protestant landowner, however, so far as they involve school rates, go to the Protestant Board, even if his tenants are Catholics, and by provincial law the maximum Protestant school rate is set at 10 mills on the dollar. The rate paid by corporations is 12 mills, and for the most part this money is divided between the Protestant and Catholic school boards in a proportion determined by the respective number of children of school age. The most prolific group gets the largest allotment. If a corporation is made up exclusively of Catholics, on the one hand, or of Protestants, on the other, the school rates paid by them are nevertheless paid into the neutral panel and from it distributed between the two systems on the basis previously indicated. If a corporation wishes to have all its taxes go to one source or the other—and there is some difference between 7 mills and 12 mills—it is necessary to vest the ownership of the property in an individual, and this is, it is reported, occasionally done, both as a means of reducing the taxes and also of retaining the power to designate the ultimate disposition of them. In a few cases, the Catholics may prefer to send their children to the Protestant schools, believing that such schools give the pupils a better preparation for ordinary life and a less purely classical education; in such a case, the students must pay tuition fees directly to the Protestant School Board at the rate of $8 a month. On the other hand, some children of Protestant parents may for various reasons— sometimes because of mixed marriage—be brought up in the Catholic schools. Once again, such children must pay tuition. There is little mixed marriage, however, in the province of Quebec.

A difficult situation was recently created in Verdun, one of the communities in Greater Montreal. Verdun has a fairly large Protestant population, but these Protestants are mostly middle-class renters and not owners of properties. Their homes are mostly owned by Catholic landlords and consequently Verdun faced the problem of providing Protestant schools for a fairly large number of children with a negligible income, and the Protestant school board of the city of Montreal proper had to come to the rescue of the Verdun schools—a clear evidence of the implicit difficulty in this method of distributing taxes.

SITUATION CREATED BY LARGE NUMBER OF JEWS IN MONTREAL

Generally speaking, however, the system worked fairly well until the Jews began to arrive in Montreal in large numbers. The first question was, should the Jews pay the Protestant or the Catholic school rate? Some Jews were at first inclined to pay the lower Catholic school rate while they sent their children to the Protestant schools. This naturally evoked Protestant protests until, in 1903, the provincial legislature passed an act to the effect that for all the purposes of education, the Jews were to be considered as Protestants. After that the Jewish school rates were all paid into the Protestant School Board. As the number of Jews increased—they number probably more than 60,000 in Greater Montreal at the present time—they began to seek further favors from the Protestant School Board, including representation on the board, a large number of Jews to be employed as teachers in the schools, Jewish religious teaching in schools which were almost entirely Jewish instead of the Protestant teaching (Jewish pupils were not required to take these classes by the terms and provisions of a conscience clause), recognition of Jewish holidays, etc. The Jews claimed that by the laws of Quebec they were regarded for education purposes as "Protestants"; the Protestants insisted that they had secured their minority rights by the British North America Act in 1867, that they had consented to Confederation only when these rights had been written into the "bond," and that it was necessary to their continued existence in Quebec to retain the control of their own schools. The Jews took their case to successive Quebec courts and everywhere lost. They then carried it to the Privy Council in England, where the decision was given that Protestants alone had the minority rights conferred upon them by the terms of the British North America Act and that the Jews could not insist on any favors other than those which the Protestant group itself was willing to confer.

After this, the dilemma before the Jews was clear; they could either accept the favors which the Protestant School Board was willing to give them and thus cease their agitation, or they could could take steps to create a dissentient board of their own and establish their own schools. Some urged the latter course, but in the end a moderate policy prevailed, and the Jews signed an agreement with the Protestant School Commissioners of Montreal which should operate for fifteen years, whereby they continue to pay their taxes to that board and the Protestant schools continue to teach their children. There are some Jewish teachers—approximately seventy out of a total of more than a thousand; the conscience clause in respect to the character of the religious teaching has been written into the agreement and is respected; Jewish children are excused on a fairly large number of Jewish holidays, and for the time being the difficult situation is eased. This is a clear situation in which the entrance of the Jews into a community in which a difficult interreligious problem had been subtly adjusted threatened to upset the delicate equipoise established.

The general statistics for the city of Montreal proper (not the Greater City) are as follows: the Catholic population is 624,209 and the Catholic school population is 117,680, together with 135 non-Catholics attending Catholic schools; the Protestant population (including Jews) is 194,368, and the Protestant school population is 34,107, together with forty-four Catholics attending the Protestant schools. It is thus seen that forty-four Catholic children attend the Protestant schools and 135 Protestant children attend the Catholic schools.

✓ Careful estimates indicate that the per capita cost of training the Jewish children is slightly in excess of the amount received by the Protestant School Board from Jewish school rates, plus the per capita amount received from the money in the neutral panel.

An interesting aspect of the situation in Montreal is that the percentage of Jewish children who continue through high school is higher than that of the non-Jewish-Protestant group, thus:[22]

Type of Pupils	In Elementary Schools	In High Schools
Protestants....................	20,687	2,979
Jews.........................	8,760	2,250
Others (including non-residents)..	1,737	244
	31,184	5,473

While the Quebec system really develops two parallel schemes of education within the province with no coördination between them, and while many undoubted difficulties arise through the extrusion of minority groups from the rural areas and situations similar to that of Verdun mentioned above, it works fairly well in the cities, except for the problems raised by the classification of the Jews as Protestants. Religious instruction is perhaps given more thoroughly than anywhere else in North America in both Protestant and Catholic schools.[23] But there are grave results as well as complications. When groups are thus kept apart, intermarriage seldom takes place and the friendly social contacts of French-Canadian Catholics and the English-speaking Protestants are almost negligible. The two groups may mix to a certain extent in business during the day, but after six o'clock they retreat to their separate quarters and live in almost complete isolation. It is difficult for one group to respect or admire the other, and thus a deep schism is created in the cultural life of Canada which complicates every effort to achieve a real national unity.

THE ONTARIO SYSTEM

The fundamental difference between Quebec and Ontario is that in Ontario there is a public-school system, paralleled by a separate school system, as opposed to the dual system of Protestant schools and Catholic schools in Quebec.

The Ontario acts provide for the establishment of a public-school system,

---

[22] Statistics for 1932.
[23] It must be confessed, however, that the curriculum in religious instruction in the Protestant schools is not very imposing.

but also permit the organization of separate schools for certain specified groups—Protestants, Catholics and Negroes. There are, however, no Negro schools, and only five Protestant schools in the province, most of these being in areas along the Ottawa River where the majority school happens to be for French Catholics. Curiously enough, in the early days, the *sine qua non* for the establishment of a dissentient Catholic school was the fact that the teacher was a Protestant, and for a dissentient Protestant school the fact that the teacher was a Catholic.[24]

Education in Ontario is compulsory. The school district is required to operate a school, and the children of school age in the district are required to attend. In case children attend private schools, the government looks the other way unless there is reason to believe that such schools are, educationally speaking, farces. If a private school is believed to be inimical to the sound enlightenment of the children, the Minister of Education has the power to step in, and while he may be unable to prevent the private school teachers from teaching, he can take their pupils away from them.

In any district, however, a dissentient minority may, if it sees fit, create a separate school, by calling a meeting of dissentients at which trustees are formally elected. The formal notification of such a meeting and the results of the election to the government are sufficient to give the trustees corporate standing. They may then proceed to secure a teacher and accommodations for a school, and to lay down local regulations, but in doing so, they must conform to the regulations for separate schools contained in special provincial acts, for the separate schools are in all respects subject to government supervision and inspection and must conform *in toto* to government standards. In this particular, there is a marked difference between the separate schools of Ontario and the parochial schools in the United States. Indeed, such separate schools are not parochial schools at all, nor are they directly under the administration of the church. They are, rather, administered locally by a board of separate school trustees who may all be laymen.

The Separate School Board may raise money by issuing bonds and the general administration of the local schools is in their hands. A minority ratepayer in Ontario who becomes dissatisfied with the separate school may, by giving due notice, cease to be inscribed as a separate school supporter, whereupon his taxes and his children both go to the public schools. (This power to change one's status from a separate school supporter to that of a public-school supporter is not allowed in Saskatchewan. In that province, if a person has once signed a petition for the creation of a minority school, and it is created in consequence of such a petition, he must continue to sup-

---

[24] For a documentary history of the struggle in Ontario over separate schools 1841-1876, see J. George Hodgins, *The Legislation and History of Separate Schools in Upper Canada* (Toronto: William Briggs, 1897).

port it so long as he resides in the community; the assumption being that the trustees of the minority schools, in offering bonds for sale, deserve the assurance that those who urge such departures will stand behind them when the time comes to pay the interest or the principal due.)

In the allocation of taxes on a given property in Ontario, not ownership (as in Quebec) but tenancy determines the destination of the taxes paid. Thus, a Catholic may live in property owned by a Protestant, but because the tenant sends his children to the separate schools, the owner of that particular building is taxed for it as a separate school supporter, and hence his tax rate may be either higher or lower (usually higher) than if the money went to the Public School Board.

In the case of tax-money from corporations, all of this money goes to the Public School Board unless the corporation specifically states its desire that it should go in whole or in part to the Separate School Board. As the religious preferences of a great company are apt to be unascertainable, and inasmuch as the personnel of the shareholders is constantly changing, it becomes impossible for most of them to provide any index of the feeling of the shareholders, and hence all the money from corporations usually, though not always, goes by default, as it were, into the public-school panel. The Catholics claim that this is unjust and at the time this report is being written are seeking to bring pressure upon the government to divide the corporation taxes, as in Quebec, on the basis of school attendance or on some other basis more equitable in their point of view. This, the Orangemen in particular are prepared to fight to the last ditch.

In addition to local taxation, all schools receive assistance from provincial funds. Formerly, this was given to all schools on the basis of school attendance. Now, however, the province has developed a very ingenious and elaborate system whereby the provincial grants are conditioned and given only in such ways as may stimulate local achievement and improvement. The initial per capita grant is very small, but more significant grants of a supplementary character are given which are based on the relation of the total amount paid for salaries by the local school to the following: the equalized assessment in that school district; additional improved equipment provided by the local school board; the character of the teaching certificates held by the teachers employed, varying from $75 for each provincial first-class certificate to only $30 for an interim second-class certificate; adequate teaching of special subjects such as music, household science, physical culture, agriculture, horticulture; the provision of fifth forms and kindergartens, etc. In addition, the province makes special grants to public or separate schools for capital expenditures if the school sections are in municipalities with unusually low assessments, while the Minister of Education has further discretionary power to make or withhold grants either to encourage fresh efforts or to discipline a school which, he has reason to believe, is not being operated in full compliance with the requirements of the provincial acts governing schools.

In this system there are often differences in the tax-rates paid by the public-school supporters and the separate school supporters in the same municipality. Of thirty-two cities in Ontario, in 1931 nineteen had the same assessments for separate schools as for public schools; ten had higher assessments for separate schools than for public schools; and three had higher assessments for public schools than for separate schools. In part this disparity is due to local conditions and to the fact that a minority group, even when it gets public funds, must pay higher for the privilege of indulging its sense of importance as a minority. It is quite clear that schools for a minority under normal circumstances cannot be maintained at as efficient a level for the same money as for the majority. Indeed, the only reason the separate school rate is not even higher than it is, is that the use of the teaching sisters in Ontario makes the aggregate payment of salaries to teachers in the separate schools proportionately less than the aggregate payment of salaries to teachers in the public schools. This is clearly evident in the following table for the entire province for 1932:

EXPENDITURES ON ELEMENTARY EDUCATION

Province of Ontario, 1931–1932

Nature of Expense	Public Schools	Separate Schools
Sites, Buildings and Permanent Improvements.......	$ 2,845,405.76	$ 641,188.08
Teachers' Salaries.................................	18,690,679.82	2,145,571.53
Pupils' Supplies.................................	839,177.44	58,205.36
Cost of keeping schools open......................	3,148,651.27	537,735.26
Cost of upkeep of buildings and grounds............	1,603,659.06	247,154.01
Cost of Administration...........................	963,259.14	155,826.99
Cost of Recreation...............................	60,493.69	4,343.89
Debt charges....................................	4,054,634.41	824,532.53
Other expenses..................................	1,499,796.89	296,412.45
	$33,705,757.48	$4,910,970.10
Number of pupils, May 31, 1931..................	474,010	95,974

This table deserves careful study as it indicates what might happen if such a system were introduced in the United States. Separate schools frequently augment the funds received from normal sources by sales, bazaars, etc., conducted by the Catholics for the sake of their schools and also by funds contributed directly by the church. They urge, however, that they be given a larger share in the distribution of corporation taxes, and this, at present, is the bone of contention.[25]

---

[25] The Catholic contention on this point is set forth in a little pamphlet by the Archbishop of Toronto, published 1931, entitled "The School Question of Ontario." The issue was injected into the political campaign of June, 1934.

In general, the people are satisfied with the system. Protestants are apt to feel that the segregation of one group of the young people is not conducive to national unity, but this is offset—at least in part—by the fact that there are no separate high schools, and that consequently in the high schools Protestant, Jewish and a good many Catholic children are trained together and thus get to know one another. Perhaps, they get to know one another too well, especially as the high schools are coeducational, for the rate of intermarriage in Ontario, as is pointed out in another chapter, is very high. Many of the separate schools, especially in rural areas and in the smaller villages, are permitted, on the other hand, to carry on continuation work equivalent to one or two years of high school.

A major advantage of the system is that all the schools are under the direct supervision of the Provincial Minister of Education and must maintain standards set by the province; the government appoints inspectors for Catholic schools directly responsible to the government and receives full and complete reports from the separate schools as from the public schools. The maintenance of such standards of achievement also prevents small minorities from too hastily demanding schools of their own, and in practically no case has a separate school, once formed, been disbanded from the disintegration of its own constituency.

Again, while the separate schools receive public money, this money does not come from the Protestant but from the Catholic tax-payers. Those who want a special kind of education pay for it, but they are not required at the same time to pay for schools, as in the United States, which they prefer not to use.

The provincial grants are distributed to public and separate schools alike on no mere per capita basis, but rather on a basis of achievement and self-effort.

While the public schools of Ontario are non-sectarian, the desire of the majority of the citizens that religion shall not be ignored is provided for in the following ways:

(a) Provision is made for the possible visits of resident clergymen who may instruct the pupils of their own denominations. This privilege, however, is only used in 185 out of 5,670 rural communities and in twenty-three of the 316 urban communities.

(b) Provision is made that school sessions shall be opened with Bible reading. This is done in 315 of the 316 urban communities in the province. There is also a place in the curriculum for the memorization of Bible passages; school is opened and closed with prayer in nearly all schools. This is done in 5,560 of the 5,670 rural communities and in 315 of the 316 urban communities.

(c) The regulations also require that it shall be the duty of every teacher to "inculcate by precept and example respect for religion and the principles of Christian morality." This might possibly be construed as standing in the way of the appointment of Jewish school-teachers.

There are practically no Catholic school-teachers in the public elementary schools, since they have their own schools to provide places for them. There are, however, Catholic teachers in the public high schools. There is little evidence of undercurrents of tension locally. There are no Catholics on public school boards where the Catholics operate their own separate schools. Factors such as these, which do complicate the American situation, are therefore absent in Ontario.

DIFFICULTIES IN THE SYSTEM

Of course, there are also difficulties in the system as well as values.

(a) The disparity in school-rates between public and separate school supporters may be a source of inconvenience to a Catholic tenant in search of a house in which to live. But the same inconvenience might challenge a Protestant seeking a house to rent in a city where the separate school rate is lower. One evidence of this kind of difficulty has been included in chapter ii.

(b) There is great tension at the present moment over the question of the proper method of distributing corporation taxes, as already indicated.

(c) In cases of mixed marriages, curious situations arise. Here, for instance, is a Protestant tenant married to a Catholic wife. As a Protestant he must pay his taxes to the Public School Board—he has no option about it. But he has promised to bring his children up as Catholics—hence he sends his children to the separate schools. The Catholic authorities in Toronto estimate that they spend $50,000 a year in educating the children of such Protestant fathers. The Privy Council ruled in 1934 that in such instances, the municipality could divert taxes paid by Protestants to the support of the separate schools.

(d) One serious complication has been created by the injection of the bi-lingual question. Canada is in a measure bi-lingual and the French peoples were given assurances in regard to their right to the use of the French language.[26] English, however, was until recently almost the sole medium of communication in Ontario until a large number of French settled along the Ottawa valley. In the schools in these areas a demand arose that French become *a*, if not *the*, language of instruction, and the provincial government issued a famous regulation, No. 17, which sought to restrict this. The regulation led to an uproar among the French, the Orangemen

---

[26] The director of the study cannot discover in the Quebec Act of 1774 any pledge given to the French people respecting their language; there were pledges regarding their freedom of worship and their use of French civil law.

and even on the part of many English-speaking Catholics in the affected areas. Court proceedings were instituted, the regulation was withdrawn, and today the Minister of Education, acting under a certain blanket authority to introduce new courses at his discretion, permits the use of French as the language of instruction in certain specific schools, at the same time doing everything in his power to increase the standards of teaching in such schools, which were at first very low. The Orangemen are still hot about the matter, however, believing that such.bi-lingualism is a threat to national unity.

(e) The fact that there are no separate high schools may perhaps be in part responsible for the fact that the number of Protestant-Catholic inter-marriages in Ontario is quite high.

(f) There does tend to be a grouping together of Catholics in certain rural communities, and the necessity of supporting separate schools may restrict the choice of residence, especially in the rural communities, of Protestants or Catholics.

(g) The ingenious system of providing provincial grants to schools, while seemingly sound, is highly complicated, and there may be instances where the salaries paid may be actually lower than those reported, in order that the provincial grant may be proportionately larger. It is, however, easier to suspect this than to prove it.

Difficulties such as these should be kept in mind in case of any proposal to modify the existing policy in the United States of no support for sectarian institutions. The whole problem of separate schools in Canada is treated *in extenso* in a recent volume by George M. Weir, entitled "The Separate School Question in Canada," published by the Ryerson Press of Toronto.

JEWISH EDUCATIONAL POLICY IN THE UNITED STATES

Most of the previous discussion has concerned primarily Protestant-Catholic relations, and it is necessary at this point, before presenting any final considerations concerning the whole problem of elementary education, to review the historic and present attitudes of the Jews to this aspect of educational life.

When the issue of parochial *versus* public schools was first argued, the Jews showed a disposition to establish parochial schools, but their endeavor was soon given up except in very few cases. In a study made by Dr. Harry S. Linfield, in 1927, the Jews living in 871 communities in the United States had only twelve parochial schools in all, and these twelve schools were all located in three large communities. They, therefore, use the public-school system almost entirely. But in nearly every city studied, the Jews were supplementing the public-school instruction by a number of communal or congregational schools which are usually held after four o'clock in the afternoon. Here Jewish children receive instruction in Jewish literature, Jewish history and culture, Hebrew (or Yiddish in some nationalist schools), and in such other subjects as make for the preservation of their interest in Jewish culture. Dr. Linfield estimated that in 1927 there were 249,409 pupils enrolled in the Jewish elementary schools of all kinds. Of these about four-fifths (194,691) were in congregational schools, while one-fifth (51,021) were in non-congregational or communal schools. Only 3,697 attended the twelve Jewish parochial schools.

Jewish attendance at such schools does not interfere in any way with the conduct of the public-school system, although the Jewish children who attend them have very little time for normal play, since they must go directly from the public school to the Jewish or Hebrew school. The funds necessary for the maintenance of such schools are of course raised entirely within the Jewish community.[27]

The presence of large numbers of Jews in certain American cities has created some embarrassing situations. On Jewish holidays some classrooms are almost emptied, while of course the Jews are absent on "Christian" holidays which are publicly observed. In some cities, the Jews have been particularly vigilant against anything that might be interpreted as Christian teaching in the schools or any teaching that might reflect on the Jews themselves. Indeed, in not a few places, they have been able to have Shakespeare's *The Merchant of Venice* eliminated from the curriculum. In one suburb of New York, as has been noted elsewhere, a Jewish rabbi spent many hours just before one Christmas visiting the public schools in an effort to see that no Christmas carols were sung and no references to Christmas made. He succeeded in making a nuisance of himself and in helping on the cause of anti-Semitism in that community.

General Observations and Possible Solutions

Before proceeding to consider some of the special problems which emerge in the field of secondary and higher education, it is perhaps well to point out that the question of religion in the public schools has not been settled with entire satisfaction in either the United States or Canada. Especially in the United States, the Catholics feel that they are left to bear a very great financial burden alone, while at the same time they must contribute to the maintenance of the public-school system in the benefits of which their children do not in any large degree share. They feel moreover, that if they had state or municipal aid, they could provide schools for all their children

---

[27] For further facts, see Dush..in, *Jewish Education in New York City* (New York: Bureau of Jewish Education, 1918), and Gamoran, E.: pamphlet on *Jewish Education in the United States* (Nashville: Cokesbury Press, 1931).

at a much lower per capita cost than that required by the present public-school system, in which all the costs have been rapidly and dangerously rising. Their contention on this point is probably correct, for the major item in public-school expense is undoubtedly involved in paying the salaries of teachers, and the teaching communities of women in the Roman Catholic Church receive a mere pittance for services, which, regarded from the purely pedagogical point of view, are undoubtedly of a fairly high order.

To these contentions, the non-Catholics reply that such is the price which any group in America must pay for its religious superiority complex just as parents who send their children to private schools must be prepared to pay for their social-superiority complex; and that if the public policy of no support for sectarian institutions were reversed, the resultant complications would be unendurable. Meanwhile, the public schools are open to all Catholics and their exclusion from such benefits is purely self-exclusion. The non-Catholics also point to impossible situations which might develop in case government grants were extended to Catholic schools in certain sparsely-populated areas where Catholics might be in a majority. It would tend either to the diminished support, or elimination, of the public school in the district, and perhaps also to the extrusion of the Protestant population, as in Quebec. Further, in many parts of the South, education is already handicapped because municipalities are required to maintain a dual school system, on account of the segregation of Negroes and whites. Either the total amount available for education is thus divided with disastrous effects between the two groups, or else the minority group is given the raw end of the deal and suffers at the expense of the majority. To impose religious segregation on the top of the existing race segregation would mean an intolerable burden. There is also a tendency within Catholic schools to segregate the sexes on the ground that boys and girls are in many respects "different animals" and require different handling. Where will such principles of segregation end? Moreover, in the light of the increasing demands being made of our schools, and the rapidly shifting populations in the city, it would be impossible to plan adequately for school facilities for all; an area dominantly Protestant today might be Catholic tomorrow, and what is now a "white" district would be "Negro" tomorrow. How many schools erected would thus become white elephants unless they were all thoroughly coördinated in one system? In short, the answer is, that educational facilities must be increasingly planned for all and as economically as possible, and when any group finds itself unwilling to fit into the central scheme, then it must be prepared to bear the financial burden of such lack of co-operativeness itself, however much this may seem to run counter to the demands of "distributive justice."

This, indeed, seems to be the fundamental position of the vast majority of non-Catholics, and while it is fairly obvious that some further reconsideration of the whole problem of "public versus parochial schools" is desirable, it is difficult to see what can be done which will satisfy all parties.

If a policy is effected which takes cognizance of the "public" character of parochial schools and consequently provides financial assistance from public funds to their maintenance, then such assistance might take one of the three forms:

(a) Money might be distributed between the Catholic and the non-Catholic schools on a per capita basis of school attendance; one difficulty in this scheme is in the obvious fact that the teachers in Catholic schools, by reason of their membership in religious communities, are paid much less than ordinary lay teachers, and such a distribution would tend to do one of two things: it might enable the Catholics to accumulate vaster proportional properties than the public schools, even though the larger share of the taxes might come from Protestant quarters; or it might tend to lower the wage standards of the teachers in the public schools.

(b) The state or the community might continue to offer nothing for the support of institutions not directly under the public schools, but might, on the contrary, give incidental assistance to the pupils in attendance at such schools provided that tuition was free and that educational standards insisted upon by the state were met. In this way, the state or community might provide text-books, as in Louisiana, or bus transportation, as in Illinois. The provision of text-books to individual pupils has been ruled by a Supreme Court decision not to contravene the state constitution forbidding allocation of public funds to sectarian institutions. The state already offers the parochial schools the services of the Health department.

(c) A distinction might be made between the disposition of state funds for education and the amounts raised locally by taxation. The latter might continue to be devoted exclusively to the public schools, while the funds available from the state might be distributed among all "free" schools, whether public or parochial, on a basis similar to that used in Ontario, which made the grants contingent upon the effort and efficiency of the individual school. This, of course, would require amendments to the constitutions in about forty states.

(d) Local school rates might be applied, in whole or in part, as in Ontario, to public or separate schools, the taxpayer being allowed to indicate his preference. While this would undoubtedly reduce the amount available for the public schools, it would obviate the apparent injustice of Catholics having to pay their taxes like other people and at the same time to support a separate system of parochial schools.

The difficulties and objections to any of these procedures are manifold, but the maintenance of the present situation is undoubtedly a trouble-breeder of the first rank.

WEEK-DAY RELIGIOUS EDUCATION ON RELEASED TIME

If it be impossible to discover any satisfactory solution of the problem along any of the lines suggested above, it may be necessary to consider more fully the possibilities in week-day religious education on released time already in operation in many states. The fundamental weakness in much American education is that it does not provide an adequate *Weltanschauung*, a philosophy of living, a just appreciation of the proper place of the individual in the great universe in which he finds himself. Techniques and skills are not enough; too many go through public school, high school and university and yet never face the larger issues of the whence and whither of their wandering days, only to enter life, fair technicians, competent perchance in the mad struggle for a living to hold their own, but without adequate appreciation of those subtler influences and ideas that link them spatially with the whole brotherhood of man and temporally with the long struggle of man to achieve peace and salvation. In short, they may get everything but spiritual culture. Hence, even the American university graduate appears to foreigners too often crude, callow, essentially uncultured. One Catholic educator put the situation in strong terms: "Better," he said, "to give our youth the *Weltanschauung* of Soviet Russia than to give them nothing at all." How, then, in a civilization which seems to have no unifying *Weltanschauung*, and which is split up by sectarian differences, can we find ways and means of supplying the deficiency in our educational structure? There are many who feel that week-day religious education, thoroughly organized and expertly provided, may show the way.

It is true that the encyclical of Pope Pius XI, issued December 31, 1929, and already quoted, condemned the mixed school (especially the so-called école unique, obligatory on all) in which students were provided with separate religious instruction, while they received their other lessons in common with non-Catholic pupils from non-Catholic teachers. Nevertheless, this condemnation might be interpreted as applying less to the separate religious instruction than to the obligatory attendance at such a school, and bishops in the various dioceses can determine for themselves, by the canon law of the church, under what conditions they may permit Catholic children to attend neutral or mixed schools. The law of the church puts it up to them. What is more, the Catholic Church has learned through history that, however desirable certain policies may be when considered ideally, adjustments and compromises must be made as they are applied to different parts of the world. What may be practicable in a country or culture overwhelmingly Catholic is quite impracticable in a country dominantly non-Catholic, and to carry through policies in the latter country which might work satisfactorily in the former is simply to invite disaster.

It does seem possible, therefore, to make arrangements within a given diocese whereby all Catholic children might attend the public school, provided that the children were excused at certain hours for definitely religious studies. Of course, if this were done, similar privileges must be offered to children of other churches, provided that a sufficient number of them were anxious to take such courses, and the churches concerned, either by themselves or coöperatively with one another, were willing to provide adequate religious instruction at the times assigned. As a matter of fact, such week-day religious instruction was being given in 1932 at 6,000 school centers in the United States to no less than 813,000 children. Problems undoubtedly arise; in some places religious instruction is not permitted to be given in the public-school buildings. The children may be taken to a church building in the neighborhood or they can go out and sit on the curbstone and receive their spiritual training, but it must not be provided in the schools. Such an attitude seems to the director of this study at once doctrinaire and childish; situations may arise where it would be frankly difficult to provide the necessary accommodation in the school building at the times desired, but in such instances a little common sense on the part of those engaged in religious instruction and a similar coöperativeness on the part of the principals of the public schools ought to solve the question. The breaking-up of mixed classes into little religiously homogeneous units also makes havoc with the time-table, but where there is a will to overcome these difficulties, they can be overcome and are being overcome, as the following statistics indicate:[28]

SUMMARY OF THE EXTENT OF WEEK-DAY RELIGIOUS EDUCATION
IN THE UNITED STATES, 1932

Religious Body	Number of Schools*	Enrolment*
Protestant churches................	4,000	400,000
Roman Catholic churches..........	360	250,000
Jews.............................	1,300	135,000
Mormons........................	400	28,000
Totals.........................	6,060	813,000

* In round numbers.

In many places where the scheme is broached the fear is expressed that this is another inroad on the public-school system, or another effort to bring together the church and the state. On such grounds religious people often oppose the effort. Protestants who are not ill-disposed to the fundamental principle have grave doubts of their own ability to prepare an adequate curriculum or to produce trained and competent teachers. Minority groups

[28] Based on a report entitled: *Biennial Survey of Education in the U. S. Bulletin 20*, Office of Education, Washington, D. C., Vol. II, p. 53.

are often suspicious. Thus, when a somewhat similar effort to integrate religious education in the public-school system was proposed for the state of Minaes Geraes, in Brazil, the Catholics enthusiastically supported it, while the Protestants, being in the minority, opposed it, fearing that this was but another effort to Catholicize the schools. In certain areas in America, the major opposition has developed on the part of Jews, Catholics and freethinkers. On the other hand, there is much in it that appeals to all three groups. Protestants feel the need of a correlation of public-school training with religious and moral instruction, and recognize the inevitable limitations of the Sunday school; the Jews are already supporting large communal schools, but the attendance after school hours takes from children their proper opportunities for healthful play and recreation in the open air; in many places, as already intimated, Catholics attend the public schools in large numbers and the Catholic Church is not wholly successful in providing religious instruction for such students.

On the practical side, perhaps the greatest difficulty is in the comparative absence of an adequate curriculum for Protestant instruction. The Jews have gradually secured in their communal schools a curriculum centering around Jewish history, literature and culture which makes it comparatively simple for them to develop excellent and meaty courses for children of different ages. The Catholics have an elaborate system of religious education already operative in their parochial schools. The Protestants, however, have not yet evolved a system at once satisfactory to all the major Protestant groups, thoroughly constructive and rich in educational values. The International Council of Religious Education is, however, at work upon the problem and has already produced some usable material. Part of the difficulty resides in the lack of integration among Protestant religious educators themselves—some crying "forward to life situations" and others shouting "back to the understanding of sound tradition."

If, however, such mixed schools prevailed, the problem of Bible-readings and prayers at various school assemblies would have to be faced afresh. These have always been moot issues, and a vast body of judicial decisions has accumulated on the problem. Perhaps a special edition of biblical selections, prepared by a joint committee of Protestant, Catholic and Jewish scholars—a sort of canon within the canon—might be issued, with in some cases an independent translation of the original. The problem of the offering of prayers is still more difficult, for, strictly speaking, Catholics are not permitted to join with non-Catholics in prayer, except when certain precautions are taken or in exceptional circumstances. If there be but one God, it is a strange anomaly if His children can not discover some supplication which they can make to Him in concert![29]

---

[29] For full particulars regarding the status of Bible reading in the schools, see *Educational Bulletin No. 2*, published by the N. C. W. C., Washington, pp. 111-154.

CHAPTER VI

Secondary and Higher Education—Federal Relations

It has already been pointed out that "academies" were a characteristic development in New England in the nineteenth century, but it is perhaps fair to say that in the early days of "public education," the most effective secondary schools were operated under private, denominational auspices, either Catholic or Protestant. At one time, indeed, many Protestant parents frequently sent their daughters to the convent-schools, believing that such schools provided not alone the most thorough education in cultural subjects but also the best discipline in general deportment. We are unable to state to what extent this earlier practice is still continued.

SECONDARY SCHOOLS

It is not easy to provide satisfactory statistics regarding secondary education, since the teaching of certain high-school subjects in advanced classes in the elementary schools and the rise of the junior high school have created no little havoc for the statisticians. There are many diverse types of high schools today, due in part to the feeling that secondary education should be an end in itself and not simply a preparation for college or university. Out of this have come the commercial or technical high schools, with their magnificent equipment and high per capita costs.

GROWTH OF PUBLIC AND CATHOLIC SECONDARY SCHOOLS

Perhaps the most outstanding feature of recent years in education has been, however, the great increase in attendance at secondary schools, due to the steadily rising age limit below which children are required by law to continue in school. This is clearly seen in the statistics for the United States provided by the federal censuses of 1920 and 1930. Of all children in the following age groups, the percentages indicated were attending school in 1920 and 1930 respectively:

	Per Cent. Attending School	
Ages	1920	1930
5–20	64.3	69.9
14–15	79.9	88.8
16–17	42.0	57.3
18–20	14.8	21.4

The attendance at public elementary and secondary schools in these two years, according to the statistics furnished by the United States Office of Education was as follows:

	1920	1930	Per Cent. Increase
Elementary schools	19,377,927	21,278,593	9.8
High schools	2,200,379	4,399,422	49.9

This necessary expansion of secondary education has put an additional load upon the Catholic Church. Having struggled against odds to provide elementary schools for its children, it must now, in accordance with its official theory, seek to provide also secondary schools. The growth of Catholic high schools may be gathered from the following figures.

Year	No. Catholic Secondary Schools	No. Students
1895	280*	12,777*
1900	361*	15,872*
1905	389*	20,150*
1910	630*	30,124*
1915	1,276	74,538
1920	1,552	129,848
1924	2,181	185,098
1926	2,242	204,815
1928	2,129	225,845
1930	2,123	241,869

* Figures marked with an asterisk are those given in government reports. Other figures are those furnished in the Directory published by the National Catholic Welfare Council.

A steady growth in the attendance of these secondary schools is indicated, although the largest number of schools, according to the official Catholic figures, was recorded in 1926, since which time there has been a slight decline in each two-year period. This would suggest that the movement towards fewer and larger Catholic high schools is gaining ground.

Certain other interesting facts become patent if we compare the numbers enrolled in the public and Catholic elementary schools with those enrolled in the public and Catholic high schools, respectively:

U. S. SCHOOL ENROLMENT, 1930

	Total	Elementary	High School	H. S. Percentage of Total
Public system	25,678,015	21,278,593	4,399,422	17.1
Catholic system (N.C.W.C. figures)	2,464,467	2,222,598	241,869	9.8

From these figures, it would seem fairly obvious that in spite of the marked increase in the attendance at Catholic high schools, a very large proportion of Catholic young people still attend the public high schools. In one diocese where Catholic education generally is well organized, a survey was made of more than 2,226 boys and girls who were attending the public high schools. They were asked to indicate the reasons why they did not attend Catholic schools. The reasons given were as follows:

	Number of Choices	Per Cent. of Total
Public schools more convenient to pupils' home....	990	44.5
Courses offered do not meet need..................	466	20.9
Cannot pay tuition.............................	374	16.8
Choice of parents..............................	274	12.3
Wish to learn a trade...........................	98	4.4
Other reasons..................................	24	1.1
Total......................................	2,226	100.00

PROBLEMS CONFRONTING CATHOLIC SECONDARY EDUCATION

Perhaps, the fundamental difficulty confronting the Catholic Church in adequately providing high schools is financial, and the financial difficulty is due principally to the following reasons:

(a) Even in public or state schools, the per capita expense of high schools is higher than that of elementary schools. Thus, in 1930, the U. S. Office of Education estimated that the average cost of the public schools per pupil in average daily attendance in cities of 10,000 or more population was:

Kindergarten...................................	$ 54.93
Elementary....................................	69.01
Junior High School............................	93.95
High School...................................	122.35
Vocational....................................	189.21
Normal.......................................	339.55

Teachers in secondary schools are more highly trained and require larger salaries; equipment is more varied and costly; subjects are more diversified and hence demand specialists. While the Catholic high schools may be operated more cheaply than public high schools, they certainly cannot be operated as cheaply as the Catholic elementary schools.

(b) It is practically impossible to conduct Catholic high schools satisfactorily on the parochial basis which, in the case of elementary schools, has proved reasonably satisfactory. The attendance is too small to justify an adequate outlay on equipment, etc., except in large and fairly wealthy parishes. Even as it is, if there be 2,123 Catholic secondary schools with an aggregate enrolment of 241,389, this means an average enrolment per school of only 113.9 which is considerably below the enrolment of the public high schools.[1] Although much may be said in favor of the greater personal at-

---

[1] The Office of Education estimates that in 1930 there were 23,930 public secondary schools, with an aggregate enrolment of 4,399,422. This would indicate an average enrolment per school of 185.01.

tention which the smaller school affords, in such schools the per capita expense becomes all but prohibitive.

The result is that the Catholic Church has been moving away from the parochial high-school idea and instead has sought to develop communal high schools. The financing of communal high schools has, however, brought with it a new set of problems. In some of these communal schools, the individual parishes pay on the basis of the children from their parishes who attend; in others, tuition fees are charged and collected directly from the children; still others are free to all Catholic children, but the diocese as a whole underwrites the operating expense up to a certain maximum per capita, and entrusts the administration to one of the religious communities, which provides the building, equipment, staff, etc., and which must put aside a certain percentage of its receipts from the diocese as a sinking fund with which to pay off the indebtedness incurred by the provision of the original building. In some instances a parochial high school with larger accommodation than the particular parish itself requires may be converted into a communal school, in which case the control of the parish priest in the work of the school may be restricted. In general, the church seems anxious to promote communal schools of this character, but encounters parochialism, vested interests of one kind and another, difficulties in financing and locating schools and other equally difficult problems.

(c) More and more the members of the religious orders of men employed in the Catholic school system have been withdrawing from teaching in the elementary schools and devoting their time to the secondary schools. Catholic statistics indicate that the teaching brothers require larger remuneration than the teaching sisters. This is an additional reason for the increased cost of operation of the high schools over the elementary schools.

(d) While a considerable number of Catholic high schools are coeducational, the tendency is clearly evident to establish, when possible, separate institutions for the two sexes. This again militates against the practicability of parochial high schools, for if it is difficult for a single parish to operate its own high school, it is no easier for it to operate two high schools.

(e) As high schools, generally speaking, must offer courses preparatory to college, their standards must be high, and various accrediting agencies refuse to accredit the Catholic high schools unless they prove themselves worthy, even if some of the standards set may at times seem artificial. Speaking of certain Catholic high schools in the West, a research worker has said:

"The standards set up by the North Central Association deal with such items as buildings, library and laboratories, records, requirements for graduation, efficiency of instruction, salaries, preparation of teachers, teaching load and pupil load. . . . On the whole such recognition is desirable, and the high schools should be encouraged to qualify for accrediting by one or other of the established agencies. For one thing, it removes the ground for the oft-heard accusation that the Catholic high schools are inferior to the public. Secondly, it gives practical assurance that the graduates of these high schools will have no difficulty in securing admission to the various colleges belonging to the association. These are, evidently, distinct advantages. None the less, accrediting has its disadvantages. When all is said and done, the main purpose of the accrediting agencies is to standardize the preparation of students for college. This was the aim that led to their organization and it is still the dominating aim. Recognition of a particular high school by the accrediting agency, therefore, often means simply that the high school is equipped to prepare its pupils for college entrance. Yet we know that only a small percentage of high school pupils actually go to college— approximately 30 per cent for the whole country. . . . Accrediting is concerned only with the interests of the minority. Hence, being accredited does not necessarily mean that a high school is meeting the need of its student body, etc."

Accrediting, whatever else it means, does set a minimum expense below which it is impossible to economize.

(f) Even if the Catholic high schools are prepared to offer sound courses of a classical nature, most of them find it quite impossible to provide the equipment demanded by technical schools, since, as has been shown above, the per capita expense of technical schools in the public system of schools is only slightly exceeded by the per capita of college education. This accounts in no small measure for the answers of the Catholic students in the public high schools when they were asked why they did not go to the Catholic schools. As we have already seen, 444 out of 2,226 stated that the courses offered in the Catholic high school did not meet their needs, while ninety-eight others expressed the desire to learn a trade. It is fairly clear from various studies made under Catholic auspices that the Catholic school constituency is drawn for the most part from the children of "large families" in "humble circumstances," who might naturally be expected, on purely economic grounds, to seek practical courses in preference to classical courses. This would probably be particularly true of the men. The following figures indicate that more girls than boys attend high schools, but that the excess is more marked in Catholic than in public schools:

STUDENTS IN SECONDARY SCHOOLS, 1930

	Boys	Girls	Total
Public high schools	2,115,228	2,284,194	4,399,422
Catholic high schools	102,094	135,120	241,869 (including 4,655 unclassified)

In fact, certain Catholic educators consulted in the course of this study stated quite frankly that they could not attempt to compete with the public technical schools; they felt that they might properly continue to provide a limited number of high schools offering excellent classical instruction, but that they would be wise to provide only a minimum of technical courses.

As to the general efficiency of the Catholic high schools, comparisons with the institutions controlled by the public may be odious and unfair. Too many factors enter into these comparisons to make them very convincing one way or the other. In 1930 a study of the freshman class at the University of Illinois indicated that of 2,291 students from the public high schools, the median record was 81.49 as opposed to a median of 78.96 from 106 students from private (including Catholic) schools. One would of course need to know whether the University of Illinois attracts the strongest students in the Catholic high schools. In 1931, the registrar of the University of Chicago had the coöperation of all public and private secondary schools in Chicago and a scholastic test was given to the seniors. The medians then established were:

> For Catholic schools............................ 120.64
> For other private schools....................... 147.78
> For public schools.............................. 126.43

These figures are given for what they may be worth.

The main point to be considered in the field of secondary education is its inevitably higher per capita expense over elementary education, and the enhanced and possibly insuperable difficulty which the Catholic Church faces in adequately providing these types of secondary education without public support. Even though the Catholic population is largely urban and hence fairly highly concentrated, the church can hardly compete with the public system. If the Catholic population were not highly concentrated, its task would be almost hopeless. Even as it is, it would seem as if it were inevitably subject to certain very definite limitations in the field of secondary education in the United States.

In Canada, Catholic secondary education is provided under provincial auspices in Quebec, but in none of the other provinces are there Catholic separate high schools supported by public funds. Certain of the separate schools do, to be sure, provide training in first-year high-school subjects and there are many Catholic academies, but these latter receive no assistance from the public treasury.

PRIVATE NON-CATHOLIC SCHOOLS

In addition to Catholic and public secondary schools, there are, in the United States, according to the statistics published by the United States Office of Education, approximately 1,165 other private secondary schools, of which 647 are non-sectarian and 518 are denominational. There were 630 such non-Catholic, denominational schools and 1,270 non-sectarian schools in 1895. Consequently, it is apparent that there has been a decline in the number of both these types of schools in thirty-five years. The increase in the number of private schools has been almost entirely Catholic. Protestant denominations, with the exception of Methodists (North), have fewer secondary schools than they had in 1895. This may be due to the abandonment of such schools, to their secularization or to their consolidation with other similar schools. Of the schools listed by the U. S. Office of Education in 1930, with more than 100 secondary pupils enrolled, twenty-six had endowments of more than $500,000. Eighteen of these had endowments of more than a million; five had endowments of more than three millions. The most largely endowed school was in Hawaii with an endowment of ten million dollars; others well-endowed were the Phillips Academy, Phillips Exeter, St. Paul's and Sacred Heart (at Detroit).

In a number of cities certain private schools are extremely exclusive, and frequently refuse to accept Jews. The excellent private schools provided by the Friends were usually exceptions to this tendency, although occasionally the Friends' schools deemed it expedient to limit the number of Jews that might be admitted. In one city, the reason was that at a certain period the public schools were in a bad way, and there was a rush to private schools. So many Jewish children applied that the Friends' school feared it might be inundated and therefore applied certain restrictions. The Jews, therefore, took the initiative in providing a school which they could control; before they had carried through their scheme they coöperated with a number of Gentiles and sought to operate a school—one of the first progressive schools to be formed in the country—which should not be for Jews only. The directors were to be drawn from both groups, and it was hoped that the student body would be equally divided between Jews and Gentiles. In recent years, however, the tendency has been toward a larger Jewish representation both in the student body and in the directorate, although efforts are being made to preserve the equilibrium. There are other schools of a similar composition in the cities studied, although it would perhaps be improper to designate them as "Jewish." Such schools are usually highly spoken of in the communities and very often they have the reputation of being the most "progressive" schools in the city. One curious fact, however, deserves note. In the schools that are practically controlled by Jews and largely attended by Jews (excluding Jewish communal schools), the teaching staff is usually Gentile. This seems to be not accidental, but intentional, and the reasons given by Jews themselves were:

(1) It was desired that the Jewish children should have, for cultural reasons, larger contacts with the Gentiles, and hence not be confined to an entirely Jewish surrounding at home, and an entirely Jewish surrounding at school.

(2) It was felt that the Gentile teacher might have a greater emotional

stability than the Jewish teacher, and consequently be better able to deal with certain types of emotional upsets experienced by the Jewish child than would a Jewish teacher who was more subject to the same kind of emotional reactions himself.

However valid these reasons may be, the fact was that about 95 per cent. of the teachers in these "Jewish" private schools were Gentiles. There are, however, other private secondary schools that are conducted under distinctively Jewish auspices, such as the Jewish People's Institute in Chicago and the Talmudical Academy (Yeshivah) in New York City which has now received a "college rank."

HIGHER EDUCATION

While elementary and secondary education is, for the most part, provided by institutions publicly owned and administered, higher education in the United States (although not in Canada) is largely carried on in private or even denominationally-controlled colleges and universities. There are, to be sure, the great state universities and there are some excellent municipal universities (e.g., University of Cincinnati); nevertheless, the biennial Survey of Education for 1928-30 provided the following table:

Type of Institution, School or Department	Publicly Controlled	Privately Controlled	Total
Universities, colleges and professional schools			
Degree-conferring institutions.................	117	684	801
Junior colleges.............................	129	148	277
Professional departments			
Theology...................................	0	75	75
Law.......................................	42	61	103
Medicine..................................	31	33	64
Dentistry..................................	12	24	36
Pharmacy..................................	34	24	58
Veterinary medicine........................	9	1	10
Independent professional schools..............	7	146	153

In 1929-30 these 1,078 universities, colleges and professional schools reporting had enrolled 971,584 students, 604,243 of whom were men and 367,341 were women. Of this student body, 390,397 were being educated in publicly-controlled institutions, while 581,187 were enrolled in privately-controlled institutions. The Biennial Survey of Education states:

"During the ten-year period 1919-20 to 1929-30 enrolments at universities, colleges and professional schools, including preparatory and special students, increased 86.2 per cent. Contrary to what might be expected, this was not the greatest increase during any ten-year period of American higher education. In the decade 1909-10 to 1919-20 there was an increase of approximately 90 per cent in college enrolments. The figures for both 1909-10 and 1919-20 contain a larger number of students in preparatory departments and in special courses."

In this decade, however, while the population increased 16.1 per cent., the enrolment in institutions of higher learning increased 86.2 per cent.

Attention has already been directed to the fact that of ten colleges founded in the thirteen colonies between 1637 and 1776, only one was non-sectarian, viz., the University of Pennsylvania. The prestige of these early institutions has hardly been shaken by the development of state universities in the nineteenth century, although many of them, originally denominational in control, have become practically non-sectarian. Many of them have secured endowments of such a magnitude that even the state universities can hardly compete with them. The endowments of Harvard and Yale, for example, both exceed $100,000,000. Such institutions, moreover, are reputedly free from the type of political interference that frequently haunts the state-controlled institution, although, on the other hand, a salutary respect for the growth of their endowments may incline them to pay undue deference to the magnates of business. There is, moreover, something to be said against state control of higher education, even as Goldwin Smith once said:

"Out of a simple and rudimentary education the State may indeed get some return, because it may say that, by reason of such an education, the citizen is enabled to discharge his duties to society with greater acceptance than he would be able to do without it; but when it comes to a matter of higher education, that is a luxury, and like any other luxury, the expense of it should be defrayed by the person who gets it."[2]

The cost of maintaining these various universities and colleges in 1929-30 was $563,547,070, of which the expense of administering public institutions was $225,816,040 and the expense of administering private institutions was $337,547,070.

There are probably too many independent colleges in the United States and the standards of some of them are, to say the least, questionable. But whatever one may think about the propriety of state-controlled institutions of higher learning in all instances, it is difficult to see how certain of the smaller and less resourceful states can adequately provide for their needs without state initiative. The situation confronting Oklahoma or Nevada, for instance, in the matter of public education may be quite different from that confronting Michigan, Wisconsin or Texas. It is highly probable that the time is ripe for a general re-examination of the best possible means of correlating these various agencies in such a way that the initiative of each may not be unduly curtailed, while they may do in common what they never could do separately. When plans are commonly discussed for the consolidation of such great institutions as the University of Chicago and Northwestern

---

[2] Quoted by Mavor, James, *My Windows on the Street of the World* (London: J. M. Dent, 1923), Vol. II, p. 132.

University, the spectacle of so many ill-equipped colleges living in a continuous state of near-bankruptcy is hardly edifying. Indeed, in Canada, during the depression, not a few expressed the feeling that the maintenance of three distinct provincial universities in the prairie provinces was an approximation to economic madness.

The multiplicity of these institutions in the United States is due in large measure to sectarian rivalry, although many private institutions were never denominational. One need only survey the various colleges and universities in the state of Ohio to realize how each denomination seemed to feel its particular responsibility to found a college. Many of these colleges have become non-sectarian, while others which remained under the wing of a particular denomination have found their financial support both within and without the denomination, by becoming all things to all men and appealing to various loyalties—the denomination, the community, the Alma Mater, and the general promotion of knowledge.

JEWS ALONE FOUND NO UNIVERSITIES

Of all the religious bodies the Jews alone have refrained from establishing institutions of higher learning. Their only colleges have been primarily theological, such as the Hebrew Union College in Cincinnati, the Jewish Theological Seminary of America in New York, Dropsie College in Pennsylvania. The Yeshivah in New York has recently begun to do work of collegiate grade. As will be shown later, Jewish students attend not only the state and non-sectarian institutions, but also the various institutions connected with Christian denominations, both Protestant and Catholic. There is some feeling, both in Jewish and Gentile circles, that it might be desirable for the Jews to develop institutions of their own, especially since—as shall be pointed out later—many private institutions have sought to establish a *numerus clausus* for Jews. In one of the largest Catholic universities in the East, 56.7 per cent. of the student body consists of Jews.

CATHOLIC COLLEGES AND UNIVERSITIES IN THE UNITED STATES

Canon 1379, of the Catholic Church, already quoted, states that "if the public universities are not imbued with the Catholic doctrine or spirit, it is to be desired that in the nation or province a Catholic University be erected." When one considers that the first colleges were almost entirely connected with Protestant denominations and that the non-sectarian institutions were at least "a-religious" in sentiment, while the state universities were "neutral," it was perhaps inevitable that Catholic colleges and universities should be founded. The first universities in the new world were of course Catholic in conception and spirit, San Marcos at Lima (Peru) and the University of

218 *Catholics, Jews and Protestants*

Mexico being founded in 1551; but the first Catholic university in the United States was founded at Georgetown only in 1787. Among the next Catholic colleges to be established were Mount St. Mary's, 1808; St. Louis, 1818; Xavier, 1831; Duquesne, 1841, and Notre Dame, 1842. The Catholic University of America, the only university to be conducted by the bishops of the United States, was established in 1889. A characteristic of this last institution is in the number of religious houses of study (twenty-three in all) near the university and integrated in its life. Many of the private institutions established since 1900 have been Catholic, so that at the present time there are 162 Catholic colleges or universities in the United States, seventy-three of these being for men and eighty-nine for women. The total enrolment, in 1930, was 105,926.

In the seventy-three institutions of university status for men, the total enrolment, excluding those who attend summer sessions and correspondence courses, is 63,424. Of this number, 39,063 are in ten institutions having 2,000 or more students enrolled in full session, and the balance, 24,361, are enrolled in sixty-three institutions. Forty-seven institutions had a total enrolment of fewer than 500 students; fourteen had fewer than 100. The following analysis is based on the returns in the Directory of Catholic Colleges and Universities for 1932-33:

	No. of Institutions for Men
Over 5,000 students....................	1
4,000–5,000.......................	3
3,000–4,000.......................	4
2,000–3,000.......................	2
1,000–2,000.......................	6
500–1,000.......................	10
100– 500.......................	33
Under 100	14
	73

The Catholic universities for men with the largest enrolment (full session) are:

Fordham......................................	6,717
Loyola.......................................	4,326
St. Johns....................................	4,806
De Paul......................................	4,008
Marquette....................................	3,721
Detroit......................................	3,561
St. Louis....................................	3,639
Notre Dame...................................	3,055
Duquesne.....................................	2,666
Georgetown...................................	2,564
Total..................................	39,063

The seventy-three institutions are in thirty states; there are no such Catholic institutions in eighteen states. One reason is in the comparative paucity of Catholic population in these states. Thus:

	Catholic Population 1926	Total Population 1930
Connecticut	557,747	1,606,903
Delaware	36,696	238,380
Florida	39,379	1,468,211
Georgia	17,871	2,908,506
Idaho	23,143	445,032
Kentucky	177,069	2,614,589
Maine	173,893	797,423
Mississippi	32,075	2,009,821
Nevada	8,447	91,058
New Mexico	174,287	423,317
North Dakota	104,195	680,849
South Dakota	97,077	692,849
South Carolina	17,871	1,738,765
Tennessee	24,876	2,616,556
Utah	14,595	507,847
Virginia	38,605	2,421,851
West Virginia	71,265	1,738,765
Wyoming	18,772	225,565

In states with large Catholic populations, the situation is different. There are eight colleges for men in Pennsylvania, and seven each in New York and Illinois. Of course, other reasons may account for such a distribution of colleges. The fact, however, that there are fourteen colleges, with an enrolment of fewer than 100 each, suggests that in all probability the Catholics have too many colleges in some states. This situation may be due in part to an over-eagerness of certain dioceses to establish institutions, whether they can support them adequately or not, and in part to the eagerness of religious communities to undertake the establishment of such colleges and their unwillingness, once the colleges are established, to yield any ground.

Another fact to be considered is the large number of *religious* employed in teaching in the 162 Catholic colleges for men and for women. The analysis of the teaching staff is as follows:

PROFESSORS AND INSTRUCTORS IN CATHOLIC COLLEGES, 1930

Religious ... 3,114
Lay ... 3,877
Unclassified ... 777

7,768

CATHOLICS, PROTESTANTS AND JEWS ON FACULTIES

A sampling made for this study of Catholic institutions with a total staff of 1,883 revealed that 260, or 13.8 per cent., of the staff were Protestants, and

59, or 3.1 per cent. of the staff were Jews. It may be that the inclusion of so many non-Catholics in the faculty is a matter of policy; it may be that for the positions the best available men at the time were non-Catholics; or the selections may have been more accidental; but the fact of their presence in these Catholic institutions is itself significant. Nevertheless, 41.3 per cent. of the entire staff consists of members of the religious communities, and it is difficult not to believe that the large number of religious so employed in teaching necessarily limits the number of positions of an academic character open to Catholic laymen in their own colleges. Will they, however, have better opportunities in non-Catholic colleges? It may be that graduates of Catholic colleges do not find that their Catholic education assists them when they seek academic positions in non-Catholic institutions. At all events, out of 179 non-Catholic universities and colleges reporting, forty-three indicated that they had no record of Catholic members of the faculty, while eighty-three, with a total faculty body of 15,389, could report only 562 Catholic members, or 3.7 per cent. of the total number of the faculty. There is some reason to believe, moreover, that many, if not most, of these 562 Catholic members received their education, not in Catholic but in non-Catholic institutions. Others are distinguished savants brought to America from Catholic countries in Europe (e.g., Austria), where they received their training and had already achieved their reputation. Of course, it must also be remembered that the Catholic population in the United States has been largely recruited from foreign immigrants who have had to take the most menial positions and often to live in the more congested areas. It would have been surprising had a group so handicapped, economically and socially, found itself "culturally" earlier.

RELIGIOUS AFFILIATION OF AMERICAN LEADERS

Two studies have been made of the religious affiliation of American leaders as indicated in "Who's Who." Dr. C. Luther Fry, of the Institute of Social and Religious Research, discovered that the denominational representation in "Who's Who" in proportion to general church-membership in the country was as follows:[3]

Unitarian	32.50
Reformed	6.52
Universalist	6.43
Episcopalian	6.07
Congregationalist	4.96
Quaker	4.40
Presbyterian	3.11
Christian Scientist	1.27
Methodist	0.89

[3] "The Religious Affiliations of American Leaders," *Scientific Monthly*, March, 1933.

```
Baptist.........................................  0.70
Disciple of Christ..............................  0.61
Lutheran........................................  0.32
Roman Catholic..................................  0.13
```

Dr. Harvey C. Lehman of Ohio University and Dr. Paul A. Witty of Northwestern University, in a somewhat similar but earlier analysis of "American Men of Science," which contains a list of 13,500 names of individuals who have carried on research in the natural and exact sciences, discovered that the number of times each denomination reaches, falls below or exceeds the quota (expected from church-membership data) among starred names in "American Men of Science," was as follows:[4]

| | Proportional |
Denomination	Representation
Unitarian......................................	81.4
Swedenborgian (1 member only)................	16.5
Congregationalist.............................	9.308
Friends.......................................	6.6
Universalist..................................	6.6
Episcopalian..................................	5.701
Presbyterian..................................	3.045
Dutch Reformed (1 member only)..............	1.0
Jewish..	0.717
Methodist.....................................	0.444
Disciples.....................................	0.291
Baptists......................................	0.244
Lutheran......................................	0.201
Roman Catholic...............................	0.048

It is quite possible to challenge the methods used by the investigators in determining the Jewish and Catholic population of the country, but even so, we may have here one of the reasons why so few Catholics or Jews are to be found on the faculties of the non-Catholic universities.

CATHOLICS IN NON-CATHOLIC INSTITUTIONS

Perhaps because of the superior "social" or academic standing of the non-Catholic colleges, we find that, despite the effort of the Catholic Church to provide higher institutions of learning under strictly Catholic auspices, a large percentage of Catholic students do not attend their own institutions. In one of the cities studied, where there is an excellent Catholic college, 31.7 per cent. of the entire student body at the secular institution was Catholic. One Baptist institution in New England reported that 13.2 per cent. of its student body was Catholic. It is difficult to obtain absolutely accurate figures on this point, but the following table indicates the distribution of Catholic and Jewish students in state universities and private, non-sectarian institutions:

[4] See article in *The Scientific Monthly*, December, 1931.

ENROLMENT OF CATHOLIC STUDENTS AT NON-CATHOLIC INSTITUTIONS
(EXCEPT DENOMINATIONAL COLLEGES) 1932–33

Type of Institution	No. Instns. Reporting	Total No. Students	No. Catholic Students	Per Cent. of Total
State universities...............	35	161,765	13,012	8.4
Other private, but non-sectarian.	63	176,481	27,736	15.7
Total......................	98	338,246	40,748	12.04

In regard to the denominational colleges, reports received from these gave only rough percentages, not the actual numbers. The returns from seventy-six such institutions may be analyzed as follows:

	Per Cent. Catholics
Quartile 1...	1.3
Median	4.0
Quartile 3...	5.0
Quartile 4...	24.0

In 1924 a Catholic investigator estimated that 7.2 per cent. of all students attending non-Catholic institutions were Catholics. He found that at that time, 36,223 Catholics were attending non-Catholic institutions against a total enrolment of 41,680 (in full sessions) in Catholic institutions. Part of this was estimate, but the estimate seemed based on fair assumptions. Since 1924, of course, enrolment in universities has greatly increased, that in Catholic institutions alone from 60,189 (including summer sessions, etc.), to 105,926. But in 1924 nearly one-half of all Catholic students were apparently to be found in non-Catholic institutions. If the total enrolment in Catholic institutions today is 105,926, and the enrolment in ninety-eight of the state universities and other non-sectarian, private institutions alone includes 40,748 Catholics, it would seem reasonable to believe that there are probably as many Catholics today studying in non-Catholic as in Catholic institutions.

According to Catholic chaplains in secular institutions who have the opportunity of discovering first-hand from Catholic students why they preferred such colleges to Catholic schools, this large Catholic attendance is mainly due to the following reasons:

(1) The academic prestige of the non-Catholic institutions is greater, and a graduate of such a college has better chances of securing a position.

(2) These institutions offer many valuable technical courses, which few, if any, Catholic colleges have the means to offer.

(3) These institutions provide larger scholarship and bursary funds than the Catholic institutions.

(4) Non-Catholic institutions carry with them greater social prestige.

NON-CATHOLICS IN CATHOLIC INSTITUTIONS

On the other hand, many non-Catholics attend Catholic institutions. Returns from twenty-four Catholic institutions, including many of the largest (with the exception of Fordham and Notre Dame), and with a total student body of 30,607, indicated that of these students 3,299 (10.8 per cent.) were Protestants and 4,722 (15.4 per cent.) were Jews. That propinquity is an important factor in college attendance may be gathered from the fact that 56.7 per cent. of the entire student body of one of these Catholic institutions in an area increasingly Jewish, were Jews. Catholic colleges in which 26.2 per cent. of the aggregate student body are non-Catholic may certainly make some claim to be non-sectarian in their operation, if not in their control.

CATHOLIC FINANCIAL PROBLEMS

Undoubtedly one great difficulty which the Catholic Church must encounter in developing centers of higher education, as it has encountered it in the promotion of elementary and secondary education, is financial. Even its great universities have endowments which are inconsiderable beside those of the larger non-sectarian, private institutions, and while this obstacle might in time be rectified in those areas where the Catholic Church is strong, it is all but insuperable in those states where the Catholic population is weak in numbers or in wealth. As already pointed out, there are no Catholic institutions of higher learning in eighteen states. What shall they do?

There are some Catholics who insist that nothing short of "an entire education of Catholics by Catholics under Catholic auspices" will suffice, and these strenuously discourage attendance of Catholics at non-Catholic institutions and seek to build up ever stronger colleges and universities of their own kind. To the outsider, however, it would seem that Catholic educationalists would be wise in limiting the number of their own institutions so that they might have, at strategically located centers, institutions worthy of comparison in financial resource, laboratory equipment, etc., with the best non-Catholic institutions. They might even offer routine classical courses in a larger number of smaller colleges, but with education so completely in flux, with the ever-increasing emphasis on technical knowledge and laboratory experimentation, it seems almost inevitable that the Catholic authorities can provide only a fraction of the higher education to be demanded by Catholics so long as the present ratio of Catholic to non-Catholic population is maintained.

ATTEMPTED SOLUTIONS

Some Catholic leaders, therefore, seek a new solution of their problem, which would not discourage Catholic students from attending non-Catholic colleges, but would rather provide facilities at each of these colleges for maintaining the religious morale of such Catholic students. They emphasize the fact that Pope Pius X, on April 15, 1905, addressed an encyclical letter on Christian education to all Catholic bishops in which he said, *inter alia:*

"We do decree and strictly command that in all dioceses throughout the world the following regulations be observed and enforced. Where there are public academies, colleges and universities, let schools of religion ('scholae religionis') be established for the purpose of teaching the truths of our faith and the precepts of Christian morality to the youths who attend such institutions wherein no mention is made of religion."

As a matter of fact, there are three distinct types of such coöperation of the Catholic authorities with non-Catholic institutions in the United States and Canada which deserve special attention:

NEWMAN CLUBS

(1) Two hundred and one Catholic Clubs, usually called Newman Clubs, with a Catholic chaplain in charge, have been organized in non-Catholic institutions. This college chaplain is recognized by the college authorities as the spiritual adviser of the Catholic students. The work in some institutions is quite small; but in other institutions, like the University of Illinois, it is most imposing. Under this system, the Catholic students mix freely with non-Catholics, and are exposed to the intellectual influences which they must inevitably encounter if they are to move freely in modern America, while at the same time they are shepherded and advised by carefully selected priests, who can deal with their intellectual and spiritual problems as they arise and thus contribute to the formation of a religious and Catholic character. Religious instruction is carried on, for the most part, by voluntary discussion groups, while masses for the students are said in private chapels reserved for the use of such clubs. In addition to these voluntary courses, however, some universities give credit for work done in courses offered by such chaplains, and the instruction of this character is often, therefore, more systematic and thorough. Newman Clubs also operate inquiry classes open to any student in the university, provide lectures by outstanding Catholic speakers, and arrange week-end retreats, etc.

SCHOOLS OF RELIGION AT UNIVERSITIES

(2) In some institutions, even state institutions, a School of Religion has been formed, with its own incorporation and financed exclusively by the denominations coöperating. Perhaps the most elaborate attempt of this kind has been made at the University of Iowa, Iowa City, where the School of Religion was incorporated in 1924. The articles of incorporation stated:

". . . the members of this corporation shall be two electors from each religious denomination which has already associated itself or may hereafter associate itself with the School of Religion at the State University of Iowa, in accordance with the constitution thereof, and a number of electors representing the State University of Iowa which shall equal in number the total number of electors chosen by said religious denominations. The electors representing the State University of Iowa are to be chosen in whatever manner said University shall decide upon and regardless of the religious belief to which said electors may subscribe. The electors to represent each religious denomination are to be chosen by such denomination in accordance with the rules, forms and usages of each said denomination."

These members selected in a prescribed manner certain trustees whose functions included the financing of the school "in so far as not provided by the budget of the State University of Iowa," the employment of the staff and the determination of the policy of this school.

At Iowa eventually the staff included three professors—one a Protestant, one a Catholic and one a Jew. After some experimentation of this character, Catholic coöperation was withdrawn.[5] The University of Iowa accredited the courses given by such professors. Other variants of this scheme have been attempted at other state or non-sectarian universities, but usually the coöperation involved has been intra-Protestant. At the University of Oklahoma, for instance, the school of religion has been regarded as the Department of Religious Education of the University's School of Education.[6] The salaries of the men engaged are contributed by the coöperating denominations, but paid to them by the university; such men are nominated by the churches for the positions, but the appointments are made by the university.

UNIVERSITY FEDERATION AT TORONTO

(3) A third method, which is actually operative in the University of Toronto, and which recently has inspired an effort at emulation at the University of Oklahoma, deserves, perhaps, fuller delineation.

In 1827, Archdeacon, later Bishop, Strachan, of the Church of England, obtained a charter for an institution to be known as King's College and to be supported out of the Clergy Reserves. The college was conceived as a distinctly Anglican institution, all the members of its council being required to subscribe to the Thirty-nine Articles, and its divinity degrees being confined to those holding Holy Orders in the Church of England. As a ma-

---

[5] Subsequent developments at the University of Iowa are treated more fully in chapter ix.
[6] An interesting analysis of the various problems which faced such Schools of Religion several years ago may be found in a small book, *The Church in the Universities*, edited by David R. Porter (New York: Association Press, 1925). More recent information will be found in chapter ix of this volume.

jority of the population of the province were non-Anglicans, a furore arose and straightway the other denominations hastened to create degree-conferring institutions of their own. The Methodists started Victoria, the Presbyterians founded Queen's, and the Catholics established Regiopolis College. So continuous was the controversy that it was impossible to launch the projected enterprise of Bishop Strachan until 1843, and in 1850 an Act of Parliament changed the name of King's College to the University of Toronto, abolished all religious tests and all denominational forms of worship in the interests of complete secularization and government control. The Anglicans thereupon established a University (Trinity) of their own.

As the provincial university grew in numbers, however, and required greater equipment, it was unable to obtain the popular financial support it needed, for the various denominations were supporting their own universities and colleges. An overture was made in 1880 to St. Michael's College (Roman Catholic), then located in Toronto, to become affiliated with the university. It did so the following year, after taking precautions in regard to the teaching of history and philosophy to Catholic students. The Provincial authorities then invited the other universities to become part of a university federation. After some six years of negotiation, Victoria University (Methodist) did so, Queen's (Presbyterian) never did so, and for many years Trinity (Anglican) also refused to belong to the federation, but finally joined forces in 1903. The result is that the University of Toronto is a federation, and a student in the faculty of arts enrols in the college of his choice—University College (non-sectarian), Trinity College (Anglican), Victoria College (formerly Methodist, now United Church) or St. Michael's (Roman Catholic). The student takes certain arts subjects in his own college, but for other arts subjects he must attend classes conducted by professors in the Faculty of Arts of the University. The four colleges provide their own instruction in Greek, Latin, Ancient History, English, French, German, Oriental Languages, and Ethics. In addition, St. Michael's provides its own instruction in History and Philosophy, including Logic, Metaphysics, Anthropology, Psychology and the History of Philosophy. All the Arts courses in the university provide for certain "religious knowledge" options in all four years. A student is not required to take Religious Knowledge, but he may take it as one of his options, and a Catholic, though enrolled at University College, would be able to take that particular option at St. Michael's. All examinations are set, and the degrees conferred, by the university.

The results of this federation are far-reaching:

(1) A student body of 4,000 in Arts alone, which would prove most unwieldy in one institution, is wisely divided among a number of colleges in which the individuality of the students may be more fully respected. Never-

theless, this division is effected, not artificially, but with respect to the real significance of the different religious and cultural backgrounds of the students themselves.

(2) While there is overlapping of certain subjects, all duplication of equipment in the teaching of those sciences which can hardly be imparted denominationally is avoided.

(3) A closer integration of the intellectual and spiritual life of the students is achieved by the definite recognition of the religious character of the three Arts colleges, and Arts students in the university are privileged to take, in connection with their course, and to receive credit therefor, some religious knowledge option in the college of their choice.

(4) St. Michael's, saved from the necessity of reduplicating laboratories, etc., now turns its attention to a specific field of scholarship in which it is seeking to build up a particularly strong department. It has created an Institute of Mediaeval Studies, which, in addition to its permanent staff, uses for part of each year such celebrated scholars as F. Gilson, and Jacques Maritain.

(5) As professors and students enrolled in these different colleges mingle together and work together at the delicate coöperative tasks which such a federation creates, they develop a spirit of tolerance and community-mindedness which has its own repercussion on the outside world. In the very week in which this is being written, the St. Michael's team is within sight of the amateur hockey championship of Canada. The writer overheard some hockey enthusiasts discussing the situation in a lunch-room. One of them said: "My grandfather was one of the greatest Orangemen in Canada, and if he could have heard me cheering for those 'mickies,' he would have turned over in his grave." They recognize, however, that St. Michael's is an integral part of their university.

(6) The whole educational life of the province is thus happily and economically coördinated in a manner that deserves the careful study, if not the emulation, of state universities in the United States. Already an effort is being made in the state of Oklahoma to effect a somewhat similar coördination there.[7]

So far as the University of Toronto is concerned, there is very general satisfaction, even pride, in the success of the federation. The quality of the work done in the federated colleges is highly regarded; the public funds available to the university as a whole are supplemented by private funds, which are enhanced by the loyalty of the several denominations to their

---

[7] See "Special Committee Report and Preliminary Proposals for the Coordinating of the Greater University of Oklahoma," printed but not published (Norman: University of Oklahoma Press, 1933).

respective colleges. The general level of scholarship in the university has received the highest rating from both the Rockefeller and the Carnegie Foundations.

JEWS AND HIGHER EDUCATION

As already indicated, the Jews have developed practically no institutions of higher learning in either the United States or Canada. A very considerable number of Jews, however, attend college and this number is steadily increasing. Even as early as 1918-19, an investigation made by the Bureau of Jewish Social Research showed that "the Jews formed 9.7 per cent. of the students at the universities and colleges, although they were only 3.32 per cent. of the population, and that in New York City alone they constituted 38.5 per cent. of the student body although only 25 per cent. of the population."[8]

The figures for 1933, obtained for this study from thirty-five state universities and sixty-three non-sectarian private institutions, indicated that with 338,246 students, the Jewish total was 38,959 or 11.4 per cent. In respect to seventy-six Protestant denominational institutions the percentages varied from 0.3 per cent. in the first quartile to 20 per cent. in the fourth quartile. These figures would seem to confirm the findings of the Bureau of Jewish Social Research in 1918-19, and indicate that probably over 10 per cent. of all students in colleges, universities and professional schools are Jewish. Even in the twenty-five leading Catholic universities, 15.4 per cent. of the student body was Jewish.

This tendency is of course what might be expected when similar conditions were found in Europe. Israel Cohen asserts that "before the war the percentage of Jews at the universities in Germany was seven times as large as the percentage of the Christian population, in Hungary it was six times and in Austria four times as large." Careful statistics concerning the number of Jews in the universities and professional schools of Europe may be found in Mr. Cohen's illuminating and informative volume. As is well known in many European countries, even before the War, the *numerus clausus* was invoked to limit the number of Jews who might be enrolled in these institutions, especially in the professional schools. Mr. Cohen says, in an illuminating footnote: "The agitation usually began among the students of the medical faculty, who demanded that the Jews should provide a proportionate number of Jewish corpses for dissection, but it soon became general." He also provides the following table showing the percentage of Jews at European universities:

---

[8] Quoted from Cohen, Israel: *Jewish Life in Modern Times,* Second Edition (London: Methuen and Company, 1929).

		Jewish Percentage of	
Country	Students	Urban Population	Total Population
Austria (Vienna)...................	24.85	10.80	...
Bavaria...........................	5.4	1.8	0.8
Czecho-Slovakia...................	15.0	5.5	2.6
Great Britain......................	2.27	....	0.7
Hungary..........................	10.8	17.2	5.9
Latvia............................	8.9	17.4	5.0
Lithuania (Kovno).................	20.8	....	7.6
Poland...........................	24.3	37.0	10.4
Prussia...........................	4.5	....	1.06
Ukraine..........................	47.4	35.0	7.0
United States......................	9.7	....	3.2

The European Jew especially patronizes the medical faculties. Thus, of all the Jewish students in Poland, 34.1 per cent. are engaged in medicine; in Prague, 68 per cent.; in Riga, 47.2 per cent.; and in Ukraine, 60.5 per cent. In the study made by the Bureau of Jewish Social Research in 1918-19, for the United States, it was found that the percentages of some 14,837 Jewish students in various departments were as follows:

	Percentage	
Department	Jewish	Non-Jewish
Commerce and Finance.............	23.2	11.8
Medicine........................	18.4	11.2
Engineering......................	16.3	30.9
Dentistry........................	12.0	4.7

Perhaps, one might quote the figures from the University of Buffalo, where, out of 1,817 regular session students in 1933, 1,024 came from the city of Buffalo, and 1,651 from the state of New York. The Jewish population of Buffalo is comparatively small, not more than 20,000 out of a total population of 573,076. Yet, in this university, among the regular students, 17.52 per cent. of those in the College of Arts and Sciences, 15.58 per cent. of those in the School of Medicine, 26.48 per cent. of those in the School of Pharmacy, 13.93 per cent. of those in the School of Dentistry and 17.97 per cent. of those in the School of Business Administration were Jews.

This is somewhat typical of conditions which exist in many of the eastern universities, even outside the city of New York, where, at one Catholic university, 56.7 per cent. of the entire student body is Jewish.

LIMITATION OF NUMBERS

In recent years a number of institutions have, therefore, introduced secretly, if not openly, a *numerus clausus*, especially into the professional schools. Among the reasons given are:

(1) Some colleges and universities, situated in the midst of a district thickly populated by Jews, do not wish to become merely a "city" college; they wish to maintain their status as a national institution which draws

students from all over the country; hence they restrict the attendance of persons resident in the city to a definite quota. There are also instances where scholarships are especially earmarked for those who come from rural areas. This, generally speaking, automatically restricts Jewish opportunities.

(2) They frankly do not wish to be inundated by Jews, fearing that if more than a certain percentage of the entire student body is Jewish, Gentiles will withdraw and attend other institutions. To date, most of the endowments of these institutions have come from Gentile, and sometimes from specifically denominational sources. The financial question is involved.

(3) Institutions which are definitely denominational sometimes find that the presence of large numbers of Jews renders more difficult the types of college activities which more definitely aim at the formation of Christian character and devotion.

(4) While some of the finest minds and most sociable persons in the student body may be Jewish, a considerable percentage of Jewish applicants have personalities which make it difficult for them to "fit in" easily into the normal social activities of the student body.

(5) Some universities report unhappy experiences in securing from Jewish students coöperation either in the promotion of the honor system at examination time, or in the prompt payment of dues.

(6) In the professional schools, such as medicine, law, etc., the profession can only absorb a certain number each year and it may be a positive disservice to encourage the attendance of Jewish students who would afterwards find it difficult to be placed professionally, often because of personality handicaps as well as because of prevalent anti-Jewish feeling outside the colleges.

(7) Again in some professional schools, especially medicine, it has been necessary to restrict rather rigidly the number of the entering class because the college does not have the facilities for training more than a limited number; in all this one must not only consider the limitations in the college proper, but also the limited hospital facilities of the city. One medical school, which strictly limited its entering class to seventy, received last year 1,563 applications. Not a few of these were from Jews, who, aware of the tendency in so many institutions to accept only such Jewish students as were superlatively qualified, made multiple applications to a number of institutions in the hope that somewhere they might find a favorable response.

There can be no doubt that the problem of sifting this deluge of applications is very great; it is no light matter to turn down students who would seem to have met the usual requirements, but are academic standards alone to be regarded?

It must be recognized that for many institutions, especially those whose ideals have been influenced by English models, a college education is far more than either a professional training or the impartation of knowledge. Wilhelm Dibelius, writing of English education, says:

"For the creation of gentlemen, two main instruments exist—corporate life in the colleges, and games. . . . The qualities England needs in the state are disciplined on the cricket and football field and in the boat-race path; here the leader reveals himself, and then the individual learns to serve as a member of the whole."[9]

If the main effort of college education is the production of men skilled in specific subjects, the college policy will be framed accordingly; but if the main effort of college education is the production of a certain type of social being, then it will necessarily consider more than academic standards in its selection of candidates.

Social assimilability seems to be one of the tests used, and certain colleges require personality tests and photographs from all applicants. Others, both colleges and professional schools, give various preferences: (a) to candidates who are themselves the children of former graduates; (b) to candidates who are especially recommended by former graduates; (c) to candidates living in those areas peculiarly served by the college. This last is the very reverse of the policy of the institutions that deliberately aim to be national in their scope.

At all events, as one of the Jewish professors at a certain institution intimated, while the university would not admit that it had a quota, it just happened each year that about 15 per cent. of the entering class were Jews. In this particular institution it also just happened that about 10 per cent. of the entering class were women.

Of course, a private, non-sectarian institution has a certain liberty in establishing a *numerus clausus* which the state university can hardly claim; on the other hand, more Jewish students attend private, non-sectarian institutions than publicly-controlled colleges, if the sampling obtained in this study properly indicates the trend, since thirty-five state universities, with a total enrolment of 161,765, only reported 6,782 Jewish students (4.2 per cent.), while sixty-three non-sectarian, private institutions, with a total enrolment of 176,481 reported 31,177 (or 17.7 per cent.) Jews. In addition to this, we must remember the large number of Jews attending Protestant denominational schools and Catholic institutions (15.4 per cent.). This tendency among the Jews to attend the private institutions may perhaps be due to a feeling on their part that the academic and social prestige of such institutions is higher than that of the publicly-controlled colleges; on the other hand, it is more probably due to the fact that the great centers of Jewish population are in the eastern states, where state institutions have always been

---

[9] *England* (New York: Harper and Brothers, 1930).

eclipsed by the private colleges; also, so far as their attendance at Catholic colleges is concerned, the Jews are likely to be numerous in the very cities where Catholics are also numerous.

While it may well be that the Jew appreciates the work of higher education more than the average Gentile, and while possibly he may be by nature more "intellectual" than the average Gentile, one incidental reason for the high percentage of Jews attending institutions of higher learning is undoubtedly to be discovered in their urban tendencies. The great colleges, especially the professional schools, are for the most part to be found in the cities, and it becomes much simpler for the ambitious Jew to benefit from these than for the Gentile living in the small towns or on the farms. There has perhaps grown up a legend about Jewish intellectuality which the apportionment of Nobel prize awards makes quite believable. Certainly, the Jews win a great many of the scholarships that are offered, and university officials recognize that while some Jews make impossible students, the majority of them show a high average of ability. It is frequently affirmed, however, that the average Jew shows greater ability in the learning to be obtained from books than in the processes of laboratory work, and that frequently his high marks are due, at least in part, to his particular ability in the field of languages where he is assisted by his inevitable bi-culturalism. Formerly, he was accused of being a "grind," although more recently he has seemed to participate quite fully in college activities.

DISCRIMINATION IN FRATERNITIES

Once admitted to the colleges, the Jew is subjected to certain discriminations. Fraternities almost universally refuse to invite Jews, and consequently Jewish fraternities have been formed, where often, it is alleged, the more fortunate Jews pass on the snubs they have received from Gentile fraternities to their own "poorer relatives." Some fraternities, to be sure, do elect Jews to membership. Such Jews usually have (a) a profile not too obviously Semitic, (b) a tidy bank account, (c) the nomenclature of Unitarians or Christian Scientists. If, perchance, a Jew has already become known for his prowess in the line of scrimmage, fraternities forget their finer sensitivities. In the honor fraternities, where membership is determined by intellectual achievement rather than by social congeniality, there is little or no discrimination against Jews.

UNDERGRADUATE ACTIVITIES OF JEWS

In undergraduate activities, the Jews are quite active, showing a preference for dramatics, debating and college journalism, but much less interest in athletics, except perhaps basketball. Some American colleges have had to reorganize their dramatic clubs to prevent them from being entirely domi-

nated by Jews, but much may be forgiven a race that has produced Sarah
Bernhardt and Max Reinhardt. They can hardly be expected to remain
"offstage." Not long since, the University of Chicago debated with Northwestern University. Each college was represented by three Jews. In reporting the event, the astute newspaper headliners in Chicago announced
"Baptists beat Methodists." Some Gentiles feel that the Jews tend to gravitate to the more exhibitionistic activities. In college journalism, some of
the Jewish editorial writers are criticized for the excessive amount of acid
which they add to their typewriter ribbons and for a certain lack of sensitivity to the feelings of the various victims of their caustic remarks. This
may be due in part to the manifestations of an inferiority complex parading
in the seats of the mighty, but it is a sin which might as easily be attributed
to the effrontery of youth as to Jewishness. In college athletics, Jews have
been less conspicuous. Some coaches seem to feel that in college athletics
there are only two types of Jewish candidates—the exceptionally good and
the exceptionally hopeless. The hopeless ones will not submit to the rigors
of training. In this connection, it must be remembered that historically the
Jew has never been interested in athletics. He repudiated the efforts of the
Seleucid rulers to "humanize" him with Hellenic innovations in the third
century before Christ, and he has on the whole acted on the assumption
that the Lord took less pleasure in the legs of a man than in his intellectual
achievements. In women's colleges, the interest of the Jewish women in
sports has been until recently even more negligible than in the case of the
men. Some of the university administrators have attributed this tendency
in part to a certain "physical laziness" of many of the Jewish women-
students. Jewish women are, however, increasingly taking their place in
"sports."

A certain number of the Jewish students keep apart and make no response to any overtures of friendliness from the Gentiles. Some of the
poorer Jewish students also complain bitterly that they are neglected both
by the Gentiles and by the Jews of a higher social status. It is even said that
in some colleges, where a number of Jews are elected to an honorary society,
they become as active as any one in restricting the acceptance of more Jews.

Among the college subjects that they pursue with unusual interest are the
social sciences, psychology and economics.

JEWISH FACULTY MEMBERS

It would be strange if a group so recently arrived in this country as the
Jews should have furnished a large proportion of the members of the staffs.
Of 179 institutions that reported, for this study, on the composition of their
staffs, thirty-six reported no record of Jewish members; eighty-seven reported
their Jewish members, and in these institutions with a total of 16,967 staff

members, only 373, or 2.2 per cent. were of Jewish faith or extraction. In sixty-two institutions, of 3,823 full professors, only seventy, or 1.8 per cent., were Jewish. While the percentage of Jewish staff members is smaller than the ratio of Jewish population to the whole population in the United States, it must not be assumed that this paucity is mainly due to discrimination. Nevertheless, the percentage is small when compared with the percentage of Jewish students in the colleges. In the Catholic colleges studied the Jewish percentage of staff members was 3.1 (fifty-nine out of 1,883).

It may perhaps be assumed that in denominational colleges—and there are, many of them—preference would be given to those whose religious orientation was more in harmony with that of the particular college, while many of the non-sectarian institutions have a long tradition of specifically Christian scholarship behind them and would naturally seek their professors from Gentile or Christian circles, other things being equal. Even in other institutions a professor is also regarded as a liaison official with the public; he is more than a professor—he is a "contact" man; his ability to mir in circles where endowments may be picked up counts as well as his scholastic eminence, and if, for some reason, he does not fit into the "social" picture, he might be passed over for someone else. In selecting their staffs, college administrators must consider public relations as well as scholastic attainment or teaching capacity. In the early days many Jews were placed on the staffs of colleges because of the traditional interest of the Christian church in Semitic languages and the difficulty of securing experts in Hebrew among the Gentiles. In more recent years, however, there has been a much wider distribution of staff positions among Jews, while in nearly every medical or legal faculty some Jewish professors or lecturers are to be found. In many instances, however, such Jewish professors are somewhat *déracinés*.

RELIGIOUS CULTURE

The religious culture of Jewish students is a more difficult matter. Even some of the outstanding non-sectarian institutions have Christian deans of religion and such religious life as there is in the colleges is tuned to a Christian note. The Menorah societies, the Hillel Foundation and other Jewish agencies have sought to preserve the interest of the Jewish students in Jewishness, but confronted with the new knowledge, many Jewish students soon adopt a cynical attitude to tenets of Judaism. In this, their experience parallels the experience of many Christians. An extended study of this tendency has recently been made by Rabbi Marvin Nathan, of Philadelphia.[10] In a few non-sectarian institutions, including Columbia University and the University of Chicago, a Jewish adviser has been integrated in the

---

[10] *The Attitude of the Jewish Student in the Colleges and Universities towards his Religion* (New York: Bloch Publishing Co., 1932).

work of the Dean of Religion and has received an official status. It is thus hoped that such men will be able to keep in contact with Jewish students, and organize such activities for them as will help them to preserve the spiritual values of Judaism.

SHOULD JEWS BUILD THEIR OWN COLLEGES

The main problem confronting the Jews seems to be implicit in the occasional proposal to develop institutions of their own. It would be quite possible, for instance, for a Jewish college to be founded at the University of Toronto, and federated with the university in much the same way as St. Michael's. This would provide an opportunity for a more intensive cultivation of Jewishness, while the Jewish students participated freely in other forms of intercollegiate life. Generally speaking, however, the Jews seem to fear anything that smacks of segregation. They wish to remain Jews—whatever it means to be a Jew—but at the same time to pay the minimum price for such resistance to "assimilation." Meanwhile, Gentiles feel that Jews take out of the colleges more than Jews put into them. They take many scholarships while they offer few; if 10 per cent. of all the students in the United States are Jews, then it may be assumed that one-tenth of the entire cost of maintaining these institutions is caused by Jewish students. If we accept the government figure of the cost of higher education in the United States in 1929-30 as substantially correct, then the annual cost of educating these Jewish students is $56,354,700. This cost is never covered by fees. The question is asked: are the Jews paying their quota of the cost, or are they demanding privileges without accepting correlative responsibilities?

FEDERAL RELATIONS TO EDUCATION IN THE UNITED STATES AND CANADA

Both the Federal Government at Washington and the Dominion Government at Ottawa are charged with responsibility for many educational projects, but the exact scope of such activity has proved difficult to adjust.

While the Constitutional Convention considered the possible responsibility of the Federal Government for education, it decided that this was a matter that each state could handle in its own way. It was, therefore, not included among the prerogatives of the Federal Government. When the British North America Act was passed in 1867, and because of the existence in Canada of religious and racial minorities, education was specifically assigned in the allotment of prerogatives to the provinces. Nevertheless, both Washington and Ottawa have been forced to assume very definite and important responsibilities for education.

In the report of the National Advisory Committee on Education (Part I, pages 116 ff.), published in Washington, 1931, we find an elaborate table of contemporary activities of the federal government in the educational field, classified under seven major heads:

(1) Education in the individual states, including land grants, national guard and naval reserve officers' training corps schools, payments to local schools for Indian education, distribution of text-books for citizenship training in public schools, certification of aeronautical schools, etc.

(2) Education in special federal areas, such as the District of Columbia, where the entire educational system is directed by the federal government, and in federal prisons and reformatories, army and navy posts.

(3) Education of Indians and other indigenous peoples in the United States, Philippine Islands, Guam, Samoa and Alaska.

(4) Education in territories outside of the United States, such as Virgin Islands, Alaska, Hawaii, Porto Rico, Panama Canal Zone, Philippine Islands.

(5) Training of government personnel in foreign service school, coast guard academy, military and naval academies, army and navy war colleges, schools in the national park service and training courses for police in the District of Columbia.

(6) Research, collection and dissemination of knowledge of various kinds, including support of national museum, national gallery of art, national zoological park, etc.

(7) Intellectual and educational coöperation with other nations, including facilitation of exchange of students, accrediting of American schools for foreign students, etc.

EFFORTS TO CREATE A FEDERAL DEPARTMENT OF EDUCATION

So extensive are these various activities that in 1929 a committee was appointed to study the situation and report on the desirable type of future scope of and organization for the existing Office of Education. A department of education, "to collect statistics and facts showing the condition and progress of education in the several States and Territories . . . and otherwise promote the cause of education throughout the country" was voted in 1867, but when the appropriation act was passed in 1868 such opposition developed that a "provision was inserted abolishing the Department of Education as a separate unit and recreating it as an Office of Education in the Interior Department," which it has remained until the present time. The National Advisory Committee, in its efforts to coördinate these various educational functions of the federal government with the work of the Office of Education, recommended "that a Department of Education with a Secretary of Education at its head be established in the Federal Government," but the plan called for leaving—

"the federal educational activities which are instrumental or incidental to proper administration of some other primary function of the Federal Government under jurisdiction of the Department which is responsible for that primary function. This applies to such activities as Indian Education, agricultural extension for adults in the Department of Agriculture, military training in the Departments of War and Navy, schooling in federal areas and in outlying possessions under the Department primarily concerned, and training of its own personnel in each of the governing Departments."

In short, the new department would perform only such functions as had been assigned to the department in 1867, but with a somewhat greater prestige and with larger financial resources than previously enjoyed by the Office of Education. The Commission further sought to limit the powers of such a department by recommending that it have—

"no legal or financial power and no regulatory or executive authority, direct or indirect, explicit or implied, by which it may control the social purposes and specific processes of education."

The committee adopted these recommendations by a vote of 38 to 11, with two abstaining from voting. Two minority reports were presented, one by a group of three, including Presidents John W. Davis, Mordecai Johnson and R. R. Moton, urging more specific methods in the fostering of Negro education, and a second by the Vice Rector of the Catholic University of America and the Secretary of the Catholic Educational Association. The latter of these minority reports interests the student of interfaith relations. These two Catholic educators expressed themselves as in accord with the fundamental principle upon which the majority report had been based, but opposed to the creation of a Department of Education in the Federal Government with a Secretary at its head, because such a department was not necessary to perform the basic functions assigned to it, and secondly "because we are convinced that the establishment of a Federal Department of Education will inevitably bring about centralization and the federal control of education."

Since the proposed Department of Education would not abolish the pluralized federal control of education, they believed that "if any change takes place it will be in the direction of the unification of such control in the Department of Education and the extension of it to general education." They offered "as an alternative mechanism the development, by means of such an increase in appropriations and enlargement of personnel as will make it fully competent to carry on the functions which the Report assigns to an adequate federal headquarters for education, of the existing Office of Education in the Department of the Interior, or in some other Department that a future reorganization of the executive branch of the Federal Government may create."

The outcome was that the effort to create a Department of Education with a Secretary of Education at its head failed; the Office of Education was retained and more amply supplied with the funds necessary to carry on a number of significant researches.

It seems reasonably clear that against the establishment of such a department of education were not alone a consideration for the retention of state rights but also a fear that such a department would inevitably eventuate in federal control and further efforts at standardization. The Catholics were opposed to such a step.

THE CANADIAN SYSTEM

In Canada, the British North America Act specifically leaves the control of education to the provinces. Here again, however, it has been necessary for the Dominion government to engage in various educational enterprises and to support others financially. The Dominion government has the responsibility for the care of the Indians in all the various reserves, in many instances allocating various stations on the reserves to different denominations, Catholic and Protestant, erecting school buildings but entrusting their administration to the denominations and giving them an annual per capita allowance for maintenance; it gives Dominion aid to vocational education in the provinces and at one time gave it to agricultural education; it supports various learned societies; it operates a military academy and other departmental training agencies; it assumes supervision of education in the territories; finally, it has a research department which seeks to gather all statistical information concerning the educational life of Canada. There has been occasional talk of a Dominion department of education, but once again the conditions surrounding racial and religious minorities in Canada, together with the specific provisions of the British North America Act, would make any such step extremely dangerous to its sponsors.

CHAPTER VII

Intermarriage

Whether marriages are made in heaven or elsewhere, propinquity is an important factor in the selection of mates, and hence to protect the marriage interests of their children, discreet parents try to limit their social relationships as far as possible to "desirable" persons. If any group, because of an alleged intrinsic superiority on the one hand, or because of a strong insistence on endogamy on the other hand, produces a social situation in which intermarriage with that group is surrounded with grave difficulties, it creates, by the nature of things, a certain measure of social exclusiveness. This is perceived in the relations of whites and Negroes. Frequently white and colored children, when quite small, play freely together, but even in poor districts the moment the age of adolescence is reached, the social lines are more rigidly drawn. As has been pointed out in Chapter III, the exclusion of Jews from social clubs, especially from golf clubs, is in part due to the fact that, although Gentile and Jewish business men might meet without inviting any serious complications, new problems arise when members of their families are thrown together. A somewhat similar precaution may determine the social attitudes of Protestants to Catholics.

The Religious Regulation of Marriage

In addition to this influence of religion on the selection of mates, one of the perennial functions of religion has been the regulation of marriage and sexual relations. Thus, the laws of marriage were for a long time in England, and later in certain of the British colonies, determined by the Established Church, and only clergymen of that church were permitted to officiate at weddings. This was undoubtedly the hang-over of the supremacy of canon law in the matter of marriage. In the early days of British occupation in Canada, the right to officiate at marriages was restricted to Church of England clergymen and Roman priests. To this day, there is no *civil marriage* in Canada, and all persons desiring to be married must be united before some clergyman of a recognized denomination.

In religiously homogeneous countries, such regulation of marriage on the part of the ecclesiastical authorities may possibly create but a few problems, but where a variety of denominations arise, complications straightway make

their appearance, such as intermarriage, the education of children born to
such marriages, divorce, and usually the State must step in to determine
questions of validity, legitimacy, and especially succession. In certain Latin
countries, a clear distinction is made between civil and ecclesiastical marriage. In France, Argentina, and some other countries, the couple must
appear first before civil authorities to be married; later, if they desire, they
may be married by whatever ecclesiastical usage they prefer. The first step
is imperative; the second optional. In Anglo-Saxon countries, there are
seldom double ceremonies, while in the United States persons who do not
wish a religious ceremony can be united in marriage before officials who
serve in a purely civil capacity. As will be pointed out later, this provision
makes it particularly difficult, if not utterly impossible, to determine the
number of intermarriages in the United States. One has reason for suspect-
ing that a good many of the Jewish-Gentile intermarriages are performed
before civil authorities, and hence are not recorded by either Christian
ministers or Jewish rabbis.

The history of human marriage reveals that while some groups are ex-
ogamous, others are endogamous. Within the Roman Catholic Church and
in many civil laws, the principle of exogamy is retained in a restricted form
in the minute regulations governing consanguinity.[1] Third cousins desiring
to marry must obtain a dispensation from the bishop of the diocese; second
cousins must obtain a dispensation approved by the apostolic delegate; first
cousins must procure a dispensation approved by the Holy See itself. Other
laws place an impediment to marriage on spiritual relationship (e.g., god-
parents and godchildren), and legal relationship (guardians and wards).
Neither is the Catholic Church endogamous in insisting on maintaining
racial purity in marriage. The Irish may marry freely with the Latin or
the black with the white, provided that canon laws and civil laws both
permit. If the civil law forbade, a priest would not venture to sanction a
given marriage; if, on the other hand, the civil law permitted, but the canon
law prohibited, a priest could not sanction such a marriage. Many Protestant churches also forbid their clergy to officiate at marriages where at
least one of the parties has received a decree of divorce on grounds other
than adultery. The civil law frequently permits the remarriage of such
persons; Protestant canon law frequently prohibits it. But there is nothing
in Catholic canon law to prohibit intermarriage on racial lines; the Catholic
opposition is on religious grounds. The Catholic Church refuses to sanction any marriage of Catholics to non-Catholics unless the marriage is performed before the parish priest and after the non-Catholic party and the
Catholic party have both made specific pledges.

[1] See Ayrinhac, *Marriage Legislation* (New York: Benzigers, 1932), chapter x.

THE CATHOLIC ATTITUDE TOWARD MIXED MARRIAGE

This attitude has been more or less characteristic of the Catholic Church throughout history. The question of mixed marriages had to be considered by the apostle Paul in one of his early epistles (I Corinthians vii:12-16). Many of the first converts were the consorts of unbelievers, and Paul instructed such to remain with their mates in the hope that they might eventually convert them; if, however, the unbelieving mate should "depart, let him depart. A brother or sister is not under bondage in such cases." The church, however, has always sought to discourage intermarriage of Catholic Christians either with pagans or with heretics and, according to the *Catholic Encyclopaedia*, was particularly averse to the marriage of Catholics with Jews, "owing to the intense Jewish hatred for the sacred name of Christ." Even to this day dispensations for marriages of Catholics with Jews are obtained with greater difficulty than dispensations for marriages of Catholics and "heretical" Christians. On this Ayrinhac says:

"In the faculties delegated to bishops there is a reservation regarding Jews and Mohammedans. If the Jew is Orthodox, it is certain that a special dispensation is needed from Rome; if he has given up the traditional Jewish beliefs and practices, it is only probable that the Holy See must be consulted. The point is disputed."

The parties seeking such a dispensation must agree that in the case of all male children born to the marriage, circumcision as a "religious rite" will not be administered.

In Eastern Europe and Russia, in much the same way, the Orthodox Church discouraged intermarriage of Orthodox with non-Orthodox, and even passed laws providing that the children resulting from the marriages of Orthodox and Roman Catholics should be always brought up in the Orthodox faith.

With the development of Protestantism, new complications arose, and the Council of Trent affirmed that all matrimonial alliances between Catholics and non-Catholics were null and void unless entered into before the parish priest or some other priest whom he might designate. It was impossible, however, to enforce these enactments, by reason of the opposition of the Protestant countries, in some of which the decree was, indeed, never promulgated. Others were specifically exempted from the provisions of the decree. Ireland, for instance, was exempted in 1785. Austria and Germany were also exempted. On April 18, 1908, the decree *Ne Temere* went into effect, which really enforced the Tridentine legislation everywhere. By a later decree, *Provida,* Germany alone was exempted from the regulations contained in the *Ne Temere* decree. This decree aroused storms of protest, notably in the province of Quebec where the peculiar recognition of the

Roman Catholic faith has been complicated by certain interpretations of the French civil law made by French-Canadian judges. At the present time, no marriage of Catholics and non-Catholics is recognized "ecclesiastically" valid unless it be performed in the presence of the parish priest or his representative, and no priest may perform such a marriage unless both non-Catholic and Catholic parties give the necessary assurances and secure a special dispensation from the bishop of the diocese.

GRANTING OF DISPENSATIONS

Dispensations are given only under the following circumstances:

(1) *There are just and grave causes.* Among the "just and grave causes" given on one of the forms on which applications for dispensation are made are (a) *angustia loci;* the place is very small and hence the choice of consorts is highly restricted; (b) *aetas superadulta feminae quae non est vidua;* the woman is of superadult age and not a widow; hence her chances of ever securing a husband are diminishing; (c) *paupertas viduae;* the widow is poor and needs some one to support her; (d) *nimia suspecta familiaritas;* the intimacy of such applicants is so suspicious that if they do not marry, worse things might happen; (e) *si jam est gravis mulier;* worse things have happened and the woman is pregnant; (f) *Periculum matrimonii mixti ver civilis ver coram ministello;* if the dispensation is not given they will probably get married anyway either before civil authorities or before a "little minister."

(2) *Promises are given by the Catholic and especially by the non-Catholic parties* which minimize the danger of the perversion from the faith of the Catholic party and assure the education of any children born to the marriage in the Catholic faith. The formula used in one large diocese is as follows:

"I, the undersigned . . . not a member of the Roman Catholic Church, wishing to contract marriage with . . . a member of the Roman Catholic Church, purpose to do so with the understanding that the marriage bond thus contracted is indissoluble, except by death; and I promise that . . . shall be permitted the free exercise of religion according to the Roman Catholic Faith, and that all children, of either sex born of this marriage shall be baptized and educated in the faith and according to the teachings of the Roman Catholic Church, even if . . . should happen to be taken away by death. I furthermore promise that no other marriage ceremony than that to be performed by the Catholic priest shall take place.

"Non-Catholic party's signature................

"I, the undersigned, a member of the Catholic Roman Church, promise that all my children shall be Catholics.

"Catholic party's signature...................."

This document must be signed in the presence of the parish priest and in the presence of two witnesses, and must accompany the application made to the bishop for a dispensation.

(3) *There is a moral certainty that the promises will be fulfilled.* In case of any dispute in the future, the church holds the document, and the non-Catholic party has formally ceded away his parental right to control the religious education of his children.

Frequently, before such marriages, the non-Catholic party takes a certain amount of instruction in the Catholic religion in order that he may be more intelligent concerning it and thus more ready not to offend the religious susceptibilities of his consort. Occasionally, such instruction may lead to his conversion before marriage in which case the marriage is not recorded as an intermarriage, and this creates obvious problems for the statistician. Conversion, however, is not required prior to the marriage or after the marriage, although Canon 1062 says: "The Catholic party is bound prudently to procure the conversion of the non-Catholic party." According to the new code, the Catholic party does not, however, formally promise to labor to effect such a conversion.

JEWISH, CATHOLIC AND PROTESTANT ATTITUDES COMPARED

One might observe at this point that a very similar attitude is taken by certain Jewish rabbis, with this exception, that most liberal rabbis refuse to officiate at the marriage of Jews and non-Jews unless the non-Jew first definitely severs his connection with the Gentile community and accepts Judaism. Certain orthodox rabbis will not marry a Jew and a non-Jew under any condition. The following form is used by one of the most liberal rabbis in the country and must be signed by the non-Jewish applicant for an intermarriage before the rabbi will officiate at the marriage:

"I, . . . in the presence of witnesses here assembled and at the time of the solemnization of my marriage under Jewish auspices, do hereby solemnly promise and swear that:

"I hereby sever all affiliation with any other religious faith except the Jewish faith.

"I shall regard my home as a Jewish home and shall do everything in my power to acquaint myself with the meaning of this term.

"Any children born to me of this marriage shall be reared by me in the Jewish faith.

"Any male children born to me of this marriage shall be circumcised according to the tradition of the Jewish religion.

"Signature. . . . ."

The names of the witnesses to the pledge are also attached.

Protestants, on the other hand, seldom draw any rigid lines at intermarriage on religious grounds, although in certain southern states which are overwhelmingly Protestant, intermarriage between whites and Negroes is forbidden by civil law. They do, to be sure, seek to discourage intermarriage between persons of different faiths, and certain of the smaller groups, such as the Mennonites, have placed under the ban of excommunication any member who contracts marriage outside the particular fold, but generally speaking their attitude is one of tolerance and is determined possibly by three major considerations: (a) a feeling that religion is essentially a personal matter, and that consequently the rights of individual consciences must be respected, whatever the social dangers in such intermarriages may be; (b) a sense, on the part of Protestant ministers, that they are, in officiating at a marriage ceremony, civil authorities as well as ecclesiastical authorities—this being probably due to the hangover from the peculiar function of clergymen of the Established Church in England in this connection, and (c) a desire, on an occasion which ought to be associated with all the sanction that a religious rite can give to it, not to withhold a religious ceremony from those who seek to be married, thus compelling them to consider marriage purely as a civil contract. The average Protestant clergyman may, therefore, seek to warn a couple desiring to contract intermarriage against the dangers and to dissuade them if possible from engaging in the ceremony, but if under an urge which is biological or psychological rather than theological, they persist in wishing to be married, he will exact no promises from them except the promise to be faithful and considerate one to another so long as they both shall live.

There are some notable exceptions to the practice of Jewish rabbis previously described. Thus, one liberal rabbi in the Middle West, has written to the director of this study:

"I officiate at mixed marriages. I do so not because I favor them—I do not. My reason for this lies in the desire to hold Jewishly as many of my people as I possibly can.

"When a Jewish and non-Jewish person desire to get married and the two come to me for the ceremony, it means, among other things, that the Jewish person still feels a religious bond uniting him with his faith and his people, and I do not want to be the one to weaken, much less to break, this bond. My refusal would mean sending such a person to a non-Jewish minister, and this I do not want to do. In more than one instance I have invited the non-Jewish minister of the denomination to which the non-Jewish person belongs or into which he was born, to share this service with me, even though I was not asked to do so. I do this for no other reason except to make the ceremony as sacred and as meaningful to the non-Jew as to the Jew.

"Under no circumstances do I permit the non-Jewish person to convert to Judaism before marriage. I suspect such conversions. They cannot possibly be based on an intelligent evaluation of the two faiths, assuming for the moment that they are sincere. It is just the price that the non-Jewish person is, for the time, willing to pay to be married to a Jew or Jewess and to have a rabbi officiate at the wedding. I much prefer sincere Christianity to a lip profession of Judaism. I usually tell these would-be converts that if they want to embrace Judaism they should come to me after they are married and I shall gladly give them instruction in the beliefs and practices of my faith. If after they have been informed they still want to join into religious fellowship with us I gladly welcome them. The fact that less than half of such people have come back for such instruction, and that of these not all wanted to accept Judaism formally, strengthens me in my view that I am right in declining to accept impulsive and emotional would-be converts."[2]

CHRISTIAN OPPOSITION TO INTERMARRIAGE INHERITED FROM JUDAISM

Perhaps, before proceeding to consider the actual degree of intermarriage in the United States and Canada, it should be stated that the recognition of the manifold complications of marriages involving mixed religions or disparities of cult were inherited, at least in part, from the Jewish nation. In post-exilic days, Nehemiah was troubled and concerned about mixed marriages, and apparently feared the total extinction of the race. Drastic regulations were pressed against intermarriage, but in the opinion of Dean Willett, these measures were futile. He says:

"If cursing men, plucking out their hair and chasing them out of the place could not bring results, what could? In reality nothing would, and nothing did. The experience of Ezra soon afterward makes that clear."[3]

The growing separatism, the sense of the mission of Israel which often became an obsession, a Semitic superiority complex which followed the wanderings of the Jews in the Diaspora and which may conceivably have been the fundamental cause of anti-Semitism—all tended against intermarriage, but as Graetz makes clear in his history of the Jews, the Jews kept intermarrying for all that. Sex proved stronger than either race or religion. With the Jews, however, it is almost impossible to distinguish race and religion, while with Christianity the opposition to intermarriage was founded not on disparity of race but on disparity of faith.

INTERMARRIAGE BETWEEN CATHOLICS AND NON-CATHOLICS

The difficulties confronting the investigator in his effort to determine the degree of intermarriage in the United States are practically insurmountable. Persons taking out marriage licenses are not required to state their religious affiliation, as in Canada, and hence no computation at all is possible. Then, as already pointed out, many intermarriages are performed before justices of the peace or civil officials who have no interest whatever in finding out the

---

[2] The director of this study feels obliged to state that in his various interviews regarding intermarriage the statement by the rabbi impresses him as a most striking utterance made on the subject. If a similar attitude were taken by officials of all three faiths, a major area of tension would be eliminated.

[3] *The Jew Through the Centuries* (Chicago: Willett, Clark & Co., 1933), p. 144.

246 Catholics, Jews and Protestants

religious affiliation of those who wish to be bound together until the divorce court gives them a decree. Non-Catholic ministers are frequently called upon to marry couples one or both of whom are Catholics, but they often make no inquiries concerning the religion of those who come before them and, even if they did, would seldom if ever make any record of it. The only possible clue in the United States to the number of marriages of Catholics to non-Catholics is in the records to be found in the various diocesan chancery offices in the Catholic Church, where records of all intermarriages are kept, as special dispensations must be issued in connection with them. Here, then, we may learn the total number of marriages performed annually by Catholic priests within the diocese which are "pure Catholic" marriages and the number which are mixed. But even when we learn this, we are confronted with two other insuperable difficulties:

(1) Some non-Catholics are converted before their marriages. Naturally, they would then appear on the record as Catholics and their marriage would be regarded as a pure Catholic marriage.

(2) Many intermarriages between baptized Catholics and non-Catholics undoubtedly take place without the knowledge of the church. There is no record of such at all, unless they are validated later by the church.

Unfortunately, however, although the chanceries undoubtedly know the ratio of mixed marriages to pure marriages in their respective dioceses they seldom publish the figures. These figures are included in the quinquennial statistics submitted to the Holy Father by the various bishops, but there is no common repository of such statistics in the United States. The *Catholic Directory* furnishes partial statistics, but often their authenticity is open to question on many counts, and while most dioceses report the total number of marriages,[4] only approximately six out of 102 published the figures for both Catholic and mixed marriages in 1929. It is quite evident that some of the bishops do not wish to give these facts to the public for reasons known best to themselves. The small sampling provided is therefore quite inadequate, but the figures for 1929 are given for what they may be worth:

Diocese	Catholic Population	Total Marriages	Catholic Marriages	Mixed Marriages
Milwaukee.....................	310,000	4,146	3,069	1,077
Portland in Oregon..............	43,599	530	278	252
Des Moines....................	38,565	341	227	114
Fargo.........................	69,871	425	291	134
Lafayette (La.).................	186,750	1,991	1,864	127
Omaha........................	94,400	907	727	180
Totals......................	743,185	8,340	6,456	1,884

[4] With the exception of Boston, Chicago, New York, Buffalo, Fall River, Great Falls and Providence.

If these figures were at all typical they would mean that out of 14,796 Catholic persons who were married in these dioceses in 1929, 1,884 (or 12.7 per cent.) married out of their faith. But the percentage varies from 3.2 per cent. in Lafayette, Louisiana, to 30.9 per cent. in Portland, Oregon. The wide range makes it particularly difficult to draw any general conclusions. While, too, the sampling thus provided does contain almost 6 per cent. of the total number of dioceses, the Catholic population of these six dioceses is only 3.7 per cent. of the total Catholic population in the country. Undoubtedly studies of intermarriage must have been made under Catholic auspices, for certain figures or estimates regarding losses have been made, but it is highly probable that the only thorough statistics —and even these will be incomplete—are on file at the Vatican and are not given to the public.

CANADIAN STATISTICS ON INTERMARRIAGE

In Canada, on the other hand, it is possible to make a fairly accurate statement regarding intermarriage year by year, for religious preference is required of all applicants for a marriage license and summaries are compiled annually by provinces and by the Dominion as a whole. Here again, of course, it is impossible to know in how many cases the non-Catholic or Catholic party may have been converted just prior to the marriage ceremony, as in such instances the marriages would not be listed as intermarriages. Certain other difficulties emerge, thus:

(1) Until 1925 the Greek Catholics (Uniats) were improperly included in the compilations with the Greek Orthodox. Since that time the Greek Catholics have been separately listed and by adding their figures to those for Roman Catholics and making the subtractions it is possible to know the total number of marriages entered into by such as acknowledge the authority of the Pope. Prior to 1925, however, any figures must of necessity exclude the Greek Catholics.

(2) Until 1926, Quebec was not included in the Dominion Registration area as its methods of gathering such data could not be harmonized with the methods used in the Dominion. Since 1926, it is possible to offer figures for the whole Dominion. For the purposes of this study, however, certain figures are included for only the eight provinces since, because of linguistic and racial differences, Quebec is entirely atypical.

(3) The Dominion Bureau makes all the tabulations, but provincial offices send in records which agree on most points. Three of the provinces, however, fail to indicate on their individual marriage records the denomination of the officiating clergyman. Had this been done, it might be possible to tell at once how many of the marriages between Catholics and non-

Catholics were solemnized before a priest and how many were solemnized before a non-Catholic minister. The writer has had to make estimates at this point on the basis of some restricted sampling.

THE TREND EXCLUSIVE OF QUEBEC

Of course, such government figures provide no clue whatever to the number of such mixed marriages later validated, nor to the future religious history of such intermarriages. Correlations between civil birth records and the records of infant baptisms in the Catholic Church throughout the entire country might furnish some clue, but only if the Catholic birth-rate was, generally speaking, similar to the general birth-rate, but it may almost be assumed that the Catholic birth-rate is higher, at least in such provinces as Quebec. The Canadian figures are, however, highly suggestive and rather fundamental. In the first table presented are listed data regarding the numbers of Roman Catholics marrying during the years 1921 to 1931 inclusive in all Canada, excluding Quebec. In this table, since it covers years prior to 1925, the word Roman Catholic does not include Greek Catholic and the marriage of a Roman Catholic to a Greek Catholic is regarded, somewhat improperly, as an intermarriage. The slight difference is, however, not very material. In later tables, Greek Catholics are all considered as Roman Catholics.

MARRIAGES OF ROMAN CATHOLICS IN CANADA (EXCLUDING QUEBEC), 1921–31

Year	Total No. Catholic Grooms	Total No. Catholic Brides	Total No. Catholics Married	No. Catholic Grooms Marrying Out	No. Catholic Brides Marrying Out	No. Catholics Marrying Out	Percentage Catholics Marrying Out
1921	9,567	9,759	19,326	1,399	1,591	2,990	15.0
1922	9,046	9,192	18,238	1,352	1,498	2,850	15.07
1923	9,538	9,851	19,389	1,383	1,696	3,079	15.8
1924	9,249	9,548	18,797	1,353	1,652	3,005	14.9
1925	9,182	9,522	18,704	1,300	1,640	2,940	15.7
1926	9,405	9,698	19,103	1,416	1,709	3,125	16.3
1927	9,702	10,102	19,804	1,486	1,886	3,372	17.
1928	10,651	11,055	21,706	1,742	2,146	3,888	17.9
1929	11,605	12,038	23,643	1,931	2,364	4,295	18.1
1930	10,846	11,377	22,223	1,829	2,360	4,189	18.8
Totals	98,791	102,142	200,933	15,191	18,542	33,733	16.78

	Males	Females	Totals
General population in area, 1931	3,927,417	3,575,114	7,502,531
Catholic population in area, 1931 (excluding Greek Catholics)	863,132	777,131	1,640,263

Such a table might be presented much more simply as follows, although it conceals certain important factors:

	Mixed Marriages	Pure Catholic Marriages
1921	2,990	8,168
1922	2,850	7,694
1923	3,079	8,155
1924	3,005	7,896
1925	2,940	7,882
1926	3,125	7,989
1927	3,372	8,216
1928	3,888	8,909
1929	4,295	9,674
1930	4,189	9,017
Totals	33,733	83,600

By thus eliminating Quebec from our computation, we have a cross-section of Canada which closely resembles the general American situation. The Catholic population in this area is 21.8 per cent. of the total population, which is approximately the per cent. of the Catholic population in the United States, especially if we eliminate there the Negroes from our computation as we have eliminated Quebec in Canada. The majority of the Protestants are of English, Scottish, Irish, German and Scandinavian descent; the majority of the Catholics are about equally divided between Anglo-Celtic and Continental European descent. In this area the Catholics are dominantly an urban group, and hence there is some reason for believing that the data here furnished might not be entirely inapplicable to the United States.

The significant facts are, first, that for every 2.47 pure Catholic marriages in these eight provinces, there is one mixed marriage, or since it takes two people to make a marriage and in a mixed marriage only one of these is a Catholic, 16.7 per cent. of all Catholics in this area who married between 1920 and 1930 married out of their faith. It is of further significance that while 16.7 per cent. of all Catholics married out of their faith, this tendency was regularly greater among Catholic women than Catholic men. Only 15.7 per cent. of Catholic grooms married non-Catholics but 18.1 per cent. of Catholic brides did so. This means, of course, that in spite of the fact that in the area there were many more Catholic males than Catholic females, more Catholic women married than Catholic men. The marriage rate, therefore, of Catholic men is lower than that of Protestant men. On the other hand, vice versa, the marriage rate of non-Catholic women must be accordingly lower than that of Catholic women.

THE TREND IN QUEBEC

When we consider Quebec, which is atypical, we find that religion, reinforced by language and race, offers a much stronger resistance to intermarriage. For this province, the following table gives only the figures since 1926 when it became part of the general registration area; and Greek Catholics are considered as Roman Catholics:

MARRIAGES OF CATHOLICS IN QUEBEC, 1926–30
(ROMAN AND GREEK)

Year	Total No. Catholic Grooms	Total No. Catholic Brides	Total No. Catholics Married	No. Catholic Grooms Marrying Out	No. Catholic Brides Marrying Out	No. Catholics Marrying Out	Per- centage Catholics Marrying Out
1926........	14,989	15,104	30,093	159	274	433	1.43
1927........	15,585	15,684	31,269	187	285	472	1.19
1928........	15,944	16,044	31,988	222	322	544	1.7
1929........	16,084	16,219	32,303	223	358	581	1.79
1930........	15,112	15,264	30,376	243	395	638	2.09
Totals...	77,714	78,315	156,029	1,034	1,634	2,668	1.70

	Males	Females	Totals
General population.........	1,447,124	1,427,131	2,874,255
Catholic population.........	1,237,199	1,225,961	2,463,160

In this province with its overwhelming Catholic population, the rate of intermarriage is very small, but the statistics indicate that it has grown during the period of five years for which figures are given. Once again, we find that in even a larger proportion the number of Catholic women marrying out exceeds that of Catholic men.

THE TREND IN ONTARIO

Further light is cast on the general problem when we consider the situation in the province of Ontario, where conditions are quite similar to those in the United States. The population of this province, in 1931, was 3,431,683, of whom 744,740 (21.7 per cent.) were Catholics. This is quite similar to the Catholic proportion of the population of the eight provinces (not including Quebec) for which figures have already been given and to the Catholic proportion of the population in the United States. While there is along the Ottawa valley a fairly heavy concentration of French-Canadians, the Catholic population is generally well-scattered over the entire province. The census indicated that of the total Catholic population in Ontario, 273,299 were of British extraction (English, Scottish and Irish), 266,460 were of French descent and 190,940 were of continental European origin other than French, the remainder consisting mostly of Indians. In the continental European groups there were 47,143 Italians, 37,827 Poles and 31,980 Germans. Such figures enable one to judge the possible application of the deductions which follow to the American situation.

The figures for Ontario indicate the number of Catholics married between 1925 and 1931 (inclusive), the year 1925 being selected as the starting-point, since from that time on the Greek Catholics and the Greek Orthodox are no longer lumped together, and the table indicates figures for both Roman Catholics and Greek Catholics, both groups being treated as synonymous:

ROMAN AND GREEK CATHOLIC MARRIAGES IN ONTARIO, 1925–1931

Year	Total No. Catholic Grooms	Total No. Catholic Brides	Total No. Catholics Married	No. Catholic Grooms Marrying Out	No. Catholic Brides Marrying Out	No. Catholics Marrying Out	Percentage Catholics Marrying Out
1925	4,535	4,603	9,138	578	646	1,224	13.3
1926	4,648	4,722	9,370	638	712	1,350	14.4
1927	4,807	4,934	9,741	653	780	1,433	14.71
1928	4,975	5,092	10,067	763	880	1,643	16.3
1929	5,759	5,968	11,727	796	1,005	1,801	15.36
1930	5,383	5,596	10,979	793	1,006	1,799	16.38
1931	5,142	5,393	10,535	779	1,030	1,809	17.17
Totals	35,249	36,308	71,557	5,000	6,059	11,059	15.4

	Males	Females	Total
General population in area (1931)	1,748,844	1,682,839	3,431,683
Catholic population (Roman and Greek)	390,963	353,777	744,740

The picture which these figures present is that of a steadily increasing trend on the part of Catholics in Ontario to marry out, although the general percentage is only 15.4 as opposed to an average of 16.7 for the eight provinces over a period of ten years. The percentage would have been slightly increased had the Greek Catholics been omitted from the statistics. Once again, we find that Catholic women marry out more than the men, 54.8 per cent. of the mixed marriages involving Catholic women and 45.2 per cent. involving Catholic men. A more significant fact in the tables is that while mixed marriages only dropped from 1,801 in 1929, to 1,799 in 1930, pure Catholic marriages declined from 4,963 to 4,590. (This resembles the figures for Quebec since in that province mixed marriages actually increased between 1929 and 1930 while pure marriages declined.) In the year of depression (1931) in the province of Ontario the number of Catholic grooms marrying non-Catholic women decreased from 793 to 779, while the number of Catholic women marrying non-Catholic men increased from 1,006 to 1,030. *This suggests an economic basis for the tendency of Catholic women to marry out.*

This theory seems also borne out by the table on page 249 giving the total number of marriages of Catholics in the whole of Canada excluding Quebec. The pure marriages dropped from 9,674 in 1929 to 9,017 in 1930, a decrease of 6.7 per cent., while the mixed marriages dropped only from 4,295 to 4,189, a decrease of only 2.4 per cent. In the same period the number of Catholic grooms marrying out dropped from 1,931 to 1,829, while the number of Catholic brides marrying non-Catholics only dropped from 2,364 to 2,360. One might hence surmise that in periods of economic depression, when the marriage rate generally falls, the number of Catholic *women* marrying out of their faith shows a negligible decline but Catholic *men* hesitate. The failure of mixed marriages to show a decline commensurate with pure marriages during the depression also suggests, in addition to the economic factor, that those who do marry out are perhaps somewhat more adventurous, reckless or improvident than those who do not.

VALID AND INVALID MIXED MARRIAGES

There still remains a difficult problem. What percentage of these mixed marriages are performed in accord with the regulations of the church, and what percentage are performed in defiance of such regulations? Figures are difficult to obtain from Catholic chanceries in Canada, but figures for the archdiocese of Toronto may, when compared with figures for the province as a whole, throw some light on this aspect of the whole question. The figures given below are for the three years 1928, 1929 and 1930:

	Population	Persons Marrying 1928-30	Pure Marriages	Mixed Marriages
Province of Ontario..............	3,431,683	159,976		
Ontario Catholics...............	744,740	32,573	13,765	5,243
Archdiocese of Toronto Catholics .	164,700	6,181*	2,753*	675*

*These figures are obtained from the Chancery records.

While the Catholic population of the province is 21 per cent. of the total population, the Catholics marrying during these three years is only 20.5 per cent. of all the persons who married in Ontario in that period.

The population of the archdiocese of Toronto is 22.1 per cent. of the entire Catholic population of Ontario, and if the same percentage were to hold good in the other figures on line 3, in the table, then we might have expected that in the archdiocese of Toronto 7,199 Catholics would have been married in these years, 3,042 pure Catholic marriages would have been performed and 1,158 mixed marriages. But the Catholic Chancery records show only 6,181 Catholics who married at all, 2,753 pure marriages and 675 mixed marriages. This disparity between the records regarding pure marriages in the Chancery office and what one would anticipate might be due to either of two causes:

(1) The marriage rate of Catholics in the archdiocese of Toronto may

be lower than the general marriage rate of Catholics in the entire province. This would seem to be indicated in the fact that the archdiocese accounts only for 20 per cent. of the total number of pure Catholic marriages while it contains 22.1 per cent. of the population.

(2) A considerable number of nominal Catholics contracting marriage with other nominal Catholics may go to a Protestant minister for the ceremony. While many instances of this character are known, especially in the case of Italians, they would hardly be sufficient to account for the difference. This might be more significant in the United States, since possibly nominal Catholics, divorced, may wish to remarry and cannot remarry in accordance with the Catholic position.

It would seem reasonable to suppose, however, that the ratio of mixed marriages in the archdiocese to the mixed marriages in the province would be the same as the ratio of the pure marriages in the archdiocese to the pure marriages in the province. Since there were 5,243 mixed marriages in the province, we should therefore expect that the archdiocese would provide us with 1,048 (20 per cent.) mixed marriages. But the chancery records know of only 675. It is reasonably safe, therefore, to assume that the difference (373) represents the total number of mixed marriages performed by other than Catholic priests. In short, we may estimate that of all the mixed marriages contracted in this diocese 675 (64.4 per cent.) complied with the regulations of the church and 373 (35.6 per cent.) did not.

While this estimate may be challenged, or even if admitted as sound, considered inapplicable to the United States, there is some apparent confirmation of the "trend" in certain studies conducted by Catholic priests in the United States in given parishes and reported in the *Ecclesiastical Review* in March, April and July, 1930. A careful census of Catholic families within parish A revealed that in 521 families there were 116 mixed marriages; and that of the 116 mixed marriages forty-two were ecclesiastically invalid, i.e., they had not been contracted before a parish priest. In parish B a similar census revealed that in 604 families there were 124 mixed marriages; of the 124 mixed marriages, forty-three were ecclesiastically invalid. In these two parishes, therefore, out of an aggregate of 1,125 families there were 240 mixed marriages, and of these eighty-five (35.4 per cent.) were invalid. A third parish reported the discovery of fifty-three invalid marriages, but the reporter failed to give the total number of mixed marriages in the parish. The similarity between the percentage of mixed marriages which were invalid in these parishes (35.4 per cent.) and the percentage of similar marriages which we have estimated for the entire archdiocese of Toronto (35.6 per cent.) is somewhat striking, although of course the sampling is too small to justify any assured statement.

It is easy, perhaps, to exaggerate another similarity, viz., that between the ratios of ecclesiastically valid and invalid mixed marriages to the ratios of Catholic women and Catholic men marrying out. In the province of Ontario over these three years, out of 5,243 Catholics marrying out of their faith, 2,352 (44.8 per cent.) were men and 2,891 (55.2 per cent.) were women. One surmises, perhaps without an adequate basis of fact, that in most cases of mixed marriage the women respect their religious status more than the men. It would be interesting to discover if the vast majority of mixed marriages *performed by Catholic priests* were not of Catholic women marrying non-Catholic men. To be sure, in one of the parish studies just mentioned, reported in the *Ecclesiastical Review,* the writer stated that of fifty-three invalid marriages in his parish, seventeen involved Catholic men and thirty-six Catholic women. He further analyzed these fifty-three marriages as to whether it might be possible in accordance with Catholic canon law, to validate such marriages, as follows:

	Where Man is Catholic	Where Woman is Catholic
Possible marriage validation (a)	76 per cent.	64 per cent.
Doubtful marriage validation (b)	12 "	17 "
Impossible marriage validation (c)	12 "	19 "

(a) implied that there was no impediment that ecclesiastical authority could not heal; (b) that there was a doubtfully valid previous marriage which required a decision from the matrimonial court of the church; (c) that prior to this marriage there had been already a marriage which, in the eyes of the church, was still valid.

FRICTION CAUSED BY ECCLESIASTICAL ANNULMENT

Of course, in no state of the United States would the civil law recognize the right of the church to annul a marriage which the civil law considered binding, or to validate a marriage which the civil law might consider invalid. In Quebec, however, on account of the indefinite status of the right to practise freely the Catholic religion and the practices of French civil law, manifold difficulties have arisen, as already indicated in chapter iii, in spite of the ruling of the Privy Council that the civil courts have no right to annul marriages on "religious" grounds. Bishop Farthing, Anglican Bishop of Montreal, discussed this matter before the annual meeting of the Anglican Synod on April 11, 1934, and stated, according to the press, that "it had been one of his major and continual difficulties during the episcopate to deal with marriage cases annulled by the court of His Grace the Archbishop of Montreal." He issued an appeal to the Catholic authorities to discontinue this practice. Perhaps one reason for the small number of mixed marriages in Quebec is the fact that should one of the mixed marriages be performed before a non-Catholic priest, and the Catholic party for any reason tire of the marriage, the Catholic authorities need not hesitate to annul the marriage, and the civil courts will follow the lead of the Catholic matrimonial court on the ground that no Catholic in Quebec has a civil right to contract a marriage with a non-Catholic before a non-Catholic clergyman, no matter what the Privy Council says about it. There can be little doubt that such an attitude on the part of ecclesiastical authorities and civil courts in Quebec is simply ruining any chance that the Catholic Church in Canada outside of Quebec may have of securing a sympathetic hearing.

WHY MORE CATHOLIC WOMEN THAN MEN MARRY OUT

At all events the Canadian statistics make it perfectly manifest that in every province, including Quebec, the number of Catholic women marrying out of their faith exceeds that of the Catholic men who do so, and in almost identical ratios in each province. Here surely one may recognize a trend, requiring some explanation. Several possible reasons may be put forth for what they are worth:

(1) The laws of the Catholic Church respecting intermarriage being so definite, someone has to yield if the marriage is to be recognized as valid in the eyes of the church. Generally speaking, the men do so and are more indifferent. The women yield less, whether they are Catholic or Protestant. Protestant men will accept the conditions imposed by the church more readily than will Protestant women.

(2) The economic status of the Catholic man is, in both the United States and Canada, generally inferior to the economic status of the non-Catholic. Women may tend to marry above their own social level. Hence, the Catholic woman is more apt to overlook the Catholic artisan of her own social class in favor of the Protestant business man. Figures quoted in chapter vi also indicated that while usually more girls than boys attend the public high schools, the excess of girls over boys in the Catholic secondary schools is even more marked. It may be that the average Catholic girl is educated somewhat beyond the level of the average Catholic boy, and this may prove a factor in the situation.

(3) It has been suggested by some that, owing to the somewhat rigid attitude of the church in relation to certain aspects of the sex relation, some Catholic women may prefer to choose Protestant husbands.

Possibly, these reasons are already placed in the order of their importance; it may be, however, that other reasons are more valid than those indicated.

WHO GETS THE CHILDREN?

The writer has discovered no adequate data dealing with this question. Father Ayrinhac, in his volume on *Marriage Legislation*, says:

"It is said by some Catholic authorities that less than half the children of mixed marriages in this country are brought up as Catholics. When a course of instruction has been given, it is found that over 70 per cent. of the non-Catholics enter the Church either before or after marriage. The losses are great in Germany— only about 40 per cent. of the children are baptized in the Church, and in strongly Protestant sections, 24 per cent." (Page 101, footnote)

In the studies already referred to and reported in the *Ecclesiastical Review,* Parish B, which had discovered within its bounds 480 Catholic families and 124 other families based on mixed marriage, reported as follows:

Per Cent.

	Miss Mass Regularly	Miss Easter Duty	Children Not Baptized	Children Reared Protestant	Children in Catholic Schools
480 Catholic marriages...........	10.5	7.0			63.0
61 valid mixed marriages, wife a Catholic.....................	20.0	16.0	2.0	6.0	45.0
20 valid mixed marriages, husband a Catholic....................	40.0	45.0	4.0	44.0	30.0
43 invalid mixed marriages.......	53.0		30.0	23.0	20.0

It would be presumptuous to build too much on one case study, but this parish is in many respects a typical and highly influential parish, and it seems to corroborate the hypothesis that the religion of the woman, even in valid mixed marriages, is a determining factor, for though twenty women had promised that they would bring their children up as Catholics, 44 per cent. of their children were being brought up as Protestants.

INTERMARRIAGE MORE SERIOUS FOR MINORITY GROUPS

It must, of course, be remembered that intermarriage is always a more dangerous source of leakage to a minority group than to a majority group. Thus, from the various figures given above, the following deductions might probably be drawn in regard to any 1,000 persons married in the United States or in Canada outside of the province of Quebec. On the basis of the general Catholic proportion of the population, approximately 225 of these persons would be Catholics, of whom 192 would marry other Catholics and thirty-three would contract mixed marriages; in the same way, 775 of these persons would be non-Catholics, of whom 742 would marry other non-Catholics and thirty-three would contract mixed marriages. The danger of exfiltration is obviously much greater for the Catholic Church than for the non-Catholic groups. Of the thirty-three mixed marriages, however, only twenty-two would probably be performed in the presence of the Catholic priest. The remaining eleven would be considered ecclesiastically invalid, and it is hardly improper to assume that most of these may be considered a dead loss to the Catholic Church. Of the twenty-two valid marriages remaining 5.5 (or 25 per cent.) would be instances where Catholic men are married to Protestant women and once again, despite the promises made by the Protestant women, there is a 50 per cent. probability that the children would be brought up as Protestants. We might perhaps say that in three of these cases the children would be brought up as Catholics and in 2.5 cases as Protestants. In the remaining 16.5 valid marriages we might estimate that in perhaps one case the children would be reared as Protestants, and in the 15.5 cases as Catholics, with the difference that at least half of these would attend the public schools.

To summarize, in the thirty-three mixed marriages, the Catholic Church could only expect that 18.5 of the families would be reared in the Catholic faith, while in 14.5 cases the children would either be reared as Protestants or would receive no religious training at all. Looking at the problem from the other angle, in the hypothetical marriage of 1,000 persons, involving 500 marriages, there would probably be 371 purely non-Catholic marriages, ninety-six pure Catholic marriages, 14.5 mixed marriages, where the children would probably be brought up as Protestants or without any religious instruction, and 18.5 mixed marriages in which the children would be brought up in the Catholic faith. The net outcome would be a non-Catholic dominance in 385.5 marriages and a Catholic dominance in 114.5 marriages. Thus, if we assume that the Catholic population is 22.5 per cent. of the total population and the general marriage trend is as indicated, Catholicism will be dominant in 22.9 per cent. of the marriages contracted and non-Catholicism dominant in 77.1 per cent.

Of course the Protestant denominations suffer from intermarriage within the denominations. In spite of the fact that the young people's societies of Protestant churches are sometimes regarded as match-making organizations, a fairly large percentage marry outside their denominations, as may be gathered from some casual figures for the Dominion of Canada for 1931:

Denomination	Total Number Grooms	Grooms Marrying Out	Total Number Brides	Brides Marrying Out
Anglicans	9,963	4,506	9,718	4,334
Baptists	3,267	1,604	3,314	1,651
Lutherans	3,252	1,119	3,128	995
Presbyterians and United Church*	19,164	5,719	18,725	5,280

* Since Church Union certain adherents of the United Church continue to call themselves Presbyterians, and hence these two churches are now considered for statistical purposes as constituting one group.

Such intermarriages do tend to break down denominational loyalty, but they present no insuperable obstacles to the discovery of some "compromise" which is perhaps characteristic of the Protestant mentality.

RESENTMENT OF CATHOLIC POLICY BY PROTESTANTS

Though the actual percentage of loss to Protestants through intermarriage with Catholics is not necessarily high, it is a source of great friction. Protestants feel that the Catholics take advantage of a "biological urge" and persuade prospective parents to sign away in a written promise the inalienable right of parents to guide the religious development of their children in accordance with their own consciences. Where, they ask, does religious liberty come in or even the right of parents to determine the spiritual culture of the child concerning which the Catholic Church itself speaks so insistently? One of the Episcopal rectors of a large city parish in the Middle West stated the issue thus:

"The Roman Catholic policy is extremely irritating and I believe that it does great harm inasmuch as it puts upon the conscience of many who, under the urge of desire to marry, make pledges which they ever after regret. If a good Catholic is married to a Protestant, not by a priest, he is uneasy and has a sense of guilt for he knows that he is an outlaw. I hold it is an iniquitous policy and I openly tell my young people so and urge them to think seriously before contracting a mixed marriage. The Roman Catholics are constantly troubled by the problem but they have brought the trouble on themselves. They lose as much as they gain by it. Many more of our boys marry Catholic women than our girls marry Catholic men; the girls often break their pledge and bring their children to the Protestant church to be baptized. The Protestant boys seldom do this."

At the same time a Roman Catholic priest interviewed in the course of the study said:

"There is a regulation that parents sending their children to public schools without the permission of their parish priests will be denied absolution at confession. The result is that parties proposing mixed marriage are less likely to have a church marriage. If the Catholic party does not intend to fulfil his pledge, the importance of the ecclesiastical marriage is rendered that much less imperative, and so the losses through intermarriage become greater."

Another Protestant minister said:

"One fundamental aspect of the situation in our city (Baltimore) is the high social standing of the old Catholic families. This made intermarriage much easier because they moved in the same social circles, belonged to the same clubs, etc. Intermarriage raised immediately difficult problems, owing to the definite attitude of the Catholic Church. One of my young girls whom I confirmed is now about to be married to a Catholic. I am not allowed to take any part whatever in the marriage ceremonies. I have to keep out of the picture, while she has to make the usual pledges to the Catholic Church concerning the education of the children. This creates family strain and an inevitable strain between me and the priest of the parish, in which the girl is to be married."

There can be no doubt whatever that the official position of the Catholic Church on the matter of intermarriage is perhaps the "hottest spot" in anti-Catholic feeling on the part of Protestants. A leading Protestant layman, socially and financially prominent, put it very frankly when he said that there could never be peace between Protestants and Catholics so long as the Catholic Church maintained its present attitude on the matter. Many Protestant ministers take the ground that if the Protestant parties in mixed marriages have made such a promise to bring their children up as Catholics they are morally obligated to keep it. Others doubt that such a promise is binding, legally or morally. They point out that any one who makes such a promise does so under a form of coercion; that the Catholic Church itself will annul a marriage if it can be proved that "coercion" was applied, and that the Catholic Church itself applies a form of coercion in insisting on these promises; that, finally, no man can morally sign away his inalienable right as a parent to determine his child's spiritual upbringing. A vow of such a nature must not be carried out if later it is believed to operate against the conscience of the person who made it.

SUCCESS OR FAILURE OF MIXED MARRIAGES

It is not possible, unfortunately, to present any satisfactory statistical material regarding the comparative success of such marriages. A careful examination of the records of the courts of domestic relations in various cities might help, although by no means all of these records give the religious connection of the parties involved. Unfortunately the limited time assigned to this study made this type of inquiry impracticable. A summary of some 500 consecutive cases in the records of the Court of Domestic Relations of Hamilton County, Ohio, made in 1923, however, indicated that 71.1 per cent. of the husbands and 43.3 per cent. of the wives concerned were not church-members at all, and that 23.1 per cent. of the husbands were Catholics and 22.8 per cent. of the wives. It was further stated on good authority that approximately 35 per cent. of all the cases handled in the court involved either Catholic-Catholic or Catholic-Protestant marriages. In an analysis of 474 cases in the records of the Family Welfare Society of Baltimore, religious difference was believed to be a significant cause of the existing domestic tension in only thirteen (2.7 per cent.) cases. It frequently complicates social work, however, as has been shown in Chapter IV.

Whether such marriages succeed or fail, it seems reasonably obvious that marriage itself offers a sufficient variety of possible tensions without complicating the difficulties with religious differences. On the other hand, as one who had himself contracted such a marriage said to the writer:

"There is some reason why a mixed marriage might be even more successful than an unmixed one. Most persons who contract them realize there are unusual difficulties to be faced, and consequently they appreciate the more the necessity of mutual consideration. Too many people get married on the crest of high emotion and never for a moment think that their married life will be marred or complicated. When the complications come, they are entirely unprepared for them. Persons who contract mixed marriages realize that adjustments have to be made and hence are inclined to be considerate."

INTERMARRIAGE BETWEEN JEW AND NON-JEW

The research worker finds quite as much, if not more, difficulty in securing hard data in regard to the number of marriages between Jews and non-Jews as concerning the marriages of Catholics and non-Catholics. In some respects, he faces even greater difficulty, since in the case of the marriages of Catholics and non-Catholics, the various diocesan chanceries at least know the number of mixed marriages which are performed in accordance with the canon law of the church, even if they do not usually publish the figures. No such figures, however, are known to the Jewish rabbis. Several suggestive studies of the subject have been made in the United States, notably one by Dr. Reuben B. Resnik, of Los Angeles, the manuscript of which was graciously put at the disposal of the director of this study, but all those who have attempted to treat the matter have found themselves restricted to the analysis of a limited number of cases. These have been extremely valuable, but unfortunately they are not sufficiently numerous to establish general trends.

Moreover, in the case of the Jews there is once again the complication created by the confusion of race and religion. Dr. Julius Drachsler, for instance, published, in 1921, the results of one of the most complete studies of intermarriage ever attempted in the United States. He analyzed the records of all marriage licenses issued in New York City in the five years, 1908-1912, and out of a total of 171,356 such licenses he selected 101,854 for further inquiry. From the latter number he excluded all marriages where either the bride or the groom (except in the case of members of the Jewish group) was born in the United States of native-born parents. This reduced the total number investigated to 79,704. Since the marriage licenses did not give any clue to the religious preference of the applicant, Dr. Drachsler determined the probable cultural origin of the applicant from (1) the name, (2) the geographic section of the birthplace of the applicant or of his or her parents, (3) the names of the witnesses to the marriage, and (4) the name of the officiating clergyman and his denomination. The possibilities of error in such a computation were very great, and Dr. Drachsler acknowledged in the course of his study that his figures probably made the intermarriage ratio lower than it is in actuality, since Jews so frequently change their names, and when they intermarry have recourse to some one other than a clergyman of either of the faiths represented in the marriage. Here again we find the general tendency to consider the Jews as a racial-cultural group rather than as a religious group, for Dr. Drachsler not only considered intermarriage from what was essentially a racial point of view, but he even distinguished, in reporting on the Jews, between Bulgarian, English, French, German, Dutch, Hungarian, Rumanian, Russian, Turkish, American and other "national" types of Jews. He thus worked out some exceedingly informative tables showing not only the intermarriage between such clear types as the Italians and the Norwegians and the Jews and non-Jews, but even between the various types of Jews, considered in relation to their recent habitat.

DRACHSLER DATA FOR NEW YORK CITY

Unfortunately, in Dr. Drachsler's excellent study, his summary figures on which he bases his various percentages do not tally with his detailed and fundamental data as contained in the copious appendix.[5] He asserted, for instance, that 364 of 32,491 Jewish grooms married out of their group, while 399 of 32,707 Jewish brides married out. It is quite obvious that a serious mistake is made here, since if one deducts the number of intermarriages contracted by grooms from the total number of grooms it will yield the same difference as when the total number of intermarriages contracted by brides is deducted from the total number of brides. It was hence necessary to subject the fundamental material contained in the appendix to his study to further retabulation with the following results:

JEWISH INTERMARRIAGES IN NEW YORK CITY, 1908–1912

	FBFP	FBFP(MO)*	NBFP	NBFP(MO)	NBNP	NBNP(MO)	TOTAL	TOTAL (MO)
Grooms	28,722	147(.51%)	3,327	200(6.01%)	642	32(4.98%)	32,691	379(1.16%)
Brides	27,709	225(.81%)	4,211	131(3.11%)	787	29(3.68%)	32,707	385(1.17%)
	56,431	372(.65%)	7,538	331(4.39%)	1,429	61(4.28%)	65,398	764(1.168%)

* MO means Marrying Out of Their Group.

Since, on the basis of these figures the total number of unmixed marriages comes to 32,312 for the grooms and 32,322 for the brides, we must postulate a slight but inconsiderable error in the compilation of the fundamental data.

[5] Drachsler, Julius, *Intermarriage in New York City* (New York: Columbia University Press, 1921).

In endeavoring to read the significance of these figures, it is necessary to take certain conditions into account:

(1) These studies were made in 1908-1912, and thus represent trends more than twenty years ago, and before the war. Beginning in 1914 Jewish immigration fell off very materially, and this would tend to reduce the number of FBFP (foreign-born of foreign parentage) Jews of marriageable age. On the other hand, since that time numerous forces have been in operation to intensify Jewish communal life and this in turn would tend, in the belief of those engaged in this study, to lessen the rate of inter-marriage among Jews.

(2) The studies were made in New York City, which is hardly typical of American conditions generally, since in this city the Jews constitute so large a percentage of the total population. Dr. Drachsler has himself inti-mated in his study that the extent of intermarriage is far greater in the smaller cities and rural districts, although exact figures are not available to substantiate such a belief. The director of the present study has found some evidence in Canada that the rate of intermarriage between Jew and non-Jew is slightly higher in the prairie provinces, where there are com-paratively few Jews, but he also discovered evidence that Jews living in the small villages and rural areas of Ontario, where there are no synagogues, showed a remarkably low marriage rate, probably because that they came to the cities to be married.

(3) Many Jews must have escaped Dr. Drachsler's method of locating them, especially the native-born of native parentage who had changed their names. He included only those Jews of whom he was reasonably certain, and it is not difficult to believe that the Jews who are more prone to change their names may also be more ready to intermarry.

Remembering these limitations in the study, his conclusions, however, seem very sound and are borne out, as shall be observed later, by Canadian government statistics. Of 65,398 Jews and Jewesses who married during these five years in New York City only 764 or 1.168 per cent. married non-Jews. Among those who were foreign-born and of foreign parentage, only .65 per cent. married out; among the native-born of foreign parentage, 4.39 per cent. married out; among the native-born of native parentage, only 4.28 per cent. married out. While the sampling of the native-born of native parentage is small, it does seem to indicate a certain hardening of Jewish communalism, and this, too, seems on the whole to be confirmed by Canadian statistics.

In the total number of cases of Jews examined in Dr. Drachsler's study, there were more women than men, and hence it is not altogether sur-prising that the number of Jewesses marrying out slightly exceeded the number of Jewish men who did so. This seems contrary to the general trend in Canadian statistics, but it is not insignificant that this excess of women over men who married out was entirely in the group of the foreign-born of foreign parentage. When we come to the native-born of foreign parentage the men who marry out are greatly in excess of the women who do so, and the same tendency is somewhat true of the native-born of native parentage.

One is inclined to believe that the trend towards a diminishing inter-marriage rate indicated in the above figures is general. There does tend to be a hardening of Jewish communalism as the group is longer domiciled, and after the second generation has broken loose for a time, it tends to find its life more largely within its own cultural group. Indeed, there is evidence that a very large proportion of the intermarriage which takes place concerns Orthodox Jews; as the Jew becomes successful, he is apt to attach himself to the liberal synagogue and finds there a social status more acceptable than he may discover either outside of Judaism or in Orthodox Judaism. He then finds his friends and his mates in that circle.

Dr. Drachsler also compared the Jews of different national backgrounds in respect to their tendencies to marry non-Jews, and offered the following figures for these various types:

INTERMARRIAGE RATES OF VARIOUS NATIONAL TYPES OF JEWS IN NEW YORK CITY, 1908–1912

Per Cent. Marrying Out

National Type	Total	FBFP	NBFP	FBFP and NBFP Men	Women
Rumanian Jew	.45	.35	2.52	.41	.48
Russian Jew	.62	.36	3.40	.50	.74
Turkish Jew	.80	.80	None	1.05	.56
Austrian Jew	.99	.57	5.68	.84	1.12
Jewish (combined group)	1.168	.65	4.39	1.16	1.17*
Hungarian Jew	2.24	2.09	3.31	.97	3.24
English Jew	3.47	4.37	2.72	3.77	3.14
Holland Jew	4.00	3.70	4.34	5.71	None
United States Jew	4.26			4.98	3.68*
German Jew	5.16	3.74	6.02	7.37	2.83
French Jew	6.54	3.44	8.06	11.11	2.17

* In the case of Jewish (combined group) and United States Jews, NBNP are included. The figures given for these types are not Dr. Drachsler's, but revision made of his fundamental data by those engaged in this study as reported above.

From these figures the trends are fairly clear. By and large the degree of intermarriage is not significant even in the case of the German and French Jews, while the Eastern European Jew marries almost exclusively within his group. It should also be said that the total number of English, Dutch and French Jews concerned was very small.

There is unfortunately little other authentic data on intermarriage in any of the cities in the United States other than New York or for a later period. Rabbi Brickner, of Cleveland, made a careful analysis of the Jewish marriages performed in Cincinnati between 1916 and 1919 inclusive and formulated the following data:

Year	Marriages Recorded	Number of Intermarriages	Per Cent. Intermarriages
1916	149	8	5.3
1917	182	8	4.5
1918	108	4	3.7
1919	143	1	0.7
Totals	582	21	3.6

If, however, we are to assume that out of 582 marriages involving Jews only twenty-one were intermarriages, then it is more correct to say that out of 1,141 Jews who married, only twenty-one, or 1.83 per cent., married out of their group. This figure, therefore, approximates the general figure given by Dr. Drachsler for New York which was 1.168 per cent. for Jews of all kinds.

Samplings of Jewish marriages for a few months have also been made in Los Angeles and San Francisco during the year 1922-23. The results of this sampling are most inconclusive:

City	Total Jewish Marriages	Grooms	Brides	Marrying Out Total	Per Cent.
Los Angeles	157	10	7	17	10.82
San Francisco	90	..	..	16	17.77

Other rough estimates have been given to the writer in various cities, but little verifiable data was offered. In general, one may believe that there is a tendency to exaggerate the extent to which intermarriage between Jew and non-Jew exists. It is highly probable that the rate of intermarriage was high in colonial days and during the pioneer period in the West. Many of the Jews in those areas at the time were single men, and they chose daughters from among the Philistines and "passed over" to the other side. Thus, in the papers of the Jewish Historical Society, one finds the following note in a brochure on the Jews of Kentucky:

"There is no frequenter of the synagogue who either lived in Kentucky or whose ancestors lived there before 1836. Whoever came, came singly, found no one to mate with. Intermarriage of the newcomers with the daughters of the land followed naturally, and the descendents of the early Jewish settlers of Kentucky are known only by their Jewish family names and their oriental features."

The degree of intermarriage around Louisville even today is quite high, but generally speaking, the general hardening of Jewish communalism is steadily decreasing intermarriage.

CANADIAN STATISTICS

We have, however, in Canadian statistics much more accurate figures than can be found anywhere in the United States. General summaries given below indicate that the degree of intermarriage between Jew and non-Jew falls quite low in Quebec, with its rigid French-Catholic culture, increases in Ontario, shows an even greater increase in the western provinces (there are few Jews in the Maritime provinces) and for the country as a whole falls slightly under the Ontario average. The first summary table gives the basic facts for different parts of Canada:

INTERMARRIAGE OF JEW AND NON-JEW IN CANADA

	Ontario 1920–30	Quebec 1926–1931	Canada Excluding Quebec 1920–1931	All Canada 1926–1931
Jewish grooms	4,846	3,212	7,935	8,169
Jewish brides	4,741	3,162	7,721	7,991
Total Jews married	9,587	6,375	15,656	16,160
Unmixed marriages	4,666	3,139	7,504	7,880
Mixed marriages	255(2.6%)	97(1.52%)	528(3.37%)	400(2.47%)
Jewish-Gentile	180	73	371	289
Gentile-Jewish	75	24	157	111

In this table, the percentage of mixed marriages is taken by dividing the total number of mixed marriages, not by the number of unmixed marriages, but by the total number of Jews married.

The fact that the intermarriage rate is almost stationary is clearly evidenced in the next table, which gives, with fundamental figures omitted and only percentages indicated, the total percentages of Jews in the various areas who married non-Jews:

Per Cent. Marrying Out

Year	Ontario	Quebec	Canada Excluding Quebec	All Canada
1921	2.91		3.85	
1922	2.58		3.52	
1923	2.68		3.75	
1924	2.75		3.70	
1925	4.1		4.31	
1926	1.8	1.54	2.96	2.33
1927	2.9	2.	3.65	3.02
1928	1.58	1.12	2.42	1.92
1929	3.01	1.4	3.58	2.73
1930	2.6	1.5	3.24	2.64
1931	2.1	1.4	2.71	2.19
Average in period designated	2.59	1.52	3.37	2.47

Of course it is not impossible that the marriage of certain Jews in Canada to non-Jews may have taken place after the Gentile party had been converted to Judaism or the Jewish party converted to Christianity. In such cases the marriage would probably be recorded as marriages between Jews or between Christians. With this exception, however, the figures seem quite credible.

It is difficult to read any evidence in these figures that the rate of intermarriage is noticeably increasing. In certain years, e.g., 1925 and 1929, there seems to be a marked increase in given areas only to be followed by a proportionate decrease the following year. By and large the rate seems fairly stable.

There is a general decline in the per cent. of intermarriage during the depression years following 1929, but there was of course a general decrease in the number of Jews, whether grooms or brides, marrying in these years. It is difficult to read any economic factor in intermarriage out of this situation, although it is true that, while the number of Jewish men marrying out in 1931 in Canada was barely half of the number that did so in 1929, the number of Jewish women marrying out actually increased from sixteen to twenty-three. The figures for the years 1929, 1930 and 1931 are as follows:

| Year | Jewish Grooms Marrying Out | | | Jewish Brides Marrying Out | | |
	Ontario	Quebec	All Canada	Ontario	Quebec	All Canada
1929	30	15	67	10	2	16
1930	24	12	50	11	8	29
1931	18	10	39	8	6	23

The total number involved is too small to speak with any assurance of a trend.

Regularly in Canada and in every portion of it, the number of Jewish men who marry non-Jews is larger than the number of Jewish women who marry non-Jewish men, and yet the Jewish group in Canada is fairly evenly divided between males and females, there being 78,505 males as against 77,101 females. Perhaps two major reasons may account for this trend:

(1) The Jewish woman has fewer opportunities for meeting Gentile men in business, etc., than the Jewish man has for meeting Gentile women. Outside of business the social line is drawn fairly sharply. It is generally asserted that many Jewish business men marry their Gentile stenographers.

(2) Generally speaking, religion may exert a greater influence with the Jewish woman than with the Jewish man, in spite of the fact—and perhaps because of the fact—that the Orthodox Jewess is not expected to keep as many commandments as the Orthodox Jew.

DENOMINATIONS INTO WHICH JEWS MARRY

The denominational spread of the non-Jewish consorts in these inter-marriages is of interest. During the six years 1926-1931, 289 Jewish men and 111 Jewish women in Canada married out of their faith, as follows:

Denomination of Consort	Jewish Grooms	Jewish Brides	Totals
Anglicans	72	27	99
Baptists	14	3	17
Christians	1	1	3
Christian Scientists	2		2
Disciples	3	2	5
Greek Catholics	6	5	11
Greek Orthodox	1	2	3
Lutheran	19	5	24
Presbyterians	32	9	41
Protestants	13	8	21
Roman Catholics	79	23	102
United Church	40	22	62
Other sects or	7		
Sects not given	—	4	11
Totals	289	111	400

Of the total number of Jews marrying out, therefore, 28.5 per cent. married Roman or Greek Catholics; 25 per cent. married Anglicans; 25.9 per cent. married either Presbyterians or adherents of the United Church of Canada; the remainder, 21.6 per cent., married into various sects.

·It is impossible to indicate which denominations win by such inter-marriage. Perhaps, the couple compromise by attending neither church nor synagogue. However, the census of 1931 provides some interesting figures which may be useful at this point. There were in the whole of Canada in that year, according to the census, 156,726 persons who claimed to be of Hebrew racial origin; there were 155,351 persons of Hebrew racial origin who were also Jews in religion and 1,375 persons (701 males and 674 females) who called themselves Hebrews but not Jews; there were 155,614 persons, whether of Hebrew or other racial origin, who claimed to be Jews in religion, i.e., 263 persons (124 males and 139 females) who were not of Hebrew descent according to father called themselves Jews. Distinguishing between the urban and rural areas, we find that in the urban areas, the Jewish faith had lost 1,016 Hebrews and gained 232 Gentiles; in the rural areas, the Jewish faith had lost 359 Hebrews and gained 31 Gentiles.

We may account in part for these 1,375 Hebrews who were not Jews in various ways. Some have been converted to Christianity through Jewish missions or they have similarly attached themselves to ordinary Christian churches in the community. Others have abandoned all religion entirely, although only seven failed to indicate a religious preference and only 112 definitely stated that they were without religion. Still others are probably the children of Hebrew fathers and Christian mothers brought up in the Christian church, and the remainder are probably Hebrew men or women converted in consequence of intermarriage.

We may similarly account for the 263 non-Hebrew Jews in various ways. Since in this category we find slightly more females than males, we may perhaps assume that most of the women at least are Gentile women converted to Judaism prior to or after intermarriage; some others may be Gentile men similarly converted in consequence of intermarriage; a few may have deliberately chosen Judaism; a larger number may be the children of Gentile fathers by Jewish mothers, who are nevertheless being reared in Judaism. To attempt to classify this group with any greater precision would be sheer speculation.

If, however, we compare the total number of non-Jewish Hebrews, classified according to the religious preferences which they gave the census-taker, with the total number of intermarriages contracted between Jews and persons of that particular religious preference for a period of six years prior to the 1931 census, we discover a fairly interesting ratio:

Denomination	Non-Jewish Hebrews (Census, 1931)	Intermarriages of Jews with Persons of Given Denomination (six years, 1926–1931)
Anglicans	255	99
Baptists	131	17
Greek Orthodox	73	3
Lutherans	66	24
Presbyterians	127	41
Roman Catholics and Greek Catholics	292	113
United Church	176	62
Others	255	41
Totals	1,375	400

The ratios are somewhat important, especially when one remembers that practically only two denominations, the Anglicans and the Presbyterians, actually conduct missionary enterprises among the Jews and their ratios are approximately the same as those for the other denominations. If one considers all the Hebrews who are not Jews, and all the Jews who are not Hebrews, we have a total of 1,638, of whom 263, or 16.05 per cent., are Jews and 83.95 per cent. are non-Jews. This may or may not provide a clue as to what happens in the case of intermarriage.

COMPARATIVE FERTILITY OF MIXED AND UNMIXED JEWISH MARRIAGES

It has sometimes been stated that intermarriage of Jews with non-Jews makes for childlessness, and on this point the Canadian statistics probably provide some light. The director of the study drew off the total number of marriages in which Jews in the whole of Canada for 1926-1929 (four years) were concerned. He divided these into three categories—Jewish-Jewish (or unmixed marriages), Jewish-Gentile and Gentile-Jewish. He then drew off all the births in Canada in the same period in which one of the parents (excluding illegitimate births to Jewish mothers) or both parents were Jews. These he classified in the same way: Jewish-Jewish, Jewish-Gentile and Gentile-Jewish. He then sought to establish ratios between the total number of marriages of a particular type and the number of births to marriages of that type. The result was an interesting table:

FERTILITY OF MIXED AND UNMIXED (JEW-NON-JEW) MARRIAGES
(All Canada, 1926–1929 inclusive)

	Marriages	Births	Ratios
Jewish-Jewish	5,040	8,049	1 to 1.6
Jewish-Gentile	200	275	1 to 1.37
Gentile-Jewish	59	144	1 to 2.44
Total mixed	259	419	1 to 1.61

Of course, the number of Gentile-Jewish marriages is a small portion of the grand total, but there would appear to be no difference at all between the fertility of unmixed Jewish marriages and those of Jewish-Gentile and Gentile-Jewish marriages taken together. It does seem true, however, that when a Jewish man marries a Gentile woman, fewer children result than from unmixed Jewish unions; on the other hand, when a Gentile man marries a Jewish woman, more children result than from a purely Jewish marriage; when both kinds of mixed marriages are considered together, the number of children resulting is approximately the same as if they had been unmixed marriages.

While the Canadian marriage statistics are summarized by the Dominion Bureau of Statistics in such a way that intermarriage can be judged only as a religious and not as a racial phenomenon, some light may be thrown on the degree of racial intermarriage between Jew and non-Jew by a consideration of the racial origins of children born to such intermarriages. To ascertain this, a sample analysis was made of such births in Ontario in the six years 1925-1931, inclusive. The results are given in the next table. Of 317 children born to such intermarriages (if we can consider the non-specified consorts as non-Jewish), 149, or nearly one-half, were the result of intermarriage of Jews with persons of English, Scotch or Irish descent, while 103 were the result of intermarriage of Jews with persons of Polish, Rumanian or Russian descent. In short the Jews, whenever they go outside of their own group, tend to marry into the "majority stock," or else with persons of Eastern European descent. The spread of nationalities is, however, fairly indiscriminate.

CHILDREN BORN TO INTERMARRIED COUPLES (JEW AND NON-JEW)

(Ontario, 1925–1931)

Race of Non-Jewish Consort	Jewish Father	Jewish Mother	Total
English	60	17	77
Irish	33	7	40
Scotch	24	8	32
French	12	5	17
German	3	5	8
Austrian	2		2
Belgian		1	1
Czech-Slovak	1		1
Dutch	1		1
Finnish	3		3
Greek		2	2
Hungarian	1	2	3
Italian	1	5	6
Negro	3	1	4
Polish	25	16	41
Roumanian	4	6	10
Russian	26	26	52
Serb Croat	1		1
Swedish	1	3	4
Ukrainian	5	2	7
Not specified	3	2	5
Totals	209	108	317

In his study of "Intermarriage in New York," Dr. Drachsler analyzed some 3,698 cases of intermarriage (apparently of various ethnic groups) where occupations of both bride and groom were given so as to determine the social level on which intermarriage usually takes place. He concluded that more than two-thirds of the intermarriages among men (67.3 per cent.) and 59.2 per cent. of the intermarriages contracted by women fell within the higher economic classes, i.e., those employed in professional service, in commerce, in manufacturing and mechanical pursuits. It is well known that not a few Jewish doctors marry Christian nurses, Jewish teachers marry Gentile teachers, while there is very considerable inter-marriage in artistic and dramatic circles. In several cases, moreover, Jewish business men marry their Gentile stenographers. Unfortunately, there is little hard data on these points, and it is more difficult to ascertain the ways in which Jewish women become acquainted with Gentile men. One of the most discussed cases of such intermarriage recently took place in England, where a Montreal Jewess married the heir of one of the largest fortunes in England. They met in a dramatic club. It would be impossible to state, although there is some evidence for believing, that women once again tend to marry above their socio-economic position. There would, of course, be notable exceptions to this rule, even if it be a rule.

SOME PROBLEMS CONFRONTING THOSE WHO INTERMARRY

Do such intermarriages work out satisfactorily? There is much conflicting evidence on this point. Many of the difficulties that arise come when one of the parties may not prove acceptable to the social set in which his partner moves and in the evitable problem of determining in which group the children resulting from the marriage shall be reared. In one of the women's colleges, it was reported that there were two sisters, children of a Jewish father and a Christian mother. The older sister was being trained as a Jew and seemed quite happy about it. The younger child, however, resented being Jewish and would frequently break into tears and express the determination, strangely enough, to be a Methodist when she was able to choose for herself. A very cultivated and well-balanced Jewish physician, who had married a Christian nurse, felt that in his marriage no outstanding problem had developed except that of arranging for the religious training of the children. Both husband and wife moved equally acceptably in Jewish or Christian circles, while as a physician he had more Christian than Jewish patients. His marriage had neither hindered nor helped his professional practice, so far as he knew. He feared, however, that the social effects of the Sunday school which the children were attending would weaken any attachment they might have to the high standards of liberal Judaism, but concluded:

"I am willing to sacrifice a little of the immediate happiness in my home if necessary in order to contribute toward solving the great problems of intermarriage, though thus far we are quite happy. When our children are older I hope to let them choose their own faith after explaining fully the teachings of both. I am anxious to avoid the prejudice of Christians toward Judaism and the even stronger prejudice of Jews toward Christianity. The latter is very deep. The Jewish-Christian marriage is a social handicap for the children, whereas the Catholic-Protestant marriage, I judge, is only a religious problem, not a social handicap."

On the very day on which the above was written, the evening paper brought the following report from Montreal:

"Montreal: May 8, 1934: A meeting of prominent members of the Jewish community was scheduled for tonight to discuss the case before the juvenile courts which involves the question of whether a 12-year-old boy should be raised as a Roman Catholic, or as a Jew.

"The boy, variously named Abraham Donnelly, and James Donnelly, had a Catholic father and a Jewess for mother. He was baptized as a Catholic and after his father's death lived for some years in the care of his paternal grandmother, Mrs. Mary Donnelly.

"Later the mother, who became Mrs. Minnie Paul, obtained custody by order of the courts and had him received into the Jewish faith.

"Recently, she claims, the grandmother took him to her home contrary to the court ruling. Judge J. Robillard will decide the religious problem next week, but has made it known that in any event the boy will go to some institution."

Without prejudging the case, one finds here a clear case of difficulty due to intermarriage. Other factors may enter into the particular case which do not appear in the press. Since the child was baptized as a Catholic, it may perhaps be assumed that the original marriage was performed before a Catholic priest, and that prior to this the prospective bride signed a statement in which she promised to bring up any children that might be born of the marriage in the Catholic faith—even if the Catholic party, so the promise reads, "should happen to be taken away by death."

The fundamental question is this: has any church or religious organization—Catholic, Jewish or Protestant—a right to claim religious liberty when it requires from a prospective parent a promise regarding the religious training of a child yet unborn which substantially takes away the right of parents to supervise their own child's religious life in accordance with their own unfolding conscience, even though the partner whose faith has required that promise may be taken by death?

On the answer to that question hangs the solution of the major religious problem in intermarriage.

CHAPTER VIII

Conversion and Proselytization

With the existing rivalry, the preservation of the integrity of the group becomes a matter of grave concern. Therefore, efforts on the part of one group to lure away the faithful from another invariably creates resentment. This is felt particularly by the Jews and towards "Jewish missions," although at one time Judaism itself was a missionary religion and welcomed proselytes.

WHY JUDAISM CEASED PROSELYTIZING

The making of Jewish proselytes practically ceased, however, mainly for the following reasons:[1]

(1) Conversion to Judaism was prohibited in the eighth and ninth centuries by Catholic Christianity in Western Europe, and by Islam in the East.

(2) The grave difficulties and persecutions to which the Jewish group was subjected made them more concerned about the preservation of their group integrity than about winning others for their faith.

(3) The Jews may have feared an inevitable adulteration of their faith through the reception of proselytes.[2] Christian missions to a given culture have almost always invited the repercussion of that culture on Christian ideas.

(4) The emphasis of Christianity on universalism probably caused the Jew to underscore his uniqueness and the peculiar mission of Israel.

(5) The coercive efforts of the Church to force Christianity on the Jews may have deepened Jewish resistance to any kind of proselytizing.

THE CENTRAL PLACE OF MISSIONS IN CHRISTIANITY

At all events, while Judaism thus ceased in large measure to be a missionary religion, Christianity maintained a perpetual crusade. Christianity is, indeed, essentially a missionary religion and Christians regard any effort

---

[1] For an interesting summary of the reasons why Judaism ceased to be a missionary religion, see paper by Rabbi Mattuck in the *Liberal Jewish Monthly* and paper No. XXXI for Jewish People published by the Jewish Religious Union for the Advancement of Liberal Judaism, at St. John's Wood Road, London, N. W. (1933) entitled "Jewish Views on Jewish Missions."

[2] In a very able paper presented to the American Sociological Society in Philadelphia (1933) Dr. Abraham Cronbach indicated a large number of borrowings of Judaism from other religions even in the last one hundred years.

to dissuade it from bringing all peoples within its influence as an invitation to apostasy. Moreover, in the Middle Ages, Catholic Christianity was highly conscious of its rôle in maintaining the integrity of Europe. It believed that the maintenance of this unity involved unity in religious belief. Consequently, it not only sought to extend the sphere of its spiritual authority through the conversion of all non-Christian peoples, but it fought against all heresies within Christianity which threatened the continuance of this spiritual unity. The Jews presented peculiarly difficult problems to the ecclesiastical coördinators and synthesizers, and while the Popes often urged a large tolerance toward them, local bishops constantly sought to incorporate them in Christendom. In this, they were sometimes abetted by the princes, and sometimes prevented. The compulsory methods used to effect their conversion were in themselves sufficient to deepen Jewish hatred of Christianity, although they must possibly be read in the light of the conscious effort of the church to "integrate" the continent.

With the rise of nationalism, the concept of religion as an integrating force was recognized in the political principle "cujus regio, ejus religio," adopted by both Catholic and Protestant princes. Dissent was crushed out when possible; force and intimidation were freely used to effect conversions, and in the ensuing wars of religion, Protestants, Catholics and Jews suffered alike. The position of the Jews was particularly difficult and their status was seldom normal. They were usually the objects of either aggressive dislike or special protection. Their gradual emancipation arose with the growth of the idea of religious liberty and the revolutionary theories that achieved their first outstanding triumph in France in 1789. The emergence of the Jews from the ghetto was the signal for a new type of missionary propaganda directed toward their conversion.

The missionary motive of Christianity mingled with the commercial motive in the discovery of the New World. This is clearly seen in the annals of South American exploration and in the Jesuit relations in North America. Today Catholics feel that the seeds of civilization on this continent were planted by their missionaries, and despite the manifold difficulties that arose in North America (notably in New France) between church and state, the early record of the church is replete with brilliant achievements and heroic martyrdoms, especially in the work attempted for the aborigines. Protestants were perhaps less daring in their work among the Indians, although John Eliot's translation of the Bible (1661-1663) is indicative of current interest. The first Protestants in the new world, however, had all they could do to establish their own theological and ecclesiastical systems—to say nothing of their political and economic systems —and the multiplicity of imported sects, inevitably inducing a live and let-live attitude, may have cooled any nascent missionary ardor. Toward the latter part of the eighteenth century—a period characterized in New England by great theological disputation—some concern was expressed for the evangelization of Africa, Samuel Hopkins of Newport proposing to use emancipated Christian Negroes in such work. Nothing, however, was done along those lines until 1826, and meanwhile the Haystack prayer meeting had led to the formation of the first American foreign missionary society, and in 1813 Adoniram Judson arrived in Burmah. The first Canadian Protestant missionary was sent out in 1845. Protestant missionary interest was soon thoroughly aroused in both the United States and Canada and in the following century missionaries were being sent to every quarter of the world.

RISE OF JEWISH MISSIONS IN EUROPE AND AMERICA

In the early days of the colonies, little pressure, if any, was put on the few Jews to effect their conversion, although there is undoubted evidence that many of them professed Christianity and intermarried with Gentiles. The Protestant churches in America were not "Jew-conscious." In Europe, however, Protestants had already been working in the Jewish field since 1676. The first indications of Christian missions to the Jews in Protestant quarters may be observed in the Low Countries where the condition of the Jews

". . . engaged the serious attention of the synods of Dordrecht, Delft and Leyden which were held in 1676, 1677 and 1678. . . . From that date conversions among the Jews in Holland were frequent. . . . In 1728 the Callenberg Institution was established at Halle, which had for its chief object the conversion of the Jew by means of tracts, Hebrew Scriptures and missionaries. The Moravian brethren about the year 1764 had their attention turned to the spiritual welfare of the Jews. . . . In 1736, 400 Jews were admitted to the evangelical church at Darmstadt. In 1739, 100 Jews embraced the Christian religion in the Grand Duchy of Hesse. The infidel revolution in Europe in 1789 put an end to all like efforts to evangelize the Jews."[3]

In 1809 the London Society for promoting Christianity among the Jews was organized. The object of the society was "to relieve the temporal distress of the Jews, as well as to promote their spiritual welfare." By 1813, seventy-nine proselytes had been made in London, and in 1818 the first foreign missionary to the Jews was sent abroad to Poland. This society, now known as the "Church Mission to Jews," still operates in various parts of the world, employing some 200 missionaries and spending approximately £45,000 a year. It is perhaps significant that not a few of the Hebrew-Christian

[3] Newcomb, *Cyclopaedia of Missions* (New York: Charles Scribner's Sons, 1854), p. 488.

missionaries now at work in America first came under the influence of Christianity in Europe through missioners employed in this oldest society.

The first effort of a similar kind in America was that of the "American Society for Meliorating the Condition of the Jews," organized in 1820. Representations had been made that Jews converted in Europe were being subjected to great persecution on the part of their kindred, and the American Society raised funds and purchased and furnished an establishment where such converts might be housed. Newcomb's *Cyclopaedia* says, however:

"Either because there were no converts disposed, or because no provision was made to enable them to emigrate, no colony of converts was ever fully organized, for want of subjects."

In 1849 a more elaborate plan for missionary activities among the Jews in America was formed, since the survey made at the time resulted in an estimate of 150,000 Jews in the country.[4]

Between 1849 and 1854 the society was able to report a total of fifty-nine converts and an annual expenditure of $14,500. It employed ten regular missionaries and seven colporteurs who travelled among the Jews in forty cities and towns.

One of the immediate results of this missionary activity on the part of Protestants was the setting-up of counter-activities by the Jews themselves. Thus, in his *Jewish Education in New York City*,[5] Alexander M. Dushkin says that the Jewish Mission Schools, established by German Jewish Congregations 1865-1881, had two purposes:

(1) To teach morality, and to exert a refining influence upon the Jewish children of the East Side, and

(2) To counteract the work of the Christian missionaries. He adds:

"In the spring of 1864 a number of Christian mission schools were opened in neighborhoods where large numbers of poor Jewish families resided. Their children were enticed by gifts of confectionery and clothing to attend classes ostensibly for instruction in the Hebrew language, but they were in reality 'nurseries of Christian teaching.' "

While there were many societies working among the Jews in Europe and Asia, there were few organizations at this time in the United States. Among the earliest societies was the Zion Society for Israel, founded in 1878 by the Norwegian Lutheran Church, which still operates in Minneapolis, St. Paul, Omaha, Chicago and Brooklyn. A list of some of the more important ventures in this field includes:

---

[4] The *Jewish Year Book* gives the estimate of 50,000, made by M. A. Berk, in 1848. In Newcomb's *Cyclopaedia* (1854) it is said that in 1851 there were 60,000 males on the synagogue rolls, and from this it is deduced that the total Jewish population would be about 150,000.

[5] New York: Bureau of Jewish Education, 1918.

1820: "American Society for Meliorating the Condition of the Jews"
1878: "Zion Society for Israel" (Norwegian Lutheran)
1884: Marcy Center, Chicago (M. E.) originally for Bohemians; now largely, but not exclusively devoted to Jewish work.
1887: "Chicago Hebrew Mission" (Non-sectarian)
1894: "American Board of Missions to Jews" (Interdenominational)
1894: "Jewish Mission Board" (Reformed Presbyterian Church of America)
1898: "New Covenant Mission to Jews and Gentiles" (Interdenominational)
1905: United Lutheran Church; Committee for Jewish Missions
1908: "New York Evangelization Society" (Interdenominational)
1909: Presbyterian Church, U. S. A. Board of Home Missions
1914: Christian Reformed Committee; Jewish Mission Committee
1917: Department of Jewish Evangelization of the Presbyterian Church in the U. S. A. co-operating with the Presbyterian Church, U. S.
1920: American Baptist Home Missionary Society
1921: Southern Baptist Convention Work among Jews under Home Mission Board.
1921: Christian and Missionary Alliance
1927: Methodist Episcopal Church South

This list, while manifestly incomplete, as there are other independent bodies at work in this field, sufficiently indicates the interest in Jewish work following the great immigration from Poland and Russia, 1880-1910. In Canada, Jewish work is carried on by the Missionary Society of the Church of England in Canada (Montreal, 1901; Toronto, 1915; Ottawa, 1914); the Presbyterian Church in Canada (Toronto, 1913) and several independent missions, one of them dating back to 1892. When the work in Canada was first attempted, Lewis A. Hart, in the *Jewish Times*, published articles against such efforts "in a language unprecedented for dauntlessness and daring in the discussion of such subjects, shattering all Christian dogma and showing the fragile basis on which Christianity rests."[6] These articles were later collected and published in 1906 under the title: "A Jewish Reply to Christian Evangelists."

CHARACTERISTICS OF MISSIONS TO THE JEWS

Many of the centers operated by missions to the Jews in the United States are quite small, and some are obviously sporadic. In one city studied a mission "for Jews and Gentiles" was supervised by a Gentile minister whose ecclesiastical standing was in the Evangelical Church. As a lad in Europe he had been employed by an Orthodox Jewish family, where he was greatly impressed by the quality of their home life. In time he gave up a prominent pulpit in his denomination to undertake special work for Jews. Inquiries elicited the fact that most of those who attended his mission were Italians

---
[6] See A. D. Hart, *The Jews in Canada* (Toronto: Jewish Publications, Ltd., 1926), p. 79.

rather than Jews, and hence the mission had been named "for Jews and Gentiles." Most of the literature issued by this particular mission was, however, directed specifically to Jews. In Cincinnati a center had been established by a man who had been a missionary in Korea. He claimed to have had a vision in Korea that he should devote the rest of his life to Jewish work, and deciding that Cincinnati was the cultural center of American Judaism, he left Korea and established a mission in the Ohio city. The work, however, lasted but a short time. There is a good deal of free-lancing in this whole field on the part of individuals or organizations not directly related to the denominations.

Another prevailing trend observed among missioners to the Jews is that towards fundamentalism. The "Biblical Research Society, Inc.," which has for its purpose "to break down anti-Semitism, and to disseminate facts and truths concerning God and Messiah," says in its literature that "it accepts the doctrinal statements of such organizations as the World's Christian Fundamentals Association, the Moody Bible Institute, the Bible Institute of Los Angeles and like organizations. It wishes to avoid every appearance of the two extremes of doctrine: modernism and fanaticism." In the Chicago area, a good many of the workers are trained in the Moody Bible Institute. In nearly all the literature published by the various organizations, much attention is devoted to Messianic prophecy and in some cases the whole course of the Jewish people, past, present and future, is treated "remnant by remnant" according to the peculiar "prophetical" inclinations of the writers. Some, though not all, of the prominent men in missionary work are unwilling to participate in good-will movements, believing that there can be little fraternizing between Jews and Christians as religious groups; it is quite evident, on the other hand, that they do not cherish any racial antagonism to the Jew, and when a Jew has "accepted Christ," they gladly introduce him to churches overwhelmingly Gentile and receive him as a "brother beloved." Liberal churches, on the other hand, are more inclined to think of the Jewish-Gentile issue in racial terms and largely to ignore the religious complications.

In not a few instances the centers were originally founded for work among non-Jews, but as the population changed, they became Jewish missions. Thus the Marcy Center in Chicago, perhaps the best-equipped institution of its kind in the country, was intended for Bohemians when it was established in 1884, but the Bohemians moved away and the Jews moved in. Other centers were in the first instance regular Christian churches which, finding themselves surrounded by Jews, tried to modify their program to meet the needs of the new arrivals. Still others are essentially neighborhood houses which work for the people of the neighborhood, whether Jewish or

Gentile, as opportunity offers. Such work is, therefore, not wholly Jewish and with further population changes it may either cease to be a work for Jews or, on the other hand, become more exclusively such. The legitimacy of the proselytizing motive in such neighborhood work is of course a moot question.

For the most part, but not always, the work of the Jewish missions is carried on by converted Jews.[7] Almost invariably these Jews have come from orthodox circles. Of eighteen Hebrew Christian workers who answered questionnaires in a previous study made about 1930, all of them were brought up in orthodox circles, the country of their birth being:

United States...............................	2
Austria.....................................	4
Germany....................................	2
Latvia......................................	1
Poland.....................................	2
Russia.....................................	7
	—
Total..................................	18

All of the eighteen insisted that their parents were observant Jews and that they themselves had attended Cheder. Only one of them, however, had gone to the Yeshivah or the Jewish High School. Only four of the eighteen reported that prior to their conversion they had received a high-school training or its equivalent, although three others specified a certain amount of high-school training. Most of them had received practically no information about Christianity in the home and, prior to conversion, tended to believe that Jesus was an impostor who had caused endless trouble to his people, that Christians were idolaters and worshippers of images, and bitter persecutors. Few of them had had any dealings with Gentiles until they had become socialists and these they found to be for the most part without any religion. Most of them had drifted from orthodoxy into Jewish nationalism, only to discover a fresh cause of discontent. One of them had lived almost exclusively with Gentiles in Vienna and these Gentiles had "impressed him" because of their truthfulness and friendliness. For the most part, however, their early experiences with Gentiles had been unhappy.

[7] A good deal of criticism has been directed against Jewish converts to Christianity who become Jewish missioners, by both Jewish and Christian groups. In the opinion of the writer, they are frequently calumniated shamefully. Some of them are obviously deeply sincere. On the other hand, some strange individuals have found their way into this fold, e.g., J. T. Trebitsch-Lincoln tells "The Autobiography of An Adventurer" in the book of that title published by Leonard Stein, London, in 1931. Lincoln was a Hungarian Jew who became a Christian missionary to the Jews in Montreal, a member of Parliament, convict, Rumanian oil-king, plotter of revolutions in Germany, adviser of Chinese war-lords. He is now a Buddhist monk and has recently brought a group of such monks to the West to convert the West to Buddhism.

REACTIONS OF JEWISH CONVERTS

In reply to a question concerning the age at which doubts concerning Judaism arose, the majority answered "seventeen," although quite a few said sixteen. One replied: "since eleven years of age," another, "when I began to study the New Testament." Still another said:

"From eleven to thirteen years of age I had to sing in the choir in the temple of Lemberg at all services. On days we had to fast, the cantor and the rabbi gave us money to buy food and fruits and told us to eat in order to sing better."

As one studies these answers further, it is clear that the first step is less an attraction to Christianity than an aversion to the formalism of orthodox Judaism, coupled with a curiosity to discover what the non-Jew lived by. A period of indifference to Judaism usually followed, accompanied by association with socialists and atheists. Then some chance contact brought the young man into touch with Christian circles, of which they say:

"I wearied of the conceit and restlessness of my atheist friends."
"Just passed a mission, saw the sign, was curious and entered."
"In a big library in Vienna, I borrowed a book—the Life of Christ. This book made a great impression on me. It was the first time I had read anything about Christ."
"Worked for a man whose wife I took to Sunday school."
"A middle-aged woman became interested in my piano-playing. We engaged in conversation which revealed she was a Christian."
"The kindly services of a Jewish missionary in Constantinople."
"The disinterested kindness of a Gentile Christian who taught me English."
"A scene in a clothing-factory of a Hebrew-Christian sweetly bearing persecution."

Most of the eighteen also indicated that the reading of the New Testament marked an important stage in their religious experience, while others regarded the reading of William James' *Varieties of Religious Experience*, Sheldon's *In His Steps* and Hall Caine's *The Master Christian*, as more or less epochal.

At this point it should be said that the Hebrew Christians interviewed in the course of this study all indicated an aversion to orthodox Judaism but a contempt for liberal Judaism. The latter they regarded as something modernistic, a mark of social status rather than a testimony to a religious experience. There are, of course, a few Hebrew-Christians who have come out of reformed Judaism, but these are seldom found in mission circles. One such, Samuel Freuder, graduated from the Hebrew College in 1886, was baptized in 1891, and announced his return to Judaism in June 1908.[8] To the con-

---

[8] See Samuel Freuder, *My Return to Judaism* (New York: Sinai Publishing Company, 1915).

verted Jews in the mission it seemed that they had to choose between Orthodox Judaism, Irreligious Socialism or Christianity, and they chose
Christianity.

The reaction of their apostasy on the members of their family is summarized by them as follows:

(a) Some were indifferent; some disliked it.

(b) They were distressed.

(c) I was away from my family. My father and mother never replied
on that matter, although our relations continued friendly.

(d) Persecution. Wife sought to divorce me.

(e) My relatives were sorry, but tolerant.

(f) I did not live at home. So had no unpleasant experiences.

(g) Ostracism.

(h) Great sorrow and shame.

(i) Father never wrote. Wife refused to come to America. It took thirteen years before we came together.

(j) Disowned.

(k) They showed me the door.

(l) I left home as soon as I made up my mind that I would be a Christian. That was one year before my baptism.

(m) Left home to live with Christian friends.

(n) They loved me greatly as the youngest in the family, and so they
lamented bitterly as if it were death to them.

(o) Cast out, cursed and disinherited.

(p) Hatred, wrangling.

(q) My people were bitterly opposed.

Others indicated that they could not obtain employment and had to leave
for another city; some were attacked by the chief rabbi and by the Jewish
press. One was turned out by the Jewish firm that employed him. Nor
was the suspicion all on the Jewish side. In the case of one convert, his
fellow-laborers (all Catholics) "looked on me as if I had become not right-
minded." Much more along similar lines, reinforced by personal interviews,
makes it abundantly clear that here is a rare field for a sympathetic novelist.
Some of the autobiographies of these Jewish missioners as given to those
making the study are full of "human interest," and it is difficult to believe
that many of them could possibly persevere in the work unless they were
sincere. Certainly, the budgets on which they operated hardly suggested
that they were motivated by financial ambition. It would be safer to assume
that persecution had only confirmed them in their resolution.

Among the values which they had discovered in Christianity were listed:

(a) Universality, love, beauty, adventure, peace.

(b) "Christ."

(c) The emphasis on universal brotherhood and on the personality of Jesus.

(d) Personal relationship to God; the joy of fellowship.

(e) Fellowship with God; the forgiveness of sins through Christ; the assurance of eternal life.

(f) God in intimate touch with man through Jesus.

(g) Prayer is the most outstanding thing to me. Never had such experiences before.

(h) A missionary duty to all peoples.

(i) Prejudices broken.

(j) Moral incentive; spiritual power; certainty of salvation; solicitude for others; a desire to serve.

TREATMENT OF JEWISH CONVERTS BY CHRISTIAN CHURCHES

Some, however, admitted that they had not received in the Christian church all the fellowship and understanding they desired, and nine stated definitely that they had encountered racial prejudice in the church, due to the superiority complex of the Anglo-Saxons. As one of the ablest men interviewed phrased it, while the Christian church may not be anti-Semitic, it is certainly not philo-Semitic! One complained that he had been refused full clergy privileges after he had successfully passed the examinations for ministerial orders. Others who had been trained for the general work of the ministry found it necessary to change their names before they secured a regular appointment, and even then they have had difficulty in securing work.

It is fairly clear that the difficulties which converted Jews find in their relationships with their kinsmen are paralleled by difficulties which they experience in the Christian churches to which they attach themselves. Because of these dual difficulties, many missionaries to the Jews postpone the administration of baptism to one who has expressed a desire to become a Christian for many months, even for years, until they are sure that the convert can make the necessary adjustments. Increasingly such converts are not baptized by the missionaries; the convert is rather referred to some local church which shows itself willing to coöperate in the assimilation of the new recruit, and here eventually he is in due time baptized and definitely enrolled in the membership of the church. However justified or unjustified may be the opposition of the Jews to missionary activities, perhaps the most serious aspect of the whole problem, from the point of view of the Christian church, is the slowness of many churches to welcome Jews "on profession" and a seeming suspicion on the part of Christians that Jews seeking admission to a Christian church are motivated by social reasons. One Presbyterian church visited in the course of this study had successfully assimilated more than a dozen Jews, but the minister, a self-confessed fundamentalist, stated that prior to accepting them, he had preached over a certain period of months special sermons designed to break down the local prejudice of his people and make them conscious of their responsibility to practice a religion which theoretically knew no race barriers.

METHODS USED BY JEWISH MISSIONS

Much of the opposition to Jewish missions on the part of the Jews is due to alleged cradle-snatching and the bribery of small children by "confectionery" and ice-cream to persuade them to attend the various classes and clubs. It is, of course, easy to interpret any social gathering at which refreshments are served as bribery, and to read sinister motives into what is really a normal mode of social intercourse. Thirty-four of the seventy-four centers, replying to the questionnaire gave definite information concerning the specific measures which they used to bring the children within reach of the Mission's influence: It seems reasonably clear that children were generally reached through their parents. One institution replied:

"We prefer to reach children whose parents are in a measure interested but we do not feel ironbound by this rule. Our display window has been used as an attraction."

One center reported that it offered a "button to the one who brings a new child." One center in New York refused to do any work for children, and stated that it was "absolutely opposed to this form of work *in every way*." Others, however, stressed their playgrounds and gymnasiums, club work, boy scout and girl scout organizations, camping, story-telling hours, woodwork classes for boys and sewing classes for girls, daily vacation Bible schools, etc. Some stated definitely that they allowed no children to come without their parents' consent, while one indicated that 95 per cent. of their children came with their parents' knowledge and consent.

The real issue here seems to be less that of any particular method, for the methods used are largely those of settlement houses, but rather the ultimate purpose of such activities. One student of the Chicago church life stated quite categorically that the great issue in that city was not so much the work of the Jewish missions, but the motivation of the neighborhood houses which were conducted under directly Christian auspices. Some of them sought to avoid mixing religion with social activities, while they provided chapels, religious services, Sunday schools, missionary bands, etc., and the real question was whether their intent should be definitely to win converts or simply to make life in the community somewhat richer.

Of course, the variety of activities engaged in is determined in no small measure by the financial resources of the institution, and for the most part these are very slender. Thirty-nine out of sixty-seven of these centers gave figures regarding their total income for the last fiscal year as follows:

Not furnished	28
Less than $1,000	1
$2,500 to $5,000	14
$5,000 to $7,500	5
$7,500 to $10,000	7
$10,000 to $15,000	6
$15,000 to $20,000	2
$20,000 to $30,000	2
Over $40,000	2
	—
	67

A conservative estimate would place the total amount expended by Protestant missions to Jews in the United States and Canada at about $600,000 a year. It will thus be seen that twenty-seven of the thirty-nine reporting had budgets of less than $10,000 a year, while fifteen, or more than one-third, of those reporting had budgets of less than $5,000. Most of the centers have very limited equipment; often they consist only of the house in which the missioner lives with the "parlors" converted into a meeting room. Others, of course are more elaborate. In one city, a center had purchased a fine old mansion and converted the garage into a gymnasium. The Lutherans, on the whole, seem to concentrate almost exclusively on religious work and center their whole ministry around the chapel and a reading-room. The finest equipment of any of these missions is Marcy Center (Methodist Episcopal) in Chicago, which has excellent facilities for dispensaries, educational work, social gatherings, together with a dignified chapel. It is located not far from the large Jewish People's Institute. Generally speaking, however, most of the centers are reduced by financial stringency to the holding of services in small chapels and in the open air, the issuing and distribution of literature, household visitation, and the provision of a reading-room. In a few centers, especially during the depression, some relief work was attempted. In one city it was alleged that Jews who could not get all they wanted from the Jewish social-service agencies would threaten to go to the mission; the Jewish missioners, on the other hand, denied that much of this happened but intimated that sometimes the Jewish agencies would "bear down" on Jews who were known to be attending the missions and these later would seek help directly from the mission. Both types of situation are not impossible. The Scott Institute in Toronto, which developed out of a Hebrew-Christian Synagogue, received wide publicity in the local press for various types of social relief provided during the depression.

The prevailing types of activity are:

(a) Regular worship on Sundays or Friday evenings; sometimes on other nights in the week.

(b) Sunday school or religious education classes for children.

(c) Occasional gatherings, social, holiday festivals, prayer-meetings for Christian friends, mother's meetings, etc.

(d) Open-air services.

(e) Reading-rooms and library.

(f) Preparation and distribution of literature.

(g) Use of dispensaries. (Some of these give as high as 2,525 treatments a year.)

(h) Field worker for the purpose of winning converts.

(i) Community visitation. One large center employs twelve visitors who make 11,000 calls a year. Another thirteen with 22,660 calls and 1,240 sick visits.

(j) Educational work, including industrial and regular classes. English classes and Americanization classes, music classes, etc.

One of the greatest needs commonly expressed is for better literature. Much of the literature issued is admittedly of a poor quality. Those interviewed expressed the belief that the most satisfactory type of literature for their purpose was that prepared by Rev. Henry Einspruch, of Baltimore, who publishes pamphlets in both English and Yiddish. He also published two small papers, one for Christians, interpreting Jewish missions to them and seeking their support and interest; the other for Jews, interpreting Christians and Christianity to them. Many of the Jewish missioners thus regard themselves essentially as mediators and interpreters. The Lutheran mission in Baltimore insists that any Jews who want Bibles or testaments pay for them; it refuses to give them away.

NUMBER OF CONVERTS

It is practically impossible to reach any conclusions regarding the number of converts made by such missions. Many of them, perhaps most of them, do not keep any records, and where records exist, the numbers are not reported. Again most of the converts are introduced to some Christian church where baptism is performed, and the missions may not in themselves develop "churches" in the ordinary meaning of the word. On this point the reports made to the Budapest-Warsaw conferences in 1927 say:

"Many societies keep no definite records and the returns are necessarily incomplete. Twenty-four missionaries in Europe have given figures and these bring the number of their converts since 1900 up to 2,184. In the Presbyterian Church of America there have been between 1,000 and 2,000 converts, 55 of whom are ordained missionaries. In the United States, it is estimated that there have been about 20,000 converts, of whom about 1,000 are Roman Catholics."[9]

[9] *The Christian Approach to the Jews* (London: Edinburgh House Press, 1927), p. 109. For those interested in statistics regarding losses to Judaism through apostasy, see Cohen, *Jewish Life in Modern Times* (second Edition, 1928), pp. 268-278. The largest number of such conversions in the nineteenth century are recorded in Russia, Austria-Hungary and the United Kingdom.

An interesting comparison is afforded by the figures given in the latest Canadian census, 1931. As indicated elsewhere in this report, the census reports individuals by racial origin and by religious preference. Under racial origin we find "Hebrews"; under religious preference we find "Jews." Out of a total population of 10,376,786, only 16,042 failed to give their *religious* preference of whom over 8,229 were Asiatics. Only 9,579 failed to indicate their *racial* origin. These figures are, therefore, reasonably complete. It is of course quite possible that the census-takers may have made certain errors; it is also possible that some "Hebrews" may have indicated that they were Russians or Rumanians, but a critical examination of the census returns tends to confirm the general reliability of the figures. It is, therefore, possible to compare the total number of "Hebrews" with the total number of "Jews" and to indicate the denominations which have gained by infiltration. It is necessary to remember that, so far as intermarriage is concerned, only the children of Jewish men and Gentile mothers would be listed as "Hebrews" since racial origin is "according to father."

In 1931 there were in Canada 156,726 persons who gave their racial origin as Hebrew; of these 155,351 also stated that they were Jewish in religion. The remainder, 1,375, gave the following religious preferences:

Adventists	7
Anglicans	255
Baptists	131
Brethren	1
"Christians"	4
Disciples	6
Christian Science	19
Evangelical Association	4
Greek Orthodox	73
I. B. S. A.	1
Lutherans	66
Mennonites	11
No religion	112
Pentecostal	1
Presbyterians	127
Protestants	53
Roman Catholics	292
Salvation Army	1
United Church of Canada	176
Other Sects	28
Not stated	7
	1,375

(Males, 701; females, 674)

Comparing another set of figures, there were in Canada 155,614 persons professing a preference for the Jewish faith, and only 155,351 of these were inscribed as Hebrews by racial origin. The racial origins of the 263 non-Hebrew Jews were:

English	41
Irish	7
Scotch	7
Other British	2
French	4
Austrian	6
Belgian	1
Czech	1
Dutch	2
Finnish	1
German	24
Icelandic	1
Italian	4
Polish	59
Roumanian	11
Russian	89
Swedish	1
Other European races	2
Total	263

(Males, 124; females, 139)

How do we account for the 1,375 Hebrews who were not Jews?
(1) Hebrews converted to Christianity, either through

(a) Jewish Missions,
(b) Local churches,
(c) Intermarriage.

(2) Hebrews who have surrendered their religious interest entirely. Only seven failed to indicate what their religion was, while 112 definitely intimated that they were without religion.

(3) Children of Hebrew fathers and Christian mothers who are brought up in the Christian Church.

How do we account for the 263 non-Hebrew Jews?

(1) Some of these are Gentiles who have been converted to Judaism by intermarriage.

(2) Some may be the children of Gentile fathers but Jewish mothers, who are being reared in Judaism.

(3) A few may be persons who have deliberately chosen Judaism.

It is fairly clear that the number of Hebrews that are converted to Christianity in Canada is fairly small. This becomes particularly evident in the study of the religious statistics in cities where Jewish missions have existed for some time.

	Number of Hebrews	Number of Jews	Hebrew Christians or No Religion
Toronto	45,305	45,140	165
Montreal	48,724	48,467	257
Winnipeg	17,236	17,150	86
Hamilton	2,636	2,599	37

Indeed, a more careful examination of the census records makes it clear that Jews are quite as apt, if not more apt, to become Christians where there are no missions as where such exist; in the towns and cities where there are but few Jews, they may easily drift into the Christian churches. (In much the same way, the Canadian census indicates that there are more Protestants of French descent *outside* the province of Quebec than *in* the province of Quebec.) Major factors, therefore in conversion, would seem to be (1) intermarriage and (2) lack of sufficient numbers of one's own group in the population. But whatever the influence, in Canada less than one per cent. of the entire Hebrew population is Christian, and there are some intimations that there are as many, if not more, Jews normally received into Christian churches directly than actually converted by the missions.

The question is frequently raised whether the expense of operating these missions to the Jews—which we have estimated roughly at about $600,000 a year—is worth it when viewed in the light of the actual number of conversions, which can hardly exceed more, perhaps, than 400 a year at the most. While many of the denominations who do not support special work for the Jews refrain from doing so only for financial reasons, one of them has stated quite frankly its policy:

"As Christians we ought to accord Jewish religious leaders first opportunity to win their own people, both children and adults, to practical religious living and we ought to coöperate with them to that end.

"In case of the large percentage of Jews who are estranged from the synagogue, if it be found, after fair trial, that they cannot be won back to the faith of their fathers, we ought to endeavor by every earnest means to gain their adherence to the Christian religion.

"In any locality where Jewish religious services are not available, Christians should offer a hearty invitation to scattered Jewish families to participate with them in religious worship.

"Where individual Jews, upon their own initiative, express a desire to join Christian churches, they should be warmly welcomed.

"In all our contacts with Jews, we should, as Christians, manifest by word and deed our consciousness of the great fact of human brotherhood and of the Fatherhood of Him who 'hath made of one blood all nations of men for to dwell on the face of the earth.'"

FEW CHRISTIANS BECOME JEWS

We have already indicated, in the Canadian statistics, 299 cases of non-Hebrews who have become Jews, but it is quite probable that in most of these cases they are the children of Gentile fathers and Jewish mothers. In recent years a considerable number of Gentiles have been attending liberal Jewish synagogues, largely attracted by the quality of the preaching with its strong social emphasis on justice. There are a few such Gentiles who have definitely identified themselves with the synagogue, but in the few instances which have been mentioned to the writer, the rabbi has assumed that they were inclined to be cranks. Certainly, they have not been encouraged. There has been one outstanding conversion from Christianity to Judaism in recent years in France, recorded in *The Unknown Sanctuary* by Aimé Pallière, who, though a Roman Catholic by birth, not only has accepted Judaism but later became a rabbi in a Jewish synagogue in Paris. Generally speaking, however, men suffer from enough difficulties in life without going out of their way, whatever their philosophical preconceptions, to accept the additional burdens and handicaps which the nomenclature of "Jews" might bring to them.

JEWS RARELY BECOME CATHOLICS

It is impossible to tell how many Jews become Catholics. In the list of conversions furnished by the various Catholic dioceses, and mentioned later in this chapter, no distinction is made between Protestants, Jews, Mohammedans and mere pagans. They are all regarded as non-Catholics. There is one prominent Jewish convert to Catholicism in Boston who has published a volume especially designed for those working with Jews, but there seems to be no way of telling how many Catholics of Jewish extraction there are in the United States, nor to what degree such conversions are due to intermarriage. In Canada, as already indicated, 292 of the 1,375 non-Jewish Hebrews are Roman Catholic. In the United States there are supposed to be approximately 1,000 "Hebrew" Catholics, although this would seem to be largely estimate.

CONVERSIONS FROM CATHOLICISM TO PROTESTANTISM

The more significant data relative to conversions from Catholicism to Protestantism are unavailable. Protestant churches do not distinguish between former Catholics who join on confession of faith and others. To gather such data would perhaps be impossible; where the overturn of ministers is so great, the ministers may not know which of their parishioners have Catholic backgrounds. It might, of course, be practicable in some of the larger denominations for the annual statistics to include a question regarding the number of persons formerly Catholic received into the church in the current year. Of course, most Protestant denominations conduct special missionary efforts among certain racial groups, largely Catholic in tradition, and their success or failure in this work has already been studied by the Institute of Social and Religious Research and reported in *Protestant Home Missions to Catholic Immigrants*,[10] to which a more extended reference will be made later. There is good reason to believe, however, that the majority of Catholics who eventually find their way into Protestant churches are not recruited by such missions but are rather "contacted" in normal church life and later attached in the normal way to normal churches.

This became evident in the course of a number of interviews with Protestant ministers in the cities studied. In nearly every Protestant church there are some persons who have come out of Catholicism, although no special effort may have been made to win them. One of the smaller dioceses in the Protestant Episcopal Church kept a record of the former Catholics who had been confirmed in that diocese alone, and in the year 1932 they numbered ninety-three. In an Episcopal church in this same diocese, the rector reported that between 1923 and 1933, he had presented for confirmation, no less than seventy-five former Catholics. During the same time he had lost approximately twelve to Roman Catholicism, most of which losses he attributed to intermarriage. He summarized his experience thus:

"Those who have come to my church from Catholicism did so mainly because (a) they reacted from the over-rigorous system of Rome, and (b) they reacted against the bigotry and unfairness of Catholic priests. Thus, recently, an old aunt of my acquaintance, a Catholic, was chiding her niece and nephew about not going to mass. She said that the priest had said he would rather see a parishioner steal or commit adultery than lapse in his fidelity to mass. The nephew simply replied: 'Yes, and because of attitudes like this, we don't go to mass.' In my opinion, there is a steady leakage from Rome, in spite of the fact that Catholics are generally capable of great loyalty. The Roman priests do not visit their people enough. That is one reason why they fail to keep in touch with them."

A Presbyterian minister in a very active church with more than 1,100 members had received about twenty former Catholics into membership. Most of them, he said, came as the result of some personal grievance with the church. They were perfectly satisfied until they ran into some form of Catholic practice that brought discontent. Often they felt themselves neglected on the part of a priest. He gave two specific cases:

(a) A Catholic man was married to a Catholic wife, and he was a most earnest and devout Catholic. The Catholic wife committed adultery, and finally he divorced her. He found that this divorce had put him in wrong with the church, and he began to attend the Presbyterian church. He attended for five years before he was willing to join. He used to prepare long lists of questions for the minister to answer, and the minister in making his answers always used the Douay version. He finally joined the church and has become very active.

(b) A Catholic woman, very devoted, was married to a husband whose Catholicism rested somewhat lightly upon him. She faced a serious operation,

---

[10] Abel, Theodore (New York: Institute of Social and Religious Research, 1933).

and sent for the priest. She delayed the operation for two hours in the hope that the priest would arrive, but he failed to come. Soon after she had pulled out of the operation, the Presbyterian minister visited her on the request of a mutual friend. She became slightly interested and after she recovered she came occasionally to service. Now she and her whole family attend. Recently, the priest called on her and said that he had not seen her much recently. She told him that she had become interested in the Presbyterian church and had been thinking for herself about religion.

Another minister of a Disciples' church which attempted with rather conspicuous success to become a "community church" stated that out of a membership of more than 1,000, he had more than one hundred members who were formerly Catholics. Most of these, he said, had drifted out of the Catholic church soon after marriage. They had settled down in a new community and at first ceased attending any church. Then, their children arrived, and they felt the need of providing some religious background for them. So they began attending the Disciples' church and soon came to enjoy the informal and friendly spirit of it. Approximately one-tenth of his entire parish was made up of such former Catholics.

While there are aggressive anti-Catholic organizations within the body of Protestants, there are, to the knowledge of those conducting this study, no Protestant organizations specifically seeking to win Roman Catholics. There are, however, several mission boards which carry on special work for "racial" groups which are presumably largely Catholic, and once again, there are under Protestant auspices neighborhood houses operating largely in districts peopled by recent immigrants from Catholic countries.

PROTESTANT MISSIONS AMONG CATHOLICS IN CANADA

In Canada missions among the French-Canadians were begun at a very early date. In 1834 the church at Lausanne, Switzerland, sent out some missionaries for work among the Indians, but these decided to devote their attention not to the Indians but to the French. After one hundred years of work attempted by various denominations, very little impression has been made on the French-speaking population of Quebec. Bulletin No. XXXV, of the Dominion Bureau of Statistics, analyzing the census of 1931 "religious denominations by racial origins," indicates that of 2,270,059 persons of French racial descent in the Province of Quebec, 2,256,817 considered themselves attached to the Roman Catholic religion. The Grande Ligne Mission has been conducted by the Baptists since 1847. In 1906 there were connected with this mission ten churches with a total membership of 497; in 1931 there were fourteen churches with a total membership of 1,008. In these twenty-six years (1906-1931) there have been 1,297 baptisms. Work has also been carried on by the Presbyterians and Methodists (later The United

Church of Canada), the Church of England and other denominations, but much of their activity has been in the support and administration of institutions providing educational facilities for the scattered French-speaking Protestant population. The Dominion Census, 1931, gives the following figures for non-Catholic persons of French racial origin in Canada and Quebec:

	Canada	Quebec
Adventists......................	390	86
Anglicans......................	22,315	4,228
Baptists......................	7,930	1,135
Lutherans......................	1,977	41
No religion......................	821	336
Presbyterians......................	10,074	1,805
Protestants......................	981	730
United Church..................	28,701	3,378
Other sects......................	4,426	510
Not stated......................	1,279	993
	78,894	13,242

An interesting aspect of the situation is that there are more non-Catholics of French racial origin outside of the province of Quebec where special missions are conducted for them than in that province, thus:

| | Persons of French Racial Origin in Canada, 1931 | | |
	All Denominations	Roman Catholics	Non-Catholics
Canada..............	2,927,990	2,849,096	78,894
Quebec..............	2,270,059	2,256,817	13,242
Canada (except Quebec)	657,931	592,279	65,652

Thus, in spite of missions in Quebec, few persons of French racial origin in that province change their faith. In the other provinces, where the Protestants are in the majority and in spite of high concentration of the French in certain counties, nearly 10 per cent. of all such persons are non-Catholics.

(1) It may be that few of these non-Catholics of French descent in the Dominion were of French-Canadian descent but came rather from Huguenot stock in France. Their ancestors may have migrated to Canada since the days of British occupation.

(2) It may be that some of these non-Catholics of French descent found the social pressure in Quebec too severe after their conversion to Protestantism and hence preferred to live in other parts of Canada.

(3) It may be that French-Canadians who went to other parts of Canada where they did not find Catholic ministrations in their own language gradually became absorbed in the non-Catholic majority group, intermarried and identified themselves with non-Catholic churches.

At all events the significant fact is that while 77.5 per cent. of the persons of French racial origin living in Canada reside in Quebec, only 16.6 per cent. of the non-Catholic population of French racial origin live in that province.

Years ago there was great excitement when the Rev. Father Chiniquy left the Roman faith and after some work among the French-Canadians in the United States conducted very vigorous missions in the Province of Quebec. He died 1899. His books had large sales not only in Canada but elsewhere. Father Chiniquy became an Orangeman in 1878. In 1876 he delivered lectures in various parts of Canada. When he lectured in a Presbyterian church in Halifax, N. S., a mob broke the windows of the Fort Massey Church. The Protestant mayor took no action to protect him. Whereupon, the Rev. George Monro Grant, later Principal of Queen's University, who himself disliked Father Chiniquy, offered him the use of St. Matthew's Church and wrote the Mayor that he was doing so, adding: "The windows of St. Matthew's are small and inexpensive; those of St. Mary's (the neighboring Roman Catholic cathedral) while quite as easily broken, are very beautiful and could not be easily replaced."

Father Chiniquy delivered his lecture in peace and when the Roman Catholic Archbishop, who had been away from Halifax, returned, he not only offered to pay all the expenses of the repairs needed at the Fort Massey Church but reproved his people for their folly.

Within the last two years, a somewhat similar defection from Catholicism followed the ministry in Montreal of the Rev. Victor Rahard, an ex-Trappist monk, who became a Protestant some twelve years ago and for the last few years has been conducting an Anglican mission among the French-Canadians in Montreal. At one service, in 1932, in the Anglican cathedral he presented no less than 427 French-Canadians for confirmation; a few months later he presented about 300 more. Some Catholics have felt that much of this was due to disaffection created in the administration of relief funds by the St. Vincent de Paul Society, which threatened at one time to become an open scandal in the city. Protestants, however, asserted that while the relief question may have provided subsidiary motives, a deeper reason for the movement was a revolt against ecclesiasticism. At all events, the Montreal police arrested the Rev. Mr. Rahard for blasphemy in January, 1934, and his case created no little excitement in other provinces of the Dominion. The case is pending at the time of the writing of the report.

So far as missions among Catholics other than French-speaking is concerned, the statistics in Canada indicate the difficulties involved in any attempt to gauge the extent of such conversions. A partial list follows for some of the groups which normally might be considered dominantly Catholic (1931).

	Persons of Racial Origin	Number Catholics	Number No Religion	Number Non-Catholic
Austrian........	48,639	32,783	121	15,956
Czecho-Slovak...	30,401	24,266	265	6,135
Hungarian......	40,582	29,425	40	11,157
Italian..........	98,173	91,742	99	6,431
Polish..........	145,503	124,252	317	21,251*
Roumanian......	29,056	11,437	51	17,619
Ukrainian.......	225,113	156,315	1,215	68,798

*Lutherans and Greek Orthodox account for 12,385 of this number.

It must be remembered that there are Protestant groups in every one of these countries and that in some, notably the Ukraine, a fairly large number belong to the Greek Orthodox Church (among the Ukrainian-Canadians, 55,386 are given as Orthodox). Many Hungarians come from the Reformed communions in Hungary, and the work among Hungarians and Czechs is in part not proselytizing but work for Protestants on the part of Protestants. There was, however, during the past year a considerable number of abjurations of Roman Catholicism on the part of Hungarians in Montreal in favor of the Lutheran Church. Here again, relief difficulties may have been part of the picture. Montreal provides some unusual opportunities for studying actual conversions, since, as already indicated, civil status depends in part upon religious faith (due to school rates), and to change one's faith, it is necessary to fill in definite forms. It is fairly evident that there is considerable leakage among the non-French-speaking Catholic population, but comparatively little, outside of the activities of Mr. Rahard mentioned above, among the French-Canadians. The Catholic Church appears to be out of touch with a fair number of its own immigrant peoples even in the large cities. Thus, the official figures of the Archdiocese of Montreal indicate that in the Catholic population of that archdiocese are 15,050 Italians. On the other hand, in the Dominion census of 1931, there were 19,834 persons of Italian racial origin who indicated a preference for the Roman Catholic faith in the city of Montreal proper alone. Some of these, however, might be connected with regular French parishes and hence reported as French.

On the other hand, the Canadian census figures seem to indicate that certain racial groups, which come from countries almost exclusively Protestant, show a surprising percentage of Catholic preference, thus:

	Total Number	Catholics
Danish.....................	34,118	1,197
Swedish....................	81,306	1,911
Norwegian.................	93,243	2,094

When one remembers that there are only approximately 4,000 Catholics out of a total population of over 6,000,000 in Sweden, only 3,200 Catholics out of a total population of 3,000,000 in Norway, and 27,000 Catholics out of a total population of 3,500,000 in Denmark, the Canadian percentage seems high. One wonders if this may not be due to intermarriage since the number of men and women for these groups is:

	Men	Women	Total
Danes	20,791	13,327	34,118
Swedes	48,049	33,257	81,306
Norwegians	53,537	39,706	93,243

This, of course, is pure hypothesis. There is, however, some confirmation of the hypothesis by examining the birth records of the Dominion for 1930 which are given by racial origin of father and racial origin of mother:

	Number of Such Children Born to Fathers of Given Racial Origin	Number of Such Born to Mothers of Same Racial Origin	Number of Such Born to Mothers of French Racial Origin
Danes	836	360	29
Swedish	1,580	644	44
Norwegian	1,973	994	56

It is quite obvious from a more detailed examination of these birth records that most persons of Danish, Swedish and Norwegian descent in Canada intermarry with women of English, Scotch or Irish descent, but there are a certain number who marry those of French and other Catholic descent and this may, possibly, account for the larger number of Catholics found in the population of these particular racial origins as a whole.

Bulletin No. XXXV, issued by the Dominion Bureau of Statistics, thus offers intriguing data which seem to indicate that the various immigrant cultural groups are, generally speaking, preserved in Canada; that infiltration from one group to the other largely follows from intermarriage, or from residence in an area where there are few people of the same cultural group to which the individual belongs; that Protestant missions to the so-called Catholic groups do not lead to any large number definitely identifying themselves with the proselytizing group; that often more conversions occur in areas where there are no missions than in areas where such missions not only exist but may become a bone of contention. On the other hand, it is quite clear that many of the special Protestant missions do perform an excellent piece of social work (e.g., the hospitals for Ukrainians in the prairie provinces), create a more favorable attitude toward persons of the non-majority stock on the part of the majority groups, and fill a rôle in the general work of Canadianization. Unfortunately, however, too often the conversionists are ill-equipped for their task and as a leading Italian Protestant minister said:

"The Protestants have lost their chance to win the Italians both in the United States and in Canada. They entrusted the work to poorly-trained men and housed it in impossible, barren mission halls. The Italian has thought of a church as a church and he cannot feel at home in a mission hall. In the days when the Vatican and the Kingdom of Italy were at loggerheads, the Italians were disaffected and many of them might have become Protestant. Now, however, the chance has gone."

The dilemma confronting the Protestant conversionist missions is clear. To establish contacts with the "alien" group they must engage in various forms of social activity—hospitals, dispensaries, gymnasia, playgrounds, post-offices, etc. The more they expend on such activities, the larger number will attend, but if they do this, it is usually desirable to keep the religious motivation in the background. The "aliens" will take what is offered to them and their children, sometimes ask for more, but still consider themselves as Catholics and turn to the priest invariably for baptisms, first communions, weddings and funerals, and while the children may be trained in Sunday schools they are, upon reaching a given age, simply removed into the church of their cultural group. On the other hand, if the missions stress the religious motive and avoid social activities, they invite bitter opposition in the locality, especially from those groups which have a strong national consciousness. Then, again, when the age of marriage comes, an Italian Protestant may marry an Italian Catholic and once again find their way back, nominally at least, into Catholicism.

PROTESTANT MISSIONS AMONG CATHOLIC IMMIGRANTS IN THE U. S.

In the study of *Protestant Home Missions to Catholic Immigrants*, made by Theodore Abel, under the auspices of the Institute of Social and Religious Research, we find much the same situation in the United States. Mr. Abel estimated that the aggregate memberships of the churches maintained primarily for Catholic groups were between 50,000 and 60,000 and consisted for the most part of five types:

(a) Immigrants who already had a Protestant background in Italy, Hungary, Czecho-Slovakia, etc.

(b) Children of converted parents brought up in the Sunday school and never in actual touch with Catholicism. (Mr. Abel on a sampling estimated these at about 25 per cent. of the total.)

(c) Immigrants dissatisfied with their church but in need of organized religion and peculiarly susceptible to a fundamentalist, emotional appeal. On this he says:

"In organizing a mission station, the Pentecostals, Russellites and others usually go after the members of mission churches first, for they find that many of them respond readily to their appeal." [11]

(d) Immigrants who join the church for the material benefits which they derive from such membership.

(e) Immigrants in need of sympathetic friendship and moral support but without social contacts.

Mr. Abel also found that "lack of adequate leadership and the difficulty of remedying this deficiency have been the most serious problems that the mission enterprise among the immigrants has had to face." Out of 114 ministers engaged in this work and whose records he was able to study, 15.7 per cent. had no professional training and 24.6 per cent. had neither college nor seminary training. He also examined the turnover of ministers in forty-six cases. Nine had left the ministry to engage in other occupations; twenty were dismissed on various grounds, more or less discreditable; eleven left the center because they became embroiled in conflicts with the congregation or because they felt that the community persecuted them beyond endurance; six were called away to other centers.

The maintenance of such churches, Mr. Abel found, was always costly to the denomination, since practically none of them were self-supporting. Each of such churches maintained by the Northern Baptists and Northern Presbyterians cost the denomination an average of $1,900 a year in subsidies, and the average annual cost of each member in those mission churches amounts to $30. "The relation of investment to membership is illustrated by the Latin American Mission, in which the total investment in land, buildings and other property amounts to nearly $500 per member." Mr. Abel estimated that in the course of the fifty years in which such work had been carried on, between fifty and one hundred million dollars had been expended. He says:

"A better understanding of Protestantism among Catholic immigrants has been achieved. But the mission enterprise has failed to realize the main purpose for which it was instituted. It has failed to accomplish to any significant degree the evangelization of Catholic immigrants and their descendants, and it has not achieved the control that it sought in directing the process of their adaptation to American life. No movement towards Protestantism has taken place as a result of these missionary efforts."

---

[11] This observation seems partly borne out by Canadian census figures:

	Total Number in Canada	British Descent	Continental Europe	Asiatic	Negro	Indian and Others Unspecified
Russellites	13,552	9,250	4,236	20	27	19
Pentecostals	26,301	18,179	7,764	13	165	180

Those originally from Continental Europe were for the most part of German or Scandinavian descent; although Ukrainians, Poles and Italians figured in the list. The Ukrainians seem to lean to Russellism and the Italians to Pentecostalism.

DO THE CHRISTIAN ASSOCIATIONS PROSELYTIZE?

In the general consideration of proselytizing activities on the part of Protestants, a brief word may be said concerning the work of the Y.M.C.A. and the Y.W.C.A. to supplement the information already supplied in Chapters II and III. There can be no doubt whatever concerning the aggressively evangelical character of the first associations.[12] The Montreal and Boston Associations were the first to be formed in the New World (1851) and the program at the Montreal Y.M.C.A. was for a time largely of a city mission character, including work for seamen, colportage and hospital visitation. As the years passed greater emphasis was placed on buildings and on physical and educational work, and the associations became largely clubs for young men and women engaged in commerce. While departments of religious work were and are retained, and while the religious motivation remains an important element in the activity of the associations, there has been a steady tendency to stress character-building rather than "evangelism," and the associations have only recently been subjected to considerable criticism within Protestant circles on the ground that their social and welfare activities have completely overshadowed their religious mission.

In a pamphlet on "La Y.M.C.A." (published by *L'Oeuvre des Tracts*, Montreal) Father Lacompte states that the distinguishing marks of the Y.M.C.A. are its laic character, its salaried personnel, and its Protestantism, and in regard to its proselytizing tendencies, he says:

"La Y M C A fait-elle du proselytisme auprès des catholiques? Il semble que non, si nous nous limitons au Canada et aux Etats-Unis. Mais si nous jetons au coup d'oeil au delà, dans l'Amerique du Sud et en Europe, nous remarquons chez la 'Y' une mobilisation générale de ses forces, pour aller délivrer de leur chaines ces pauvres catholiques courbes sous le joug de Rome. . . . La *Civiltà* de Rome et le *Tablet* de Londres ont fait entendre de vigoreuses protestations contre ce qu'ils appellent l'achat des âmes."

It hardly seems, therefore, that the Catholic Church is troubled by any proselytizing influences of the Associations in the United States and Canada, but is concerned about trends in other countries. This whole issue involving foreign work of the Y.M.C.A. and Y.W.C.A. is treated *in extenso* in the *International Survey*. A chart given on page 81 of that report indicates that in eight countries dominantly Roman Catholic the total membership of the Y.M.C.A. is 68 per cent. Catholic and 15 per cent. Protestant; in Argentina and Brazil the total membership of the Y.W.C.A. was 58 per cent. Catholic and 41 per cent. Protestant.[13]

---

[12] For brief history of the Y.M.C.A. and Y.W.C.A.; see *International Survey of Y.M.C.A. and Y.W.C.A.* (New York: International Survey Committee, 419 Fourth Avenue, 1932.)

[13] For proselytizing tendencies in various forms of social work, see section on this subject in Chapter IV.

Conversions from Protestantism to Catholicism

In considering conversions to Catholicism, there is much more material for study and there are even more statistics. So many converts have transcribed their experiences in confessions and spiritual autobiographies that it is possible to observe some of the reasons that led to their conversion. In the new *Catholic Dictionary* (1929) a number of such autobiographies are listed, including Newman's *Apologia*, Kinsman's *Salve Mater*, Brownson's *The Convert; or Leaves from my Experience*, Kent Stone's *The Invitation Heeded*, Ronald Knox's *A Spiritual Aeneid*, Mrs. Anstice Baker's *A Modern Pilgrim's Progress*. Two comparatively recent volumes are Stanley B. James' *The Adventures of a Spiritual Tramp* and W. E. Orchard's *From Faith to Faith*. Gilbert K. Chesterton has also included some autobiographical matter in his book on *The Catholic Church and Conversion*, in which he says:

"It is impossible to be just to the Catholic Church. The moment men cease to pull against it they feel a tug towards it. . . . The moment they try to be fair to it they begin to be fond of it. But when that affection has passed a certain point it begins to take on the tragic and menacing grandeur of a great love affair." (Page 62.)

In his book *Will America Become Catholic?*, John F. Moore states that he has read over two hundred stories of conversion to the Catholic Church written either by the convert himself or by some one familiar with the facts of the case, and he classifies these two hundred stories into five major groups:

(1) Those won by literature.
(2) Those led into the Church through her schools.
(3) Those summoned by an inner light they could not refuse to follow.
(4) Those who refer indirectly to the influence of Catholic wives, husbands, or members of their families.
(5) Miscellaneous.

The number of such converts can be estimated with a fair degree of accuracy from the statistics provided annually in the Catholic Directory. For the past few years, the following figures of conversions have been reported for the United States:

```
1918.......................................... 24,552
1919.......................................... 23,625
1920.......................................... 28,379
1921-26....................................... Not given
1927.......................................... 35,751
1928.......................................... 33,991
1929.......................................... 36,376
1930.......................................... 38,232
1931.......................................... 39,528
1932.......................................... 40,269
1933.......................................... 40,226
```

It is necessary, however, to ask just what is meant by a convert to Catholicism. Baptism once duly administered is not repeated, and hence it might be possible, by comparing the figures for adult baptisms with those for converts, to determine the percentage of converts to Catholicism who had grown to manhood and womanhood without ever being baptized. Examination of the statistics by dioceses in the United States, however, indicates that in 1929 the number of converts received approximately equals the number of adult baptisms. One cannot assume, nevertheless, that most of the converts were never identified with any church before such conversion, because it is quite probable that most converts would neither have their baptismal certificates in their possession nor care to solicit certifications that they had been baptized according to the required formulae. Under such circumstances, the priest may consider it simpler to take no chances and administer baptism a second time.

Again, these converts may have come into the church from Judaism or from a practical paganism as much as from Protestantism. There is no way of telling just what proportion of these converts had been actively identified with the Protestant church. Some indeed were obviously reared in a Catholic atmosphere but drifted into indifference. Such a convert was the author of *The High Romance*.[14] The numbers of such converts at first blush seems imposing, but when such numbers are compared with the total number of priests in the United States, the number of converts per priest is not very great. Thus, in 1922, Father Coakley stated that the converts for the previous year averaged but 1.78 for each priest, and in 1927 he said:

"One thing is certain; either the Faith is not making tremendous headway in America, or else the figures in the *Catholic Directory* are wrong. . . . We will never get anywhere by closing our eyes to the fact that the figures of convert-making in this country would almost warrant the conclusion that the priests in the United States are losing the missionary spirit. How else explain the fact that 25,773 of them, upon whose education a huge fortune has been spent, succeeded in one year in making only 1.3 of a convert per each?"

The figures in the Catholic Directory may perhaps be incorrect, but if they are substantially correct and if the Catholic population of the United States is correctly estimated at between 20,000,000 and 25,000,000, then it is fairly clear that it takes over 500 Catholics a whole year to make a single convert. The growth of Catholicism in the United States must have been almost entirely due to immigration and natural increase, and not to conversion.

This is perhaps the more surprising since the rigid regulations of the Catholic Church in respect to intermarriage of Catholics with non-Catholics

[14] Williams, Michael, *The High Romance* (New York: The Macmillan Company, 1926).

tend to put the non-Catholic at a disadvantage. As has been pointed out in the last chapter, there are no available statistics regarding intermarriage of Catholics and non-Catholics in the United States. Each bishop has these figures for his own diocese and takes them with other statistics with him to Rome on the occasion of his quinquennial visit. Probably, therefore, only the Holy Father has access to the facts, but the seriousness of intermarriage is recognized by both Protestants and Catholics. One may make an estimate as to its extent. It is highly probable that the ratio of mixed marriages in the United States to the total Catholic population is no less than the ratio of mixed marriages in Canada (exclusive of Quebec, which is atypical) to the total Catholic population. We know that in these eight Canadian provinces there were, in 1930, no fewer than 4,063 such intermarriages.[15] The Catholic population in 1931 was 1,822,228. The number of intermarriages was therefore 2.23 per 1,000 Catholic inhabitants. If we estimate the Catholic population of the United States in 1929 at 21,000,000 and assume that the rate of intermarriage is the same (it may be much higher) as in the eight Canadian provinces, then it would seem that the number of intermarriages in the United States in 1929 would have been approximately 46,830. But if the number of converts in that year was 36,376, then it is clear that, even if all the converts were the results of intermarriage—which is certainly not true—there would still remain approximately 10,000 non-Catholics who had married Catholics without changing.

CATHOLIC EFFORTS AMONG PROTESTANTS

There are many Catholic organizations which address themselves principally to the conversion of non-Catholics. One of the most conspicuous of these societies is the Missionary Society of St. Paul the Apostle (Paulists), founded by Father Hecker in 1858. The new *Catholic Dictionary* (published in 1929) states that the membership of the society in that year consisted of seventy-five priests and fifty novices. Emphasis is laid on lecturing, preaching, the holding of special missions and the wide use of literature, notably pamphlets. Perhaps, the Paulists have been foremost in the effort to study the psychology of the Protestant majority and to discover an apologetic suited to "Anglo-Saxon" needs. The Converts' League was founded by Father Conway, author of "The Question Box," himself a Paulist, in 1895, with the object of familiarizing converts to the church with Catholic associates and of aiding for a time those who on account of change of faith suffer pecuniary or social disadvantage.[16]

---

[15] Excluding all instances of marriage where the non-Catholic party became a Catholic prior to the marriage ceremony, and holding all Greek Catholics to be Roman Catholics.

[16] *New Catholic Dictionary*, 1929, p. 254.

RESULTS AMONG NEGROES

During the War there were numerous stories afloat that the Catholic Church was planning to win the Negroes in the United States, the vast majority of whom are Protestants, but who might be attracted by the colorful ritual of the Catholic Church. After the War the dual animosity of the Ku Klux Klan to Negroes and to Catholics might also have served to bind the two groups more closely together in spite of the traditional antipathy of the Irish to the colored people. But there seems to be little evidence of any serious Catholic encroachment on this particular Protestant preserve. There are about 12,000,000 Negroes in the United States, and the Government census of 1926 gave the number of colored Catholics in the country in that year as 124,324. Other estimates vary. An article in *America* for September 28, 1929, claimed that there were 204,000 colored Catholics in the country, "either in colored congregations or worshipping with their white brethren," and this estimate was based on what purported to be the "first accurate, official and national census of colored Catholics in the United States as of January 1, 1928."[17] Colored Catholics are found in significant numbers in Baltimore, New Orleans, and Memphis. In Baltimore, out of a total Negro population of 142,106 there are some 8,000 to 10,000 Catholics. In Canada the Negro population is very small and totals only 7,361 in the 1931 census. Of these 429 were Catholics, and 330 of these were in the Province of Quebec. Of the balance 4,510 were Baptists and 1,425 were Anglicans.

There does not seem to be any great movement of Negroes into the Catholic Church. If there is any marked movement out of the Negro church at all, it is of certain radicals who are "fed up" with the church and are rather anti-religious in general. While it may seem surprising that the Catholic Church has not worked harder to secure a Negro clientèle, there was sufficient for it to do to hold the vast number of immigrants from Catholic countries. There was also little money to spare for special efforts for non-Catholics and from all accounts the contributions made in northern cities for the work of colored Catholics were never very significant.[18] Strategically, also, a large colored Catholic population in the United States might have brought new problems into the bosom of the church, and in the end the maintenance of separate institutions for them would have required vast expenditures of money. One sometimes wonders, moreover, if white Catholics really desire a large ingress of colored converts.

---

[17] For various estimates of the number of Colored Catholics in the United States, see Moore, J. F., *Will America Become Catholic?* (New York: Harper and Brothers, 1931), pp. 185-199.
[18] The annual collection in the Catholic Church for Negro and Indian work aggregates only about $250,000. The American Missionary Association of the Congregational Churches, despite the fact that there are few colored Congregationalists, spent over $625,000 for the Southern Negroes in 1930-31 alone.

THE INFLUENCE OF CATHOLIC HOSPITALS AND COLLEGES

This section on conversion from Catholicism must simply note certain other agencies which may exert some influence. Comment has already been made in Chapter VI on the number of Protestant and Jewish students in Catholic universities. It is perhaps impossible to estimate the extent of such an environment on their religious life and ideals. In twenty-four Catholic universities 10.8 per cent. of the student body was Protestant and 15.4 per cent. was Jewish. Those directing this study have not learned of any religious work being undertaken in these institutions under either Protestant or Jewish auspices. Then one must also remember the Protestants who attend Catholic academies, convent schools, etc. Certain duties required of Catholic students are, to be sure, not required of non-Catholic students. Thus, in the calendar of Canisius College, Buffalo, it is stated:

"Catholic students are required to make the annual Spiritual Retreat, and they are expected and urged to receive the Sacraments of Penance and Holy Communion at least once a week. *Non-Catholics are not required to take part in the exercises of religion.*"

Again, it is stated

"Apologetics is prescribed for all Catholic students. Non-Catholics may substitute other elective courses in place of the courses in Apologetics."

On the other hand, in this college thirty-two out of a total of 130 semester hours, required for graduation with the degrees of Bachelor of Arts or Bachelor of Science, are prescribed in the department of philosophy under which is included Logic, Epistemology, Ontology, Cosmology, Fundamental Psychology, Rational Psychology, Natural Theology, Fundamental Ethics, Individual Ethics, Social Ethics, Sociology, Special Questions and the History of Philosophy. It will thus be seen that such students are inevitably exposed to the philosophical backgrounds of Catholicism.

Once again there is the matter of hospitalization. All hospitals, whether secular, Catholic or Jewish, emphasize that they limit their ministry to no particular creed, but medical missions have always been under suspicion of exerting definitely religious influence. In an article in *The Commonweal* (April 6, 1927) the Rev. J. Elliot Ross stated:

"Moreover, our hospitals reach numbers of non-Catholics who would never enter a Catholic church. And if they are not converted, at least they rarely leave the hospital as bigots. Prejudice is broken down, and some preparation made for later conversion."

Apparently corroborative evidence of the use of hospitals for the purpose of predisposing to conversion may be found in Mr. Moore's book, already cited, *Will America Become Catholic?* (pp. 157-162). In this connection, it must be stated that in some parts of the country, especially in the smaller cities and towns, Catholic hospitals are often welcomed even by the Protestant community, since the expense of maintenance is usually much less than that of Protestant or secular institutions. Generally speaking, moreover, there is expressed a very sincere regard for the gentleness and care exercised by the sisters.

THE RÔLE OF THE RADIO IN PROPAGANDA

Another form of propaganda, the success of which it is impossible as yet to gauge, is through the radio. Protestants were among the first to utilize the radio, and Catholics seemed at first at a loss to know how to transmit their services over the air. However, they have made the necessary adjustments with great skill and on the whole maintain their radio services at a high level. On the other hand, while some Protestant hours are characterized by aesthetic taste and intellectual vigor, many of the spiritual sharpshooters who have their time "on the air" can hardly commend the Protestant faith to the unseen audiences. One great difficulty exists in the whole question of radio. Can one form of religion be successfully promoted without attacking another form? The rules of the Canadian Radio Commission state:

"No broadcasting station may broadcast any speech, printed matter, program or advertising matter containing abusive or defamatory statements with regard to individuals or institutions, or statements or suggestions contrary to the express purpose of any existing legislation."

On this regulation, Judge Rutherford of the Russellites was deprived of the use of the air on January 18, 1933. Local stations are held responsible for such utterances, and consequently religious addresses have to be noted carefully and when anything suspiciously slanderous sounds in the offing, "transmission trouble" may suddenly develop. It is needful for all religious organizations using the radio, therefore, to watch their step, and this development may perhaps mean a new and fairer emphasis in preaching, both in Protestant and in Catholic circles. At all events, many Protestants listen with interest to the Catholic hour, while the reverse is also probably true. Whether such radio addresses make converts or not, they may develop a greater mutual respect especially when they are delivered with force, dignity and magnanimity. The religious uses of radio are fraught with great opportunities and immense dangers.

On the whole, the evidence does not indicate any very extensive movement from Protestantism to Catholicism, in spite of much publicity on the occasion of more or less sensational conversions. By and large, both groups seem more concerned to abide by the motto "what we have we hold," and whatever leakage may exist in one direction is probably balanced by a parallel leakage in the opposite direction.

CHAPTER IX

Coöperation

THE FIELD OF COÖPERATION

"The wolf and the lamb shall feed together" was the Hebrew prophet's picture of reconciliation. Had he lived in modern Europe he might with equal pertinence have written that Catholic and Protestant, Christian and Jew shall overcome their aversions and clasp hands in brotherhood. Even in this land of religious liberty there have been periodic outbursts of religious intolerance, particularly by Protestants against Catholics, and while the Jews in the United States have never been subjected to violent persecution they have suffered from popular prejudice and discrimination.

It is in such rocky soil that the tender plant of coöperation among the three faiths has had to struggle to take root. The marvel is not that there is so little coöperation today among members of the three faiths, but that there is any whatever.

Certain obstacles to the closest coöperation among strict believers in the three faiths seem insurmountable in any predictable future. The most formidable is the conflict between irreconcilable absolutes: the Catholic claim of Papal infallibility, the Jewish insistence on maintaining a communal integrity in which race, religion and culture are interlocked, the Protestant insistence on the supremacy of private judgment. These are manifestly irreconcilable. Accordingly, speaking broadly, full official coöperation in worship and in religious instruction by orthodox representatives of the three faiths is impossible. In such activities only progressive Protestants and Reform Jews can participate freely.

Coöperation by the official leaders of the three faiths has, therefore, been limited almost entirely to such non-inflammable fields as civic betterment, social work, studies and pronouncements regarding the ethics of social issues, the promotion of mutual appreciation and the safeguarding of religious liberty. To the "modernist" or the "liberal" these, after all, form a large part of religion—the "loving mercy and doing justice" of which Micah wrote. Be that as it may, these zones where the absolutes seldom intrude give wide play to the coöperative spirit, yet even in them the coöperators are not, as a rule, national ecclesiastical bodies of any of the faiths, but only aggregations of individuals, or local congregations. In the case of the

305

Jews, there are no national ecclesiastical authorities. The various "unions" and "conferences" of Jewish congregations and rabbis, while influential, exercise not mandatory but moral authority, for the local congregations jealously guard their independence. In the case of the Roman Catholics, the recent interdiction of Pope Pius XI against equal relations with other religious bodies stands in the way. In the case of the Protestants, the Federal Council of the Churches of Christ in America has authority within narrow limits to speak and act for its constituent bodies. Locally, on the other hand, the barriers to ecclesiastical coöperation are absent in the case of many of the Jewish congregations and Protestant churches. The Roman Catholic barriers are only occasionally lowered by a liberal bishop. Social work and participation in raising community funds seem to be among the few spheres where the Catholic clergy feel free to coöperate with other faiths on a permanent and equal footing. One obstacle to coöperation by Roman Catholics is their reluctance to be paired with Protestants only. An Episcopal bishop credited the coöperation by Catholics in his city to avoidance of this dilemma:

"The absence of friction and the presence of such a high degree of Catholic coöperation is partly due to the fact that in all coöperative efforts all three—not only two of the faiths—have been called in. This has pleased the Roman Catholics because they then could coöperate on a broad religious basis without being lured into any exclusively Christian line-up with Protestants, where their own interpretation might be compromised. The Roman Catholics here have played fair and never sought advantage by underhanded means."

Having thus defined the field of coöperation in general terms, we are ready to consider more fully the philosophies that largely delimit interfaith coöperation.

THE PHILOSOPHIES CONDITIONING COÖPERATION

Few men have a thought-out philosophy. Most of them are content to follow the leader, whether that leader be tradition and upbringing, or a dominating personality. Others are content to follow the line of least resistance, to accommodate themselves so as to live on tolerable terms with their immediate fellows. It is alleged by social psychologists that the mass of people, even in an era of well-nigh universal schooling, are unreflective and impulsive in their social relations. In the age of isolation, before steam and electricity and radio, uncritical living constituted no special menace to social harmony and health. Today, when whole peoples can be subjected to the pressure of propaganda by press or radio, it becomes supremely important to make all the people critically minded, lest, like the Gadarene swine, they hurl themselves in blind passion over some cliff. When designing military and political leaders in more than one country, within recent years, have converted a civilized nation into an unreasoning herd, contemptuous of civil and religious liberty, then religious leaders in America can hardly afford not to try to immunize their people against such hazards.

If one thinks through the reasons why the three faiths as a whole or their individual adherents do or do not coöperate, one will find that the reasons fall naturally under three heads, described by the cumbrous words: theological, sociological and psychological.

The theological barriers to interfaith coöperation, briefly alluded to in the preceding section, call for further consideration. Just because differing theological beliefs are held on such high sanctions, as decreed by the divine will, they form perhaps the most solid and unyielding of all barriers. Theoretically, the high-churchman—of whatever faith—is estopped from giving the right hand of fellowship to any dissenter. Practically, there are very few intransigent high churchmen. The milk of human kindness dissolves their hard theories. The percentage of "low" or "broad" churchmen is possibly much greater among Protestants and Jews than among Roman Catholics, but numbers of Catholic laymen and some of the Catholic clergy fall in that category. It is they who are eager to go as far in religious fellowship with believers of other names as they can without destroying the integrity of their own body. Faithful Catholics and orthodox Jews, however, regardless of their kindly feeling for non-Catholics, base their refusal to join in common worship on reasons which need to be understood by Protestants. If they are understood they will presumably command respect even if not assent. One Catholic priest has thus stated the case:

"It is not a question of Catholics believing that those outside the visible organization of the Catholic Church cannot be saved. Rather, it is that Catholics feel they cannot, with loyalty to Christ, take formal part in a worship that denies His divinity—at least implicitly—or any of His essential teachings, such as the Real Presence."

The protagonists of coöperation in religious fellowship place stress on the basic beliefs which are common to them all: a personal God of righteousness and love, the sacredness of all men as children of a common Heavenly Father, the obligation to realize God's will by practicing social justice and brotherhood. The protagonists of non-coöperation in religious fellowship place stress on the precious beliefs which are peculiar to each faith. Among them are these: salvation only by faith in the sacrifice of Jesus Christ; the supreme authority either of the Church councils, or of the Vicar of Christ, or of the New Testament, or of the cumulative Christian conscience, or of the Hebrew Scriptures and recognized Jewish tradition; the unique mission of the children of Israel. These peculiar beliefs probably hold a warmer, more intimate place in believers' affections than the beliefs common to all; and just because they are shot through with deep-seated feeling, far below the zone of rational demonstration, they are grasped with an instinctive tenacity which the more reasoned, less intimate tenets common to all do not command.

If this analysis is substantially true, then the possibility of whole-hearted coöperation by the three faiths in the realm of religion is inevitably limited. Unrestricted coöperation would require the relinquishment by each of the three faiths of beliefs whose roots are intertwined with a venerable cultural heritage. To do this appears both rationally and emotionally impossible. Our examination later of the various national interfaith organizations will show that none of them pretends to achieve thoroughgoing religious coöperation.

The nine organizations described below fall into two categories: The first includes those that promote mutual respect among the three faiths and assume their continuing integrity; their motto might be "coöperation without compromise." They do not ignore differences, indeed, they recognize and almost glory in them. They dwell not on uniformity or combination but on wealth in variety. Whether intentionally or not, they encourage cultural pluralism rather than cultural monism. In this category belong five agencies: the National Conference of Jews and Christians, the World Fellowship of Faiths, the Religious Education Association, the North American Board for the Study of Religion in Higher Education and the united religious cabinets of university pastors at Iowa, Cornell, Columbia and the University of California at Los Angeles. The second category includes those that have a pragmatic object and pay little or no direct attention to creedal matters. In this category belong the occasional coöperation among the social-service organs of the Federal Council, the National Catholic Welfare Conference, and the Central Conference of American Rabbis, for the purpose of making studies and pronouncements concerning the ethical aspects of social and industrial issues, the World Alliance for International Friendship through the Churches, the Church Peace Union, the Community Chests, and other intermittent interfaith activities like the United War Work Drive.

The sociological philosophy of coöperation and non-coöperation may be put in brief and untechnical language. Unless there is close articulation and free interchange among all the member groups in the body politic, the health of the body as a whole will inevitably suffer. Organized coöperation for the good of the whole means lowering the barriers among different heredities so that each cultural group can readily make its contribution to the common weal. Interstimulation of diverse ideas and customs, unified by underlying common ideals and loyalties, rather than suppression of difference, may contribute greatly to cultural growth and the development of a richer American civilization. Association in common tasks for the general good is a sure road to the removal of ignorance and its evil progeny. On the contrary, isolation from and ignorance of one another among religious and racial groups may lead to mutual distrust, friction and schism. Since all of the agencies discussed in this chapter are dedicated to promoting acquaintance and coöperation among groups which tend somewhat to be isolated from one another, they qualify as unifying and socializing forces just in the proportion that they achieve their aim. No exact measure of their efficacy in this respect is possible, but among those that rank high in the judgment of many competent witnesses, are the Community Chest and Councils of Social Agencies, the National Conference of Jews and Christians, the united staffs and programs at various universities, and the North American Board for the Study of Religion in Higher Education.

The psychological principles involved in interfaith relations center in the moot question, whether the obstacles to mutual respect and coöperation can be best removed by direct or indirect methods. It is generally agreed that among the chief obstacles are: the tendency to generalize about a whole group on the basis of a few individuals; prejudice; suspicion or aversion toward people and ideas that are strange and different; distorted or misinterpreted information. Should agencies like those already named remove these obstacles indirectly, by getting people of different faiths to work together, or directly by dissecting and discussing the mind-sets and misinformation and fallacies that make up the obstacles, or by using both direct and indirect methods?

The whole trend of experimental psychology and pedagogy supports a combination of the direct and indirect methods. Attitudes toward persons of different faiths and races are formed and re-formed either by imitation or by agreeable or disagreeable contacts with the differing persons. In most adults, as well as in children, the capacity for analysis and reasoning is too limited and too strongly overbalanced by unreflecting reactions for the direct method to be as effective as the indirect.

At this point digression is in order. While this volume has been concerned primarily with relations among adults of the three faiths, the importance of efforts to develop in children attitudes favorable to intelligent and coöperative relations with persons of other faiths can hardly be overstated. Manifestly, the work of the church and synagogue schools, of the public and parochial schools, and of the other youth organizations is exerting tremendous influence for or against coöperative interfaith relations. The text-books studied and the activities engaged in by the children may engender in them undesirable attitudes toward other faiths by what is omitted as well as by what is included. It is, therefore, to the credit of the National

Conference of Jews and Christians that it has sponsored a critical study of allusions to the Jews in the curricular material published by six of the large Protestant bodies.[1] Such unjust or mistaken points as are discovered are being privately called to the attention of the respective editors, most of whom are eager to make corrections and to add material calculated to foster appreciation of the Jews. If a similar policy is applied in the text-books of all three faiths and also in those of the public schools, there surely ought to be much less prejudice and lack of coöperation among the faiths in the next generation than in the present.

Resuming now the main thread of the argument, additional psychological reasons will be given for and against the direct and the indirect methods of removing obstacles to mutual respect and coöperation. At the beginning of this psychological section, four obstacles were named. One was, the tendency of some persons to make snap judgments about a whole group, say Roman Catholics, on the basis of contact with a few individual Catholics. Obviously, an excellent way to correct this tendency is to give the "judges" authentic information about a much larger number of Catholics. This may be called direct or conscious education. There is, however, ample justification for using the indirect method by helping the "judges" to broaden their contacts with Catholics, and thus be unconsciously reëducated.

The protagonists of the indirect method argue that, from the viewpoint of social harmony, ignorant antipathies are pathological, and when a patient is obsessed by them he should be diverted from himself and his obsessions and engaged in absorbing activity with the very persons toward whom he is antipathetic. Thereby he will discover how like himself and how likeable are those whom in his ignorance he had distrusted or disliked. This argument by analogy is challenged by some experts as oversimplifying the case and giving only part of the corrective process. They say the treatment of obsessions calls first for helping the victim identify the obsession or "complex," trace its origin, recognize its falsity, and then replace it by a truer concept—to be "reconditioned."

Another obstacle named was distorted or misinterpreted information. The psychologists say that information about anything needs to be interpreted, that is, set forth in its relation to the larger whole; that unrelated, uninterpreted bits of information and of experience are more apt to mislead than to orient one. The very word "orient" means relating the spot where one stands to the entire environment. Suppose, for example, that a Protestant and a Jew are brought into contact in planning a community assemblage on behalf of disarmament and the Jew absents himself from a committee meeting on account of a religious festival or because he cannot eat non-

---

[1] This unpublished study was directed by Professor J. V. Thompson, of Drew University, and was completed early in 1934.

kosher food. Unless the significance of the Jewish observances is interpreted to the Protestant he is likely to form an aversion to rather than a respect for the Jew. The psychologists lay stress on learning by "life-situations," such as the one just described. Sometimes the participants unaided catch the lesson of the situation, but often they need to have it interpreted and supplemented by some more widely-informed guide. So, here again, we are driven to conclude that not only the indirect method of removing obstacles to coöperation by getting people of different faiths to work together, but also the direct method of interpreting what happens when they associate are both needed.

A final psychological principle, akin to the life-situation, is "specificity," by which is meant that our attitudes and concepts are built out of specific or particular experiences. They are not born full-fledged. The Character Education Inquiry tended to show that few children are honest in general; they are honest in certain respects and dishonest in others. Resounding general resolutions about religious freedom, or exhortations about the brotherhood of man, are apt to be water off a duck's back; whereas a visit by a Christian to a cultured Jewish home or the defense of the Y.M.C.A. by a Catholic priest before a Community Chest meeting is likely to make a lasting difference in the attitudes of all concerned. This principle lends support to those who hold that the sovereign specific for interfaith prejudices is to get Protestants, Catholics and Jews to adjourn their differences and join hands in worthy enterprises. Among the organizations that emphasize this view are the Federal Council of the Churches of Christ, the Religious Education Association, the Church Peace Union, and the University Religious Conference. The failure of the last to deal directly with differences of belief and causes of prejudice among the faiths is one of the chief criticisms levelled against it. The sponsoring by the National Conference of Jews and Christians of coöperative enterprises, like the joint speaking pilgrimage across the country by a Catholic, a Jew and a Protestant, entitles the Conference to be included in this list, although the main emphasis in its seminars and publications, as will be pointed out later, has been to remove prejudice, distrust and intergroup conflict by a critical analysis of their causes. Frank discussion of ways to remove or control sources of irritation has naturally ensued, and at times its seminars have resulted in plans for action.

Our discussion of the philosophies conditioning coöperation has been intended to do two things: to show the importance of defining the factors that help and hinder interfaith coöperation, and to consider the relative merits of the direct and the indirect methods of overcoming the obstacles to coöperation. In so far as we have succeeded in this intent, we are prepared to examine and evaluate the various organizations and activities that exemplify interfaith coöperation.

Coöperation of National Scope

The national organizations now to be reviewed are arranged very roughly in an ascending scale, as their importance for interfaith coöperation is judged by the investigators.

OF A TEMPORARY CHARACTER

War Work Campaign: The psychology of wartime was conducive to the submerging of religious differences in common devotion to the national aims. When, therefore, the government suggested, in 1918, that representatives of the three faiths should conduct a joint campaign to raise funds for service to the enlisted men, they promptly complied. While this campaign was marked in many localities by the most friendly relations, it was also accompanied by some friction between Protestants and Catholics, but there appears to be no proof that the strain between the two groups during the drive was the cause of the criticisms made by Catholics of the Y.M.C.A. work among the troops in France. The fact is that similar criticisms were also made by non-Catholics.

Goodwill Committees: Efforts toward understanding and coöperation between Christians and Jews were inaugurated soon after the World War by the *American Hebrew*, when the Ku Klux Klan and the *Dearborn Independent* were stimulating religious and racial hatreds in the United States. To combat these sinister influences this journal devoted a series of issues to promoting understanding of the Jew and overcoming religious prejudice. This material was summarized in the *Literary Digest* and it helped to arouse secular and religious journals to carry on a similar campaign.

One of the indirect outcomes of this campaign was the inauguration, in 1924, in Arkansas of Better Understanding Week, in which churches, schools and commercial companies joined to decry intolerance and promote understanding among all faiths.

At about the same time the Central Conference of American Rabbis formed a Good-Will Committee and instituted close coöperation with the similar committee which had been formed by the Federal Council of the Churches of Christ, but which was later merged in the National Conference of Jews and Christians. In this connection the President of the Central Conference, on March 27, 1925, wrote as follows:

"The season which brings the doctrine of the Resurrection into the joyous foreground of the Christian consciousness dramatizes to the sharpening edge of divisive illwill the relations between Jews and Christians.

"It is easy enough for people of the same faith to coöperate. Real progress is evidenced when individuals and organizations of diametrically opposite principles have so learned to curb their antagonisms and to minimize their differences as to rejoice in the fellowship which an appreciation of their fundamental agreements inspires.

"The Central Conference of American Rabbis has entered joyously into a coöperative relationship with a Committee of the Federal Council of the Churches of Christ in America not merely to cultivate goodwill in the committee room, but also to generate it as a directing power in the social life of the nation."

In the fall of 1925 *The American Hebrew* availed itself of radio station WRNY to present a series of broadcasts by eminent Jews and Christians in order to build bridges between the faiths. As a climax to these efforts, came the creation of the American Christian Fund for Jewish Relief, in 1926, in connection with which a meeting was held in the Cathedral of St. John the Divine, in which Bishop Manning, General Pershing, Major General O'Ryan, Dr. Cadman, and the late Mr. Louis Marshall participated, possibly the first occasion when, in a great Christian Cathedral, Catholic, Protestant and Jew met in the same pulpit to bring tidings of a great humanitarian project, fathered by Christians in behalf of suffering Jews.

The Inquiry and the Fairfield Experiment: The idea of fostering dispassionate conferences between Catholics and Protestants in order to remove ignorance and prejudice regarding one another's faith was originated in March, 1927, by the Inquiry into the Christian Way of Life. It happens that the lead in the experiment was taken by the director of the study reported in this volume. At that time considerable effort was expended on working out a technique for group discussion concerning the beliefs of Catholics and Protestants and their attitudes toward one another. To that end an experimental group of Protestants was conducted in Fairfield, Connecticut, for several months. The results were embodied in a booklet which became a guide for similar groups in other communities. Father J. Elliot Ross collaborated in the experiment and later conducted a similar group for Catholics. Although the Inquiry was dissolved after a few years, having fulfilled its original purpose as an experimental enterprise, the Fairfield Experiment was not lost, but supplied much of the impetus in the development of the National Conference of Jews and Christians and provided the pattern on which the Interfaith Seminars of the National Conference have been conducted.

Sustained coöperation on a national scale by either agencies or individuals of the three faiths appears to have been virtually unknown until the Religious Education Association was founded in 1908.

OF A PERMANENT CHARACTER

The World Fellowship of Faiths: In 1924, by the coming together of the Union of East and West and the League of Neighbors, the World Fellowship of Faiths was established in the United States. The leaders in bringing this about were its present general executives, Kedarnath Das Gupta and Charles F. Weller. Although the Fellowship embraces individuals of many faiths beside Christianity and Judaism, its significance for this study lies in the fact that it has fostered intercourse and understanding among Catholics, Jews and Protestants. Its declared purpose is "to unite people of all religions, races, countries and classes, by building bridges of appreciation across the chasms of prejudice. It is not its purpose to merge all religions into one, to convert adherents of one faith to another, or to prove the equality, superiority, or inferiority of any religion. Our aim is unity in variety, not uniformity."

For the attainment of this purpose it has relied chiefly upon conferences, platform meetings and joint worship by representatives of many faiths, plays portraying the character of the East to the West, celebrations of the sacred festivals of the various faiths participated in by adherents of other faiths, and a quarterly journal entitled *Appreciation.* During the Century of Progress Exposition in 1933 it held sixty gatherings in Chicago where some two hundred representatives of many religions spoke regarding the contribution of their respective faiths to the solution of man's present problems. Catholic participation in the Fellowship has been very slight, being inhibited, no doubt, by such things as the joint services of worship.

A few years ago the Fellowship staged in Boston a meeting in which both Protestants and Jews paid public tribute to the Roman Catholic faith. Cardinal O'Connell wrote afterward to express his appreciation of the event, but it did not prove possible to persuade Roman Catholics to reciprocate by paying similar tribute to Protestantism or to Judaism.

Among the few active local centers of the Fellowship is Cleveland, where both Christians and Reform Jews have coöperated in holding several symposiums on current problems during the last two years. The meetings have been held in various church auditoriums. On each occasion the speakers have comprised a Catholic as well as a Jew and a Protestant. Among the topics discussed have been "How my faith helps toward an effective brotherhood in a united world," "Spiritual security in the midst of economic insecurity," and "What can we do about racial and religious prejudice."

The investigators heard both favorable and unfavorable comments about the Fellowship. In one city, three Jewish rabbis, including one of orthodox views, praised it warmly, and several Protestant ministers spoke well of it, but the Catholic clergy were lukewarm, although both priests and laymen had spoken at Fellowship meetings. The attitude of the local Catholic bishop was thus characterized by a rabbi:

"The Bishop has been cold to the whole idea. He can't tolerate fellowship with other faiths. No doubt we could get his support if we dropped the name

'Fellowship' and used 'Forum.' But so far as I have heard he has not rebuked the Catholic speakers."

A prominent Catholic layman who was formerly active in the Fellowship gave as his reason for withdrawing, that "I felt it was religiously too dilute and besides it was too much of a hippodrome."

The most frequent criticism was akin to that voiced by a Reform rabbi:

"The Fellowship is superficial and artificial. I thought we had got beyond patting each other on the back. We need to work together on common problems."

That this idea is not shared by some of the Fellowship leaders in the same city is indicated by the remark of another rabbi:

"When some one proposed combining the Fellowship here with the Conference of Jews and Christians, the Fellowship leaders opposed it, saying that the Fellowship stressed appreciation, not coöperation."

National Council on Religion in Higher Education: A quite different form of interfaith coöperation is represented by the National Council on Religion in Higher Education. Though started and maintained almost entirely by Protestant laymen, it has to some extent served Catholics and Jews and enlisted their support. The unostentatious but significant nature of the Council's activities will be evident in a sketch of its history. It was founded in 1923 by the late Professor Charles Foster Kent, of Yale University.

"Its primary purpose is to make a qualitative contribution to the religious life of the colleges. Especially it is seeking to discover and develop for colleges, without regard to their religious or secular character, teachers and administrators, who with a genuine interest in religion, combine learning with culture.

"Because of this central concern with *persons*, the Council competes with no existing organization or institution, and is attached to no ecclesiastical body or theological position. In one capacity or another, its officers and Fellows will be found identified with all societies working in this field. It has no particular program which it seeks to have adopted by colleges and universities. Its resources and energies are concentrated on the important task of improving the quality of leadership of religion as it functions in education, chiefly by the provision of fellowships for men and women pursuing graduate study.

"The total number of Fellows appointed up to April 1934 was 137, of whom seven were Jews and one a Catholic.

"Ninety-six Fellows are now located in teaching, administrative, or other positions in connection with educational institutions, chiefly in colleges and universities. 51 different colleges and universities and 6 preparatory schools are represented on the list.

"The Board of Directors has generally included a Catholic and a Jewish member, and other Jewish leaders have coöperated closely with the Council."

Among the activities conducted by the Council, supplementary to its selection and maintenance of Fellows, are the Week of Work, the annual gathering of the Fellows for intensive discussion of pertinent problems; the provision of courses at the University of Chicago and Yale-Union Summer Schools on the moral and religious development of undergraduates and on student counselling; in coöperation with the Hazen Foundation the holding of a week's conference on personal relations with students; and the placement of Fellows in academic positions. The Council has had a simple, unspectacular program. It has been no part of its policy to attempt to influence public opinion or directly to ameliorate relations among the three faiths. Within its limited sphere, it has done quiet, thorough work, and the ultimate influence of its Fellows on interfaith relations may be termed a by-product.

Religious Education Association: Its basis is entirely non-ecclesiastical, but from the outset it embraced individuals of the three faiths in both Canada and the United States. Its executive officer has said:

"Inasmuch as persons have been sought for their ability and not because they are members of any faith, this has placed the relationships in the R.E.A. on a personal rather than a faith basis. We never think of one as representing a faith but as standing on his own feet as an individual among other individuals. This has brought about unique relationships within the R.E.A."

The years that have followed have witnessed no narrowing of its basis, but in fact the large majority of its members have been Protestants. Reform Jews in its membership have been fairly proportionate to their numbers in the two countries as a whole, but Catholic members have been very few. Nominating committees have often taken pains to include a due proportion of non-Protestants on the governing board and on the programs of the Association, but the emphasis on experimentation and discovery and the absence of any fixed dogmas have been repugnant to Catholic critics and have led some Catholic members to feel ill at ease in Association conferences and even to let their membership lapse.

A characteristic example of this reaction was an editorial criticizing the Association written by a member of the faculty of Notre Dame University and published in the April, 1933, *Religious Bulletin* of the University. The gist of his charges was that the Association had no faith in an infallible revelation from God and no accepted system of religious education, whereas the Catholic Church had both, and consequently its communicants had nothing to gain from approaching religious issues in the exploratory and tentative spirit of the Association. Representatives of the Association quite sincerely met these charges by pleading that the Association was officially neutral, but that it offered a forum to which the non-Catholics were eager to have Catholics contribute their convictions and experiences and to compare the results in terms of the character values produced by the different systems. This plea apparently fails to satisfy the generality of Catholic leaders. It appeals only to a limited number of Catholic educators and laymen in whom the scientific spirit or the desire for interfaith coöperation is particularly strong.

The educational philosophy underlying the relations of members of whatever faith in the R.E.A. has been thus stated by its executive officer:

"The R.E.A. has never attempted in a direct way to relate the various faiths. Instead, it has attempted to tackle significant problems with members from the various faiths working together at them, thus making the interfaith relation incidental to the work in hand. I personally feel that we need more of this approach. There are so many things that we need to accomplish in which we need all hands. Furthermore, I do not believe we accomplish interfaith relations so well in a direct way as in this indirect way."

An excellent illustration of this principle was the promotion by the Religious Education Association of the great Jewish pageant entitled "The Romance of a People," which was first presented in connection with the Century of Progress Exposition at Chicago in 1933. Upon learning of the proposed pageant, the officers of the Association offered to form a strong committee of Christian sponsors, both Catholic and Protestant, and to promote attendance upon the pageant by Christians. Had the Association not rendered this service the pageant might have been stigmatized by anti-Semites as merely another illustration of self-glorification by the Jew. The sponsorship of so many eminent Christians and the sympathetic notice of the pageant in religious as well as secular papers fostered appreciation for the achievements of the Jewish people and sympathy for them in face of the recent German persecution.

International Relations: The World Alliance for International Friendship through the Churches stands squarely for the inclusion of members of the three faiths, and of other faiths as well, but they participate as individuals not as official representatives. The Alliance

"was organized in the summer of 1914 to mobilize into a conscious force for international goodwill men and women who subscribe to the Christian ideal of international relationships, whatever may be their religious faiths, political affiliations or diversified views as to instruments and forms of organization for promoting peace."

The American Council of the Alliance is one of thirty-three in various countries. In its membership and activities Protestants greatly preponderate, but the Executive Committee includes a few Catholics and Jewish laymen, and all three faiths are represented on the Advisory Boards of Laymen and Clergymen. A similar balance is generally maintained in the list of speakers at the meetings of the Alliance. The Alliance finds it difficult to secure official coöperation by Catholic authorities, but the laymen coöperate heartily, and a considerable number of the more liberal and outspoken priests go as far as their superiors allow. One high ecclesiastic allowed his name to appear on the letterhead of the Alliance until after the issuance of the Pope's encyclical against coöperation. No difficulties have been encountered in enlisting the participation of Jewish leaders, although occasionally a committee has been genially called to account for using such a phrase as "we Christians."

The Church Peace Union is a body with aims almost identical with those of the World Alliance, and the officers and directors of the two are interlocking. Naturally they collaborate closely. The Union is as religiously inclusive in its membership as the Alliance. One of the chief projects which the Union has in hand is the assembling of a World Conference on International Peace through Religion. In connection with the preparations for this conference, one of the leading Protestant members of the committee of arrangements made these significant observations:

"We have been able to hold the representatives of eleven faiths, including Roman and Greek Catholics, back of the plans for the Conference because we have avoided definitions of doctrine and have stressed our common interests and objectives, not each man's explanation of why he held those objectives. Instead of trying to get agreement on general principles and moot points, it is far better to tackle practical issues one by one, and to keep as far as possible in the wide field of common convictions. Also, I have great faith in our practice of getting men to act not as representatives, but as individuals."

Association of American Colleges: This Association includes among its 464 member institutions no less than eighty-nine Catholic colleges and universities, and the Executive Committee has approved the membership application of Yeshivah College, the only college of liberal arts and sciences conducted under Jewish auspices. On the Executive Committee is one woman president of a Catholic college. While the employed staff has always consisted of Protestants, their services have been placed at the disposal of the Catholic institutions as fully as of any others. The Executive Secretary has expressed special satisfaction at the number of first-grade Catholic colleges developed in recent years and now identified with the Association. He also has written: "There is a fine spirit of camaraderie between the representatives of the various groups affiliated with this Association and many lines of coöperative work." It is, therefore, not surprising that the university secretary of the Association became one of the pioneers in developing permanent interfaith coöperation in state universities.

United Staffs and Programs at Universities: The idea of aligning the professional religious workers at a university in one combined staff originated at the University of Pennsylvania, in 1901. Some years later, at the University of Texas, the President of the Austin Presbyterian Theological Seminary took the initiative in drawing Catholics, Protestants and Jews together in order to introduce courses in religion in the curriculum of the university. The teachers of these courses organized the Religious Teachers Association. A parallel Religious Workers Union has also been formed in order to coördinate the activities of all denominations on the university campus. At Cornell University the Student Y.M.C.A. in 1919 took the lead in introducing, with slight modifications, the plan in operation at Pennsylvania. Variants of this scheme have been adopted at other state universities, among which are Alabama, Illinois, Missouri and Oregon. In several instances the Student Christian Association is the core of the organization, its general secretary being the executive of the united work. The essential characteristic of these united staffs is that the program is jointly framed and executed, each member being responsible for one phase of it. Much remains to be done separately by the respective religious groups and the students are encouraged to be loyal to their own churches while they learn to coöperate with men of other faiths. Six years ago a favorable appraisal of this plan was given in the volume "Undergraduates,"[2] and recent estimates by outside observers are likewise favorable, except that student initiative is thought sometimes to be overborne by the professional staff, a defect, however, from which other types of religious organization in the colleges are by no means free.

The University of Iowa was the first place where the plan of an interfaith school of religion as an official part of the University was joined with the plan for a coördinated staff of religious workers. During 1924 and 1925 the national Council of Church Boards of Education, through its university secretary, Dr. O. D. Foster, worked out with the university authorities and the religious bodies a plan for a School of Religion whose faculty and student counsellors would be supplied by the coöperating Catholic, Jewish and Protestant bodies, but whose courses would be a part of the university curriculum. The plan has been in regular operation since 1927.[3]

The management of the School is vested in a Managing Board on which the religious bodies and the university are represented. Relations with the university as a whole have been increasingly harmonious. The School is invited to participate in introducing relevant religious material into courses in other departments, and the University faculty last year voted unanimously to reverse its action of six years ago and to authorize the School of Religion to offer an optional course, "Religion and Ethics," to freshmen. Teachers

[2] New York: Institute of Social and Religious Research, 1928.
[3] Cf. Chapter VI, p. 224.

of the three faiths have participated in the course and the enrolment has numbered forty-five for the first semester and fifty for the second.

While the early emphasis of the School was laid on the courses of instruction, it has paid increasing attention to the extra-curricular religious activities of the students and faculty, and one member of its faculty gives most of his time as coördinator and adviser of the work of the seventeen organized denominational and interdenominational groups on the campus.

The Administrative Director, Dr. M. Willard Lampe, writes as follows of the relationships and influence of the School, and most of his statements have been confirmed by other authorities:

"So far as is known, the School enjoys the goodwill of every religious group in the state of Iowa.

"Officials in many responsible positions, from the governor of the state down, have heartily approved it. This is especially noteworthy in view of the fact that a special committee of the legislature has recently made a thorough-going study of every phase of the university's program and policies.

"It is very significant that whereas three years ago the Catholics withdrew from the School because of the lack of a sufficient volume of favorable sentiment, they have now officially returned, and are cordially coöperating in all of the activities. While there is, as yet, no full time Catholic professor, Catholic lecturers are furnished, from time to time, and in every other way their coöperation is complete.

"Jewish, Catholic, and Protestant students, faculty, and professional religious workers, meet at regular and frequent intervals for fellowship and the construction of common plans.

"There is much evidence that the very presence of the School of Religion on the campus, with its happy relationships of respect and tolerance, and with its academic and extra-academic program, has increased student respect for religion even when students have not formally participated in its work. Many students have testified to the School's value in mediating between their early religious training and the broader outlooks of university life.

"Has the principle of 'coöperation without compromise' been found to be practicable? As I think back over the relationships of the last five years I can recall many altercations and differences of opinion, but it has been a trail of widening and deepening friendship, without a single instance so far as I can recollect of anything suggesting personal animosity or estrangement. So far as my experience goes, our fellowship has been as genuine as that commonly found within any single religious group, and it has stood the test of daily association and the meeting of many unexpected and difficult problems."

A Catholic priest, who is thoroughly familiar with the Iowa situation, makes these confirmatory comments:

"The most interesting experiment, however, because of the lengths to which the university has gone, is in Iowa. Here a School of Religion has been made a constituent part of the university with the same prerogatives as any other school. Its board of trustees is made up of equal numbers from the university, Catholics, Protestants and Jews. Teaching is done in one of the university buildings, and offices are maintained there. The teachers, nominated by their respective groups, have the rank of full professor in the university and vote on all matters coming before the faculty. They are paid by their own groups, but the administrative expenses are met by Mr. J. D. Rockefeller, Jr. Thus no public funds go to the School of Religion.

"In addition to giving courses on the same academic basis as other schools of the university, the School of Religion has placed religion on a dignified plane before the whole university. The professors have acted as a leavening influence on the faculty. In fact, the indirect effects far outweigh the direct results of getting a small percentage of the student body in the classes.

"Although the Catholic bishop withdrew the Catholic professor in 1929, Catholics are still on the Board of Trustees and coöperate in other ways. And as one ground for the bishop's action—the requirement of sophomore standing for taking courses—has been removed, he has expressed himself as willing to provide a professor whenever the number of Catholic students wishing to take the courses seems to justify this.

"Besides the actual work of teaching, the School of Religion has served to bring Catholics, Protestants and Jews together in various coöperative undertakings. The whole religious field of the campus is discussed jointly. And while each group continues to maintain its special student organization, their work has been unified in many ways. For instance, one annual drive for funds is made through a campus chest representing all religious work."

Columbia University, being a private institution, has been able to organize the united religious work as an official and integral part of the university. The professional religious workers on the campus are nominated by Protestant, Catholic and Jewish authorities, but since 1928 have been formally appointed by the university and listed as members of its administrative staff. Close coöperation is facilitated by an executive director. Unlike the "university pastors" at tax-supported institutions, who are attached to some local church staff, the staff at Columbia devote their entire time to work on the campus. They emphasize personal counselling with students and give courses from their respective standpoints in the department of education in Teachers College, these courses being open to students in any department of the university. Their salaries are derived chiefly from alumni contributions and no gifts are solicited from the students. The expense of the headquarters is borne by the university. In view of this set-up it is not surprising to have some students and outsiders declare that the plan is bureaucratic and unfavorable to student initiative. But it should be stated that the student-controlled Association which preceded the present plan was far from satisfactory, and from the viewpoints of interfaith coöperation and of numbers of students served the present plan is generally recognized as superior.

The promising inauguration of the School of Religion at the University of Iowa led Dr. Foster soon after, in 1928, to bring about the establishment of a somewhat similar plan in Southern California, primarily in connection with the University of California at Los Angeles, under the name "The University Religious Conference." As will later appear, however, the emphasis in the work of the Conference for the time being has been necessarily confined almost entirely to extra-curricular activities.

It seems worth while to review the University Religious Conference in considerable detail for various reasons: the extension of the Conference to other tax-supported universities in the West is being contemplated; and the problems at Los Angeles are typical of those faced at some other state university centers, for instance, as to the legality of allowing a School of Religion to give courses on religion in a state university, when the state constitution prescribes that the university must be "independent of sectarian influence."[4]

The exact nature of the Conference can best be conveyed by making abstracts from its own published statements:

"The Conference is a California corporation, formed by official representatives of the Catholic, Episcopal, Jewish and Protestant church groups for work among their students at public educational institutions . . . which enables them to work together without any compromise of the faith of any one, to put the power of all behind the work of each, and to mass the forces of religion against the danger of irreligion and atheism, among the students who will be the leaders of the next generation. The University Religious Conference, therefore, has two primary purposes:

"To bring about tolerance, understanding and harmony between all religious groups at the campus.

"To secure for each student the religious training which will enable him to take his place as an educated member of the religious group to which he traditionally belongs, and to graduate with his religious knowledge on a par with the development which the college and university have given him.

"The Conference in the first unit of its building at Westwood, and in New-

---

[4] In order to multiply this type of organization, at state universities particularly, Dr. Foster and others formed, in 1932, the North American Board for the Study of Religion in Higher Education. Its activities have naturally centered in the western regions where tax-supported institutions are so prominent. Apart from fostering the University Religious Conference idea, the Board has recently pressed two specific projects. One was the conduct by the President of the Pacific Division of the Board of an illuminating Survey of Religious and Character Influences on ten state university and college campuses, which is editorially summarized in the *Christian Century* of April 4, 1934. The other was the coördination of all the universities and colleges in Oklahoma, a scheme conceived by the Chairman of its Directing Council, Bishop Francis C. Kelley (a Catholic) and its secretary, Dr. Foster. In this scheme the state university occupies a central place and extends facilities to the denominational colleges, both Protestant and Catholic, while the colleges retain administrative autonomy.

man Hall at the Los Angeles Junior College, provides partial equipment for all the agencies and groups connected with the three faiths.

"The programs of these agencies at the campus are in part coöperative, in part separate. They consist of classes in religion, forums, Bible study, international interest, social work, vocational instruction, recreational activities under religious leadership, inter-group friendships, etc., while the intensively religious expressions of worship and sectarian interpretation are carried on in the churches and synagogues."

There are eleven paid pastors and secretaries, known as "advisers," of whom four are clergymen, and seven are laymen, including five women. The chairmanship of the board of trustees has been held in rotation by a representative of each of the three faiths.

Opinions regarding the Conference, as far as the investigators were able to learn, were on the whole distinctly favorable. There was no outright hostility and even the most sceptical participants and observers felt kindly toward it. Churchmen said that their interests were adequately safeguarded and that sustained collaboration among the groups was superior to the gingerly and spasmodic coöperation that would otherwise prevail and would be likely to veil underlying competition.

The motto of the Conference is "Coöperation without Compromise," but as to the reality in practice there is some difference of judgment. A veteran Protestant minister expressed a favorable opinion:

"As long as we adhere to 'coöperation without compromise' we need not fear. Each faith and denomination can, and I hope will, bear witness and teach in accordance with its own historical beliefs and standards."

A qualified judgment was voiced by another Protestant leader:

"All are coöperating in a fine friendly spirit. The leaders are very considerate of one another. The Conference necessarily takes a negative attitude toward all coöperative religious efforts because it must keep off joint worship and doctrinal teaching."

In this connection Executive Secretary Evans called attention to the policy followed in assembling a library in the headquarters building of the Conference.

"The Faculty and Church Committee in selecting books to go into the Library believe that religion thrives in an atmosphere of friendliness and appreciation, more than in one of competition and dispute. Therefore, in the general library, controversial books are ruled out, but in the various offices of the denominational representatives, they have as many partisan and controversial books as they see fit. The late Mr. Iden, the 'Upper Room' worker among students at the University of Michigan, followed the same non-controversial policy with notable success."

A Protestant leader implied that the motto sometimes was watered down to "coöperation *with* compromise":

"The constant attempt to avoid offending men of different faith does restrain men, especially in prayer. 'Coöperation without compromise' is apt to be over-shadowed by tolerance, which is negative and leads to suppression of cherished beliefs."

The Catholic authorities have staunchly backed the Conference, and a Catholic millionaire gave $30,000 toward the $75,000 Conference Building Fund, but one of the most loyal Catholic supporters confessed to some doubts and fears in words to this effect:

"The Conference is a noble attempt at coöperation for religion and high ethical ideals, but I sometimes have deep misgivings about it. Will it tend to pull us down to the level of the Jews and some Protestants, who have thrown overboard the supernatural? If our getting together imperils what we believe deepest and truest, of what avail will it be?

"Last year, for example, it was proposed that the Conference send to all the faculty of the university a letter begging them to speak kindly of religion in their classrooms. To us Catholics that seemed preposterous and humiliating. We don't want to ask favors from any one for our faith. It stands on its merits and needs no patronage. The letter was never sent.

"To speak frankly, we are anxious for our people because of the degenerate religious atmosphere they have to breathe—partly due to Protestants who lean to humanism and deny the supernatural. But even such Protestantism is better than the paganism which prevails so widely in America. That is one reason why I favor the idea of the Conference."

If it be asked what holds the Conference together, notwithstanding such misgivings, the answer is that perhaps the strongest bond is the friendship between the representatives of the different faiths. Repeatedly, the investigator heard men of sharply contrasted religious convictions speak affectionately of one another. A rabbi exclaimed: "I love Bishop ——." Once a Catholic father smilingly remarked in an intimate interfaith committee: "Why couldn't we have corporate communion—if you'd all come back where you belong!" A rabbi, quick as a flash, replied: "How far back?" and the father joined in the laugh.

The Student Young Men's and Young Women's Christian Associations have taken less kindly to the Conference than have the church leaders. The reason given by a friendly critic of the Association was that they were "ambitious to be 'inter-confessional' and to represent the church as a whole on the campus, which is impossible from the point of view of Catholics and Jews, and unacceptable to the Protestant churches, which increasingly wish to be represented by their own university pastors."

Coöperation 325

Spokesmen for the Young Men's Christian Association, both students and older men closely in touch with it, revealed a charitable attitude toward the Conference and an unusual absence of self-perpetuating institutional ambition. Their apparently honest concern was lest the spontaneity and vitality of student initiative be stifled under the weight of ecclesiastical authority and of leadership by older adults. This will appear in the following questions and answers taken from various interviews and letters.

Q. Does it cramp the style of the Y.M. and Y.W.C.A. to be tied up to a denominational set-up like the Conference?

A. Yes, because the student leaders are so busy with denominational and united work, they haven't time for the special Y.M.C.A. program.

Q. Are the students smothered by the overhead machinery, by the fact that it has been set up by ecclesiastics, from above, not from below?

A. The students who have joined in the work are not restive or apparently repressed, but others outside are apt to be repelled. The Conference program draws most men and women of a certain type who like this set-up.

It depends on the skill of the Church representatives in stimulating student initiative. We push loyalty to the Church, but not to denominational standards or sectarianism.

The degree of church emphasis and adult domination depends largely on the national church executive's attitude. I am left entirely free and I try not to dominate but keep behind the students and use their language.

The student is admitted by all church workers to be the point of reference, but in any issue, the church authority takes precedence. Even the "Y" has to be on guard against this institutionalism, and take extra care to draw students to the front.

Financially, the Y.M.C.A. has a tough problem because it must raise funds practically in competition with the Conference and the denominational representatives. I don't see any solution. The situation is aggravated by the fact that the university authorities oppose any drive among students and faculty on the campus.

The conference has been criticized for slighting the women, but a Y.W.C.A. representative who studied the situation at first hand found points in it to praise as well as to deprecate.

"One thing that acts to prevent the kind of working together to which we in the Y.W.C.A. are accustomed is the influence of the ecclesiastical tradition of 'from the top down.' . . . It is precisely here (utilizing student initiative) that the working methods of the Conference are faulty; tradition and the staff supply the motive power, and if there is any room left student initiative can operate, which is not a plan calculated to stimulate student initiative. This, it seems to me, is the first task of the Conference, to set about *cultivating* this attitude on the part of the students, in order to make even a start toward the accomplishment of its purpose, which is to make religion vital on the campus, for if students remain content to be spoon-fed in matters of organization and program, they will partake of religion in the same fashion.

"As for the intangible values of 'harmonious coöperation' (which words are mentioned so often they have come to draw a smile from the more irreverent), it is a fact that one cannot sit at Board meetings for over a year and see the clerical and lay leaders of three faiths working together with increasing understanding and respect without feeling that sentiment sometimes reveals more real values than statistics. Perhaps one of the most beneficial influences of the Conference will be enabling more students and more church leaders to feel that they are a part of a wider group than those whose individual names they bear, a group made up of differing creeds and traditions, characterized by a common concern for the things of the spirit."

One person not officially connected with the Conference but acquainted with the situation deplored the tendency of the church representatives to hold the center of the stage, remarking that at the public gatherings of the Conference which he had attended, students were little in evidence either as listeners or as speakers. A Jewish undergraduate said:

"The Conference has a long way to go to reach and hold the mass of students. We now reach directly only forty Jewish students out of 600 Jews in the student body of 5,500. But the small group now in are rather strong and should gradually influence others in sororities and fraternities and other groups."

A neutral observer remarked: "I think the students get as much chance at expression and initiative as they are able to use."

The judicial attitude of several Association representatives is reflected in these observations by one of them:

"The Conference has not solved the problem of religious work by students for students, even though it may have lifted the repute of religion as a whole in their eyes. It requires a good deal of time to keep the machinery of good relations between the sects well oiled and it calls for so much money for the Conference and the salaried denominational workers that the student Y.M.C.A. and Y.W.C.A. find very slim pickings. But I think we ought to try the plan in good faith and see how it comes out after a few years more of operation."

The officers of the Conference are not blind to the need of making special efforts to ensure student initiative and activity. In the history of the Conference entitled "After Five Years," it is pointed out that the students go on deputations to churches, schools and other outside organizations, and that the publication of the handbook or Freshman Bible and many other phases of the campus program are handled by the Student Religious Board.

There is general agreement that the Conference has served to dignify religion on the campus. The President of the University Student Body speaking at the dedication of the Conference headquarters building declared that "now, on this campus you will find no contempt for religion. . . ." One proposed activity by means of which the Conference has from its inception hoped to enhance the standing of religion in the university is the provision of comprehensive courses in the field of religion, for which academic credit would be given, as at the University of Iowa. Some of the leaders of the Conference have therefore been disappointed over the delay in putting the plan into effect, and have been disposed to place all the blame on the university. It is true that the university authorities have not seen their way clear to approve the plan, but they claim that the law stands in the way, because Article IX of the state constitution contains these explicit words:

"The State University shall be entirely independent of all political or sectarian influence and shall be kept free therefrom in the appointment of its regents and in the administration of its affairs."

One of the University authorities commented on the article to this effect:

"You can see that we are left no choice. But we do wish to foster a strong spirit of essential religion in the university, free from dogmatism and from sectarian competition. In achieving this the Religious Conference can prove to be very effective provided it operates as from the outside and is not allowed to fasten itself on the university as such. It is ideally housed on the fringe of the campus and it has free access to both students and faculty, but it can't be given a formal status in the university."

The critics of the university attitude maintain that other educational authorities in California interpret the article quite otherwise, holding that it was not intended to prohibit non-sectarian, scholarly instruction in the field of religion, but was aimed primarily against the intrusion of sectarian influence in the administration, and secondarily against propaganda in the curriculum.

Regardless, however, of which school of constitutional lawyers is right, it is doubtful whether the Conference would be fully prepared to avail itself of the privilege of giving courses in religion, even if it were offered. The reason is, according to Protestant informants, that the Protestants would not be able to agree upon the content of certain courses to be given by their representatives. On this score the Catholics and Jews have no difficulty.

The Conference, furthermore, is a prime example of the solution of interfaith prejudices and irritations by indirection, by avoiding competition and controversy and focussing attention on coöperative effort to attain the objectives desired by all.

Thus far the discussion of the University Religious Conference has dealt only with the situation at Los Angeles, but active steps in the same direction have been taken at the University of California, in Berkeley, and a brief account of the attitudes of leaders there may be of value in itself and also for the light it throws on the situation in Los Angeles. The university authorities at Berkeley declare their readiness to proceed as soon as all the major religious representatives have formally agreed to a workable plan. As yet no such agreement has been reached, although it seems to be only a matter of time. The Protestant church representatives endorsed the plan in 1932, but the attitude of the Student Christian Association, both Men's and Women's, is one of watchful waiting. One woman graduate said:

"It would take a great demonstration of success at the U.C.L.A. to make us wish to see the Religious Conference started here. It has been imposed at Los Angeles by ecclesiastical and administrative authorities, without any student initiative. Furthermore, there is a tendency in interfaith enterprises to leave women out. This is true of the East Bay Religious Fellowship and of the North American Board for the Study of Religion in Higher Education."

The hesitation of the Catholics to endorse the Religious Conference appears to be due to scruples which have been successfully overcome at Los Angeles. They were phrased in this way by a liberal-minded Catholic:

"As long as religious bodies differ on fundamental dogma, there is no alternative but to maintain our identity and separate programs. But we can unite on some things, such as the Union Forum here, which sponsors speakers on religion acceptable to all groups in an effort to introduce a spiritual emphasis throughout the University. President Sproul and Provost Deutsch support it heartily."

One of the influential Protestant pastors made these suggestive observations:

" 'Coöperation without compromise' is a wise slogan. It will mean that all three faiths will be given due recognition. The minority groups will not be penalized. When religious courses are offered in the curriculum by the three faiths, the Roman Catholics and Jews can hold up their head as high as we Protestants can.

"Even if the united plan is adopted, some of the groups will still need their own chapels and social centers, because there are sharp differences among them regarding liquor drinking and other social customs as well as regarding religious observances. But there is a broad field for coöperation on common religious and ethical convictions.

"It would be a mistake to plunge hastily into the formal organization of the Conference. We need to feel our way. There are many things to be tested, many doubts to be overcome."

Another Protestant leader expressed the novel opinion that the Director of the Religious Conference at Berkeley should be directly accountable only to the President of the University, although he should be nominated by or entirely acceptable to the religious groups; and he should of course be as competent as the deans of the university and might himself be Dean of Religion.

The university authorities have made no formal commitment regarding the plan, but the President is known to have the matter deeply at heart and to desire that whatever may ultimately be done shall place religious instruction and activities on as high a plane as that occupied by other disciplines. So far as could be learned, the authorities do not construe the state constitution as interposing any obstacle to courses in religion which would be accorded academic credit.

Studies and Pronouncements on Social and Industrial Issues: Beginning in June, 1923, three national agencies widely representative of Protestants, Catholics and Jews have collaborated in the making of studies and the issuance of pronouncements regarding current social issues, especially those concerning relations between employers and employees, and unemployment. These agencies have been the Federal Council of the Churches of Christ in America, through its Department of Research and Education, the Rev. F. Ernest Johnson, director, and its Social Service Department, Industrial Division, the Rev. James Myers, secretary, the Social Action Department of the National Catholic Welfare Conference, the Rev. John A. Ryan, director, and the Social Justice Commission of the Central Conference of American Rabbis, of which Rabbi Edward L. Israel and Rabbi Sidney E. Goldstein have been chairmen.

The joint studies have been as follows:

The Enginemen's Strike on the Western Maryland Railroad. A report, issued February, 1927.

Industrial Relations in a Hosiery Mill. A study of industrial relations at the Real Silk Hosiery Mills, Inc., Indianapolis, Indiana, and of the relations between employers and the American Federation of Full Fashioned Hosiery Workers in the Philadelphia District, issued in *Information Service*, May 19, 1928. The National Catholic Welfare Council did not collaborate on this study.

The Centralia Case. A joint report on the Armistice Day Tragedy at Centralia, Washington, November 11, 1919, issued October, 1930.

Another important study made only by the Federal Council, but containing a joint statement denouncing the 12-hour day was: The Twelve Hour Day in the Steel Industry: Its social consequences and the practicability of its abolition. Research Bulletin No. 3, issued June, 1923.

The major official pronouncements and other projects intended to voice the ethical judgment of the three constituencies and to educate the public regarding social justice have been as follows:

A public statement with reference to conditions in the textile industry, on December 28, 1929.

A national conference jointly sponsored by the three bodies on the subject of Permanent Preventives of Unemployment, held in Washington, D. C., January 26-27, 1931.

A joint public statement on unemployment in January, 1932.

In June, 1932, when unemployment conditions were very grave and the federal government was reluctant to take any action on them, Rabbi Edward L. Israel, Father R. A. McGowan, and the Rev. James Myers, together with representatives of the American Federation of Labor, and of a national farmers' organization, spoke at Washington before a committee of Senators and Congressmen, and broadcasted over a national radio hook-up demanding adequate attention by the federal as well as local governments to the critical unemployment situation at that time. This was toward the close of Congress, which subsequently voted the first funds for federal aid.

On July 13, 1933, shortly after the National Industrial Recovery Act was passed, Dr. John A. Ryan, Rabbi Edward L. Israel and Rev. James Myers issued a statement on the social implications of the N.R.A.

On December 18, 1933, Rabbi Sidney E. Goldstein, newly appointed chairman of the Social Justice Commission of the Central Conference of American Rabbis, Father R. A. McGowan and the Rev. James Myers appeared before the Committee on Ways and Means of the House of Representatives which was considering methods of taxation, and made statements on the position of their respective bodies concerning the necessity of a more equitable distribution of wealth and income.

Another form of coöperation is the printing of the Federal Council's Labor Sunday Message in some Catholic and Jewish papers, and the printing of similar Jewish and Catholic statements in the Federal Council's *Information Service* and some Protestant papers.

It is naturally impossible to determine the precise effects of these joint activities, but it is common knowledge that they receive prominent notice in the press of the country and supply information and stimulus to a large number of public speakers and writers. The widespread and effective popular demand for the abolition of the twelve-hour day in the steel industry was generally attributed in considerable measure to the research study and pronouncement on that issue.

It should be noted that coöperation has been limited to ethical issues, and that matters of religious doctrine and ecclesiastical authority have been avoided. Whatever difficulties in reaching an accord have been met by the collaborators have arisen not so much over differences in ethical conviction as over harmonizing the particular categories and terminology of the distinctive Catholic system of industrial ethics with those held by the Protestants and liberal Jews. One of the collaborating officials thus summarizes the matter:

"Such difficulties as we have had are of a sort calling for closer rather than less close contacts, and for intenser coöperation in determining points of view and perfecting methods of work."

This close collaboration by these three agencies, speaking for tens of thousands of churches and synagogues, is considered by thoughtful men to have done much toward educating the conscience of the nation and toward demonstrating the courageous concern of all the creeds with justice and the good life for all men. It has helped to disprove the charge that the religious bodies are class organizations, the tools and defenders of special interests. There is little doubt that the positions taken in the pronouncements of the three agencies are more advanced than those held by many of their constituents, but the fact remains that their actions have not been repudiated by the church judicatories. Furthermore, the impartial array of facts and of opinions undergirding most of the pronouncements has given the critics no ground to stand on, except the old assertion that the church should preach "religion" and let economics alone.

The National Conference of Jews and Christians: The National Conference of Jews and Christians is the only organization of a national character whose sole purpose is the promotion of "justice, amity and understanding among Protestants, Catholics and Jews in America." It is composed of adherents of the three faiths acting as individuals and its co-chairmen are a Protestant, a Catholic and a Jewish layman. One of these co-chairmen, Mr. Roger W. Straus, some years ago recounted the origin and nature of the Conference in these words:

"The history of the formation of the National Conference of Jews and Christians is interesting. For some time following the World War a number of thoughtful clergymen associated with the Federal Council of the Churches of Christ in America felt that the after-war phenomena of race and religious prejudice was contrary to the tenets of Christianity and to the spirit of America. In 1924, these gentlemen organized the Good-will Committee of their organization to combat this spirit of intolerance, and to take such positive action as they could to bring about better understanding amongst the various cultural groups throughout the country. This committee naturally consulted from time to time with various individuals who they felt could give them advice and assistance in carrying on their program.

"These discussions became more and more frequent, and it was suggested that a more formal organization might be able to carry on the work more effectively, and so the National Conference of Jews and Christians was brought into being in 1927. The leadership in this movement has come, as it should come, from the Protestant group, who are in the majority in this country, and others have accepted their invitation to join in the effort to bring about better understanding and goodwill.

"It was decided that the National Conference should have three co-chairmen, one representing the Protestant group, one the Catholic, and one the Jewish group. I, as a Jew, am glad to be serving with the Hon. Newton D. Baker and Prof. Carlton J. H. Hayes, as co-chairmen. We number amongst our membership Christian clergymen, rabbis, and lay leaders, all actively interested in furthering these ideals.

"The National Conference has evolved an informal procedure whereby Jews, Catholics and Protestants can talk things over. As members of three culture-groups, we can talk over the 'rubs' between us, as Professor Kilpatrick put it in a meeting of the leaders. 'What are the rubs? Why are the rubs? How do they rub?'

"More than that, in conference we can discover how many things we all are interested in achieving as American citizens. Christians and Jews alike want justice to characterize American community life. There are many tasks in that area on which we can work together. As Americans also, we want what has come to be called 'the good life' to continue in its development, and the Jew and the Christian each can share its contribution in science, the arts, and in philosophy, for the progress of civilization."

Toward the realization of its purpose the Conference has carried on a varied and vigorous program of activities, among which these have been prominent: parleys and seminars, an information bulletin, news releases, addresses over the radio and in local centers, pronouncements on current events and issues, fellowship dinners, discussion groups and preparation of materials for them, the formation of local interfaith round-table groups. It derives moral and financial support from a membership of several thousand individuals plus a National Laymen's Advisory Council numbering over one thousand members and from a smaller but growing Women's Advisory Council. The central office is in regular communication with persons or groups in 200 cities and towns.

The National Conference program for the year 1934 includes these elements, among others:

1. *Research.* A study of the relationships of Protestants, Catholics and Jews in American history. This study describes, (a) prejudices and social strains imported from Europe in Colonial times; (b) the development of federal and state constitutional parity among Protestants, Catholics and Jews as American citizens; (c) early 19th Century Nativist riots against Catholics; (d) three organized movements, nominally Protestant, against Catholics, the last, also against Jews—Know Nothingism (1850's), American Protective Association (1890's), and the Ku Klux Klan (1920's); (e) generalizations, particularly in anthropology, social psychology and sociology, re intergroup relations, drawn from these data; (f) suggestions for educational approaches to the problems raised by cultural pluralism. This study was made by Dr. Everett R. Clinchy and was published in November, 1934, by the John Day Company under the title, *All in the Name of God.*

2. *The creation of materials* intended to cultivate appreciation of the various groups, racial and religious, comprising the United States: (a) for high schools, supervised by a committee for service in education in human relations, associated with a number of faculties of education in American universities; (b) materials for Y.M.C.A.'s, K. of C.'s, Y.M.H.A.'s and Y.W.H.A.'s, and church and synagogue discussion groups, with assistance of the personnel of the former Inquiry, and its files; (c) for adult community groups, a discussion outline by Dr. B. Y. Landis, making the Silcox Fisher study, *Catholics, Jews and Protestants,* available for local consumption.

3. *Guidance and assistance for local community groups.* Programs in school, church, and civic educational and coöperative ventures, such as, (a) a minister, priest and rabbi appearing before high school assemblies to speak on American Tradition of Religious Freedom; (b) subject matter instruction on contributions of each group to the arts and sciences of our common civilization; (c) local radio broadcasts; (d) local "clearing-house" programs for the communication of aims, beliefs, aspirations, and knowledge, leading to common understanding so necessary for *community* life in a democracy; (e) ethically significant common undertakings *as citizens.*

To the extent that funds are available the National Conference will plan and execute (with local leadership) demonstrations of education and coöperation in intergroup relations.

4. *College and city seminars* in additional centers.

5. *A News Service,* which is now reaching 600 editors of religious and secular press, each week, with items and articles, questions and answers, re Protestant, Catholic, and Jewish news and current information.

The anti-Semitic events in Germany during 1933 occasioned extraordinary activity by the leaders of the Conference. They issued pronouncements to influence public opinion, held conferences with government officials, and most spectacular of all, during November and December of 1933 they sent three speakers, a Catholic priest, a Jewish rabbi, and a Protestant minister as a team to speak in thirty-eight western and southern cities. The dramatic quality of this pilgrimage everywhere caught popular attention and won extraordinary newspaper space and editorial approval. Besides addressing some 54,000 people at 129 meetings, this triumvirate conveyed their message to a vast audience through twenty-one radio broadcasts. In many of their platform meetings they found the trialogue, or three-cornered conversation, an effective method. A by-product of the tour was the formation of thirty-five additional local committees to foster interfaith fellowship and education. While this pilgrimage was being planned some doubts were expressed as to its wisdom, particularly lest an over-emphasis on the persecutions suffered by the Jews should cause not sympathy but a feeling that Jews are "always asking special treatment and looking out for number one." In order to check on these doubts trustworthy observers in several cities visited by the team were asked by the writer to give their confidential judgment on the results of the addresses. The replies received were almost entirely commendatory.

The Conference has by no means been free from criticisms, but its leaders have faced them in a teachable spirit. It will be illuminating to state a number of criticisms gleaned by the investigators and the rejoinders to them.

Attention at seminars and parleys is sometimes focussed on religious prejudices, their cause and cure. Some critics hold that this is bad psychology, like invalids rehearsing their ailments; that it only aggravates the trouble; that the Conference would be on firmer ground if it placed more emphasis on getting adherents of the three faiths to work together on worthy projects. As one man put it:

"An ounce of coöperation will cure more prejudice than a pound of psychoanalysis. When we analyze our attitudes toward people of other faiths, we think of them in the mass as 'they'; when we work with them shoulder to shoulder on something for the common good we think of them as partners, as a part of the 'we' group, and without our knowing it our suspicions and prejudices are dissolved."

A leader connected with an active interfaith organization in California has written:

"Our entire group are more firmly convinced than ever that public discussions of differences between groups are undesirable. We are finding that the other process of ignoring differences is increasingly successful. Of course, we recognize that the discussion of things which the groups may do together, is altogether desirable."

To these strictures the rejoinder is: It is not an "either-or," but a "both-and." Working together and thus rising above suspicion based on differences into the zone of respect based on a common altruism is undeniably a good way to replace an offensive stereotype of Jews in general or Christians *en masse* by a concrete and likeable individual who, on second thought, happens to be a Jew or a Christian. The Conference leaders recognize the soundness of this principle, but also maintain that if a man can be led to look squarely at the stereotype-caricature in his mind and discuss it until he recognizes its absurdity, he will laugh it away once and for all.

Another criticism is that so long as Protestants, Catholics and Jews differ so sharply on some of their deepest religious beliefs, it really does little good to keep harping on the few important beliefs they hold in common. As one Protestant lay leader observed:

· "I respect the Catholics and the Jews, but I'm too busy to attend pretentious meetings to tell them so *ad nauseam*. I would enjoy worshipping with them, but most of them would decline to worship with me. Since no amount of palaver will lessen our religious differences, hadn't we better quit discussing them and confine our attention to coöperation in social work or civic affairs?"

On this point an officer of the Conference has said:

"We would be fooling ourselves if we did not state the fact that Protestants and Catholics and Jews each hold fundamentally opposing philosophies which, though they meet at many points, contain certain elements that are distinct and which cannot be fused. We must accept the facts of the existence of such incompatibilities and stop fretting about them. We shall never think exactly alike. We must find a meeting place on another plane than that on which we do our theological thinking. We must develop that high quality of respect for unlikeness which is the work of true cultivation of spirit. Cultural pluralism in America is not to be deprecated but welcomed."

In other words, the Conference does not directly seek to abolish religious differences, but to overcome the mutual prejudice and fear that spring from ignorance, misinformation and clannishness. It holds no brief for eclecticism, hybridism or the weakening of church loyalties, but believes it is vital to the solidarity and peace of the American people to stress the fact that on at least three pivotal matters the three faiths stand absolutely together: the principle of religious liberty, belief in a loving, righteous God, and acceptance of the ethics of Amos, Hosea and the Golden Rule. Points of disagreement and difference are constantly played up by bigots bent on recruiting "Silver Shirts" and other equivalents of the Ku Klux Klan. The Conference believes that the best way to prevent outbursts of violent fanaticism is to knit men and women of all faiths together in friendship and in devotion to the fundamentals on which they are agreed. The Conference holds no brief for religious and cultural uniformity but urges understanding and appreciation. A cogent expression of this viewpoint is at hand in the statement of purpose issued in March of 1934 by the Inter-Faith Good-Will Committee of Rochester:

"The Catholic, Protestant and Jewish communions in this city, through official representatives, have organized a permanent body known as the Inter-Faith Good-Will Committee to express their sense of comradeship and to consider such issues as may arise which are of common concern. The confusion of the time offers to these communions an opportunity to achieve a deeper understanding and appreciation of one another. It also challenges them to emphasize in their moral and religious outlook the great common principles they believe to be the basis of our civilization.

"The members of these communions, for instance, share the belief in the spiritual nature of man and in man's supreme responsibility to God. They are also united in the desire to maintain the rights of men, civil and religious, which are the foundation pillars of the Republic, and which are guaranteed to our citizens by the Constitution. The purpose of the Inter-Faith Good-Will Committee will be to express this belief and desire, shared alike by Protestants, Catholics and Jews, and to engage in such activities as will remove prejudice and bigotry and make for an increasing fellowship in the service of the common good."

Among the minor criticisms of the Conference heard in several cities was the complaint that in forums and seminars the Catholics and Jews were apt to place all the blame for interfaith friction on the Protestants. As one eastern business man put it:

"I get weary of going to hear us Protestants made 'the goat.' We are so anxious to make amends to the 'minority faiths' for what some Protestants have said or done that we refrain from referring to the bigoted or sectarian things Catholics or Jews are doing. We are too humble. We take the punishment lying down."

A western Protestant minister who felt the Conference was "toadying to the Jews" added remarks to this effect:

"The Conference publishes articles that dwell on Protestant offenses, but no Catholic or Jewish offenses are mentioned. If the rabbis would only preach the great messages of the prophets they could make a notable contribution to the spiritual life of their own people and all of us, but instead they harp on persecution and prejudice and Zionism. This makes a lot of Protestants sore. It's no wonder some of us resent being kicked this way and then urged to coöperate."

Perhaps the most pertinent rejoinder to this type of criticism is made in the following extracts from the *Information Bulletin* of the Conference for October, 1929, and for June-July, 1933:

"Society is divided into cultural groups, each with peculiar values and attitudes. Each group fortifies its own beliefs and practices, and commonly constructs unfortunate mental images of differing people. Many Christians picture Jews *en masse* as inferior immigrants from Eastern Europe. Many Catholics fail to comprehend the behavior of Protestants. The American Catholic still seems 'foreign' to most Protestants. Jews often read-in offensive interpretations which Christians never intended in their actions or sayings. The National Conference is experimenting in a variety of ways with the round-table method when cultural groups meet face to face. On these occasions frankness is encouraged, so that all shall hear what otherwise might be said behind their backs; fairness is required, that facts may lead one to admit his own wrongs as quickly as he states injustices done against him; humor is essential, not only that one may see a joke even if on himself, but also that unpalatable truths may be stated in good-humored friendliness.

"The National Conference, in accordance with the principles which it has often proclaimed, stands committed to the only permanently effective method of dealing with such situations as have now arisen (in Germany), that of joint study. We are primarily concerned with causes. The National Conference has long departed from a merely sentimental re-statement of the need for fellowship and is bending its efforts to develop methods of making that fellowship more intimate and real in the day-by-day contacts of practical life. Concerned as it is with conspicuous and obvious instances of injustice and discrimination, it seeks to deal also with the less dramatic misunderstandings and maladjustments in everyday life of which such conspicuous outbreakings are the flower and fruit, and to reinterpret these in terms of the theory of religious liberty and tolerance which is fundamental to the whole structure of American life."

In the judgment of the investigators, the Conference has been marked by capable leadership, both lay and professional and by resourcefulness in program. In its educational technique it has used both the direct and the indirect methods. Such coöperative enterprises, for example, as the pilgrimage of priest, rabbi and minister illustrate the indirect method. The seminars where the discussions are focussed on sources of prejudice and suspicion illustrate the direct method. In these seminars, however, the Conference has resolutely steered clear of basic theological differences. A similar avoidance, indeed, characterizes all the interfaith organizations except possibly the Religious Education Association, probably for the reason pointed out earlier, that it seems futile to attempt to reconcile competing absolutes. It may be, however, that in its seminars the Conference, instead of assembling numbers of believers in the three faiths who keep silent about their conflicting absolutes, should persuade smaller groups to engage in a frank interchange of their respective religious concepts and experiences. The chief difficulty in this matter might be to overcome the reluctance of Catholics and of conservative Protestants and Jews.

It would also be well for the Conference to remove ground for the charge that it is too exclusively concerned with the grievances and the rights of the minority faiths, on the one hand, and on the other, with the offenses of the Protestant majority. The Conference deserves commendation for steering a middle course amidst the partisanship aroused in the United States by the Hitler persecutions and for turning it to account in a nationwide campaign for amity and religious liberty.

LOCAL COÖPERATION

The manifold forms of local coöperation among adherents of the three faiths will be passed in review, with little attempt at evaluation, the chief purposes being to indicate their ingenious variety and to provide a reservoir of suggestions for local program-builders. The various activities fall roughly into ten categories.

SOCIAL WORK

The most common and aggressive coöperation occurs in the field of social work, in connection especially with the Community Chest and the Council of Social Agencies or similar bodies. Since these have been fully dealt with in Chapter **IV** no further mention is called for, except to state that in the judgment of the investigators, this type of coöperation forms the strongest evidence that can be cited to support the advocates of mitigating religious prejudice and schism by indirection.

By means of Good-Will Dinners the churches have taken the lead in fostering acquaintance and friendship among men and women of the three faiths.

The Student Christian Associations on many campuses, the International Houses at Philadelphia, New York, Chicago and Berkeley, the Church Federations and other agencies bring students of various faiths and races into friendly contact.

In Philadelphia a group of three rabbis and three ministers, with their wives, for several years made a point of attending the theater together. In this city also there flourished until recently a fraternal group called the Forty Club, composed of rabbis and Protestant ministers. They agreed that at their meetings every one should be addressed as "rabbi" although only one-third of them were Jews.

The interchange of pulpits between Reform rabbis and Protestant ministers is practiced in many cities. The investigators were told in Cleveland, San Francisco, Toronto, Los Angeles, and elsewhere of liberal rabbis who were repeatedly invited to Christian pulpits. The canons of the Catholic Church forbid the opening of its pulpits to non-Catholics.

Inquiries in several places failed to discover any rabbi who had specifically asked a Christian minister to expound Christianity to his people, whereas several cases were discovered of ministers who had asked rabbis to expound Judaism to their congregations and young people's societies. By way of explanation, it was said that while this would be welcomed by some rabbis, it was too soon to expect people who inherited an ancestral tradition of Christian persecution to wish to know any more than they must about Christianity.

Instances of a synagogue or church auditorium being offered to a congregation of the other faith when it had lost its own place of worship have occurred in several cities, but the most striking series of such courtesies in any one city was found in Buffalo: both St. Paul's Protestant Episcopal Church and the Delaware Avenue Methodist Episcopal Church at different times availed themselves of the hospitality of Temple Beth-Zion, and the Temple congregation, in turn, worshipped in Central Presbyterian Church while their own building was being erected.

At Plainfield, N. J., St. Mary's (Catholic) Church offered the use of a hall to a Protestant church when its building was burned. In New York City a Catholic pastor held Mass in a neighboring Jewish hospital while his church was being erected.

In Newark, New Jersey, a community memorial service, in which several Protestant clergymen participated, was held a few years ago, in the Old First Presbyterian Church, in honor of a Jewish philanthropist and merchant, Felix Fuld.

In the Kenwood-Hyde Park Council of Churches, in Chicago, certain synagogues are included.

Good Friday Observance Committees, consisting of Catholics and Protestants, are found in Toledo, where the idea originated eleven years ago, and in Philadelphia. The working of the plan in Philadelphia is clearly set forth in a letter received from the chairman of the Committee, Mr. John J. McNally, a Catholic:

"For some years the thought of promoting the more reverent observance of Good Friday has been expressed within the ranks of the Knights of Columbus and efforts made occasionally to do so with rather limited success. About six years ago an invitation was extended to prominent clergy and laymen of different Christian denominations to join in the effort. Thanks to the splendid support of Dr. Palmquist, secretary of the Federation of Churches, a very successful meeting was held at one of the central hotels, and the Citizens' Committee was born.

"Active work is started about two months prior to Good Friday and usually two meetings of the entire Committee are called. All meetings are held on neutral ground, so to speak, with luncheon at one of the hotels, and we confine ourselves strictly to the matter of Good Friday observance. As to difficulties, I cannot recall having encountered any."

EDUCATIONAL MEASURES

Efforts to displace ignorance and prejudice by knowledge and appreciation of one another's faith take diverse forms. Perhaps the commonest is the historical and interpretative lecture given at schools, religious societies, and conferences or over the radio.

At Detroit, in March, 1934, more than 18,000 students in sixteen high schools were addressed by Catholic priests, Protestant ministers and Jewish rabbis, all of whom stressed the principle of religious liberty.

Theological seminaries and Young Men's and Women's Christian Associations arrange courses for the study of various faiths in which Catholic and Jewish speakers appear.

Small groups of ministers and rabbis meet regularly to discuss religious and philosophical questions, using such names as the Cosmic Club, in Cincinnati, the Alethian Society, in Cleveland, and no name at all, in Toronto.

Two hundred and fifty Protestant and Roman Catholic clergymen were guests of Euclid Avenue Temple when Jewish scholars gave historical addresses on the Rise of Judaism, the Rise of the Sermon in the Synagogue and the Jews in this Changing Civilization.

Forums and seminar discussions are another variant of the educational method. In a Baltimore Disciples church this took the form of an Institute of Human Relations. In Cincinnati an annual gathering known as the Jewish Institute is participated in by many Protestant ministers. At various universities seminars on relations among the religious groups are held. At the latest seminar held at the University of California the attendance aggregated some 3,000 persons. The seminar plan took root in Canada, at Toronto, in April, 1934, when the Lieutenant Governor of Ontario made an impressive address and the press carried extensive reports of the proceedings.

In the important field of week-day religious education there are obvious obstacles to interfaith coöperation on account of the divergent theories as to the public-school system already noted in Chapter V. Nevertheless, in New York City there has been for some years excellent coöperation of Catholics, Jews and Protestants in fostering week-day religious instruction.

MASS MEETINGS ON RELIGIOUS LIBERTY

The plight of both Jews and Christians of late in Germany has given rise to numberless meetings and messages of protest by adherents of all the faiths. At the beginning of the Hitler Semitic persecution there was danger lest Jewish leaders in America hurt their case by excessive clamor, but Christians soon stepped to the front and joined with the Jews in organizing meetings where religious liberty for all creeds as well as for the Jews was demanded.

CULTURAL APPRECIATION

Two unique devices for enhancing the general appreciation of diverse cultures have been successfully employed in Cleveland. The one is the Theater of the Nations, sponsored by *The Plain Dealer*, where the Yiddish Culture Society and many other cultural groups have for several years presented dramatic offerings. The other is the Cultural Gardens at Rockefeller Park, in which the Jews, the Germans, and several other groups have erected statues and planted trees and flowering shrubs reminiscent of their history and literature.

At New York University, in 1932, the Interfaith Council presented, in three sessions, music distinctive of the three faiths, and a week before the Christmas of 1933 the Council held a musical festival in which the Feast of the Candles, a Jewish celebration, was followed by the singing of Christmas carols.

The Romance of a People, the grand pageant presented at Chicago, New York, Detroit and elsewhere, by a large Jewish cast and chorus, has already been mentioned in another connection. It appears to have made a powerful impression on Jewish and Christian spectators alike and occasioned many sympathetic references in the press to the Jewish people and their culture.

SOCIAL ETHICS

Men of all the faiths have often made common cause against forces that threaten the moral health of the body politic, but under the stimulus of the various national agencies already described, such joint efforts seem to have taken on new vigor.

At Plainfield, New Jersey, early in 1933, a representative citizens' committee summoned Catholics, Jews and Protestants to spend two days in considering how to apply the "social ideals" to which they have subscribed to the moral disintegration now facing individuals and the community. The conference was centered around the nation-wide data presented in "Social Trends," the report of the commission of social scientists appointed by President Hoover, but it also considered local conditions and the obligation of religious people to better them. One of the speakers, Rabbi Philip Bernstein of Rochester said: "The American churches and synagogues will die as in Russia if they, in the presence of social maladjustment, turn their backs like Peter who 'sat by the fire, warming himself.'"

In Washington, the Monday Evening Club, with a three-faith membership of nearly 400, discusses local social problems and makes its influence felt in official quarters.

Joint attacks have been made in New York against obscene literature and theatrical performances. The initiative was taken by the Catholics, but they have been supported by the United Synagogue of America and the Greater New York Federation of Churches. At the instigation of these bodies the Commissioner of Police took action against certain publications and performances. At Philadelphia, a few years ago, Catholic and Protestant leaders coöperated in suppressing salacious literature, but for some reason the Jews declined to coöperate. The local press opposed the movement. In other centers representatives of the three faiths have attempted to secure cleaner motion pictures. It is often charged that most of the cinema producers are Jews, and that the quality of the pictures they sponsor damages the reputation of all Jews. When, however, a local group, representing the three faiths, investigated this matter at Hollywood, they discovered that Gentile producers were as prominent as Jews, some of whom have been second to none in standing for high moral standards.

In May of 1934 the bishops of the Roman Catholic Church in the United States inaugurated a movement to boycott salacious motion pictures, organized under the name, the Legion of Decency. By the latter part of June it was said by Archbishop John T. McNicholas of Cincinnati, the chairman of the committee in charge, that more than one million persons had taken the pledge. It is estimated that one-third of this number were enrolled in the Archdioceses of Cincinnati and Philadelphia alone. The pledge reads as follows:

"I wish to join the Legion of Decency, which condemns vile and unwholesome moving pictures. I unite with all who protest against them as a grave menace to youth, to home life, to country and to religion. I condemn absolutely those salacious motion pictures which, with other degrading agencies, are corrupting public morals and promoting a sex mania in our land. I shall do all that I can to arouse public opinion against the portrayal of vice as a normal condition of affairs, and against depicting criminals of any class as heroes and heroines, presenting their filthy philosophy of life as something acceptable to decent men and women. I unite with all who condemn the display of suggestive advertisements on billboards, at theater entrances and the favorable notices given to immoral motion pictures.

"Considering these evils, I hereby promise to remain away from all motion pictures except those which do not offend decency and Christian morality. I promise further to secure as many members as possible for the Legion of Decency.

"I make this protest in a spirit of self-respect, and with the conviction that the American public does not demand filthy pictures, but clean entertainment and educational features."

This crusade of the Catholic hierarchy was promptly endorsed by the executive committee of the Federal Council of the Churches of Christ in America and also by leading Jewish rabbis. In the past Protestants have almost invariably taken the initiative in enlisting the three faiths behind social reforms, but the fact that the Catholics led off in this instance did not appear to diminish the cordiality with which the Federal Council followed suit. If the moral control exercised by the Catholic clergy over their people is as strong as is generally believed, the Legion of Decency may form. a spearhead for one of the most influential coöperative efforts ever undertaken by the religious forces.

CIVIC INTEREST

A house-to-house religious census of San Francisco was made in February, 1934, by men and women in every walk of life and of the three faiths. The information gathered was used in an effort to revive the loyalty of indifferent and unattached adherents.

When a two-day conference on Childhood and Youth was held at Buffalo in 1933, papers were read not only by officials of the municipal departments of education and police, but also by lay and clerical leaders of the three faiths, especial attention being given to the relation of the church and religious education to public education.

Thanksgiving Day services in which Jews and Protestants unite are held in many communities, but Catholics almost invariably decline to participate if the program includes public prayer.

An Armistice Day celebration in which the three faiths coöperated was held in Chicago for ten years beginning in 1918, but in 1928 the Catholics withdrew, ecclesiastically speaking, although a Catholic layman is always on the program. No official explanation was given, but it was surmised that the reason might be either the change of the meeting place from a public auditorium to the Methodist Temple, to save expense, or the resentment caused by the attacks on Al Smith as a Catholic aspirant to the presidency.

On Memorial Day, at Cincinnati, the graves of the Heroes of Peace are publicly decorated, care being taken to recognize all who have sacrificed their lives for others in times of peace, regardless of their religious affiliation.

Early in 1925 the Chicago (Protestant) Church Federation proposed to the City Council that sessions of the Council be opened with prayer offered in turn by Roman Catholic, Jewish and Protestant clergymen. The Council promptly adopted the proposal and ever since then Protestant and Jewish clergymen have officiated. The Catholic authorities have declined to respond to repeated invitations, even though some of their own laymen have interceded with them. Cardinal Mundelein has made no official statement, but it is understood that his opposition rests on three points: formal ministration outside a consecrated place; performing such a service in a mixed crowd assembled for other purposes; mixing religion in politics. The persons to officiate are selected by the secretary of the Church Federation, in collaboration with the Episcopal bishop and the President of the Rabbinical Association.

Brotherhood Day was inaugurated in 1934 by the National Conference of Jews and Christians in order to dramatize the two transcendent facts that unify America's heterogeneous population—a common citizenship and a common Heavenly Father. The idea was first suggested by a Catholic priest, but it was at once eagerly endorsed by spokesmen of many Christian bodies and vigorous plans for its initial observance on Sunday, April 29, 1934, were made throughout the country. The dominant purposes of the day were stated by the executives of the National Conference in these words:

"Emphasis should be placed on human relations and united work as citizens, not on religious systems; Brotherhood Day does not deal with doctrinal differences, it does not promote worship in common, and it does not seek to water down anyone's religious convictions.

"A disillusioned and a weary world is listening to the seductive promises of tyrants and mobocrats who are openly contemptuous of democracy and religion.

"America is not free from this danger. There are forces within it that, in the fair names of patriotism and Christianity, are playing herd against herd. They are using the rich differences in the human make-up of this country as entering wedges for the poisonous shafts of race and religious prejudice. Organized religion of every creed must scotch this danger by holding fast to its fundamental doctrine, the Fatherhood of God, and its inevitable corollary, the brotherhood of man. Organized religion must not be content with merely defending the principles which it has long maintained. It must summon the best energies of America to face the major tasks of social reconstruction—the elimination of poverty, the clearing of our slums, the promotion of peace, the curbing of criminality, and the cleansing of our theatres, our movies and our press. Jew, Catholic and Protestant must forget their minor differences in the face of this challenge which threatens all religion and civilization. In the fellowship of good works, they must build the Great Society."

Early in April the National Conference prepared a card, to be distributed and signed at meetings held on the Day, which bore the following statement:

A Declaration of Brotherhood

God being my Father and all men being my brothers, I make this declaration:

1. I intend to do unto others, of whatever race or creed, as I would have them do to me.
2. It is my purpose to respect the rights of human beings, and to judge each fellow-man on his individual merits alone.
3. I will oppose every organized effort to evoke fear or hatred of any religious or racial group.

FEDERATION OF YOUTH SOCIETIES

The young people's groups in Protestant churches and Jewish synagogues in Baltimore are bound together in the Federation of Church and Synagogue Youth. Begun in April, 1931, it now unites two Jewish and fifteen Protestant groups. Overtures have been made to enlist a group from a Roman Catholic college. The presidency of the Federation has been held alternately by a Christian and a Jew. So far as the officers in 1933 were aware, there was no friction or dissatisfaction in the Federation. The Jewish president thus summarized the program:

"In addition to holding occasional forums on vital questions efforts are made through the year to promote intervisitation among the various units and to hold religious services in which the points held in common by Jews and Christians are stressed. It is hoped that in time it will be possible to help the Christians understand and appreciate the distinctive teachings and ceremonies of Judaism and also to have the Jews understand and appreciate Christianity more fully."

LOCAL FELLOWSHIPS AND COUNCILS

The formation of local fellowships has from the beginning been promoted by the National Conference of Jews and Christians, and today there are scores of them across the country. Their purpose is to realize in their own communities the objectives of the National Conference. A concrete idea of their activities may be gained from the program of the East Bay (Oakland-Berkeley) Fellowship for 1934: A series of addresses by goodwill teams at high-school assemblies, service clubs and women's clubs; a mass meeting at the University of California with addresses on Religion and the Social Order; promotion of discussions in young people's religious societies; broadcasting on a local station; Fellowship luncheons to take counsel on program and on specific cases of religious intolerance or discrimination; readiness to supply arbitrators in case of local industrial conflicts.

In several universities there have sprung up councils dedicated to purposes similar to those of the local fellowships. In the Washington Square departments of New York University the Interfaith Council is composed of an equal number of representatives from each of the three religious groups. It presents a united front to the university by means of three or four impressive events each year, such as music festivals to present the music of the three communions, and seminars to consider and dispel prejudice and misunderstanding regarding the respective faiths.

At another metropolitan university, originally Protestant but now nonsectarian, a Pan-Religious Council was formed in 1932, with the three faiths equally represented. During the first year it sponsored a successful program, two of whose events were a convocation addressed by a religious leader of national repute and a drive on behalf of the milk fund of the University Medical Center toward which nearly every student contributed. The Council had just entered on a promising second year when the Catholic Cardinal dealt it a body blow by forbidding the participation of the Catholic students and professors.

GROWTH OF TOLERANCE AND COÖPERATION

Today the persons of all three faiths who care particularly about interfaith coöperation probably constitute only a small minority, but a quarter of a century ago, when organized interfaith coöperation on a national scale was begun, the numbers interested were very much smaller. Growth was to have been expected in view of the general increase of religious tolerance, but it has apparently been stimulated by the recurrent bursts of religious intolerance, such as the Ku Klux Klan and the Nazi agitation in America. There may be a law of social dynamics by which any organized religious intolerance will by counteraction give impetus to the forces of tolerance.

Much of the vigor of the various movements for interfaith coöperation has been due to a few able and courageous leaders. It would be invidious to attempt to name the honor roll, but it would include men and women of all three faiths.[5] Honesty, however, compels mention of the relative failure of most of these movements, as compared with other contemporary social movements, to enlist the energies of either women or youth.

COMPARATIVE APPEAL OF MOTHER CHURCH AND INTERFAITH ORGANIZATIONS

Even after reviewing the growth and activities of the interfaith organizations as set forth in these pages, it would not be surprising if the average reader, of whatever faith, should say that the whole story left him cold. For one thing, the story has been told in general terms, lacking in dramatic or emotional appeal; but the deeper reason may be that interfaith organizations, after all, are like cousins once removed. They do not arouse the warm affection that a man feels for mother church. One of the sources of that affection is the complex of emotions and associations connected with corporate worship, but participants in interfaith enterprises are deprived of that source because they cannot worship together. Is there, then, no substitute for joint worship? Yes, in part, at least, it is to be found in the formation of personal friendships and the accumulation of precious memories with men of the other faiths by means of engaging with them in enterprises for the common good. Friendships based on planning, striving and sacrificing together can transcend creedal and cultural barriers.

BARRIERS TO COÖPERATION IN EACH FAITH

Each of the three faiths presents some barriers to interfaith coöperation which are hard to scale. In addition to the theological absolutes tenaciously held by all three, there are certain barriers peculiar to each. Many Christians resent what seem to them the hyper-sensitiveness and self-assertiveness of the Jews, and they feel that friendly and coöperative relations between Jews and Christians are retarded by the Jewish insistence on communal integrity. Catholics and Jews are offended by the tendency of certain Protestant leaders to set themselves up as censors of public morality, and to assume that the standards evolved by Protestantism should be accepted without question by the whole nation. For example, the zeal of Methodists,

---

[5] The *American Hebrew Medal* is bestowed annually, in honor of the nine founders of the publication, "on that American man or woman who during the year has achieved most in the promotion of better understanding between Christian and Jew in our country." The medal was first presented on November 21, 1930, to the Honorable Newton D. Baker. Subsequent recipients have been Archbishop Edward J. Hanna, Dr. John H. Finley, and Mrs. Carrie Chapman Catt. The medal, designed by Ernest Wise Keyser, is in bronze and portrays two figures, personifying the Jew and Christian together ascending the steep mountain of misunderstanding toward the heights of mutuality.

in particular, on behalf of prohibition has made many Catholics transfer their dislike of prohibition to Methodists, and is said by an influential priest to have interposed an impediment to friendly and coöperative relations with all Protestants. Protestants and Jews regret the way Catholic bishops often block the participation of their laity as well as their clergy in co-operative enterprises where questions of joint worship and doctrinal differences are not at all involved.

CULTURAL VARIETY IN UNITY

One principle which has emerged more than once in earlier chapters, as well as in this, is that the strength and wealth of national life may be enhanced by cherishing, within a fundamental unity, the cultural richness resulting from diverse racial and religious heritages. If this principle is sound, it means not mere toleration, but positive appreciation of religious and other cultural variations.

COÖPERATION IN RELATION TO GEOGRAPHY, POPULATION, AND SOCIAL LEADERSHIP

It is sometimes assumed that the willingness of Catholics to coöperate religiously increases from the Atlantic to the Pacific Coast and also in proportion to the smallness of the Catholic population in a city. The investigators made no attempt to subject either of these assumptions to precise checks, but their general observations discovered no close correlation in either case. Speaking broadly, Catholic policy, East or West, in Catholic strongholds and in weak centers, has been to abstain from all interfaith relations that are likely to involve doctrinal matters. The situation, however, has various angles, on which a brief discussion may throw some light.

There appears to be more ground for the geographical than for the proportional population hypothesis. Consider first the geographical factor. Apart from the levelling of social barriers which is always characteristic of the frontier, economic competition was a factor. In the eastern cities the influx of large numbers of Catholics—first the Irish, then the Italians and others—intensified the economic struggle for the older and predominantly Protestant inhabitants, thus arousing resentment against the newcomers, primarily on economic, but indirectly on religious, grounds; whereas, on the frontier, all inhabitants were on an equal footing and religious groups were not identified with economic competition.

In the West, on the other hand, the Protestant barriers to coöperation have been by no means negligible. The fault has lain not entirely at the Catholic door, for Protestant sectarian ambitions everywhere inhibit coöperation and those ambitions have been aggressive on the frontier as well as in the eastern cities. Furthermore, the new West has been at least as susceptible to anti-Catholic propaganda as the old East. The net result of all these influences seems to have been that the Protestants and Catholics have coöperated very little better in the West than in the East.

A more potent determinant of coöperation than the frontier has been the attitude of the ecclesiastical and community leaders. If a Catholic bishop is friendly, approachable and community-minded, then the path of interfaith coöperation is smoothed. If he is the opposite, then Catholic laymen, however coöperative, have an uphill road to travel. In Protestant circles, the clergy play a far less dominant rôle and the laymen a correspondingly greater one.

In respect to ratios of religious population in a city, there seems to be no direct correspondence between the strength of the Catholics and their coöperativeness. In all cases, as already observed, non-coöperation in religious matters is the basic policy. But the temper and character of the ruling Catholic ecclesiastic makes a great difference. One bishop can say "no" with such graciousness and manifest regret as to make the word sound as sweet as another bishop's "yes" might be. For example, the exceptionally cordial feeling between the Catholic and non-Catholic ecclesiastics in the Catholic strongholds of San Francisco and St. Paul is to be explained in large measure by the personal equation of the local Catholic archbishops. On the other hand, one hears of no such cordial relations either in other Catholic strongholds, such as Boston, New York, Philadelphia, Baltimore and Chicago, or in most of the cities where the Catholics are a small and uninfluential minority.

The discussion thus far has excluded reference to the South, which calls for special mention. In the East and the West the Protestants, as a rule, are ready to take the lead in effecting interfaith coöperation and in removing interfaith prejudices and misunderstanding. In the South, however, religious coöperation of any sort is still in its infancy. The Protestants are notably deficient in coöperation among themselves, whether between the white and colored churches, or between the predominant denominations, the Baptists and Methodists. The Catholics constitute only a small minority, in most states, and the places with a considerable Jewish population are very few. In the cities the characteristic Protestant attitude probably is not aversion but indifference toward the Catholics. In the remote places where Catholics are practically unknown there is latent distrust of them, a tradition from the historic strife between Catholics and Protestants in Europe, which can be played upon by agitators, especially in times of political excitement. At any rate, the presence of an overwhelming Protestant majority in the South has not, to say the least, noticeably fostered interfaith coöperation. It is a fair question whether or not a preponderance of Catholics would have any different outcome. A Catholic priest who has resided for years in both the South and the North characterizes the situation in these piquant sentences:

"There is considerable prejudice against the Church in the abstract or as an organization, but the animus against the individual Catholic is likely to be less in the South than in the North. There is an epigram about race relations that applies largely to religion. It runs: the difference between the North and the South in regard to the Negro, is that in the South they hate him as a race, but love him as an individual; in the North they hate him as an individual, but love him as a race. So in the South they may hate the Catholic Church, but they love the individual Catholic; in the North they may have more respect for the Church, but I believe they have less for the individual Catholic."

COÖPERATION IN SOCIAL WORK

When it comes to coöperation in social work, the absence of theological complications has led to happier results. The general tendency has been for the Catholics to coöperate heartily wherever the Catholic Charities are in charge of trained professionals, although a particularly conservative bishop may place impediments in their way. In the case of the Jews, the "coöperation index" is not the total strength of the local Jewish community, but the strength of the Reform or liberal congregations. The orthodox congregations everywhere seem disposed to keep pretty much to themselves.

SOCIAL UNITY

The fundamental justification for fostering interfaith coöperation in any country is that it promotes social unity. Every age down to our own has witnessed the tragic disunity caused by religious intolerance and strife. In so far as this is true, the promotion of understanding and coöperative endeavor between Christians and Jews and among Catholics, Jews and Protestants in the United States and Canada should therefore not be considered a hobby to be pursued by a few sentimentalists, but rather be made a major objective of the statesmen of all three faiths. To neglect it is to expose the nation to the perils of interreligious distrust and factional strife.

CHAPTER X

Epilogue

No thoughtful student of current affairs can meditate long on the various tensions created by religious differences without at some time feeling an infinite regret that religion, which has been so often a most significant means of social integration, has in the New World become more commonly a divisive and disintegrating force. The Jewish state was for the most part theocratic; its unity was essentially a religious unity, and consequently to this day it is difficult to distinguish between the Jewish race and the Jewish religion. The Jewish state was in a sense totalitarian, and to the Jew religion was not simply a method of personal life but an expression of group solidarity. Christianity, on the other hand, gave a larger expression to the place of the individual as its universalism seemed to transcend all groups and to cut horizontally across the known cultures of the Mediterranean world. Some careful students of Judaism and Christianity have expressed their belief that the bitter struggle between the two in the first few centuries of the present era was, therefore, a tragedy of the first rank, since Christianity, by its emphasis on the worth of the individual, tended at times to minimize the importance of the corporate life, while Judaism, in its aversion to Christianity, overemphasized the worth of the group at the expense of the individual.

There may be something in all this—at least in the respective emphases of the two religions—although the statement is perhaps too apt to be true. However much apostolic Christianity may have stressed the individual, certainly Catholic Christianity deliberately sought to integrate all society, both in this life and in the life to come, under the banner of the cross, and to this end developed a system of law and discipline which still challenges the attention of all who are interested in forms of organization and administration.[1] Indeed, from one point of view, Protestantism may be adjudged a protest against the complete subordination of the individual to the Catholic system. Judaism, on the other hand, did not wholly disregard the individual.

Today, however, organized religion makes for divisiveness rather than for

---

[1] The fundamental principles of Catholic administration have been suggestively treated in Mooney, James D., and Reiley, Alan C., *Onward Industry* (New York: Harper and Brothers, 1931), pp. 217-272.

integration, and because of this divisiveness the people look for their social safety less to the organized churches than to the secular state. But the secular state is actuated more by sheer expediency and political chicanery than by fundamental philosophical principles. Religion tends to give way to patriotism; the sacred scriptures yield to the constitution; divine revelation is undermined by the rational empiricism of modern science; the life to come is forgotten as the modern man cynically recalls the words of Thoreau, "one world at a time." In Russia, irreligion has been exalted into a religion; in Mexico and Uruguay anti-clericalism is active and in the ascendent; in our own cultures many thoughtful people, weary of religious strife, find refuge in the secularist philosophy, even though secularism may, as Ozanam says, promise men an earthly paradise at the end of a flowery path only to lead them to a premature hell at the end of a way of blood. In the face of the great struggle between a secularist and a religious philosophy of life, the differences between the struggling religious denominations may seem to many to be of little consequence. To them, the cynic may feel inclined to use the old adage: "Gentlemen, if you do not hang together, you will hang separately."

The Jew of today may exclaim, "We have survived the bitterest persecution for at least three thousand years; we are the chosen vessels of divine truth; we have a peculiar mission to all mankind and we have a right to believe that we shall not utterly perish until that mission is fulfilled." The Roman Catholic may insist, "Our church is founded upon a Rock and the gates of hell cannot prevail against it, for we have nearly 2,000 years of history during which there are manifold evidences of infallible guidance." The Protestant may say, "What if institutions do collapse? A religion which has given to men the gift of personal liberty and made every man a priest before God need not perish with the institutions. No man can take our personal faith from us, even as the Stoic of old replied to the nobleman who threatened to take off his head, 'that is the only part of me you can't take away.'" Nevertheless, all three faiths are threatened and indeed in some portions of our modern world the very right to believe is in itself challenged. On the brink of such an abyss one may sing lustily and with faith: "magna est veritas et praevalebit," but no amount of singing will obviate the ugly situation confronting organized religion. Certain rights can only be assured as we stand together and stress those spiritual values which seem to transcend our differences.

When all this has been said, however, it still remains true that behind the minor differences are some significant differences to ignore which is mere madness, and in conclusion we can but point to certain of the differences in philosophy which have seemed to hound our entire study.

MINORITY RIGHTS VERSUS TOTALITARIANISM

First, we must consider the concept of society held by many—though not all—Jewish leaders as a Group of Groups. The social theory is more commonly called cultural pluralism, as opposed to totalitarianism. The assumption underlying such a pluralism is that the true development of man is in the direction not of homogeneity but of heterogeneity, and it is urged in consequence that instead of stressing the melting-pot and the obliteration of racial lines we should encourage the perpetuation of unlikeness and seek a society in which the rights of each cultural variety, however small, to growth and perpetuity, should be frankly recognized. Many Jews regard their group as the "spearhead" of this philosophy in the modern world, and such deem it to be the "mission of Israel" to stand for the rights of minorities the world over.

Certain historical factors may have tended to explain their peculiar insistence on cultural pluralism. In the first place, the Jews were an unusually vital but comparatively small people set down on one of the great highways between the mighty powers of Babylonia, Assyria, Egypt and Greece. Whenever one of these powers went forth to war, Palestine felt the power of its heel, and hence the people of Israel were all but annihilated on more than one occasion. Only "remnants" survived, and after the return of the exiles from the Babylonian captivity some far-seeing souls had reason to wonder whether any remnant at all could survive another such disaster. They determined, nevertheless, that there should be such a remnant, that Israel had its peculiar place in the economy of God, and they took strong action, which was reinforced by every conceivable form of ritual law, to ensure survival. In his recent book, *How Odd of God,* Lewis Browne says on this point:

"The rabbis seem to have built up the Law by watching the behavior of the Gentiles and commanding the contrary. Thus they hoped to wall in the Jews, to set them apart as a 'peculiar people.' A well-established ghetto had to be almost a self-contained world, with its own house of prayer, house of learning, marriage-hall, hospital, bath, slaughter-house, bakery, inn, and burial ground. Such elaborate segregation was necessary because, even if (a very grave *if*) the Gentiles were ready to mingle with the Jews, the Jews dared not mingle with the Gentiles. They dared not do so because every phase of their life was weighted down with ritual."[2]

Even in our own day, the investigators observed plans in certain cities for the completion of the communal organization of the Jews in that city, some of them so carefully made, at least on paper, that the Jewish popula-

---

[2] New York: Macmillan, 1934, pp. 25-26.

tion would be almost as thoroughly a unit of society as it was in mediæval Europe. Again, when Jerusalem finally fell, Israel became a nationality without a national home—an almost unique people in the whole world, but their religious ritual combined with the deep sense of their distinctive mission to prevent them from being absorbed in other peoples despite the inevitable intermarriage and apostasy. If any group is historically justified in propounding cultural pluralism, then it seems reasonably clear that the Jews have that right.

But there are two things which the exponents of cultural pluralism underestimate. First, while minorities may have their rights, minorities must also accept their responsibilities and the presence of a minority does, moreover, complicate as we have pointed out in this volume, the life of the majority. It does constitute an "imperium in imperio"; it must be dealt with often as a separate entity through its leaders; by reason of its cohesion and clannishness and its location at strategic centers it may exercise a control out of all proportion to its actual numbers or even its actual contribution to the well-being of society; it does prevent the full and efficient functioning of many social institutions; it raises barriers such as intermarriage to normal social life. Further, if minorities have their rights, majorities also have their rights. A minority may say, "We wish to live in good-will with the majority and to deal freely with them at points *a, b, c and d,* but we wish to live to ourselves at points *e, f and g.*" What is to prevent the majority from saying, "We also wish to live in good-will with the minority and to deal freely with them at points *d, e, f and g,* but we prefer to live to ourselves at points *a, b and c.*" A minority must expect to pay the price of its self-exclusion, and it can hardly claim the right to practise seclusion or exclusion where such a policy suits its fancy and at the same time deny a similar privilege to the majority.

Secondly, the problem of minorities in the New World is substantially different from the same problem in Europe. Since the treaty of Versailles, the number of minority peoples in Europe living under majority domination has been reduced, it is maintained, from more than eighty million to approximately twenty million. The difficulties of administration when minorities are involved have been so clearly recognized that what has taken place is practically a segregation along national lines. Whether this is a step in the right or wrong direction, it has been reasonably practicable because minority groups had already for the most part been segregated in given areas. In the New World, however, we are little else than a congeries of minorities. Every race in the New World has poured into the United States and Canada and secured a certain footing in these two countries. To permit the perpetuation of cultural differences here is to challenge the possibility of any kind of national unity and to make the proper functioning of political organization almost impossible. A close study of the Canadian situation makes this particularly clear. Where special privileges are granted to the French-Canadians in Quebec, they are soon demanded for French-Canadians in other provinces, and soon with the rise of other cultural blocs, new situations develop in which it looks as if everybody but the majority is to receive special consideration. Thus, if the Jewish group in the United States wishes to ensure its own separatism, the same privilege must also be granted to the Germans, the Italians, the Poles, the Czechs, the Japanese in California, the Mexicans in the Southwest, the Negroes in in the South, and out of it all comes something that can only be deemed a nation by wishful thinking. Already, the existence of national blocs in many cities does undoubtedly complicate political life and contribute powerfully to the vicious management of American cities.

While members of the majority group may frankly recognize an interim or transitional stage in which cultural cross-fertilization may take place, influencing both the majority and the minority, it deeply resents a philosophy which postulates the permanence and perpetuation of cultural pluralism. They say with Robert Frost that something in nature seems to hate a wall, and that the slow erosions of time level it to the ground. They recognize the importance of allowing for time to remove the difficulties, but they resent the conscious effort to maintain and perpetuate walls when nature is doing its best to eliminate them.

Meanwhile the profound student of cultural relations cannot fail to see that the erection of the walls that separate Jews and Gentiles is the work of both Jewish and Gentile groups. Jewish seclusion, as Lewis Browne points out in the book to which reference has just been made, led, in part at least, to Gentile exclusion, while today the anti-Semitism in Germany is causing a rebirth everywhere of Jewishness. The problem, therefore, is essentially this: are we to maintain and perpetuate a philosophy of cultural pluralism in the New World or are we frankly to seek cultural unity, recognizing that interim adjustments must necessarily be made slowly, but that the resulting cultural unity will involve less an assimilation of minority cultures to the majority culture than the creation of a new and hybrid culture in which the best strains of each will be diligently retained? Can we achieve this in the United States or Canada, or will Russia, by reason of its irreligion, achieve this before we do?

AUTHORITY OR FREEDOM

While we have urged in the main body of this book that the fundamental difficulties between the Jews and the non-Jews are but slightly religious and mostly social, racial or economic, the perennial quarrel between the Protestants and the Catholics is largely religious, philosophical and political. A

Catholic priest was recently pursuing an argument with certain public officials in the matter of social work and decided to draw up a statement of his position. He laid down certain fundamental premises, truly Catholic in their nature, and from these premises he deduced quite logically that such and such a course inevitably followed. He then showed this statement to a Protestant friend, asking him if he could see anything wrong with the general course of the argument. The Protestant friend read the document and replied simply, "If one accepts your premises, there is no fault with it, but since I refuse to accept your premises, the whole thing seems false to me."

Once assume certain fundamental premises regarding the necessity of salvation, the inevitability of revealed religion, the theological doctrine of the Deity of Christ and there is little escape from the logical deductions of the Catholic Church, for even the heretic Loisy can point out that what is explicit in the historic church is implicit in the gospel, asking, for instance, why one should gladly admit the impeccability of Jesus and at the same time deny the infallibility of the Pope.[3] The Protestant difficulty is, however, less with specific doctrines than with the assumptions on which the whole theory of the church is erected, and consequently tension is apt to develop at almost any point. Tom Kettle once said that "the Catholics take their beliefs *table d'hôte* and the Protestants theirs *à la carte*." One might add that there are many times when men of judgment will trust a good cook and eat what is set before them with a grateful heart, but Protestants do not see why they should always be required to accept the judgment even of a good cook when he urges upon them something against which their whole digestive system rebels, especially when they strongly suspect that the motives of the cook in insisting on *table d'hôte* are not entirely unmixed. In short, the liberal Protestant insists on freedom and rejects authority, and tends to believe that the authority assumed by the church and grounded on alleged facts of doubtful historicity springs less from divine truth than from the skill of political manipulators anxious to enlarge the sphere of their power and authority. To such Protestants, the Catholic doctrine of authority is simply the Nietzschean will to power parading behind a crucifix. Possibly, the average Protestant is quite ignorant of a large measure of personal freedom safeguarded in the Catholic system, but at all events he fails to see it.

Moreover, the Protestant would be quite willing to let people believe anything they cared to believe provided that it did not threaten the existing moral sanctions of his particular society or seem to clash with existing political policy. But on this point he is inevitably suspicious of the Catholics,

---

[3] Loisy, *The Gospel and the Church* (New York: Charles Scribner's Sons, 1912).

even when he may be substantially at one with them on certain major aspects of fundamental doctrine. In short, he senses in the imposing edifice of the Catholic Church essentially a super-state, which, however much it may seek to distinguish between the temporal and the spiritual, is actually always confusing the two, as in all probability any vital religion which is not entirely other-worldly must. He, therefore, sees in Roman Catholicism a bid for universal power, founded on the wreckage of the Roman Empire and bearing countless evidences of its Italian origin in its spiritual imperialism, yet marvellously sustained throughout history by philosophical acumen, political tact, psychological insight, administrative genius and a certain unyielding intransigence. He sees, moreover, the political action of his own country complicated by various decrees regarding education, social work, industrial reconstruction, intermarriage, etc., issued by a spiritual potentate who is almost always an Italian and whose fundamental mentality is Latin and not Anglo-Saxon. To the average Protestant, the Catholic Church is, in its political genius, essentially a dictatorship, while he, on his part, is trying so to educate the rank and file that they may worthily and intelligently live in a democracy.

Here, then, seems to be the crux of the matter. The Protestant believes in religious liberty but he winces when the Catholics take him at his word and demand liberty to practise their own religion, since he recalls the formulation of the famous demand made by Louis Veuillot, the French clericalist, who asked freedom for his church from the French liberals: *"Nous vous demandons la liberté au nom de vos principes; nous vous la nions au nom des nôtres."* (We demand liberty from you in the name of your principles; we deny it to you in the name of ours.) What can be done with a demand like that?

But in all social philosophy, one must start on some premises, and the group that does so and lays down certain fundamental principles even if they are only supported by myth has a great tactical advantage over another group which avowedly seeks inductively nothing but the truth. The difference becomes increasingly clear even in a seminar. The liberal Protestant is willing to approach Roman Catholicism dispassionately to discover some unsuspected truth in it and to appropriate such a truth. The loyal Catholic, however, if he thinks it worth while to attend the seminar, feels rather that he is there to expound the Catholic position, to clear up any "misunderstandings" about such a position, but always in the temper of "take it or leave it. I couldn't change it or modify it if I would; I wouldn't change it or modify it if I could."

This makes it extremely difficult to effect any *modus vivendi* between Protestants and Catholics. It is difficult to conduct intellectual negotiations with a group that refuses to allow its fundamental principles and premises to be inserted in the agenda for consideration, or insists that all problems are in the last analysis theological problems. If we live together in peace and harmony, it is not because of our respective principles but in spite of them; because Protestants know Catholics, and Catholics know Protestants, who are mighty good fellows in spite of their curious religious ideas, and especially because we know full well that we have to live together in peace whether we want to do so or not. But the peace is too often but an armed truce; the ancient suspicions eternally project themselves into our political musings and an occasion is usually around the corner when the Protestant majority will ask itself again, "Are we justified in extending the full measure of religious liberty to the Catholic group in the 'name of Protestant principles' when we are far from sure that the Catholic group, were the numerical conditions reversed, would extend the same liberty to Protestants in the 'name of Catholic principles'? Can democracy really endure if one group is educating its children for freedom while an influential minority in its midst continues to educate its children for authority?"

The religious issue, therefore, becomes essentially a political issue, as the Protestant refuses to accept the Catholic theory of the modern state, believing rightly or wrongly that he is the custodian of the fundamental principles upon which American political institutions repose.

Is the United States a Protestant Country?

This brings us to another consideration, viz., the frequent assumption on the part of Protestants that the United States is a Protestant country and that the perpetuation of its unique institutions requires the perpetual dominance of the Protestant mentality. There is no doubt whatever that there is a tendency in education, social work, etc., to postulate the prevailing Protestant point of view, even in its approximation to secularism, as the American point of view, and to regard other points of view as substantially "minority reports." This identification of Protestantism with Americanism is extremely irritating to the minorities, but can be paralleled in South American countries by the readiness of Roman Catholics to assume the rôle of defender of the national culture. The missionary activities of Protestants among Catholic immigrants were frequently justified not on the main grounds of religious conversion but on the grounds of Americanization.

All this raises the fundamental question of what is an American, and what are the great underlying American assumptions? Is the American still in the making, and if so, whither are we bound? There has, perhaps, been much inconsistency in the past between our philosophical pretensions and our practices, for even in 1776, when the Declaration of Independence was launched and its social philosophy expounded, the manifesto of Samuel Hopkins and Ezra Stiles, both ministers of Newport, urging that the

American people apply to the Negro people what they had just declared about the inalienable rights of individuals to life, liberty and the pursuit of happiness fell on deaf ears. Perhaps, too, in all our emphasis on "rugged individualism" we were reflecting only the necessities of the pioneer and not following the postulates of a reasoned philosophy such as an advanced and sophisticated culture demands. At all events, the time is more than ripe for a reappraisal of Americanism. It is hardly sufficient to note recent trends as if we had no pattern of social organization, no fundamental *Weltanschauung* to motivate our political action. Unless our pattern is recovered or a fresh pattern discovered, our destiny may be more "manifest" than we may care to think.

The function of religion is to help the individual to find his proper place. Philosophy makes him at home in the universe; history helps him to see himself as the heir of the ages; ethics ought to make him the good neighbor in the world of men. Is not our fundamental task, then, the recovery of a distinctive religious philosophy, drawn from the lessons of our own American experience and our own peculiar needs as children of the New World? In this new discovery we cannot be limited by the experience of ancient Judea or of Imperial Rome or of the Anglo-Saxon peoples. Ours is, for better for worse, a mixed culture; we are the heirs of all races and all strains, but out of this appalling variety we must achieve two things: first, we must secure a real national unity, and secondly, we must grow a sincere national soul. And we must achieve that for ourselves.

New days require new duties, and while new and superlative loyalties can hardly unfold out of the wreckage of old loyalties, it seems to those who have engaged in this difficult but fascinating study that all three groups are immediately challenged to look beyond themselves, to learn from one another, to seek increasingly and sympathetically to understand one another, and then to work in a far greater unison to build here in this New World a city of God whose walls shall be called Salvation and whose Gates shall be called Praise.

APPENDICES

APPENDIX A

Birth Control

Undoubtedly, birth control is at the present time one of the most debated problems in religious circles. The issue, unfortunately, is too often confused with other more or less related problems such as abortion, sterilization, free love, divorce, the home, feminism, Malthusianism, adultery, fornication, and even infanticide. The discussion about it is muddled to a certain extent by a confusion between the practice of birth control within the married relation and a similar practice outside the married relation—some believing that the sole end of sex intercourse is procreation and other insisting that within the married relation the sex-act may be considered as an end in itself and, when not abused, may prove beneficial to both parties physiologically, psychologically and even spiritually. The discussion is further complicated by a difference of opinion as to whether the world in general and the United States in particular is reaching the "saturation point" in population, or whether, on the other hand, our greatest need is not that of a larger consuming population to use the increased store of products made possible both in industry and in agriculture by our machine age. Some may thus approach the problem from a purely sociological angle; while others attack it from a physiological, psychological, moral or spiritual angle.

Neither the Protestants nor the Jews have any official position on the matter, for neither of these groups has any recognized central authority capable of making a pronouncement on their behalf. Within these groups, therefore, there is a diversity of opinion. Some Protestant denominations have given a qualified approval to birth-control measures; others have withheld such approval. Within Judaism, there are differences between the liberal and orthodox positions. A responsum on Birth Control prepared by Rabbi Jacob Z. Lauterbach at the request of the Central Conference of American Rabbis, appears in the Conference Yearbook for 1927, pages 369-384. This responsum formulates four major principles based on the halakic teachings of the Talmud as accepted by medieval rabbinic authorities. The fourth principle is an essential summary of the rest: "In case a man has fulfilled the duty of propagation of the race, as when he has already two children, he is no longer obliged to beget children and the law does not forbid him to have intercourse with his wife even in a manner which would not result in conception. In such a case the woman certainly is allowed to use any kind of contraceptive or preventive."[1] Within orthodox Judaism there seems to be a variety of points of view. In general it is held that the male, since he must obey the whole law of Israel, must take no steps in the direction of

---

[1] This is paralleled in modern Russia by the laws establishing state clinics for abortion; abortion is not permitted in the case of the first pregnancy.

contraception, but the female, who is not required to obey the whole law, is free to take whatever steps she deems wise to prevent conception.

The position of the Roman Catholic Church is well known and has been set forth in recent years in many books and pamphlets. The church is opposed to the use of all artificial measures to thwart the processes of nature. It has consequently sought to prevent the establishment of contraceptive clinics and has worked against the abrogation of laws which made the impartation of contraceptive information a criminal offence.[2] The Roman Catholic Church has thus become the focal point of attack on the part of those persons who are promoting birth control and who believe that the "social question" sooner or later must concern itself with the vital problems of population, and that the only effective means of eliminating crime and feeble-mindedness is through cutting off the supply at the source by means of sterilization—or birth control. More recently, however, a book has appeared with a certain ecclesiastical sanction by Dr. Latz, entitled *Rhythm*, which suggests as a proper means of birth control intercourse only in the "safe period" of the menstrual cycle, when, it is alleged, conception rarely ensues. The Post Office states that this book is mailable, while certain books put forward by the birth-control promoters are ruled unmailable. The advocates of birth control retort that the "safe period" is not "safe."

It has been stated by some scholars that part of the difficulty is resident in the fact that while the Catholic mind demands very clear and concise definitions of terms in order to legislate wisely, it has failed in its pronouncements regarding birth control to define its terms with precision. Are methods which do not *absolutely* assure the prevention of conception, for instance, to be considered strictly speaking "birth control"? If not, then who is to judge what methods *absolutely* prevent conception? The experts do not claim 100 per cent. success for their methods, although they sometimes do claim 98 per cent., whatever that means. Again, if the "safe period" is absolutely safe, then does not any sanction given it really sanction sexual intercourse within the marriage relation without any end of procreation in mind? On the other hand, if this is not entirely reliable as a precautionary method, is it sanctionable because (a) it does not involve a positive interference with nature or natural processes, or (b) it still presupposes the responsibility of the parties concerned to fulfil their parental obligations should conception take place despite their precaution? If the sanction is implicit in the fact that there is no positive interference with nature, then it might be argued that we are interfering with nature in almost every stage of human development. If, on the other hand, the sanction is implicit in the fact that absolute contraception cannot be guaranteed, and that, consequently, the parties concerned accept their full measure of responsibility for any consequences that may follow, then this would provide a possible argument for a measure of contraception within the married relation but within the marriage relation *only*, since it might be assumed that those who are willing to accept responsibility for such acts should do so before the act and not after it.

---

[2] See Sanger, Margaret, *My Fight for Birth Control* (New York: Farrar and Rinehart, 1931).

It is quite obvious that the issue is complicated and requires careful definition and clarification.

Whatever may be argued for or against contraception, the Catholic attitude on this matter has created tremendous opposition in liberal circles. The investigators discovered clear instances where leading Protestant clergymen had looked with suspicion on birth control until the Catholic bishop in the region had openly attacked the movement and made various threats, direct or indirect, if certain projected clinics were established. This attack forced the crystallization of their views in favor of such clinics. The opposition to the Catholic position on birth control among non-Catholics has, in addition to honest differences of opinion, certain subsidiary elements in it, thus:

(1) Non-Catholics tend to doubt the moral sincerity of the Catholic Church at this point. They believe that the church is deliberately seeking to "outbreed" the lesser faiths, believing that there is safety and supremacy in numbers. There can be no doubt, for instance, that the Church has put a good deal of faith in the breeding capacity of the French-Canadians in Quebec to enable it to offset its minority status in the Dominion, just as Hitler and Mussolini today are urging large families with what seem to be sinister motives.

(2) Whatever justification there may be in the claim of the Catholic Church to legislate for its own communicants in matters of this character, non-Catholics resent the effort of the church to prevent the repeal of laws directed against the communication of information regarding contraception to such as desire that information, thus inflicting its particular moral code on non-Catholics.

(3) Non-Catholics believe that the Catholics provide more than their quota of delinquency, crime, poverty and feeble-mindedness. It is difficult to reach accurate factual conclusions in regard to this allegation so far as the United States is concerned, on account of deficiencies in fundamental statistics and the even greater difficulty in attributing the proper recognition to the various causes of given tendencies toward crime or feeble-mindedness. Statistics included in Appendix B, dealing with crime statistics, throw some light on this situation. Non-Catholics, however, whether they are right or wrong in their surmises, are not disposed to acquiesce in the assumption that undesirable breeds should not be restricted, especially when there is everywhere an increasing effort made to load the state with the responsibility of caring for such unfortunates.

(4) Non-Catholics, moreover, resent the effort of the Catholic priesthood to determine the nature of the sexual relations within marriage, when the priesthood itself is celibate and has only second-hand information or tradition on which to base its conclusions. If the priests were not celibate, they would be taken more seriously when they denounce contraception, but at this point to the average non-Catholic they suffer from an "invincible ignorance."

These, therefore, are contributory factors to the present excitement, but when all this has been said quite frankly, it must not be supposed that all non-Catholics support birth-control measures. Some of them, perhaps most of them, are quite conscious of grave dangers which may harass our social organization if the information regarding contraception is widely circulated among unmarried persons with no fundamental sex idealism. They realize that such information would probably remove one of the general restraints on promiscuity. On the other hand, many such unmarried persons have the information anyway, and hence it seems wiser to offset the dangers by a fresh emphasis on the beauty and dignity of such relationships within marriage, the reaffirmation of the sacramental nature of marriage, a vigorous insistence on the centrality of the home as the unit of society, established not in coercion but in freedom, not on lust but on love, and the impregnation of the minds of the adolescents and pre-adolescents with the ideals which prove the best antitoxins to libertinism.

It is incontrovertible that birth-control methods are being widely used. The birthrate is rapidly falling and the decline has apparently been accentuated by the untoward economic conditions of the past few years. It is, of course, quite impossible to gauge the extent to which the declining birth rate is due to contraceptive measures, although one might gather facts regarding the actual number of contraceptive appliances sold annually. Only a comparatively small number of persons visit the various contraceptive clinics in the country. One of the largest of these —the Illinois Birth Control League, operating six clinics in Chicago—gave advice in 1932 to 2,406 patients. Of these, 1,769 sought advice for economic reasons; 258 for economic and health reasons; 153 for health reasons; 217 in order to "space" their children and the remaining 11 because of various domestic difficulties, etc.

The religious preferences of the applicants at these clinics is not without significance. In the 2,406 cases in Chicago, 1,265 (or 52.68 per cent.) were Protestants. Some of these were undoubtedly colored women, of whom there were in all 270. Eight hundred cases (33.25 per cent.) were Roman Catholics, 13.30 per cent. were Jewish and the small balance (0.77 per cent.) were Mormons, Mohammedans or persons without any religion.

Dr. Raymond Pearl, of Johns Hopkins University, is at present engaged in a study of the relation of religious affiliations to contraceptive practice which may throw further light on the situation.

From such fragmentary statistics as were furnished the investigators at the clinics visited, there seems to be no doubt that Catholic attendance at the clinics is growing. At one of the smaller centers it increased from 20 per cent of the total attendance in 1930-31 to nearly 50 per cent. in 1932-33. In this same center, where the Jewish population is about 12 per cent. of the total population, the Jewish applicants numbered about 10 per cent. of the total number of cases.

Most interesting statistics were furnished by a city in the Middle West. In the first four years of its existence this clinic had dealt with 1,735 cases, divided religiously as follows: 1,395 Protestants (80.40 per cent.); 33 Jews (1.90 per cent.); 279 Catholics (18.08 per cent.) and 28 others (1.62 per cent.), who either professed no religion or for whom there were no records. In eight of the thirty-three Jewish cases, the husband was a Protestant. In 134 of the 279 Catholic cases, the husband was a Protestant and in two cases the husband was Jewish. In 141 cases, however, both husband and wife were Catholics. In this particular city, the opposition of the Catholic bishop seemed to give unusual publicity to the clinic and after his attack the attendance almost doubled while the percentage of Catholic attendance increased from 9.74 per cent. in the first year to 17.10 per cent. in the second. The workers at this clinic, as at other clinics, reported that their Catholic patients had occasionally said that they were no longer going to confession, while others intimated that they were taking particular care to "choose their confessors."

The issue is a burning one in social-work circles, and is regarded as an additional reason why Catholic charities should look after all Catholic cases. In a mental hygiene clinic we were told of a Catholic wife who came to them nervous and unhappy. Part of her difficulty seemed undoubtedly due to sex problems, and were she not a Catholic, contraceptive measures would have been recommended. Under the circumstances the mental hygienist did not feel free to recommend the course he considered most necessary.

Again, a prominent judge in the juvenile delinquency courts stated quite frankly that in his opinion religion had little to do with delinquency even if the figures in his own city showed a very high rate among Catholics. He attributed delinquency essentially to bad economic conditions and lack of a living wage, to demoralized homes resulting from poor standards of living, to inability of parents born abroad to deal with children growing up under American institutions, and to a high percentage of mental deficiency among certain of the immigrant groups. Whereupon he added: "The greatest solution possible is along the lines of sterilization or the promotion of voluntary birth control. But here, of course, we run up against the Catholic philosophy."

APPENDIX B

Crime, Insanity and Religious Affiliation

The relation of religious affiliation to crime and mental instability deserves careful study, although it is doubtful if it would be possible in the United States to secure the fundamental statistics necessary to such a study. The investigators made some effort to do so, but found that the available data were too incomplete to warrant any sound deductions.

Information was sought concerning the religious affiliation of inmates of states' prisons in the United States, but out of twenty-nine states from which information was sought, eight gave no information concerning religion, and even where the religious affiliation was given there were never any correlations between such affiliation and the types of crime committed.

In the Juvenile Courts, the statistics compiled locally usually include an analysis of the religious affiliation of those brought before the courts, but occasionally the delinquents and dependents are lumped together in the statistical tables. There is usually a correlation between religious and racial statistics at one point—that of color. This makes it quite possible to see that in several communities the heavy Protestant load is largely a Negro load. It is also possible in some cities to compare the statistics for colored Protestant delinquents with those for colored Catholic delinquents.

In the city of Washington, Negroes constitute only 27.1 per cent. of the total population, but of 1,174 children brought before the Juvenile Court in that city in 1932, 733 (or slightly over 62 per cent.) were colored. In 1926, in the city of Baltimore, 1,106 of the 3,184 delinquent or dependent children dealt with in the Juvenile Court were colored. In Baltimore the Negroes constitute approximately 16 per cent. of the total population, while nearly 35 per cent. of these cases in the courts came from that racial element. In Baltimore, too, 121 of the 1,106 colored children were Catholics, although the colored Catholic population is probably not more than 6.5 per cent. of the entire colored population of the city. Wherever there is a large Negro population, there seemed to result inevitably a heavy Protestant load.

Where the Negro population is small, as in Buffalo, and the number of foreign-born Catholics is large, the situation is of course quite different. In Buffalo and Erie County, out of a total of 902 cases handled in the Children's Court, 621 were Catholics, 260 were Protestants and only seven were Jewish. Here only fifty-five colored children appeared in court. Buffalo's population is probably 60 per cent. Catholic and less than 3 per cent. colored.

It is thus rather hopeless to reach any precise conclusions, because the religious affiliations are intertwined with such other considerations as racial origin, economic and social status, etc.

One fact was fairly clear in all the cities studied. The number of Jewish juvenile delinquents in American (though not in Canadian) cities was consistently small, and the reasons usually given for this was the excellent standard of social work carried out by Jewish agencies. The Jewish Big Brothers and Big Sisters seem to leave no stone unturned to restore the occasional delinquent to his full status in society, while the many Jewish educational agencies seek to prevent the first outbursts of delinquency. An additional reason may perhaps be found in what seems to be the low Jewish birth rate.

In regard to crimes committed by adults, the Jewish Statistical Bureau issued a report on September 25, 1933, giving statistics for offences committed by Jews chiefly in nine states—New York, California, Connecticut, Illinois, Maryland, Michigan, New Jersey, Ohio and Pennsylvania. In New York State, during the year 1932, a total of 70,630 persons were committed to prison. These included 3,492 Jews, or 4.9 per cent. of the total, although the Jews constitute over 15 per cent. of the total population of the state. Of 2,379 persons convicted for serious offences, only 188, or 7.9 per cent., were Jews, while the Jewish prisoners committed to reformatories constituted 8.6 per cent. of the total.

The detailed statistics are as follows:

NEW YORK STATE (Jewish population, 15%)

	Total	Jews	Percentage
Committed during 1932 to:			
State prisons	2,379	188	7.9
Reformatories	1,233	107	8.6
Institutions for Defective Delinquents	186	11	5.9
Penitentiaries	10,469	89	0.8
County Jails	56,363	708	1.3

NEW YORK CITY

	Total	Jews	Percentage
Committed to city prisons	73,352	14,352	19.5

OTHER STATES

	Total	Jews	Percentage
California (Jewish population, 2.78%):			
Received at Folsom Prison, 1929 and 1930	995	9	0.8
Connecticut (Jewish population, 5.59%):			
Admitted to state prison, 1929-30	457	19	4.1
Committed to farm for women, 1929-30	279	2	0.7
Illinois (Jewish population, 4.74%):			
Committed to state prisons, 1930-31	9,368	135	1.4
Maryland (Jewish population, 4.44%):			
At Maryland Penitentiary, Oct. 1, 1932	1,106	13	1.1
Admitted at House of Correction, 1931-32	5,007	20	0.3
Michigan (Jewish population, 1.99%):			
In state prisons, January 1, 1929	7,063	91	1.2
New Jersey (Jewish population, 6%):			
At state prison, July 1, 1930	1,796	87	4.8
Received at Reformatory, Rahway, 1929-1930	992	21	2.1
Received at Reformatory for Women, 1929-30	347	7	2.0

Ohio (Jewish population, 2.59%):
Received at State Penitentiary, 1929-30.........	4,213	33	0.7
Received at State Reformatory, 1929-30.........	3,312	122	3.6
Received at Reformatory for Women, 1929-30...	469	3	0.6

Pennsylvania (Jewish population, 4.16%):
Committed to Eastern penitentiary, 1928-29.....	1,425	38	2.6
Committed to Western penitentiary, 1930.......	588	3	0.5
Committed to industrial reformatory, 1927-28...	1,543	10	0.6

It is thus seen that, generally speaking, the record of the Jewish group is one of which they may be proud. Some who were consulted during the study made two observations on the above trends: (1) Jewish social agencies are most assiduous in getting Jews out on parole or in securing a reduction of the term of sentence, while Protestant and Catholic workers are less solicitous for their prison population; (2) Jewish lawlessness or evasion of the law is of the subtler quality that does not usually lead to states' prisons.

The criminal laws of Canada are directly administered by a federal Department of Justice, and the Dominion gathers statistics for the entire country and includes religious affiliations among them. Consequently it is possible to offer fairly complete tabulations for several years of all persons convicted of indictable offences:

RELIGIONS OF CONVICTED PERSONS, DOMINION OF CANADA, 1922-1931

Year	Total Convictions	Denomination Not Given	Roman Catholics	Jews
1922..............	15,740	2,464	5,077	407
1923..............	15,188	3,297	4,620	340
1924..............	16,258	4,326	4,171	408
1925..............	17,219	3,597	5,057	354
1926..............	17,448	3,838	5,437	422
1927..............	18,836	3,474	5,977	433
1928..............	21,720	3,894	6,938	592
1929..............	24,097	3,698	7,784	470
1930..............	28,457	3,582	9,804	497
1931..............	31,542	4,590	10,141	618

In 1931 (the census year), the Jewish population was shown to be 1.5 per cent. of the entire population, but in that year the Jewish group furnished 1.96 per cent. of all those convicted of indictable offences. In much the same way the Canadian figures show that of 5,311 juvenile delinquents found guilty of major offences in 1931, 107, or 2.01 per cent., were Jewish. It may be that the Jewish rate is slightly higher since sometimes Jews refrain from giving their religious affiliations when called before the courts. The fact that the Jewish group is so highly urban might be one factor worthy of consideration in accounting for this higher criminal rate, but perhaps the most important is the shortcoming of Jewish social agencies in Canada to provide the preventive and curative measures which such agencies have undertaken with conspicuous success in the United States.

Figures of the Dominion Bureau of Statistics as of June 1, 1931, show that Jewish inmates of penitentiaries were 130.9 per 100,000 of the Jewish male population in the Dominion, against an index number of 85 for those of British (English, Scottish and Irish) descent; 59.1 for those of Scandinavian descent; 143.2 for Indians, and 166.1 for those of Asiatic stock.

In regard to all Catholic criminal statistics due attention must be paid to the racial status of the indicted, and especially to the length of residence of their families in the country of their adoption. The Canadian statistics throw some interesting light on this point. In 1931, there were 10,141 Catholic cases among the 31,542 convictions for indictable offences in the entire Dominion. This is low when it is remembered that the Catholics constitute over 40.88 per cent. of the population (including Greek Catholics). But although 57 per cent. of the Catholic population of the Dominion is highly concentrated in the province of Quebec, Quebec furnished only 3,848 (37.9 per cent.) of the 10,141 Catholic cases. In Quebec one finds a Catholic community with more than 300 years of consecutive indigenous history behind it, and apparently the Catholic minorities in the other provinces furnish the bulk of Catholic criminality in Canada. In the juvenile courts the Catholics furnished 2,234 of the 5,311 convictions for major offences, or 42.06 per cent., which is just slightly higher than their percentage of the entire population.

In regard to the inmates of mental hospitals, there were in the Dominion of Canada, in 1931, 31,172 inmates, of whom 12,933 (41.4 per cent.) inscribed themselves as Catholics and 420 (1.34 per cent.) as Jews. The French number about 28.4 per cent. of the total population and they furnished to the mental hospitals 8,497 inmates, or 27.2 per cent. of the total. It would therefore seem that the Jews furnished slightly less than their proportion—unless a disproportionate number of those who failed to give their affiliations (721 in all) were Jewish— and the Catholics slightly more than their proportion, while the French furnished slightly less than their proportion.

It is also not without interest that the Catholic rate of criminality is high in Ontario, which is largely Protestant, while the Protestant rate of criminality is high in Quebec, which is overwhelmingly Catholic. In the latter province the Protestant group furnished, in 1931, 1,132 of the 5,737 persons convicted for indictable offences, although the entire population of the province, after deducting the Catholics and the Jews, contains only 351,359 persons. (The total population is 2,874,255.)

Such figures as are given above perhaps prove nothing; but they do sound a warning to any who jump to conclusions and make unwarranted deductions from fragmentary crime statistics involving religious affiliations.